PERSONALITY IN THE DEPRESSION

UNIVERSITY OF MINNESOTA
THE INSTITUTE OF CHILD WELFARE
MONOGRAPH SERIES NO. XII

PERSONALITY IN THE DEPRESSION

A STUDY IN THE MEASUREMENT OF ATTITUDES

BY

EDWARD A. RUNDQUIST

Assistant Director, Psychological Laboratory
Cincinnati Public Schools

AND

RAYMOND F. SLETTO

Assistant Professor in Sociology, University of Minnesota

GREENWOOD PRESS, PUBLISHERS
WESTPORT, CONNECTICUT

Library of Congress Cataloging in Publication Data

Rundquist, Edward Alfred, 1906-
Personality in the Depression.

Reprint of the 1936 ed. published by the University of Minnesota Press, Minneapolis, which was issued as no. 12 of Monograph series of the Institute of Child Welfare, University of Minnesota.
Bibliography: p.
1. Attitude (Psychology)--Testing. 2. United States--Social conditions--1933-1945. I. Sletto, Raymond Franklin, 1906- joint author. II. Title. III. Series: Minnesota. University. Institute of Child Development and Welfare. Monograph series ; no. 12.
HB3726.R8 1975 155.2'5 72-142315
ISBN 0-8371-5903-2

Originally published in 1936 by the University of Minnesota Press, Minneapolis

Reprinted by Greenwood Press, Inc.

First Greenwood reprinting 1975
Second Greenwood reprinting 1977

Library of Congress catalog card number 72-142315
ISBN 0-8371-5903-2

FOREWORD

In 1933 the Institute of Child Welfare initiated a series of projects to study the effects of the depression on family life and the adjustment of children. This series included a comparison of the behavior of a group of young children in 1933 with that of a similar group upon which data had been obtained in 1926; a study of the home activities of junior and senior high school girls in 1933 compared with similar data obtained in 1929; and the study which resulted in this monograph. The latter sought to measure the attitudes of adolescents of both sexes--of whom, some were continuing their education, some were employed full time, some half time, and some not at all--toward the family, the law, education, and the economic situation, and to determine the factors conditioning such attitudes. Morale and inferiority measures were included as checks. Not only was the relation of attitudes in these areas to employment status to be analyzed, but their relation to a wide variety of other factors, such as the socio-economic and educational level of the parents of the adolescents studied, the employment status of parents, and various measures of family disorganization were also to be examined.

This monograph describes the derivation and standardization of the attitude scales used in this project and presents the results obtained on many different groups and the relation of the findings to many different factors. As with many studies in new areas, the project involved a methodological study in which new techniques and devices had to be formulated, tested, evaluated, and then eliminated or retained on the basis of objective criteria. Extensive studies were made of the efficacy of the criterion of internal consistency, of the overlapping between scales devised for different purposes, of the effect of the form of statement upon the generality of specificity of the attitude measured, and of the interrelations of attitudes. The result is a thoroughgoing analysis of many of the techniques used in attitude measurement, which should go far to clarify our conceptions both of the methods to be employed and the results to be expected from their use. Incidentally the study offers a clear demonstration of the rationale of existing attitude scales, which are so largely composed of negatively stated items.

An important practical outcome of the study is the well-standardized Minnesota Scale for the Survey of Opinions, which can be given either to groups or to individuals. The results of the specific attitude scales, and of a very sensitive general adjustment scale incorporated in the total scale, can be quickly converted into standard scores which enable the examiner to determine the relative standing of the person examined and construct a psychograph that will picture his attitudinal relation to his environment in striking fashion.

In carrying through this project Dr. Rundquist, a psychologist, and Dr. Sletto, a sociologist, have shown themselves to be an effective team in bringing the resources of their respective sciences to bear on a complex and difficult problem which laps both fields. If their efforts carry us a bit further on the road to the measurement and the understanding of personality, they will feel well repaid for their persistence, energy, and insight.

JOHN E. ANDERSON, Director
Institute of Child Welfare

ACKNOWLEDGMENTS

This study is one of several made possible through fellowships for advanced research granted to the authors by the Institute of Child Welfare, University of Minnesota. These fellowships permitted them to leave their usual professional positions for a year--the one as psychologist for the Minneapolis Public Schools, the other as instructor in the Department of Sociology of the University of Minnesota.

We are especially indebted to Dr. John E. Anderson, Director of the Institute of Child Welfare, whose unfailing encouragement and wise counsel have been indispensable to the completion of the project. Generous assistance, freedom for independent work, and competent statistical aids made working conditions ideal.

To Miss Katherine Kohler, Director of Adult Education, and to Miss Prudence Cutright and Walter E. Anderson of the curriculum department, Minneapolis Public Schools, we are indebted for permission to give scales to classes under their direction. The interest and cooperation of the principals of three Minneapolis high schools, Edison, Marshall, and West, made possible the gathering of high school data of much value.

Our thanks are extended to the members of the University Departments of Sociology and Psychology who granted permission to administer the scales in their classes. Dr. H. P. Longstaff of the Department of Psychology generously permitted giving the scales twice in his classes to provide retest data.

Miss Blanche Anderson of the statistical staff of the Institute gave much valuable assistance in the making and checking of statistical calculations, which we gratefully acknowledge.

This has been a completely cooperative study since its inception; the arrangement of the authors' names on the title page is alphabetical. Limitations of the monograph are to be ascribed solely to the authors. The complexity of the problems leave them with increased admiration for the contributions of their fellow explorers in this fascinating, perplexing field.

TABLE OF CONTENTS

L I S T   O F   F I G U R E S

LIST OF TABLES

Chapter I

INTRODUCTION

The chief purpose of this investigation has been to develop and apply instruments for measuring the effects of the depression on the personality and family life of young people. Loss of morale, development of feelings of inferiority, disharmonious family relationships, increased disrespect for law, economic radicalism, and disillusionment concerning the value of education are among the effects most commonly alleged to result from unemployment. Case studies demonstrate that unemployment does sometimes lead to these results, but, while there are many qualitative estimates of such effects, there is little quantitative evidence.

Our special interest was in the extent of such effects among recent high school graduates. Can unemployment alone produce unfavorable personality manifestations, and if not, what are the other circumstances that are associated with such manifestations?

The need for quantitative measures is particularly urgent at this time in view of the various educational and recreational programs that are being widely instituted to prevent the disintegration of personality that is presumed to accompany prolonged unemployment. Furthermore, quantitative measures devised now will permit the detection of future trends with respect to the traits measured.

Among the possible methods of making a quantitative study of the effects of unemployment, one of the most promising, it seemed, was to utilize the existing techniques for measuring attitudes. In making this decision we were greatly aided by O. Milton Hall's report (9) of a comparative study of the occupational morale, attitude toward employers, and attitude toward religion of employed and unemployed engineers. Hall found no differences in the attitudes of the two groups toward religion, but he reported striking differences in occupational morale and attitude toward employers.

TRAITS TO BE MEASURED

In an effort to extend this study to younger people and to measure a greater variety of traits that might be affected by unemployment, six general fields were chosen for exploration: general morale, inferiority, family relationships, respect for law, economic conservatism, and attitude toward the value of education. It is apparent that measuring devices in the first three fields may more properly be regarded as general tests of personality adjustment than as attitude scales.[1] Since Hall had successfully applied the technique developed by Likert (13) to a phase of morale, it seemed worth while to attempt a further extension of the technique to the problem of measuring morale in its more general aspects, feelings of inferiority, and family adjustment. In the absence of more appropriate designation the six fields listed above serve as labels for the scales developed. These designations may be evaluated from the validating data presented later.

It was decided that an investigation of several similar fields by the same general method was preferable to an investigation of several traits by

---

1. In this study the morale, inferiority, and family scales would ordinarily be referred to as personality inventories, whereas the law, economic conservatism, and education scales seem more strictly social attitude scales. As usually used in the literature, social attitude scales are those intended to measure the individual's position on controversial social problems or the degree to which existing social institutions are approved. Examples are scales to measure attitude toward war, birth control, the League of Nations, communism, etc. Personality inventories are designed to measure generalized differences in psychological reaction to a wide variety of specific situations, self-estimates, or the tendency to assume certain roles in the interaction process. Scales of this type are designed to measure feelings of inferiority, introversion-extroversion, dominance-submission, neurotic tendencies, timidity, self-sufficiency, etc. We are using the two terms "attitude scale" and "personality scale" almost interchangeably in order to avoid monotonous repetition.

different methods, for two reasons: (1) it would lead to a better understanding of the technique employed, and (2) it would yield information on the interrelationships between traits, a field of personality study that has not received the attention it deserves.

TECHNICAL PROBLEMS TO BE STUDIED

Such were the original purposes of the investigation. Problems of method and interpretation, however, have a tendency to loom large in studies in the personality field. This study is no exception. The nature of the problems encountered made necessary not only a critical examination of the method but also an exploration of problems fundamental to the correct interpretation of the results. The study was therefore carried far beyond the limits originally set. Investigation of the technique employed assumed at least equal importance with the initial purpose of the study. As will be seen, such problems inevitably became the major point of interest. An attempt was made to provide at least tentative answers to such questions as these: Are items selected from one group applicable to a dissimilar group? Do positively and negatively stated items yield different results? If so, what is the significance of such differences? Are the scales as reliable when applied to different groups? What is the nature of the relationship between discriminative values, standard deviations, and split-half reliability coefficients? Does the technique of internal consistency as usually applied select items that are actually consistent in their measurement of a common element? These and many other questions of method will be considered in detail throughout this work.

GROUPS GIVEN THE SCALES

The six scales were administered to 560 University of Minnesota students, of whom 200 were in the elementary sociology class, 200 were in the General College psychology class, 100 were law freshmen, and 60 were students receiving federal aid; to 1,024 persons in the night school classes in the Adult Education Department of the Minneapolis Public Schools; to 412 in the special classes for unemployed supervised by the same department; to 642 high school seniors and 71 high school juniors; to 21 high school teachers; and to 52 men on the rolls of the Minneapolis Department of Public Relief. In all, the scales were administered to approximately 3,000 individuals. Elimination of incomplete papers reduced the total number to 2,882.

It is apparent that the administration of the scales to so wide a variety of groups offers an unusually good opportunity for an investigation of many technical problems concerning personality measurement. The character of the groups tested is such that, if our measures are valid, depression affects can also be evaluated. The groups range from married men receiving public aid to high school seniors subjected to no severe economic deprivation.

CONSTRUCTION OF THE SCALES

The six scales were constructed according to the general method applied to attitude measurement by Likert (13) and utilized by Hall (9)--the method of internal consistency. The use of total score as the validating criterion for an item, which is essentially what internal consistency implies, is not new. It was used at least as early as 1916, when Terman (18) applied it to the Stanford-Binet Scale. The term "internal consistency", as applied to the construction of personality scales, seems to carry the implication that no outside criterion for validating total score is available and that each of the items meeting the criterion is a measure of a common element. The Thurstones (21) in discussing the criterion of internal consistency as applied to their neurotic inventory state (page 14): "This is an application of the criterion of internal consistency which the authors consider to be more essential in establishing the validity of the schedule than correlations with the available outside criteria." Allport and Vernon (1) credit Heidbreder (10) with first utilizing the criterion of internal consistency in scale construction, presumably having personality scales only in mind. Vernon and Allport (22) used the method in constructing their Scale of Values. Likert, however, seems to have been the first to emphasize its utility in attitude measurement, to emphasize the unit variable nature of the resultant items, to utilize more purposefully each item as a scale in itself, and to compare arbitrary and sigma methods of scoring the items of this type of scale. He was also the first to compare it with the method of constructing attitude scales developed by Thurstone.

Although the merits and defects of the method of scale construction will become evident as various problems are discussed, one or two advantages may be mentioned here. The method does not require judges and hence is less laborious than that developed by Thurstone. It is flexible, i.e., it is not dependent for scoring weights upon the adequacy of the standardization group. It gives very satisfactory reliability with few items. (See Table I.)

TABLE 1.-COMPARISON OF THE THURSTONE AND THE 1 TO 5 METHOD OF SCORING THE THURSTONE-DROBA WAR SCALE (LIKERT'S TABLE IX)

(N = 54.)

Method of Scoring	Form A vs. B	
	Raw	Corrected
Thurstone-Droba scale scored 1-5 method (18 questions only used in each form instead of 22)	(18 vs. 18) .88	(36 items) .94
Regular Thurstone scoring (44 items) . .	(22 vs. 22) .78	(44 items) .88

COEFFICIENT OF CORRELATION BETWEEN THE TWO METHODS

	Raw	Corrected for Attenuation
Thurstone scale (44 items) vs. 1-5 scoring of Thurstone scale (36 items)	.83	.92

That the Likert method compares favorably with the Thurstone is indicated by Table 1. This is Likert's Table IX, appearing in the work to which reference has already been made. Having found that his Scale of Internationalism yielded as high reliability as did the Thurstone-Droba War Scale, despite the fact that there were fewer items in the Internationalism Scale, Likert applied his technique to the items of the Thurstone-Droba War Scale. Four statements in each form of the Thurstone-Droba War Scale were not adapted to Likert's method and were omitted. In this case Likert's method when applied to Thurstone's scale yielded higher reliabilities with fewer items than did Thurstone's own method.

A technique that will yield such high reliability with few items is of considerable practical importance. If it can be extended to such personality fields as inferiority, family adjustment, and general morale, it has still more significance; for interrelations of various personality traits may be studied in a more satisfactory manner within the limits of time which are usually at the disposal of an experimentor or of a subject.

While several of Thurstone's attitude scales may be administered in a short time, most instruments for the measurement of such personality traits as inferiority, neurotic tendencies, and the like are so long that their research utility is considerably diminished. Smith's inventory for the measurement of inferiority feelings (16) contains 200 items, Thurstone's Neurotic Tendency Inventory, 223 items. With scales of this length it is impossible to obtain more than one measure when the subjects are available only once and then for not more than an hour.

CHOICE OF ITEMS

Study of the various scales already published was of assistance in devising items for our scales. Since scales were not available for the exact purposes desired, most of the items were drawn from the general knowledge of the writers. The only items taken verbatim from a scale already in existence were three items from Hall's Scale for Measuring Occupational Morale, a copy of which he kindly made available for our use. All five statements in his scale were tried out in a preliminary series of items; three met our criteria of selection and were retained in the final scale. That two of the items did not meet the criteria is not surprising in view of the fact that we were dealing with a group that had had little or no employment experience.

In phrasing the statements an attempt was made to state the essential idea in a conversational or colloquial manner rather than in the language of formal discourse. Statements in informal, conversational language are within the comprehension of a greater proportion of potential subjects and more in conformity with their usual speech reactions.

One hundred and sixty-two items were first tried on a small group of graduate students in psychology and child welfare and on a group of advanced students in sociology. Both groups were asked to comment on these items and in particular to indicate which were ambiguous. They were also requested to indicate which statements were responded to on the basis of their own personal experience. The number of cases involved in these groups was so small and the groups so homogeneous that it was not thought worth while to subject the results to a completely quantitative analysis. A semi-quantitative analysis gave us many helpful lessons in the formulation of later items.

All items indicated as ambiguous were rephrased or eliminated. It was discovered that statements containing the words all, always, none, never, and other terms universal in scope were often unsatisfactory. One of the most persistent comments coming from the graduate students was that such a statement was disagreed with because of the universal term, although it otherwise had the commentator's complete approval.

The greater number of the statements asserted to have been answered on the basis of personal experience were statements in the morale, inferiority, and family scales. It was desired to evoke responses that were based on personal experience but to phrase statements impersonally, i.e., without the use of the personal pronoun. This attempt to measure personal reactions by simple declarative sentences was motivated by the fact that Smith (16) in his inferiority inventory found striking differences between the responses to items phrased negatively and those phrased positively. He states (page 103): "Form P [positively stated--i.e., 'feels people speak well of him and like him'] showed no evidence of unreliable responses; Form N [negatively stated--i.e., 'feels people criticize him or dislike him'] considerable evidence on certain papers. Form N appeared to introduce the subject into a much more highly charged emotional atmosphere than Form P, thus fostering unreliability and evasion." It is particularly interesting, therefore, to ascertain whether morale and inferiority feelings can be measured by simple impersonal statements that carry little emotional tone and that appear to be designed to measure majority opinion rather than to discover deviations of the individual from group norms. In other words, we are attempting to obtain a response based on personal feelings without sharply focussing the attention of the individual on his personal problems.

A further criterion utilized in this tentative preliminary selection of items was that of reliability. This was determined by giving the scales twice, one week apart. If individuals' responses to an item fluctuate widely during the period of one week, it is a poor item, unless such short-time variations are the subject of study. Such items were eliminated.

The procedure described above may be termed pre-experimental. Profiting from the lessons learned, we added enough items to those retained to increase the number to 212. These were presented to 184 junior students in sociology classes, 72 men and 112 women. The results were analyzed for internal consistency. For convenience in treating the data, 22 items were retained in each scale. These 22 were chosen on the basis of their ability to discriminate sharply between the upper and lower quartiles on each scale. The test papers were scored on the basis of uniform arbitrary weights to be described later, and the highest and lowest quartiles were segregated. The mean score on each item was obtained for each quartile; the size of the difference between these means was taken as a measure of the discriminative value of the item. This difference in terms of the five-point item scale will be referred to hereafter as the item scale value difference (s.v.d.), or as the discriminative value of the item.

For the morale and inferiority scales the procedure involved one further step; the carrying out of the inductive procedure of this method of item selection to its logical conclusion. The discriminative value of each item of the _morale_ scale was computed for the upper and lower quartiles of the _inferiority_ distribution; and the discriminative value of each item of the _inferiority_ scale was computed for the upper and lower quartiles of the _morale_ distribution. Each item was scored in the scale in which it discriminated best. Had time permitted, this procedure would have been applied to all the scales, i.e., the discriminative value for each item would have been computed for each of the six scales.[2]

In phrasing the alternative responses to the statements we followed Hall in using the expressions _strongly agree_, _agree_, _undecided_, _disagree_, and _strongly disagree_ rather than Likert, who used the words _approve_ and _disapprove_ where Hall used _agree_ and _disagree_. It seemed to us that Hall's expressions were better adapted to the meaning of the statements we were using. For example, it is more understandable to agree or disagree with the statement "The future looks very black" than it is to approve or disapprove of it.

ALTERNATIVE RESPONSES TO ITEMS

Under the Likert technique each item is a scale in itself. It is scored by giving the response at one end of the scale an arbitrary weight of 1, the next phrase 2, and so on up to 5. Whether the _strongly agree_ or the _strongly disagree_ response is assigned the weight of 1 is determined on the basis of a judgment

---

2. This was done for each statement after the scales were in their final form. See Chapter III.

which is objectively checked by applying the test of internal consistency. The important consideration is not whether one decides that a low or high score shall indicate good morale, but whether one is consistent in assigning the values from item to item. Anyone who works with this method soon discovers that it is a simple matter to assign the values consistently. Below are two statements from the morale scale together with the score assigned to each response. In this scale a high score indicates poor morale.

THE FUTURE LOOKS VERY BLACK
Strongly agree^{5} Agree^{4} Undecided^{3} Disagree^{2} Strongly disagree^{1}

IT DOES NOT TAKE LONG TO GET OVER FEELING GLOOMY
Strongly agree^{1} Agree^{2} Undecided^{3} Disagree^{4} Strongly disagree^{5}

Likert did not include the numbers assigned as scores in the printing of his scales; the present authors did. It simplifies the tabulation and, judging from our experience with the scales given anonymously, it does not seem to affect responses. Although the scales have been administered to more than 3,000 individuals, we have yet to hear an inquiry as to significance of the numbers, which are printed very inconspicuously.

Inspection of the alternative phrases underneath each item reveals that there is a decided advantage in using such phrases as compared with assigning a single weight to an accepted statement. Not only is it possible to estimate the individual's position on the attitude distribution, but it is also possible to ascertain his position more precisely on each individual item.

The authors devised these scales primarily for research purposes. All possible precautions were taken to secure honest responses. In administering them, therefore, particular emphasis was laid upon the fact that it was not necessary for the subject to sign his name. Whether the responses obtained would have been different had the subject felt that his paper could be identified, the authors do not know. This point is probably of more importance for groups outside a university, the students of which are accustomed to filling out schedules of every variety. Since the authors were particularly interested in applying the scales to other groups, they have consistently followed the procedure of emphasizing the anonymous nature of the responses. The fact that the responses were anonymous made a particularly favorable impression on the group of relief clients to whom the scales were administered. Since the procedure eliminates the possibility of obtaining further information about the subjects, it has occasionally been a source of regret.

FINAL SELECTION OF ITEMS

The method used in the final selection of the items for the morale scale was employed in selecting the items for all six scales. Scores on the individual items in the second preliminary form of the scale were totaled to determine roughly the individual's position on the attitude continuum. Responses to each item were then tabulated for individuals in the upper and lower quartiles.[3] The group contained 72 men and 112 women. The discriminative value of each item was then computed by obtaining the difference between the average scores for the quartiles on each item. The method of computing discriminative values is illustrated in Table 2 for the male group. In Table 3 are given the discriminative values for the sexes combined and the statements in the second preliminary form of the scale.

We may note from Table 3 that the items selected for the final form of the morale scale have fairly high discriminative values, considering that the differences are those between the extreme quartiles. Likert and Hall report some discriminative values that are higher than these, but they were dealing with only the upper and lower 9 per cent of the distribution.

---

3. The percentage of cases to be included in the highest and lowest groups is a matter of judgment. Likert used the 9 per cent at each extreme. The authors believed that by using the upper and lower quartiles the results would be more stable. Vernon and Allport (22) and Heidbreder (10) also used the upper and lower quartiles.

TABLE 2.—COMPUTATION OF SCALE VALUE DIFFERENCE

Item 49: No One Cares Much What Happens to You

Response	Weight	Lowest Quartile		Highest Quartile	
		Frequency	Frequency x Weight	Frequency	Frequency x Weight
Strongly disagree . .	1	2	2	0	0
Disagree	2	14	28	3	6
Undecided	3	1	3	3	9
Agree	4	1	4	8	32
Strongly agree . . .	5	0	0	4	20
Total		18	37	18	67
Mean			2.056		3.722
Item Scale Value Difference = 3.722 - 2.056 = 1.666					

An additional fact emerges from Table 3; negative statements in this scale discriminate better than do positive. The eight statements having the highest discriminative values are negative. The significance of this will be considered later.

The nature of the items in Table 3 raises the question of how adequately material of this kind could be scaled by the Thurstone method. Consider item 43: A person's thinking soon turns into daydreaming about what he would like to have happen, which has a very low discriminative value (.210). Nearly all the college sophomores agreed with it when reacting on a personal basis. Not so many years ago a group of psychological judges would perhaps have considered this item as indicative of low morale, the general belief being that daydreaming had an adverse personality significance. The likelihood of all the judges being wrong because of prevailing conceptions is probably not great, so far as regards most traits that have been measured by the Thurstone technique. It is possible, however, that in evaluating more generalized personality traits than attitudes the Thurstone technique may be inapplicable. The authors have no particular conviction in the matter and merely raise the problem as one deserving of experimental attention.

TABLE 3.—MORALE ITEMS ARRANGED IN ORDER OF THEIR CAPACITY TO DISCRIMINATE BETWEEN THE UPPER AND LOWER QUARTILES

(N = 184; sexes weighted equally.)*

Item No.**	Scale Value Difference	Statement
115	1.514*	The future is too uncertain for a person to plan on marrying.
191	1.441*	The future looks very black.
169	1.441*	No one cares much what happens to you.
181	1.297*	Life is just a series of disappointments.
67	1.264*	There is really no point in living.
207	1.229*	These days one is inclined to give up hope of amounting to something.
140	1.210*	Life is just one worry after another.***
215	1.177*	Success is more dependent on luck than on real ability.****
55	1.165*	Real friends are as easy to find as ever.
79	1.139*	There is little chance for advancement in business or industry unless a man has unfair pull.****
139	1.137*	The young man of today can expect much of the future.
26	1.125*	The day is not long enough to do one's work well and have any time for fun.***
61	1.095*	Any man with ability and willingness to work hard has a good chance of being successful.****
213	1.074*	A person can plan his future so that everything will come out all right in the long run.
38	1.020*	A man does not have to pretend that he is smarter than he really is to get by.***
145	0.996*	It does not take long to get over feeling gloomy.
133	0.985*	It is difficult to think clearly these days.
1	0.973*	Most people can be trusted.
49	0.972*	Times are getting better.
19	0.909	It is hard these days to find recreation which will take a person's mind off his problems.
186	0.875	Hard times are here to stay.

Table 3.-Continued

Item No.**	Scale Value Difference	Statement
214	0.863*	One seldom worries so much as to become very miserable.
37	0.830*	This generation will probably never see such hard times again.
73	0.784	Young men of today cannot expect to earn as much as their fathers did.
209	0.780*	It is great to be living in these exciting times.
198	0.725	A person can be happy on very little money.
216	0.681	Standards of conduct should not be lowered in an attempt to make a living.
157	0.665	There is not much sense in trying very hard to make good.****
205	0.655	The efforts of the government to end the depression will be successful.
85	0.653	Training for special work is useless because one cannot find a job anyway.
163	0.635	Hard times destroy a man's confidence in himself.
91	0.629	Ambition is all right for youngsters, but a man gets to realize it is all the "bunk."****
195	0.624	The future is so uncertain that it does not matter what anybody does.
7	0.617	It is easy to maintain one's self-respect.
211	0.552	After the depression times will be more prosperous than ever.
175	0.525	Conditions are seldom as bad as they seem at the moment.
109	0.508	It is easy to keep up one's courage.
97	0.481	Most people are ready to give a fellow a helping hand.
121	0.470	Such strange things happen today that life seems like a dream.
151	0.466	Looking for work is a waste of effort.
31	0.443	It is easy to make decisions at this time.
201	0.437	It is more fun to strive when the going becomes difficult.
25	0.415	People's ideals are as high as ever.

Table 3.-Continued

Item No.**	Scale Value Difference	Statement
127	0.365	There is absolutely nothing of more importance than having a job.
203	0.254	One should take advantage of being out of work to have a "swell time."
43	0.210	A person's thinking soon turns into daydreaming about what he would like to have happen.
103	0.163	A person gets about as far if he doesn't try as if he does.
13	0.125	Keeping up one's personal appearance won't help one much to get along in the world.

*Items retained.

**The numbers here given are those used to identify the items in the preliminary forms, and not those used in the final form.

***These items were originally included in the inferiority scale. All the items in the inferiority scale were tabulated in terms of morale quartiles, and all the items in the morale scale were tabulated in terms of inferiority quartiles. The items were placed in the scale in which they discriminated best.

****Hall's items.

To eliminate the possibility that items discriminating well between the quartiles would do so more because of a sex difference in response than because of individual differences within each sex, the sexes were treated separately. Once it had been ascertained that an item discriminated well between the upper and lower quartiles for each sex, the ideal procedure would have been to combine an equal number of each sex and again determine the discriminative value of each item. This procedure would have eliminated the papers for 40 women, and the authors were reluctant to reduce the reliability of their measures by eliminating these cases. It was therefore decided to compute the discriminative values for each item by sex and then weight each sex equally by averaging these values. Whether the items are selected on the basis of their discriminative value for either sex or on the basis of the unweighted average of these values, substantially the same items are retained. The maximum number of items that would be changed in any scale by selecting on the basis of either sex alone is 7. For most scales it was 2 or 3.

One further factor in the selection of these items must be considered. To minimize the effects of suggestion, it appeared desirable to balance positive and negative statements--that is, to have as many items to which strongly agree represents an unfavorable response as items to which it represents a favorable one. Thus individuals standing at opposite extremes in their attitudes should indorse about equal numbers of statements.

Table 3 illustrates how it was sometimes necessary to make a slight sacrifice in discriminative value in order to retain an equal number of positive and negative statements. The first 19 statements in order of discriminative value include 11 negative and 8 positive statements. To reach the arbitrarily chosen number of 22 items for the scale, we simply took the next three positive statements, numbers 214, 37, and 209. Items numbered 19, 186, and 73 were rejected because stated negatively. The morale scale furnished the major problem in this respect. For none of the remaining scales was it necessary to change more than one item in order to balance positive and negative statements. In some of the scales the two types of statement balanced themselves.

Table 4 shows that there is a fairly large sex difference in the discriminative capacity of several of the items; it has been pointed out that each sex has been given equal weight in the selection of items. Hence sex differences that may be found later cannot be attributed to the method of item selection.

DISCRIMINATIVE VALUE OF ITEMS

Did the method of selecting the 22 items for the morale scale include items yielding $Q_1 - Q_4$ discriminative values that might be accounted for on a

TABLE 4.-SCALE VALUE DIFFERENCE OF MORALE ITEMS FOR EACH SEX

(N = 72 men, 112 women.)

Item	Male	Female	Item	Male	Female	Item	Male	Female
115*	1.78	1.25	133*	1.11	0.86	195	0.89	0.36
191*	1.67	1.21	1*	0.94	1.00	7	0.56	0.68
169*	1.67	1.21	49*	0.94	1.00	211	0.39	0.71
181*	1.67	0.93	19	0.89	0.93	175	0.72	0.32
67*	1.78	0.75	186	1.00	0.75	109	0.44	0.57
207*	1.28	1.18	214*	0.83	0.89	97	0.39	0.57
140*	1.28	1.14	37*	0.94	0.71	121	0.33	0.61
215*	0.89	1.47	73	0.89	0.68	151	0.61	0.32
55*	1.22	1.10	209*	1.17	0.39	31	0.28	0.61
79*	1.28	1.00	198	1.06	0.39	201	0.44	0.43
139*	1.17	1.10	216	0.61	0.75	25	0.72	0.11
26*	1.00	1.25	157	0.72	0.61	127	0.44	0.29
61*	0.83	1.36	205	0.67	0.64	203	0.22	0.29
213*	1.11	0.93	85	0.56	0.75	43	0.28	0.14
38*	1.11	0.93	163	0.56	0.71	103	0.11	0.21
145*	1.28	0.71	91	0.72	0.54	13	0.00	0.25

*Item retained.

chance basis? The data in Table 5 show conclusively that this is not the case. Even with an N as small as 18 in each extreme male quartile the D/σ diff. ratios average 4.236 for the 22 items in the morale scale. In no case is the difference less than twice its standard error, and in only six cases is it less than 3. Only one of these cases is less than 2.5 (item 55). The results for women are similar. For the 22 items the average of the D/σ diff. ratios is 4.277. Only one item has a ratio of less than 2.00 and only two of less than 3.00. Clearly the critical level for the discriminative values was set sufficiently high. Since the discriminative values for the remaining scales were equally good and the N remains constant, it was not considered necessary to evaluate the differences statistically for any of the other scales.

Data on the additional scales may be briefly presented. Table 6 gives the discriminative values of

TABLE 5.-CRITICAL RATIOS FOR THE DISCRIMINATIVE VALUES OF THE ITEMS

(N = 18 men, 28 women in each quartile.)

Item	Male	Female	Item	Male	Female
1	5.619	4.676	67	5.376	4.618
7	3.603	3.327	73	4.948	4.355
13	6.419	5.811	79	4.172	5.009
19	4.021	4.423	85	2.973	2.714
25	2.605	4.042	91	3.166	3.638
31	2.963	4.427	97	6.173	3.865
37	5.137	3.228	103	2.806	3.270
43	2.532	4.642	109	5.920	3.896
49	6.054	5.329	115	3.081	7.602
55	2.453	5.266	121	5.022	4.681
61	4.244	1.674	127	5.911	3.597

Mean (Men) 4.236
Mean (Women) 4.277

the items retained in the six scales. Since the same number of items were retained in each scale, simple addition of the values will provide a rough measure of the discriminative power of each scale. It may be noted that the economic conservatism scale appears to have the most, and the law scale the least discriminative power. All scales, however, possess fairly good capacity to discriminate between the upper and lower quartiles.

For convenience in analyzing the data, and in the hope of developing comparable forms of the test to use in measuring changes in these attitudes, each scale was divided into two forms on the basis of the discriminative value of the items. It was also attempted to place items that appeared to carry much the same idea in different forms. Table 7 indicates that the two forms may be considered equal in discriminative capacity. In all scales except those measuring feelings of inferiority and economic conservatism the sex difference is in the same direction for each form. In this table the sum of the sex differences for the 11 items in each form is given. The differences are so small in relation to

TABLE 6.-DISCRIMINATIVE VALUES OF THE ITEMS RETAINED IN THE SIX SCALES

(N = 184.)

	Morale	Inferiority	Family	Law	Economic Conservatism	Education
	1.514	1.439	1.846	1.226	1.748	1.566
	1.441	1.312	1.693	1.215	1.693	1.439
	1.441	1.302	1.513	1.149	1.889	1.215
	1.297	1.264	1.447	1.070	1.683	1.091
	1.264	1.242	1.373	1.064	1.552	1.060
	1.229	1.240	1.272	1.030	1.544	1.056
	1.210	1.153	1.270	1.010	1.465	1.032
	1.177	1.147	1.242	1.000	1.440	1.008
	1.165	1.145	1.197	0.979	1.417	1.002
	1.139	1.074	1.197	0.961	1.363	0.940
	1.137	1.061	1.185	0.960	1.341	0.925
	1.125	1.049	1.163	0.917	1.282	0.891
	1.095	1.024	1.111	0.907	1.278	0.889
	1.074	1.010	1.084	0.875	1.261	0.853
	1.020	1.008	1.050	0.856	1.254	0.810
	0.996	0.949	1.036	0.843	1.230	0.794
	0.985	0.937	1.030	0.766	1.210	0.792
	0.973	0.926	0.978	0.756	1.187	0.792
	0.792	0.905	0.963	0.753	1.175	0.782
	0.863	0.844	0.963	0.687	1.147	0.778
	0.830	0.770	0.952	0.674	1.038	0.776
	0.780	0.758	0.804	0.659	0.966	0.764
Total...	24.697	23.559	26.369	20.357	30.163	21.255

a scale running from 11 to 55 points on total score that they probably can be neglected.

DISGUISING THE CONTINUITY OF SCALES

In these scales, values were assigned to the responses in such a way that a low total score indicates high morale, absence of inferiority feelings, favorable family attitudes, respect for law, economic conservatism,

TABLE 7.-SUM OF THE SCALE VALUE DIFFERENCES OF THE ITEMS AND TOTAL SEX DIFFERENCE FOR THE 11 ITEMS IN FORMS A AND B OF EACH SCALE

(N = 72 men, 112 women.)

Scale	Sum of Scale Value Differences		Sex Difference	
	Form A	Form B	Form A	Form B
Morale	12.347	12.379	1.105M*	0.763M
Inferiority	11.540	12.019	1.008M	0.104F
Family	13.374	12.995	0.682M	0.448M
Law	10.117	10.240	1.290M	0.487M
Economic Conservatism . . .	15.328	14.635	0.209F**	1.126M
Education	10.456	10.799	2.514M	1.317M

*Men exceed.

**Women exceed.

and high regard for the value of education. The items were arranged in the final form of the survey in random order except that every sixth item belongs to the same scale.

When only every sixth item is in the same scale, the personality continua involved are less obvious than if all items of a single scale were printed consecutively. The subject's difficulty in identifying the continua involved presumably avoids a spuriously high reliability resulting from an attempt to make responses intellectually consistent. Spacing of responses to items in the same attitude scale is also advantageous from the viewpoint of the theory of sampling. The scales as they were given are presented in the Appendix. The form in which an item is included can be ascertained from the tabulation sheet, which is also appended.

THE FINAL SCALES

In order that the reader may perceive the scales as units, the 22 retained items of each are given here, numbered in the position each appeared in the Survey of Opinions. An item followed by (N) is a negative item in the sense that agreement with it indicates the unfavorable attitude. The implications of this will be considered later. The scales are named on the basis of the ideational continuity of the items.

No attempt will be made to define this ideational continuity until the data have been considered. It will be noted that all statements are declarative in form and that many of the items are so stated as to arouse a personal reaction without sharply focussing the individual's attention on his own personal problems.

THE MORALE SCALE

1. THE FUTURE IS TOO UNCERTAIN FOR A PERSON TO PLAN ON MARRYING. (N)*

7. IT IS DIFFICULT TO THINK CLEARLY THESE DAYS. (N)

13. THE FUTURE LOOKS VERY BLACK. (N)

19. LIFE IS JUST ONE WORRY AFTER ANOTHER. (N)

25. MOST PEOPLE CAN BE TRUSTED.

31. TIMES ARE GETTING BETTER.

37. IT DOES NOT TAKE LONG TO GET OVER FEELING GLOOMY.

43. THE DAY IS NOT LONG ENOUGH TO DO ONE'S WORK WELL AND HAVE ANY TIME FOR FUN. (N)

49. NO ONE CARES MUCH WHAT HAPPENS TO YOU. (N)

55. ANY MAN WITH ABILITY AND WILLINGNESS TO WORK HARD HAS A GOOD CHANCE OF BEING SUCCESSFUL.**

61. IT IS GREAT TO BE LIVING IN THESE EXCITING TIMES.

67. THESE DAYS ONE IS INCLINED TO GIVE UP HOPE OF AMOUNTING TO SOMETHING. (N)

73. THERE IS LITTLE CHANCE FOR ADVANCEMENT IN INDUSTRY AND BUSINESS UNLESS A MAN HAS UNFAIR PULL.** (N)

79. THE YOUNG MAN OF TODAY CAN EXPECT MUCH OF THE FUTURE.

85. THIS GENERATION WILL PROBABLY NEVER SEE SUCH HARD TIMES AGAIN.

91. REAL FRIENDS ARE AS EASY TO FIND AS EVER.

97. LIFE IS JUST A SERIES OF DISAPPOINTMENTS. (N)

103. ONE SELDOM WORRIES SO MUCH AS TO BECOME VERY MISERABLE.

109. A MAN DOES NOT HAVE TO PRETEND HE IS SMARTER THAN HE REALLY IS TO "GET BY."

115. SUCCESS IS MORE DEPENDENT ON LUCK THAN ON REAL ABILITY. (N)**

121. A PERSON CAN PLAN HIS FUTURE SO THAT EVERYTHING WILL COME OUT ALL RIGHT IN THE LONG RUN.

127. THERE IS REALLY NO POINT IN LIVING. (N)

---

*(N) indicates that agreement with the statement was regarded as an unfavorable attitude.

**Item taken from Hall's Scale of Occupational Morale.

THE INFERIORITY SCALE

2. AFTER BEING CAUGHT IN A MISTAKE, IT IS HARD TO DO GOOD WORK FOR A WHILE. (N)*

8. IT IS EASY TO EXPRESS ONE'S IDEAS.

14. IT IS DIFFICULT TO SAY THE RIGHT THING AT THE RIGHT TIME. (N)

20. ONE CAN USUALLY KEEP COOL IN IMPORTANT SITUATIONS.

26. IT IS EASY TO GET ONE'S OWN WAY IN MOST SITUATIONS.

32. IT IS EASY TO HAVE A GOOD TIME AT A PARTY.

38. MEETING NEW PEOPLE IS USUALLY EMBARRASSING. (N)

44. IT IS EASY TO KEEP UP ONE'S COURAGE.

50. IT IS EASY TO IGNORE CRITICISM.

56. IT IS EASY TO ACT NATURALLY IN A GROUP.

62. IT IS HARD TO BRING ONE'S SELF TO CONFIDE IN OTHERS. (N)

68. IT IS HARD TO DO YOUR BEST WHEN PEOPLE ARE WATCHING YOU. (N)

74. IT IS EASY TO GET ALONG WITH PEOPLE.

80. IT IS EASY TO FEEL AS THOUGH YOU HAD A WORLD OF SELF-CONFIDENCE.

86. MOST PEOPLE JUST PRETEND THAT THEY LIKE YOU. (N)

92. SO MANY PEOPLE DO THINGS WELL THAT IT IS EASY TO BECOME DISCOURAGED. (N)

98. IT IS HARD NOT TO BE SELF-CONSCIOUS. (N)

104. IT IS NO TRICK TO BE THE LIFE OF THE PARTY.

110. IT IS EASY TO KEEP PEOPLE FROM TAKING ADVANTAGE OF YOU.

116. MOST PEOPLE ARE TOO CRITICAL OF ONE'S BEHAVIOR. (N)

122. FEAR OF SOCIAL BLUNDERS KEEPS ONE FROM HAVING A GOOD TIME AT A PARTY. (N)

128. IT IS EASY TO LOSE CONFIDENCE IN ONE'S SELF. (N)

---

*(N) indicates that agreement with the statement was regarded as an unfavorable attitude.

THE FAMILY SCALE

3. HOME IS THE MOST PLEASANT PLACE IN THE WORLD.

9. PARENTS EXPECT TOO MUCH FROM THEIR CHILDREN. (N)*

15. ONE OUGHT TO DISCUSS IMPORTANT PLANS WITH MEMBERS OF HIS FAMILY.

21. IN MAKING PLANS FOR THE FUTURE, PARENTS SHOULD BE GIVEN FIRST CONSIDERATION.

27. A MAN SHOULD BE WILLING TO SACRIFICE EVERYTHING FOR HIS FAMILY.

33. PARENTS TOO OFTEN EXPECT THEIR GROWN-UP CHILDREN TO OBEY THEM. (N)

39. ONE CANNOT FIND AS MUCH UNDERSTANDING AT HOME AS ELSEWHERE. (N)

45. ONE OWES HIS GREATEST OBLIGATION TO HIS FAMILY.

51. IT IS HARD TO KEEP A PLEASANT DISPOSITION AT HOME. (N)

57. PEOPLE IN THE FAMILY CAN BE TRUSTED COMPLETELY.

63. ONE BECOMES NERVOUS AT HOME. (N)

69. THE JOYS OF FAMILY LIFE ARE MUCH OVER-RATED. (N)

75. ONE'S PARENTS USUALLY TREAT HIM FAIRLY AND SENSIBLY.

81. ONE SHOULD CONFIDE MORE FULLY IN MEMBERS OF HIS FAMILY.

87. ONE FEELS MOST CONTENTED AT HOME.

93. FAMILY TIES ARE STRENGTHENED WHEN TIMES ARE HARD.

99. PARENTS ARE INCLINED TO BE TOO OLD-FASHIONED IN THEIR IDEAS. (N)

105. MEMBERS OF THE FAMILY ARE TOO CURIOUS ABOUT ONE'S PERSONAL AFFAIRS. (N)

111. PARENTS KEEP FAITH IN THEIR CHILDREN EVEN THOUGH THEY CANNOT FIND WORK.

117. PARENTS ARE TOO PARTICULAR ABOUT THE KIND OF COMPANY ONE KEEPS. (N)

123. OBLIGATIONS TO ONE'S FAMILY ARE A GREAT HANDICAP TO A YOUNG MAN TODAY. (N)

129. SO FAR AS IDEAS ARE CONCERNED, PARENTS AND CHILDREN LIVE IN DIFFERENT WORLDS. (N)

---

*(N) indicates that agreement with the statement was regarded as an unfavorable attitude.

THE LAW SCALE

4. THE LAW PROTECTS PROPERTY RIGHTS AT THE EXPENSE OF HUMAN RIGHTS. (N)*

10. A PERSON SHOULD OBEY ONLY THOSE LAWS WHICH SEEM REASONABLE.(N)

16. IT IS ALL RIGHT TO EVADE THE LAW IF YOU DO NOT ACTUALLY VIOLATE IT. (N)

22. THE SENTENCES OF JUDGES IN COURTS ARE DETERMINED BY THEIR PREJUDICES. (N)

28. ON THE WHOLE, JUDGES ARE HONEST.

34. JURIES SELDOM UNDERSTAND A CASE WELL ENOUGH TO MAKE A REALLY JUST DECISION. (N)

40. ON THE WHOLE, POLICEMEN ARE HONEST.

46. A MAN SHOULD OBEY THE LAWS NO MATTER HOW MUCH THEY INTERFERE WITH HIS PERSONAL AMBITIONS.

52. COURT DECISIONS ARE ALMOST ALWAYS JUST.

58. IN THE COURTS A POOR MAN WILL RECEIVE AS FAIR TREATMENT AS A MILLIONAIRE.

64. PERSONAL CIRCUMSTANCES SHOULD NEVER BE CONSIDERED AN EXCUSE FOR LAW-BREAKING.

70. A MAN SHOULD TELL THE TRUTH IN COURT, REGARDLESS OF CONSEQUENCES.

76. A PERSON WHO REPORTS MINOR LAW VIOLATIONS IS ONLY A TROUBLE-MAKER. (N)

82. A PERSON IS JUSTIFIED IN GIVING FALSE TESTIMONY TO PROTECT A FRIEND ON TRIAL. (N)

88. A HUNGRY MAN HAS A RIGHT TO STEAL. (N)

94. ALL LAWS SHOULD BE STRICTLY OBEYED BECAUSE THEY <u>ARE</u> LAWS.

100. LAWS ARE SO OFTEN MADE FOR THE BENEFIT OF SMALL SELFISH GROUPS THAT A MAN CANNOT RESPECT THE LAW. (N)

106. ALMOST ANYTHING CAN BE FIXED UP IN THE COURTS IF YOU HAVE ENOUGH MONEY. (N)

112. IT IS DIFFICULT TO BREAK THE LAW AND KEEP ONE'S SELF-RESPECT.

118. ON THE WHOLE, LAWYERS ARE HONEST.

124. VIOLATORS OF THE LAW ARE NEARLY ALWAYS DETECTED AND PUNISHED.

130. IT IS ALL RIGHT FOR A PERSON TO BREAK THE LAW IF HE DOESN'T GET CAUGHT. (N)

---

*(N) indicates that agreement with the statement was regarded as an unfavorable attitude.

THE ECONOMIC CONSERVATISM SCALE

5. THE GOVERNMENT SHOULD TAKE OVER ALL LARGE INDUSTRIES. (N)*

11. LABOR SHOULD HAVE MUCH MORE VOICE IN DECIDING GOVERNMENT POLICIES. (N)

17. LEGISLATURES ARE TOO READY TO PASS LAWS TO CURB BUSINESS FREEDOM.

23. FOR MEN TO DO THEIR BEST, THERE MUST BE THE POSSIBILITY OF UNLIMITED PROFIT.

29. POVERTY IS CHIEFLY A RESULT OF INJUSTICE IN THE DISTRIBUTION OF WEALTH. (N)

35. THE GOVERNMENT SHOULD NOT ATTEMPT TO LIMIT PROFITS.

41. THE MORE A MAN LEARNS ABOUT OUR ECONOMIC SYSTEM, THE LESS WILLING HE IS TO SEE CHANGES MADE.

47. THE GOVERNMENT OUGHT TO GUARANTEE A LIVING TO THOSE WHO CAN'T FIND WORK. (N)

53. LARGE INCOMES SHOULD BE TAXED MUCH MORE THAN THEY ARE NOW.(N)

59. MEN WOULD NOT DO THEIR BEST IF GOVERNMENT OWNED ALL INDUSTRY.

65. MOST GREAT FORTUNES ARE MADE HONESTLY.

71. PRIVATE OWNERSHIP OF PROPERTY IS NECESSARY FOR ECONOMIC PROGRESS.

77. WITHOUT SWEEPING CHANGES IN OUR ECONOMIC SYSTEM, LITTLE PROGRESS CAN BE MADE IN THE SOLUTION OF SOCIAL PROBLEMS. (N)

83. ON THE WHOLE, OUR ECONOMIC SYSTEM IS JUST AND WISE.

89. LABOR DOES NOT GET ITS FAIR SHARE OF WHAT IT PRODUCES. (N)

95. WHEN A RICH MAN DIES, MOST OF HIS PROPERTY SHOULD GO TO THE STATE. (N)

101. IF OUR ECONOMIC SYSTEM WERE JUST, THERE WOULD BE MUCH LESS CRIME. (N)

107. THE INCOMES OF MOST PEOPLE ARE A FAIR MEASURE OF THEIR CONTRIBUTION TO HUMAN WELFARE.

113. A MAN SHOULD STRIKE IN ORDER TO SECURE GREATER RETURNS TO LABOR. (N)

119. A MAN SHOULD BE ALLOWED TO KEEP AS LARGE AN INCOME AS HE CAN GET.

125. MONEY SHOULD BE TAKEN FROM THE RICH AND GIVEN TO THE POOR DURING HARD TIMES. (N)

131. OUR ECONOMIC SYSTEM IS CRITICIZED TOO MUCH.

---

*(N) indicates that agreement with the statement was regarded as an unfavorable attitude.

THE EDUCATION SCALE

6. A MAN CAN LEARN MORE BY WORKING FOUR YEARS THAN BY GOING TO HIGH SCHOOL. (N)*
12. THE MORE EDUCATION A MAN HAS THE BETTER HE IS ABLE TO ENJOY LIFE.
18. EDUCATION HELPS A PERSON TO USE HIS LEISURE TIME TO BETTER ADVANTAGE.
24. A GOOD EDUCATION IS A GREAT COMFORT TO A MAN OUT OF WORK.
30. ONLY SUBJECTS LIKE READING, WRITING, AND ARITHMETIC SHOULD BE TAUGHT AT PUBLIC EXPENSE. (N)
36. EDUCATION IS OF NO HELP IN GETTING A JOB TODAY. (N)
42. MOST YOUNG PEOPLE ARE GETTING TOO MUCH EDUCATION. (N)
48. A HIGH SCHOOL EDUCATION IS WORTH ALL THE TIME AND EFFORT IT REQUIRES.
54. OUR SCHOOLS ENCOURAGE AN INDIVIDUAL TO THINK FOR HIMSELF.
60. THERE ARE TOO MANY FADS AND FRILLS IN MODERN EDUCATION. (N)
66. EDUCATION ONLY MAKES A PERSON DISCONTENTED. (N)
72. SCHOOL TRAINING IS OF LITTLE HELP IN MEETING THE PROBLEMS OF REAL LIFE. (N)
78. EDUCATION TENDS TO MAKE AN INDIVIDUAL LESS CONCEITED.
84. SOLUTION OF THE WORLD'S PROBLEMS WILL COME THROUGH EDUCATION.
90. HIGH SCHOOL COURSES ARE TOO IMPRACTICAL. (N)
96. A MAN IS FOOLISH TO KEEP ON GOING TO SCHOOL IF HE CAN GET A JOB. (N)
102. SAVINGS SPENT ON EDUCATION ARE WISELY INVESTED.
108. AN EDUCATED MAN CAN ADVANCE MORE RAPIDLY IN BUSINESS AND INDUSTRY.
114. PARENTS SHOULD NOT BE COMPELLED TO SEND THEIR CHILDREN TO SCHOOL. (N)
120. EDUCATION IS MORE VALUABLE THAN MOST PEOPLE THINK.
126. A HIGH SCHOOL EDUCATION MAKES A MAN A BETTER CITIZEN.
132. PUBLIC MONEY SPENT ON EDUCATION DURING THE PAST FEW YEARS COULD HAVE BEEN USED MORE WISELY FOR OTHER PURPOSES. (N)

---

*(N) indicates that agreement with the statement was regarded as an unfavorable attitude.

Chapter II

DESCRIPTION OF THE SUBJECT GROUPS

The personality scales were administered to the several groups listed in Table 8. The characteristics of each group, where the label is not self-explanatory, will be described when necessary. It is the four main groups--the university students, the high school seniors, the members of Minneapolis evening classes, and those of Minneapolis day classes for the unemployed--which will be described in this chapter. The information concerning these groups was obtained from the face sheet of the attitude scales. (See the Appendix.)

TABLE 8.-CLASSIFICATION OF 2,882 SUBJECTS GIVEN PERSONALITY SCALES

Group	Male	Female
General College	100	100
Sociology I (College of Science, Literature, and Arts	100	100
First year College of Law	100	...
Students receiving federal aid	60	...
Employed high school teachers	10	11
University high school juniors	37	34
Minneapolis public high school seniors.	359	383
Minneapolis public evening schools . .	346	678
Classes for the unemployed	152	260
Men receiving public relief	52	
Total	1,316	1,566

THE UNIVERSITY GROUP

The university group consists of 100 of each sex from the elementary sociology classes in the liberal arts college, and 100 of each sex from classes in beginning psychology in the General College. The students of these General College classes fall, for the most part, within the three lower deciles on the Minnesota College Aptitude Test; the sociology group constitutes a sampling of the complete range. Since there were no conspicuous differences in attitude scores (see Table 17) nor with respect to age, parental occupation, and the other variables for which information was available, the two college groups have been combined. The absence of differences between the attitude scores for these groups argues strongly that the traits measured are little affected by absolute intelligence.

PARENTAL OCCUPATIONS

As may be seen from Tables 9 to 16, the university group is typical of the general run of college students. The ages are typical and the parental occupations are weighted toward the upper socio-economic levels. The revision of the Barr-Taussig Occupational Scale on the basis of the Barr Scale ratings as developed by the University of Minnesota Institute of Child Welfare (6), was used in classifying the occupations, the distribution of which is given in Table 9. The occupational distribution of the Minneapolis population in 1930 has been expressed in terms of this scale by the University of Minnesota Employment Stabilization Research Institute (7). The percentage of male persons in each occupation, taken from this source, is given in Table 9 under the heading Standard Sample. Groups selected to approximate this sample in composition will be referred to as standard or as controlled samples. In general, Class I represents the professional groups; Class II, the business executive groups; Class III, the clerical and skilled trades; Class IV, the farmers; Class V, the semi-skilled trades; Class VI, the relatively unskilled trades, the positions in which have the characteristic of permanency; and Class VII, the unskilled laboring group.

TABLE 9.-OCCUPATIONAL DISTRIBUTION OF PARENTS OF THE VARIOUS GROUPS

(Single persons only)

Occupational Class*	Evening Classes				Day Classes				High School Seniors				University Group				Minneapolis Standard Sample**
	Men		Women		Men		Women		Men		Women		Men		Women		
	No.	%	No.	%	No.	%	No.	%	No.	%	No.	%	No.	%	No.	%	
I . . .	7	2.98	19	3.81	5	4.20	5	2.66	38	13.72	22	7.48	30	19.11	26	15.20	4.20
II . . .	32	13.62	66	13.23	10	8.40	25	13.30	57	20.58	72	24.49	41	26.11	54	31.58	10.00
III . . .	81	34.47	172	34.47	41	34.45	71	37.77	96	34.66	116	39.46	49	31.21	56	32.75	22.90
IV . . .	25	10.64	80	16.03	2	1.68	12	6.38	4	1.44	16	5.44	8	5.10	18	10.53	.20
V . . .	66	28.07	110	22.04	48	40.37	50	26.60	65	23.47	51	17.35	23	14.65	15	8.77	42.60
VI . . .	11	4.68	29	5.81	9	7.56	15	7.98	10	3.61	10	3.40	4	2.55	1	.58	7.60
VII . . .	13	5.53	23	4.61	4	3.36	10	5.32	7	2.53	7	2.38	2	1.27	1	.58	12.70
Total .	235	99.99	499	100.00	119	100.02	188	100.01	277	100.01	294	100.00	157	100.00	171	99.99	100.00
Unclassified	48	16.96	107	17.66	26	17.93	42	18.26	82	22.84	89	23.24	43	21.50	29	14.50	
Grand Total	283		606		145		230		359		383		200		200		

*I, professional groups; II, business executive groups; III, clerical and skilled trades; IV, farmers; V, semi-skilled grades; VI, relatively unskilled but permanent trades; VII, laboring group. See Goodenough and Anderson (6), Appendix A.

**1930 Census.

THE HIGH SCHOOL GROUPS

Graduating classes of three senior high schools were tested. Two of the schools draw largely from the upper socio-economic levels, and one from the lower. Table 9 shows the weighting in the direction of the upper socio-economic levels. In the absence of information concerning the distribution of occupations among parents of all graduating seniors, it is impossible to say how much of this weighting is a result of the location of the schools tested. Certainly some weighting in this direction is to be expected for high school seniors. Inspection of the additional tables describing the groups shows nothing to distinguish this population from that of any other city high school.

CLASSES FOR EMPLOYED AND UNEMPLOYED

The entire populations of the Minneapolis evening classes and of the unemployed day classes were tested. These classes are under the supervision of the Adult Education Department of the Minneapolis Public Schools. A very nominal fee is required in the evening classes and no fee at all in the day classes. Educational costs therefore play a very minor role in the selection of these students. It is difficult to say in what way the willingness to attend such classes indicates that they differ from random samples of the population. Possibly they are more ambitious, harder working, more alert, and have higher general morale. Data on other characteristics are presented in Tables 10 to 16. It may be stated that whatever the selective nature of this population, it does not cause the mean scores on the attitude scales to differ appreciably from those of the high school or university groups.

MARITAL STATUS

Data on the marital status of the groups is presented in Table 10. The high school seniors and the

TABLE 10.-MARITAL STATUS OF THE VARIOUS GROUPS

Marital Status	Evening Classes				Day Classes			
	Men		Women		Men		Women	
	No.	%	No.	%	No.	%	No.	%
Single	283	82.74	606	89.64	145	96.03	231	89.19
Married . . .	56	16.37	58	8.58	5	3.31	26	10.04
Divorced . . .	3	.88	12	1.78	1	.66	2	.77
Total . . .	342	99.99	676	100.00	151	100.00	259	100.00
Omitted . .	4	1.16	1	.15	1	.66	1	.38
Grand Total	346		677		152		260	

university group were all single persons. The largest proportion of married persons existed among the men of the downtown evening classes, 16.37 per cent (56 cases) of the number whose marital status was known. The women of the evening classes included the largest number of divorced persons, though they constituted only 1.78 per cent of the group. The information concerning marital status is virtually complete, the largest proportion of omissions, 1.16 per cent, occurring among the men of the evening classes.

TABLE 11.-EMPLOYMENT STATUS OF THE VARIOUS GROUPS

(Single persons only)

Employment Status	Evening Classes				Day Classes			
	Men		Women		Men		Women	
	No.	%	No.	%	No.	%	No.	%
Employed Full Time	159	56.18	306	50.50				
Employed Part Time	43	15.19	71	11.72	18	12.41	1	.43
Unemployed . .	81	28.62	229	37.79	127	87.59	230	99.57
Total . . .	283	99.99	606	100.01	145	100.00	231	100.00

EMPLOYMENT STATUS

Since the relation of marital status and attitude will be considered separately, the remaining information tabled is for single persons only. Table 11 gives the employment status of the groups. The high school seniors and the university groups were naturally composed entirely of nonemployed. Approximately 12 per cent of the men and less than 1 per cent of the women in the afternoon classes reported that they were employed part time. The classes serve, then, those for whom they were intended, the unemployed. Slightly over half of each sex in the evening classes were employed full time. Between 12 and 15 per cent were employed part time, and approximately 30 per cent were unemployed. Both the full-time employed and the unemployed groups included a large enough number to permit of an adequate comparison between the two groups on the measures of personality.

AGE DISTRIBUTION

Table 12 confirms the statement previously made that the high school and university groups were typical with respect to age. The evening groups were slightly older, the median age being between 20 and 24 years for both men and women. Almost 94 per cent of the men and 90 per cent of the women were between 17 and 29 years old. The day groups were younger than the evening groups, over half being less than 20. This suggests that the classes for unemployed were drawing largely upon the very recent high school graduates. The preponderance of women in both groups suggests that women are more interested in the educational program offered, as does the fact that there were so many more women over 30.

The information given in Table 13 concerning the amount of education of the several groups, not only confirms the conclusion that the classes for the unemployed were drawing largely upon the recent high school population but indicates also that the evening schools

TABLE 12.-AGE DISTRIBUTION OF THE VARIOUS GROUPS

(Single persons only)

	Evening Classes				Day Classes				High School Seniors					University Group				
	Men		Women		Men		Women		Age	Men		Women		Age	Men		Women	
Age	No.	%	No.	%	No.	%	No.	%		No.	%	No.	%		No.	%	No.	%
17-19	78	27.56	194	32.01	73	50.69	128	55.90	15			2	.52	15-16			1	.50
20-24	144	50.88	244	40.26	60	41.67	74	32.31	16	25	7.04	51	13.32	17-18	38	19.10	58	29.15
25-29	43	15.19	99	16.37	7	4.86	17	7.42	17	171	48.17	243	63.45	19-20	105	52.76	104	52.26
30-34	15	5.30	36	5.94	2	1.39	5	2.18	18	129	36.34	69	18.02	21-22	42	21.11	21	10.55
35-39	3	1.06	17	2.81	2	1.39	4	1.75	19	25	7.04	16	4.18	23-24	9	4.52	5	2.51
40+			16	2.64			1	.44	20+	5	1.41	2	.52	25+	5	2.51	10	5.03
Total	283	99.99	606	100.03	144	100.00	229	100.00		355	100.00	383	100.01		199	100.00	199	100.00
Omitted					1	.69	1	.43		4	1.11				1	.50	1	.50
Grand Total	283		606		145		230			359		383			200		200	

TABLE 13.-EDUCATION OF THE VARIOUS GROUPS

(Single persons only)

Grade Completed	Evening Classes				Day Classes			
	Men		Women		Men		Women	
	No.	%	No.	%	No.	%	No.	%
8 or less . .	29	10.66	39	6.63	2	1.40	7	3.12
9-12	214	78.68	450	76.53	116	81.12	189	84.37
13-16	29	10.66	99	16.84	25	17.48	28	12.50
Total . . .	272	100.00	588	100.00	143	100.00	224	99.99
Omitted . .	11	3.89	18	2.97	2	1.38	6	2.61
Grand Total	283		606		145		230	

get the greatest response from people with this amount of education. There were some who had had a year or more of college or university training, persons who apparently had found it necessary to supplement their education in order to meet the demands of the business world.

INTELLIGENCE COMPOSITION

Intelligence test scores, while not particularly necessary to demonstrate that the high school and university groups were selected groups, might assist in understanding the composition of the evening and day classes. No information is available for the day classes. For the total population of the evening classes, scores on the Iowa Silent Reading Test were kindly furnished by Mr. Walter Anderson of the Curriculum Department of the Minneapolis Public Schools. This test is reported to have a correlation of .827 with the Terman Group Test of Mental Ability. The authors (8) remark that "this correlation is high enough to indicate that the reading test may be reasonably substituted for tests of a general mental ability type for classification purposes." On most of the subtests of the Iowa Silent Reading Test the median score of the evening classes approximates that of the twelfth or thirteenth grade. The median total comprehension score of the evening classes is 126.6; of the twelfth grade, as reported by the authors of the reading test, 123. As is to be expected in view of the range of educational experience represented, the evening classes are slightly more variable in their reading comprehension than are the normative twelfth graders. Q_1, Q_3, and Q for the evening classes are 97.6, 152.4, and 27.4; for the normative twelfth graders, 96, 147, and 25.5. The only subtest on which the evening classes fall appreciably below the norms of the twelfth grade is rate of reading. The evening classes, as a group, read more slowly than does the median ninth grader. This indicates that the evening classes are not atypical so far as intelligence is concerned. It also suggests that the majority of them have not been in constant contact with educational institutions; if they had, their reading rate would not be so low.

DEPENDENCE UPON FAMILIES FOR SUPPORT

Were these groups independent of their families? Table 14 indicates that they were not. About a quarter of the university group were from out of town. In the evening classes 82.13 per cent of the men and 74.6 per cent of the women lived with their parents. Information concerning home residence was obtained from a blank, additional to the personality survey, which was not given to all the day classes.

EMPLOYMENT STATUS OF PARENTS

The data given thus far do not indicate that the groups were under any considerable economic stress. Most of the members of the day and evening classes had recently been graduated from high school and were still living at home. Were their fathers employed? Table 15 gives the answer to this question. The evening classes included the greatest proportion of persons with deceased parents, as was to be expected in view of their greater age. As compared with the other groups the

TABLE 14.-RESIDENCE OF MEMBERS OF THE VARIOUS GROUPS

(Single persons only.)

Residence	Evening Classes				Day Classes				High School Seniors				University Group			
	Men		Women		Men		Women		Men		Women		Men		Women	
	No.	%	No.	%	No.	%	No.	%	No.	%	No.	%	No.	%	No.	%
At home . . .	216	82.13	422	74.69	52	96.30	41	95.35	50	98.04	62	95.38	37	67.27	44	77.19
Not at home .	47	17.87	143	25.31	2	3.70	2	4.65	1	1.96	3	4.62	18	32.73	13	22.81
Total . . .	263	100.00	565	100.00	54	100.00	43	100.00	51	100.00	65	100.00	55	100.00	57	100.00
Omitted . .	20	7.07	41	6.77	91	62.76	187	81.31	308	85.79	318	83.03	45	45.00	43	43.00
Grand Total	283		606		145		230		359		383		100*		100	

*Data on residence obtained for students in Science, Literature, and Arts College only.

TABLE 15.–STATUS OF FATHER FOR VARIOUS GROUPS

(Single persons only.)

Status of Father	Evening Classes				Day Classes				High School Seniors				University Group			
	Men		Women		Men		Women		Men		Women		Men		Women	
	No.	%	No.	%	No.	%	No.	%	No.	%	No.	%	No.	%	No.	%
Dead	53	19.27	139	23.92	17	11.97	43	19.11	39	11.47	43	11.75	34	17.62	18	9.14
Retired	29	10.55	52	8.95	1	.70	6	2.67	10	2.94	8	2.19	7	3.63	17	8.63
Employed	157	57.09	290	49.91	107	75.35	135	60.00	259	76.18	277	75.68	144	74.61	156	79.19
Unemployed . . .	36	13.09	100	17.21	17	11.97	41	18.22	32	9.41	38	10.38	8	4.15	6	3.05
Total	275	100.00	581	99.99	142	99.99	225	100.00	340	100.00	366	100.00	193	100.01	197	100.01
Omitted . . .	8	2.83	25	4.13	3	3.07	5	2.17	15	4.23	17	4.44	7	3.50	3	1.50
Grand Total .	283		606		145		230		355		383		200		200	

evening groups included a rather large number whose fathers had retired. This certainly does not suggest edonomic stress, although they may have retired for other than economic reasons--ill health, for example. From 60.00 to 79.19 per cent of the fathers of the day classes, university groups, and high school seniors were employed, a good percentage in these days of depression. The university groups show the smallest incidence of parental unemployment, 3 and 4 per cent. The day school and evening school groups show the largest incidence of parental unemployment, ranging from 12 to 18 per cent.

SIZE OF FAMILY

That the groups do not differ appreciably with respect to the size of family they come from, as measured by the number of children, is shown in Table 16. The largest families among the evening and day classes are slightly larger than among the high school and university groups, but the difference is so slight that it cannot be considered a factor of importance.

COMPLETENESS OF DATA

For the most part the data presented are complete, indicating that the scales were taken with good cooperation. Table 9, the occupational distribution of parents, includes a considerable percentage under the heading Unclassifiable. This is chiefly due not to a large proportion of omitted responses, but to responses so worded as to make classification difficult. Only those occupations were classified that were adequately described. The unclassifiable group, therefore, is probably spread fairly evenly among the seven classes. There was no evidence that more of the unclassifiable occupations belonged to one-half of the occupational scale than to the other. Since the scales were given anonymously, there was no motive for concealing occupations that might be considered undesirable. As already remarked, the high school and university groups show the expected weighting in the direction of the three upper socio-economic levels.

TABLE 16.–SIZE OF SIBSHIP IN FAMILIES OF SINGLE PERSONS OF THE VARIOUS GROUPS

Size of Sibship	Evening Classes				Day Classes				High School Seniors				University Group			
	Men		Women		Men		Women		Men		Women		Men		Women	
	No.	%	No.	%	No.	%	No.	%	No.	%	No.	%	No.	%	No.	%
1	30	10.83	48	8.05	19	13.38	22	9.82	44	13.17	47	13.02	28	14.14	35	17.77
2	65	23.47	123	20.64	26	18.31	61	27.23	81	24.25	79	21.88	54	27.27	41	20.81
3	59	21.30	112	18.79	32	22.54	50	22.32	84	25.15	87	24.10	43	21.72	41	20.81
4	47	16.97	98	16.44	25	17.61	28	12.50	54	16.17	59	16.34	33	16.67	39	19.80
5	28	10.11	58	9.73	15	10.56	19	8.48	30	8.98	40	11.08	10	5.05	18	9.14
6	22	7.94	57	9.56	13	9.15	16	7.14	18	5.39	22	6.09	17	8.59	11	5.58
7	11	3.97	32	5.37	6	4.23	11	4.91	15	4.49	11	3.05	7	3.54	4	2.03
8	7	2.53	32	5.37	2	1.41	7	3.12	6	1.80	5	1.39	4	2.02	2	1.02
9 and over	8	2.89	36	6.04	4	2.82	10	4.46	2	.60	11	3.05	2	1.01	6	3.05
Total	277	100.01	596	99.99	142	100.01	224	99.98	334	100.00	361	100.00	198	100.01	197	100.01
Unknown	6	2.12	10	1.65	3	2.07	6	2.61	25	6.96	22	5.74	2	1.00	3	1.50
Grand Total . .	283		606		145		230		359		383		200		200	

The evening and day classes depart most conspicuously from the standard sample in Classes V, VI, and VII--these classes being less well represented than in the general population. These groups are not nearly so overweighted in the upper three occupational groups as are the high school and university groups. It is worth noting that Class IV, the farmers, is well represented, considering that this is an urban population. This may be part of the explanation of the rather high frequency of retired fathers in this group. Another possible explanation is the migration to the city of farmers' sons and daughters. But since most of the group are living at home, migration cannot be the only factor.

To summarize, the Minnesota Survey was administered to four main groups--high school seniors, university sophomores, evening class students, and day classes for the unemployed. The high school seniors and university sophomores were typical members of their groups. The evening and day classes more closely approximated a random sample of the population, so far as parental occupation is concerned, than did either the high school or the university group. The day classes were composed mostly of very recent high school graduates; the evening classes were also composed largely of high school graduates, but they were somewhat older than any of the other groups. The evening classes did not differ greatly from the high school seniors so far as intelligence is concerned. Both day class and evening class groups were, for the most part, living at home whether they were employed or not. The groups contained a reasonable sampling of employed and unemployed persons. There is no evidence to suggest that any group had been severely affected economically.

It will be possible, then, to make a comparison of the attitudes of the typical high school senior, the typical university sophomore, and the recent high school graduate, employed and unemployed, for the purpose of evaluating any widespread differential effects, if they exist, of the depression.

The single persons in the total groups do not differ in the central tendency of their attitudes. The mean standard score for all scales is 50. Table 17 shows that no group deviated much from the standard mean.

Since the day classes were composed almost entirely of recent high school graduates who were unemployed, absence of difference might indicate that the personality of members in this group was not affected by unemployment. Such a conclusion must await further analysis. Table 17 is presented to emphasize the general similarities of the groups. Differences will be considered later.

TABLE 17.-MEAN STANDARD SCORES OF THE VARIOUS GROUPS ON ALL SIX SCALES

(Single persons only.)

Group	Morale	Inferiority	Family	Law	Economic Conservatism	Education	N
			Single Men				
Evening classes	50.31	50.20	50.44	51.06	53.10	46.95	283
Day classes	49.70	48.30	50.49	48.17	52.13	50.48	145
Sociology I	50.36	47.91	49.54	50.88	49.14	53.91	100
General College	48.09	47.85	49.21	52.42	46.73	50.07	100
High school	49.50	50.76	50.10	50.83	50.93	48.56	359
			Single Women				
Evening classes	51.32	51.88	51.67	48.78	50.44	49.21	606
Day classes	51.88	51.16	51.02	47.09	51.60	51.63	231
Sociology I	50.29	49.86	49.83	52.47	51.27	49.79	100
General College	48.40	48.46	48.33	49.34	47.80	50.28	100
High school	50.13	52.16	50.08	47.50	50.05	47.62	383

THE STANDARD SAMPLES

To answer such questions as whether the items are applicable to groups somewhat dissimilar to the original standardization group and whether the scales are equally reliable for all groups, comparable samples were selected from each of the groups. Sampling the university students offered no problem. It is reasonably certain that the classes selected were a representative group. The high school seniors and the evening and day classes might have been selected at random. It was desired, however, not to have a sampling of the groups that happened to be tested but to obtain samples that might more nearly resemble the total population of high school seniors and recent high school seniors. It was further desired to obtain comparable samples of unemployed and of employed recent high school graduates. Selection from each group of a sample whose distribution of parental occupations would correspond to the distribution of occupations in the city of Minneapolis appeared the most feasible method of accomplishing these ends. One hundred of each sex were chosen from the high school seniors, from the employed of the evening classes, and from the unemployed of the day and evening classes combined. These samples will hereafter be called standard or controlled samples. Table 18 shows the extent to which we were successful in approximating the occupational distribution that existed in the city of Minneapolis. Classes VI and VII present the

TABLE 18.—OCCUPATIONS OF PARENTS OF PERSONS IN THE CONTROLLED SAMPLES

Occupational Class*	High School Seniors		Employed Sample		Unemployed Sample		Standard Sample
	Men	Women	Men	Women	Men	Women	
I . . .	4	4	2	4	4	4	4.20
II . . .	10	10	12	10	10	10	10.00
III . . .	23	23	23	23	23	23	22.90
IV . . .	..	..	..	..	..	..	.20
V . . .	47	47	44	42	42	42	42.60
VI . . .	9	10	10	10	11	9	7.60
VII . . .	7	6	9	11	10	12	12.70
Total .	100	100	100	100	100	100	100.20

*I, professional groups; II, business executive groups; III, clerical and skilled trades; IV, farmers; V, semi-skilled trades; VI, relatively unskilled but permanent trades; VII, laboring groups. See Goodenough and Anderson (6), Appendix A.

most marked deviations from the standard sample. Since these two classes could well be treated as one, this discrepancy is probably not a serious one. Although marital status has little or no effect on the attitudes measured, the attempt was made to select only single persons. Only 3 per cent of the employed and of the unemployed sample were married. In selecting the samples of the employed and unemployed, persons under 25 were chosen wherever possible. Ninety-nine per cent of the unemployed women and 98 per cent of the unemployed men, and 92 per cent of the employed women and 78 per cent of the employed men, were less than 25 years old. Since the employed men as a group were older, it was impossible to match the ages of the standard sample of the employed with those of the unemployed. Age makes little difference on these scales, however, for these groups until 30 is reached, and since virtually none of the members of these groups were over 30, it is not probable that this age difference invalidates the comparisons to any great extent.

In Table 19 are given the scores of the standard samples and those of the university groups. The groups do not differ markedly; a comparison with Table 17 shows that this method of sampling did not cause the scores to deviate much from the means for the total groups.

TABLE 19.—MEAN STANDARD SCORES AND STANDARD DEVIATIONS OF STANDARDIZATION GROUPS

(N = 1000; 100 in each subgroup)

Group	Morale		Inferiority		Family		Law		Economic Conservatism		Education	
	Mean	σ	Mean	σ	Mean	σ	Mean	σ	Mean	σ	Mean	σ
Males:												
500 males	49.12	9.57	48.96	9.81	49.82	9.33	50.59	10.24	50.20	11.04	50.29	10.11
Sociology I	50.36	11.02	47.91	10.11	49.54	8.99	50.88	10.01	49.14	12.19	53.91	11.38
General College	48.09	9.57	47.85	10.75	49.21	8.87	52.42	10.49	46.73	9.93	50.07	9.75
High school seniors (C)*	49.06	8.25	49.82	9.81	49.66	9.40	50.07	9.41	51.55	11.13	48.52	9.32
Employed (C)	47.70	9.30	49.97	8.91	49.57	9.26	50.41	11.35	50.47	9.82	50.65	9.69
Unemployed (C)	49.93	10.27	48.77	8.78	51.09	9.80	49.04	10.17	53.32	10.51	49.37	10.75
Females:												
500 females	50.87	10.24	51.07	9.94	50.23	10.67	49.39	9.73	50.13	8.74	49.64	9.90
Sociology I	50.29	9.36	49.86	9.38	49.83	10.10	52.47	7.85	51.27	11.62	49.79	8.07
General College	48.40	9.63	48.46	9.13	48.33	9.61	49.34	9.87	47.80	7.18	50.28	9.93
High school seniors (C)*	51.77	11.05	53.47	11.24	49.62	11.64	47.91	9.88	51.12	8.51	47.88	11.12
Employed (C)	49.87	9.85	51.79	9.09	52.49	11.67	49.29	9.37	50.19	7.93	48.66	10.49
Unemployed (C)	53.23	10.36	51.78	9.99	50.88	9.65	47.95	9.36	50.29	7.27	51.58	9.21

*C = Controlled sample.

Chapter III

DISCRIMINATIVE VALUES OF THE ITEMS FOR VARIOUS GROUPS

Four of the standard or controlled samples described in the previous chapter, including both sexes, were utilized for an exhaustive item analysis. These four groups are the Sociology I students and the controlled samples of high school seniors, of employed, and of unemployed. The discriminative values of each item in each scale were computed for each group.

The first question to be considered in this analysis is whether items chosen on the basis of one group are applicable to somewhat different groups. That is, do items chosen on the basis of results obtained from a fairly typical group of college sophomores discriminate as well when the resultant scales are applied to high school seniors and to groups of young employed and unemployed persons?

In Table 20 are given the scale value differences $Q_1 - Q_4$ obtained for the original standardization group, A, and for the remaining groups combined, B. The data on the two sexes have been combined in this table.

Consider first the mean discriminative value of items in each scale, as given in the last line of the table. It is clear that each scale considered as a unit discriminates as well for groups other than the standardization group as it does for that group. Three of the mean discriminative values are higher for group B than for group A, and in three of the scales the difference is in the reverse direction. The mean item discriminative values of all scales are above 1.00 for group B. A discriminative value of 1.00 implies excellent discriminative power when differences between quartiles are used as the measure. Only two items fall below .60 in discriminative value. Even with 25 cases in

TABLE 20.—SCALE VALUE DIFFERENCES OF ITEMS IN GROUP A, USED TO SELECT ITEMS, AND IN GROUP B, GIVEN COMPLETED SCALES

(N, group A = 184; N, group B = 800.)

Morale			Inferiority			Family			Law			Economic Conservation			Education		
Item	A	B	Item	A	B	Item	A	B	Item	A	B	Item	A	B	Item	A	B
1	1.514	.825	2	.905	.950	3	1.846	1.495	4	.687	.520	5	1.689	1.650	6	.778	1.125
7	.985	.945	8	1.312	1.145	9	.963	1.265	10	.843	1.050	11	1.187	1.250	12	1.566	1.325
13	1.441	1.425	14	1.242	1.145	15	1.197	.870	16	.960	.765	17	.966	.485	18	.792	.915
19	1.210	1.485	20	1.024	.760	21	.978	1.165	22	.766	1.035	23	1.038	.275	24	1.060	1.210
25	.973	.825	26	1.008	.600	27	1.163	.965	28	.753	1.025	29	1.465	1.510	30	.764	.945
31	.972	1.075	32	1.049	1.130	33	.804	1.135	34	.917	1.180	35	1.278	1.330	36	.853	.895
37	.996	1.125	38	1.061	.970	39	1.513	1.680	40	1.149	1.275	41	1.230	.660	42	1.008	1.055
43	1.125	1.120	44	1.010	1.350	45	1.030	1.230	46	1.030	.970	47	1.440	1.240	48	1.056	1.190
49	1.440	.985	50	.758	.680	51	1.185	1.485	52	.961	1.295	53	1.683	1.495	54	.925	1.020
55	1.095	1.080	56	1.264	1.480	57	1.447	1.305	58	.875	1.455	59	1.341	1.140	60	1.032	1.030
61	.780	1.030	62	1.074	.825	63	1.084	1.235	64	1.010	1.050	65	1.261	1.185	66	.810	1.125
67	1.229	1.615	68	1.153	1.305	69	1.270	1.745	70	1.064	.900	71	1.282	.805	72	1.439	1.460
73	1.139	1.250	74	1.147	1.015	75	1.242	1.230	76	.659	.865	77	1.552	.895	78	1.002	.985
79	1.137	1.375	80	.770	1.120	81	1.272	1.365	82	.979	.835	83	1.417	1.075	84	.794	.900
85	.830	.605	86	.949	.800	87	1.693	1.430	88	1.000	1.135	89	1.147	1.150	90	.940	1.255
91	1.165	.900	92	1.145	.990	93	1.036	.905	94	.907	1.100	95	1.693	1.530	96	.776	1.010
97	1.297	1.360	98	1.439	1.400	99	1.197	1.250	100	1.070	1.060	101	1.363	1.095	102	.891	.865
103	.863	.765	104	.844	1.070	105	1.373	1.630	106	1.226	1.255	107	1.175	.840	108	.889	.825
109	1.020	.870	110	.926	1.115	111	.952	.805	112	.756	.970	113	1.254	1.000	114	.792	.88[illegible]
115	1.177	1.070	116	.937	.870	117	.963	.885	118	1.215	1.160	119	1.544	1.615	120	1.215	.[illegible]45
121	1.074	.915	122	1.302	1.195	123	1.111	.905	124	.856	1.175	125	1.210	1.460	126	1.091	1.105
127	1.264	.985	128	1.240	1.435	129	1.050	1.570	130	.674	.615	131	1.748	1.170	132	.782	1.240
Mean	1.124	1.074		1.071	1.061		1.199	1.252		.925	1.031		1.362	1.130		.966	1.059

each quartile (instead of the 200 in group B), a discriminative value of .60 yields a D/σ diff. ratio of 2 or better on virtually every item for which the authors have tested the statistical significance of the difference. Each scale then is applicable to groups other than the standardization group.[1]

CONSTANCY OF DISCRIMINATIVE VALUES FOR SINGLE ITEMS

Whether or not an item retains its relative discriminative power within a scale is another question. In Table 21 are given the rank order correlations for the discriminative values of the morale items for the various groups. While the general tendency is for the correlations to be positive, negative signs do appear, and few of the correlations are over .50. It is of some interest to note that the correlations between the original standardization group and the employed and unemployed groups are higher than those between the original group and the Sociology I class, the student group which seems, a priori, most like the original group. There appears to be no consistent sex difference in the size of these coefficients. The male sociology group yields the most negative correlations with other groups. Low correlations are not unexpected, since we are dealing with a restricted range of items, items that have proved to discriminate well for one group. Even when rejected items are taken into account, the relationship is not appreciably higher. Figure 8 on page 219 shows the relationship of discriminative values for a general scale extracted from the 132 items of the survey. The relationship is not at all close.

A more detailed analysis of the fluctuations in discriminative value for the groups that were given the final scales is possible from Tables 22 to 27,

1. As will be shown later, a better procedure for determining this fact would be to administer all the items to all the groups to determine whether substantially the same items would be retained. The procedure, as applied, is one step in the right direction.

TABLE 21.-RANK ORDER CORRELATIONS FOR SCALE VALUE DIFFERENCES OF MORALE ITEMS

(N = 72 men and 112 women in second preliminary group. Elsewhere N = 100.)

Group	Second Preliminary Group		Sociology I		High School Seniors (C)*		Employed (C)		Unemployed (C)
	Male	Female	Male	Female	Male	Female	Male	Female	Male
Second preliminary group (men)									
Second preliminary group (women)	+.01								
Sociology I men	+.03	+.33							
Sociology I women	+.17	-.12	-.23						
High school senior men (C)* . .	+.31	+.07	-.05	+.53					
High school senior women (C) .	+.26	+.23	-.06	+.37	+.45				
Employed men (C)	-.01	+.41	-.07	+.17	+.64	+.29			
Employed women (C)	+.41	+.28	-.01	+.30	+.73	+.44	+.54		
Unemployed men (C)	+.46	+.27	-.04	+.39	+.45	+.36	+.58	+.52	
Unemployed women (C)	+.28	+.29	+.15	+.33	+.43	+.61	+.49	+.48	+.74

*(C) = Controlled sample.

which present the discriminative values for each item for all groups, sexes treated separately. On the average the items of the morale scale (Table 22) hold up rather well. No female group averages less than 1.00. Two male groups fall below 1.00, the lowest being .873 for the controlled high school sample. The morale scale as a whole is applicable to all the groups considered. A study of the table will show that the items do not maintain such consistency. Item 25, for example, varies from .32 to 1.32 in its discriminative value, being of practically no value for the controlled sample of unemployed men. While an item could have a discriminative value of zero and still be a good item if the group were sufficiently homogeneous with respect to the attitude being measured, the evidence on variability to be presented later indicates that this argument is not applicable to the groups considered here. Although some items in the morale scale might be profitably replaced, no item is consistently poor in discriminative value. Item 103 is one of the least satisfactory from this point of view, particularly for men. If the scale were revised, this statement could well be eliminated.

In Table 23 are the scale value differences for the inferiority scale. The mean discriminative values again are consistently good, the lowest being .940 for men in the controlled sample of employed. Again we note a tendency for the female groups to have slightly higher mean discriminative values. The discriminative values of individual items vary widely from group to group, item 2 varying from .04 for the unemployed men to 1.44 for the high school men. No item is consistently poor, item 50 being the least satisfactory.

The family scale (Table 24) shows the same trends. The mean discriminative values are generally higher than for the scales thus far considered. The mean discriminative value is above 1.00 for every group. The same tendency for female groups to show higher discriminative values is evident. No item is consistently poor.

Data for the law scale (Table 25) are similar save that the sex difference is reversed. The discriminative values for males are slightly higher than those for females in three of the four groups. Item 4 is the poorest, particularly for females.

TABLE 22.-SCALE VALUE DIFFERENCES FOR MORALE ITEMS

(N = 400 of each sex 100 in each group.)

Item	Male Groups					Female Groups					Mean (N=800)
	Sociol- ogy I	High School Seniors (C)#	Unem- ployed (C)	Em- ployed (C)	All Males	Sociol- ogy I	High School Seniors (C)	Unem- ployed (C)	Em- ployed (C)	All Females	
1	.76	.72	.96	.96	.85	.68	.92	.60	1.00	.80	.825
7	.56	.96	1.00	1.04	.89	.96	.96	.72	1.36	1.00	.945
13	1.28	.96	2.00	1.00	1.31	1.12	1.60	1.88	1.56	1.54	1.425
19	1.36	1.24	1.76	1.20	1.39	1.20	1.76	1.56	1.80	1.58	1.485
25	1.32	.64	.32	.60	.72	1.20	1.04	1.00	.48	.93	.825
31	1.32	.80	1.44	1.16	1.18	.72	.80	1.52	.84	.97	1.075
37	1.24	1.20	.80	.72	.99	1.08	1.44	1.24	1.28	1.26	1.125
43	.88	1.08	.96	1.44	1.09	.88	1.60	1.12	1.00	1.15	1.120
49	1.64	.80	.88	.88	1.05	.64	1.00	.92	1.12	.92	.985
55	1.80	.76	1.04	1.12	1.18	1.00	.52	1.20	1.20	.98	1.080
61	1.28	.84	1.04	.76	.98	.96	1.36	1.04	.96	1.08	1.030
67	.68	1.44	1.92	1.84	1.47	1.48	2.12	1.44	2.00	1.76	1.615
73	1.40	1.60	.96	1.48	1.36	1.16	.96	.96	1.48	1.14	1.250
79	1.56	1.16	1.72	1.00	1.36	1.24	1.56	1.48	1.28	1.39	1.375
85	1.08	.12	.44	.36	.50	.76	.56	.56	.96	.71	.605
91	1.28	.44	1.28	.44	.86	1.20	1.00	1.04	.52	.94	.900
97	.84	1.20	1.80	1.28	1.28	1.32	1.48	1.76	1.20	1.44	1.360
103	.60	.80	.48	.48	.59	1.32	1.00	.52	.92	.94	.765
109	1.36	.72	.88	.92	.97	.68	.96	.60	.84	.77	.870
115	1.36	.60	.88	.96	.95	.56	1.68	1.28	1.24	1.19	1.070
121	1.36	.60	.84	1.08	.97	.76	1.20	.96	.52	.86	.915
127	1.04	.52	1.28	.92	.94	.88	1.00	1.24	1.00	1.03	.985
Total	26.00	19.20	24.68	21.64	22.88	21.80	26.52	24.64	24.56	24.38	26.360
Mean	1.182	.873	1.122	.984	1.040	.991	1.205	1.120	1.116	1.109	1.074

#(C) = Controlled sample.

TABLE 23.-SCALE VALUE DIFFERENCES FOR INFERIORITY ITEMS

(N = 400 of each sex 100 in each group.)

Item	Male Groups					Female Groups					Mean (N=800)
	Sociol-ogy I	High School Seniors (C)#	Unem-ployed (C)	Em-ployed (C)	All Males	Sociol-ogy I	High School Seniors (C)	Unem-ployed (C)	Em-ployed (C)	All Females	
2	.96	1.44	.04	1.20	.91	1.28	.88	.60	1.20	.99	.950
8	1.40	1.40	1.00	1.52	1.33	1.04	.96	1.16	.68	.96	1.145
14	1.04	.72	1.08	1.44	1.07	1.04	1.28	1.04	1.52	1.22	1.145
20	1.04	.68	.60	.40	.68	1.24	1.20	.44	.48	.84	.760
26	1.04	.36	.84	.48	.68	.44	.60	.40	.64	.52	.600
32	1.68	.52	.88	.96	1.01	1.32	1.40	1.16	1.12	1.25	1.130
38	.68	1.08	.76	.76	.82	.88	1.36	1.16	1.08	1.12	.970
44	1.36	1.20	1.36	1.40	1.33	1.16	1.76	1.56	1.00	1.37	1.350
50	.36	.76	.64	.96	.68	.92	.80	.48	.52	.68	.680
56	1.36	1.28	1.24	1.48	1.34	1.48	1.88	1.84	1.28	1.62	1.480
62	1.12	1.48	.80	.12	.88	.80	.88	.72	.68	.77	.825
68	1.48	1.36	.96	1.04	1.21	1.24	1.48	1.16	1.72	1.40	1.305
74	.80	1.16	.76	1.12	.96	.48	1.68	1.52	.60	1.07	1.015
80	1.24	1.12	1.24	.88	1.12	1.16	.96	1.32	1.04	1.12	1.120
86	.84	1.12	.88	.52	.84	.40	1.08	.92	.64	.76	.800
92	.32	.88	1.44	1.12	.94	.72	1.32	.76	1.36	1.04	.990
98	1.40	1.44	1.24	.88	1.24	1.40	1.64	1.76	1.44	1.56	1.400
104	.76	1.16	.84	.72	.87	1.36	1.40	1.40	.92	1.27	1.070
110	1.16	1.08	1.04	1.24	1.13	.96	1.12	1.52	.80	1.10	1.115
116	.68	.36	.72	.72	.62	1.00	1.64	1.16	.68	1.12	.870
122	1.32	1.60	1.08	.80	1.20	1.40	1.12	.88	1.36	1.19	1.195
128	1.68	1.16	1.48	.92	1.31	1.36	1.40	1.80	1.68	1.56	1.435
Total	23.72	23.36	20.92	20.68	22.17	23.08	27.84	24.76	22.44	24.53	23.350
Mean	1.078	1.062	.951	.940	1.008	1.049	1.265	1.125	1.020	1.115	1.061

#(C) = Controlled sample.

TABLE 24.-SCALE VALUE DIFFERENCES FOR FAMILY ITEMS

(N = 400 of each sex; 100 in each group.)

Item	Male Groups					Female Groups					Mean (N=800)
	Sociol-ogy I	High School Seniors (C)#	Unem-ployed (C)	Em-ployed (C)	All Males	Sociol-ogy I	High School Seniors (C)	Unem-ployed (C)	Em-ployed (C)	All Females	
3	1.40	1.40	1.72	1.00	1.38	1.72	1.16	1.92	1.64	1.61	1.495
9	1.52	.72	1.12	1.12	1.12	1.52	1.52	1.16	1.44	1.41	1.265
15	.84	.64	.56	1.28	.83	.80	.60	1.20	1.04	.91	.870
21	1.20	.72	1.28	1.08	1.07	.96	1.20	1.60	1.28	1.26	1.165
27	1.00	.76	1.04	.80	.90	1.04	.52	1.40	1.16	1.03	.965
33	.88	1.16	1.00	1.00	1.01	1.24	1.20	.96	1.64	1.26	1.135
39	1.60	1.64	1.36	1.64	1.56	1.60	2.16	1.36	2.08	1.80	1.680
45	1.32	1.04	1.32	.88	1.14	1.24	1.04	1.32	1.68	1.32	1.230
51	1.20	1.56	1.48	1.72	1.49	1.44	1.68	1.20	1.60	1.48	1.485
57	1.28	1.04	1.20	.88	1.10	1.24	1.72	1.04	2.04	1.51	1.305
63	.84	1.12	1.48	1.04	1.12	1.40	1.40	1.12	1.48	1.35	1.235
69	1.48	1.84	1.56	1.68	1.64	2.20	2.12	1.52	1.56	1.85	1.745
75	1.20	1.00	.96	.96	1.03	1.16	1.80	1.04	1.72	1.43	1.230
81	1.36	1.16	1.24	1.16	1.23	1.32	1.40	1.68	1.60	1.50	1.365
87	.84	1.40	1.28	1.12	1.16	1.80	1.96	1.36	1.68	1.70	1.430
93	.40	.84	.88	1.16	.82	.60	.92	1.12	1.32	.99	.905
99	1.04	1.32	1.12	1.56	1.26	1.84	1.84	.96	.32	1.24	1.250
105	1.36	1.96	1.52	1.84	1.67	1.24	1.88	1.44	1.80	1.59	1.630
111	.48	.52	1.12	.68	.70	.40	1.12	.96	1.16	.91	..805
117	.84	.88	.92	.68	.83	.92	1.32	.72	.80	.94	.885
123	1.08	1.04	.56	1.00	.92	.80	1.20	.76	.80	.89	.905
129	1.36	1.52	1.80	1.20	1.47	2.00	1.72	1.24	1.72	1.67	1.570
Total	24.52	25.28	26.52	25.48	25.45	28.48	31.48	27.08	31.56	29.65	27.550
Mean	1.115	1.149	1.205	1.158	1.157	1.294	1.431	1.231	1.434	1.348	1.252

#(C) = Controlled sample.

TABLE 25.-SCALE VALUE DIFFERENCES FOR LAW ITEMS

(N = 400 of each sex; 100 in each group.)

Item	Male Groups					Female Groups					Mean (N=800)
	Sociol-ogy I	High School Seniors (C)#	Unem-ployed (C)	Em-ployed (C)	All Males	Sociol-ogy I	High School Seniors (C)	Unem-ployed (C)	Em-ployed (C)	All Females	
4	1.16	.32	.84	.88	.80	.72	.20	.16	-.12	.24	.520
10	1.12	.92	1.28	.84	1.04	.80	.84	1.24	1.36	1.06	1.050
16	.68	.68	.84	.76	.74	.44	.88	.80	1.04	.79	.765
22	1.00	1.04	.92	1.08	1.01	1.00	1.24	1.08	.92	1.06	1.035
28	.84	1.08	1.28	1.24	1.11	.64	1.00	1.32	.80	.94	1.025
34	1.48	1.16	1.28	1.88	1.45	1.12	.88	1.12	.52	.91	1.180
40	1.48	1.60	.92	1.24	1.31	1.20	1.16	1.32	1.28	1.24	1.275
46	.88	1.16	1.12	1.12	1.07	.68	.72	1.04	1.04	.87	.970
52	1.32	1.24	1.12	1.76	1.36	1.28	1.24	1.52	.88	1.23	1.295
58	1.48	1.76	1.48	1.92	1.66	1.16	1.24	1.48	1.12	1.25	1.455
64	.56	1.20	.60	1.52	.97	1.16	1.32	.72	1.32	1.13	1.050
70	1.08	.68	.76	1.00	.88	.96	.56	.84	1.32	.92	.900
76	.72	1.28	.80	.84	.91	.28	1.60	.48	.92	.82	.865
82	.48	.28	1.12	1.20	.77	.64	.80	1.32	.84	.90	.835
88	.80	.84	1.72	1.24	1.15	1.48	1.16	1.20	.64	1.12	1.135
94	1.36	1.32	1.08	1.20	1.24	1.40	.96	.28	1.20	.96	1.100
100	.84	.96	1.12	1.64	1.14	1.36	1.36	.44	.76	.98	1.060
106	1.04	1.12	1.56	1.20	1.23	1.12	1.56	1.52	.92	1.28	1.255
112	.80	.84	.88	1.08	.90	1.24	1.16	.80	.96	1.04	.970
118	1.36	.84	1.12	.84	1.04	1.04	1.20	1.28	1.60	1.28	1.160
124	1.24	1.56	1.04	.92	1.19	1.28	1.32	1.28	.76	1.16	1.175
130	.52	.60	.52	.48	.53	.56	.60	.84	.80	.70	.615
Total	22.24	22.48	23.40	25.88	23.50	21.56	23.00	22.08	20.88	21.88	22.690
Mean	1.011	1.022	1.064	1.176	1.068	.980	1.045	1.004	.949	.994	1.031

#(C) = Controlled sample.

TABLE 26.-SCALE VALUE DIFFERENCES FOR ECONOMIC CONSERVATION ITEMS

(N = 400 of each sex; 100 in each group.)

Item	Male Groups					Female Groups					Mean (N=800)
	Sociol-ogy I	High School Seniors (C)#	Unem-ployed (C)	Em-ployed (C)	All Males	Sociol-ogy I	High School Seniors (C)	Unem-ployed (C)	Em-ployed (C)	All Females	
5	2.44	2.20	1.48	1.72	1.96	1.68	1.48	1.04	1.16	1.34	1.650
11	1.64	.88	1.56	1.56	1.41	1.12	1.44	1.00	.80	1.09	1.250
17	1.24	.96	.64	.36	.80	1.16	-.08	-.36	-.04	.17	.485
23	.12	.40	.32	.00	.21	.68	.16	.00	.52	.34	.275
29	1.68	1.36	1.48	1.68	1.55	1.92	1.36	1.00	1.60	1.47	1.510
35	1.72	1.88	1.64	1.20	1.61	1.48	1.20	.72	.80	1.05	1.330
41	.80	.52	.44	1.04	.70	.72	.68	.24	.84	.62	.660
47	1.64	1.32	1.20	1.44	1.40	1.84	.88	.80	.80	1.08	1.240
53	1.68	1.56	2.00	1.36	1.65	1.84	1.08	1.04	1.40	1.34	1.495
59	1.72	1.64	.68	.72	1.19	1.12	.76	1.20	1.28	1.09	1.140
65	1.00	1.44	1.24	1.08	1.19	1.28	1.24	1.72	.48	1.18	1.185
71	1.32	.96	.64	1.00	.98	1.04	.64	.04	.80	.63	.805
77	1.28	.88	1.32	.84	1.08	.88	.60	.60	.76	.71	.895
83	1.44	.96	1.16	1.24	1.20	1.32	.96	.76	.76	.95	1.075
89	1.48	1.20	1.48	.84	1.25	1.24	1.24	.60	1.12	1.05	1.150
95	1.88	1.76	1.60	1.04	1.57	2.12	1.44	1.20	1.20	1.49	1.530
101	1.40	1.24	1.52	1.40	1.39	.84	.96	.36	1.04	.80	1.095
107	.68	.80	.88	.44	.70	1.08	.88	1.28	.68	.98	.840
113	1.04	1.40	.92	1.16	1.13	1.08	.76	.92	.72	.87	1.000
119	1.64	1.96	1.68	1.60	1.72	1.92	1.48	1.32	1.32	1.51	1.615
125	1.12	1.56	1.20	1.80	1.42	1.56	1.32	1.56	1.56	1.50	1.460
131	1.44	1.56	1.20	1.44	1.41	1.40	1.16	.32	.84	.93	1.170
Total	30.40	28.44	26.28	24.96	27.52	29.32	21.64	17.36	20.44	22.19	24.855
Mean	1.382	1.293	1.194	1.134	1.251	1.333	.984	.789	.929	1.009	1.130

#(C) = Controlled sample.

TABLE 27.-SCALE VALUE DIFFERENCES FOR EDUCATION ITEMS

(N = 400 of each sex; 100 in each group.)

Item	Male Groups					Female Groups					Mean (N=800)
	Sociol-ogy I	High School Seniors (C)#	Unem-ployed (C)	Em-ployed (C)	All Males	Sociol-ogy I	High School Seniors (C)	Unem-ployed (C)	Em-ployed (C)	All Females	
6	1.00	1.16	1.60	.80	1.14	.76	1.56	1.16	.96	1.11	1.125
12	1.92	1.16	1.28	1.40	1.44	1.52	1.04	1.16	1.12	1.21	1.325
18	1.24	.52	.96	1.04	.94	.92	.92	.56	1.16	.89	.915
24	1.52	1.36	1.32	.84	1.26	1.00	1.04	1.08	1.52	1.16	1.210
30	1.00	.80	.92	1.04	.94	.84	.72	1.08	1.16	.95	.945
36	.20	.56	1.28	.92	.74	.52	.88	1.48	1.32	1.05	.895
42	1.12	.84	1.28	1.48	1.18	.40	1.12	.88	1.32	.93	1.055
48	1.36	1.24	1.28	.96	1.21	.72	1.44	1.20	1.32	1.17	1.190
54	1.56	.88	1.12	1.00	1.14	.56	.96	.80	1.28	.90	1.020
60	1.12	.80	1.12	1.00	1.01	.84	1.36	.84	1.16	1.05	1.030
66	1.16	1.08	1.00	.92	1.04	.96	1.28	1.40	1.20	1.21	1.125
72	1.12	1.08	1.88	1.36	1.36	1.36	1.36	1.68	1.84	1.56	1.460
78	.68	.68	1.20	.92	.87	1.00	1.68	.72	1.00	1.10	.985
84	1.16	.60	1.04	1.04	.96	.36	1.36	.72	.92	.84	.900
90	.96	1.44	1.88	1.20	1.37	.76	1.56	1.12	1.12	1.14	1.255
96	.92	.92	1.16	1.08	1.02	.84	1.32	.92	.92	1.00	1.010
102	.96	1.28	.76	.72	.93	.60	.88	.76	.96	.80	.865
108	1.00	.84	.64	.88	.84	.80	.88	.68	.88	.81	.825
114	.56	1.44	.64	.84	.87	.92	1.04	1.08	.52	.89	.880
120	1.24	.72	.80	1.00	.94	.80	1.28	.72	1.00	.95	.945
126	1.20	1.04	1.36	.84	1.11	.80	1.64	.72	1.24	1.10	1.105
132	1.08	1.52	1.16	1.08	1.21	.96	1.12	1.64	1.36	1.27	1.240
Total	24.08	21.96	25.68	22.36	23.52	18.24	26.44	22.40	25.28	23.09	23.305
Mean	1.094	.998	1.167	1.016	1.069	.829	1.202	1.018	1.149	1.050	1.059

#(C) = Controlled sample.

Additional points worth noting about the discriminative power of the economic conservation scale (Table 26) are that the sex difference is in favor of the men and that two items, 17 and 23, are poor items for practically all these groups. Number 17 actually discriminates in the reverse direction for some groups. These items could well be eliminated from the scale.

The education scale (Table 27) also shows uniformly high mean discriminative values. No consistent sex difference appears in the discriminative power of the scale. No item is consistently poor.

To summarize this material: there is a slight but consistent tendency for the morale, inferiority, and family scales to yield higher discriminative values for women; the law and economic conservatism scales exhibit a reverse tendency; there is no consistent sex difference for the education scale.

The most significant finding here is that the scales, considered as units, have excellent discriminative power for both sexes of all groups, whereas the several items fluctuate markedly in their discriminative values. It is pertinent to inquire whether the fluctuation observed in the discriminative values of the items is due to the unreliability of the individual items. Fluctuation in the discriminative values of the items, and approximately the same mean discriminative values for the scale as a whole, are exactly what is expected if it is assumed that the fluctuation in the discriminative values of the items is a chance phenomenon.

ITEM DISCRIMINATIVE VALUES AND RELIABILITY

Since test-retest (60 days) correlations are available for each item, an analysis of the relation of the variability in the discriminative values of the items from group to group and the unreliability of the items will provide a partial answer to this question. Among the several measures of the variability of an item, the range or the average deviation may be used. In Table 28 are given the discriminative values, the range of variation, and the average deviation of the discriminative values for each sex and for both sexes for the 10 items having the least reliability and the 10 items having the greatest reliability. For males the items with the greatest reliability show the least fluctuation in discriminative value, whether the range or the average deviation is used as a measure of variability. Although the average deviation of discriminative values for females is smaller for the most reliable items, the range of variability is larger. The differences are so small that it does not appear that unreliability is chiefly responsible for the fluctuation in the discriminative values of the items. The rank-order correlation between the unreliability of an item and its variability in discriminative value (the item with the lowest reliability and the greatest variability receiving the rank of 1) is .153 for the 22 items in the morale scale when range is used as a measure of variability and .116 when the average deviation is used. The corresponding correlations for the economic conservatism scale are .140 and .056. Although the range is the less reliable measure of variability, it gives the highest correlation. When unreliability and variability of the 132 items were correlated, the range was used as a measure of variability in order that the maximum apparent effect of chance could be detected. This correlation is only .068. The fluctuation in scale value differences of items from group to group, then, does not seem to be caused to any appreciable extent by the unreliability of the items.

With chance ruled out as the major factor in the variability in discriminative value of items, the implication of these data may be considered. The variation in discriminative values makes it improbable that the scoring can be improved by weighting an item according to its discriminative value. No attempt, therefore, has been made to so weight the items.

Attitude being dependent on social conditioning, it would be surprising if the discriminative values did not vary from group to group, according as different social stimuli are operative. These data do not support the argument that such scales are applicable only to the standardization group or one very similar to it. Nor do they substantiate the claim that individual

TABLE 28.-RANGE AND AVERAGE DEVIATION IN DISCRIMINATIVE VALUES OF 10 ITEMS WITH HIGHEST AND 10 ITEMS WITH LOWEST TEST-RETEST RELIABILITIES

(N = 100 in each group)

Item	r	Scale Value Differences for Males: Sociology I	High School Seniors (C)#	Unemployed (C)	Employed (C)	Range	Average Deviation	Scale Value Differences for Females: Sociology I	High School Seniors (C)	Unemployed (C)	Employed (C)	Range	Average Deviation	Both Sexes: Range	Average Deviation
		10 Items with highest Reliabilities						10 Items with Highest Reliabilities							
127	.916	1.04	.52	1.28	.92	.76	.220	.88	1.00	1.24	1.00	.36	.145	.76	.182
96	.902	.92	.92	1.16	1.08	.24	.100	.84	1.32	.92	.92	.48	.160	.48	.133
6	.875	1.00	1.16	1.60	.80	.80	.240	.76	1.56	1.16	.96	.80	.250	.84	.233
13	.864	1.28	.96	2.00	1.00	1.04	.345	1.12	1.60	1.80	1.56	.68	.190	1.04	.325
103	.829	.60	.80	.48	.48	.32	.110	1.32	1.00	.52	.92	.80	.220	.84	.245
39	.773	1.60	1.64	1.36	1.64	.28	.100	1.60	2.16	1.36	2.08	.80	.320	.80	.220
49	.763	1.64	.80	.88	.88	.84	.295	.64	1.00	.92	1.12	.48	.140	1.00	.201
125	.751	1.12	1.56	1.20	1.80	.68	.260	1.56	1.32	1.56	1.56	.24	.090	.68	.185
25	.745	1.32	.64	.32	.60	1.00	.300	1.20	1.04	1.00	.48	.72	.225	1.00	.315
18	.730	1.24	.52	.96	1.04	.72	.210	.92	.92	.56	1.16	.60	.165	.72	.188
Mean	.815	1.18	.95	1.12	1.02	.66	.218	1.08	1.29	1.10	1.18	.596	.191	.82	.223
		10 Items with Lowest Reliabilities						10 Items with Lowest Reliabilities							
41	.014	.80	.52	.44	1.04	.60	.220	.72	.68	.24	.84	.60	.190	.80	.195
55	.113	1.80	.76	1.04	1.12	1.04	.310	1.00	.52	1.20	1.20	.68	.230	1.28	.250
10[illegible]	.165	.96	1.28	.76	.72	.56	.190	.60	.88	.76	.96	.30	.120	.68	.155
71	.[illegible]25	1.32	.96	.64	1.00	.68	.180	1.04	.64	.04	.80	1.00	.295	1.28	.275
46	.301	.88	1.16	1.12	1.12	.28	.095	.68	.72	1.04	.87	.36	.127	.48	.161
64	.303	.76	1.20	.60	1.52	.96	.390	1.16	1.32	.72	1.32	.60	.205	.96	.318
92	.322	.32	.88	1.44	1.12	1.12	.340	.72	1.32	.76	1.36	.64	.300	1.12	.320
1[illegible]	.350	1.08	1.04	.56	1.00	.52	.180	.80	1.20	.76	.80	.44	.155	.64	.186
8	.358	1.40	1.44	.04	1.20	1.40	.400	1.28	.88	.60	1.20	.68	.250	.84	.339
50	.359	.76	.76	.64	.96	.60	.180	.92	.80	.48	.52	.44	.180	.60	.180
Mean	.276	.95	1.00	.73	1.08	.78	.249	.89	.90	.66	.99	.574	.205	.87	.238

#(C) = Controlled sample.

items will give nearly identical results when applied to appreciably different groups. That these scales, considered as units, are applicable to various groups is encouraging to the research worker. Group differences as well as individual differences may be studied.

Since the method of scale construction adapted by Likert to attitude measurement differs markedly from that developed by Thurstone, certain problems may be raised. Both methods involve a check of internal consistency. Thurstone calling his the criterion of irrelevance. The essential difference is that Thurstone assigns a definite scale value to an item according to a group of judges' opinions of the item's placement on a scale. The Likert method does not require judges, nor does it assign a definite scale value to the items. It simply weights arbitrarily the responses to each item.

Now our data make it difficult to believe that stable scale values can be assigned to individual items. If the members of different groups do not associate an item with a trait to the same extent, it appears unreasonable to expect judges selected from diverse groups to assign essentially the same scale value to an item. Since this point can be experimentally settled, the argument will not be enlarged. It is of some interest, however, to consider the effect on the results obtained by the two methods of such fluctuation in the association of items to the trait measured. The Thurstone method, as elaborated by Thurstone and Chave in 1929 (20), does not require a response to every item. Therefore an item that would not meet the criterion of relevance (it is assumed that the scale has already been constructed) for the particular group concerned may well cause greater unreliability of the scale as a whole. This may be the reason that Likert found higher reliabilities with fewer items when he applied his method to one of Thurstone's own scales than the Thurstone method of scoring yielded. Naturally the reliability of both methods will be reduced by the inclusion of an irrelevant item, but the greatest effect would be expected where the fewest responses are made. For the same reason one might expect a greater deviation from the individual's true position on the attitude continuum when an item is inapplicable to the particular group tested. With the method of scale construction used in this study the variations in the applicability of the items tend to cancel each other, so that the scale as a unit maintains its discriminative power. This cancellation process, would apparently operate so that two individuals possessing a given trait to the same degree would tend to receive the same score, even though the items differ for the two individuals in significance for the trait measured.

This process would tend to take place under the Thurstone method or, for that matter, under any other method of scale construction. But if some items are not responded to, the chances for greater misplacement in total score by the inapplicability of a single item are greater than if every item evoked a response. The assignment of definite scale values to an item on the basis of judges' opinions may be not only unnecessary but actually undesirable, particularly if the criterion of relevance is applied only to the standardizing group. In other words, it does not seem that the Thurstone method permits of cancellation of the variation in the significance of items from individual to individual or from group to group to so great an extent as does the method used in this study. The latter method is the more flexible and may prove to be the more desirable when group comparisons are the major interest of a study.

The problem would be considerably clarified and both methods would be more useful if it could be demonstrated that essentially the same trait could be measured with items that vary from group to group. Items that did not meet the tests of internal consistency employed in the two methods could be eliminated from the scoring for the particular group concerned. This problem is capable of experimental solution. For the present it appears necessary to score all items for all groups in order to make adequate comparisons of them.

DISCRIMINATIVE VALUE OF ITEMS IN EVERY SCALE

In addition to analyzing for all groups the discriminative values of the items in the scale in which they are placed, the discriminative values of the 132 items were evaluated in each of the six scales. That is, the papers of the group were separated into quartiles on the basis of the morale scores and the average difference between Q_1 and Q_4 computed for all items, not merely the items in the morale scale. The process was repeated for the remaining five scales; thus each item was evaluated in each scale for each group. This analysis allows us to consider the question whether an item functions most effectively in the scale in which it is placed. Would a morale item yield better results if scored in the education scale? This analysis yields forty-eight tables, six scales for four groups of each sex. Since these tables conform to a general trend, three of the twenty-four tables for men are chosen at random and, with the three similar tables for women, are presented here (Tables 29 to 34).

One of the most striking features of the tables giving the detailed analysis of three of the scales is the scarcity of inverse discriminative values. Every item tends to discriminate in every scale. It is evident that a general factor is operative in these scales. The fundamental importance of this general factor and its implications for the measurement of personality will be clearly appreciated as the analysis proceeds. For the present only the improbability of securing items measuring one trait and that one alone need be noted.

Table 36 summarizes the differences in the discriminative values of all scales for all groups. It is to be read as follows: Of the 22 items in the morale scale 4 items discriminate better in one of the other scales for Sociology I men, 2 for the controlled samples of employed men, none for Sociology I women, and so on. By far the greater proportion of the items are correctly placed, so far as these six scales are concerned. This table should not be interpreted as

TABLE 29.-SCALE VALUE DIFFERENCES OF ECONOMIC CONSERVATISM ITEMS COMPUTED FOR EVERY SCALE

(Sociology I men; N = 100)

Item	Economic Conservatism	Morale	Law	Inferiority	Family	Education
5	2.44	.36	.32	.52	.08	.16
11	1.64	.44	.12	.52	-.24	.00
17	1.24	.24	-.08	.08	-.28	-.20
23	.12	-.16	-.28	-.24	-.40	.00
29	1.68	1.00	.72	.76	.20	.60
35	1.72	.88	.72	.36	-.04	-.68
41	.80	.04	.44	.40	-.24	-.28
47	1.64	.40	.00	.36	.32	.44
53	1.68	.16	.24	.36	-.44	.28
59	1.72	.68	.48	.44	.16	.72
65	1.00	.80	1.12	.40	.32	.36
71	1.32	.84	1.12	.32	-.32	.84
77	1.28	.48	.12	.16	.40	.76
83	1.44	.88	.64	.68	.16	.40
89	1.48	.60	.60	.36	.48	.28
95	1.88	.48	.52	.32	.32	.16
101	1.40	1.00	.64	.88	.68	.72
107	.68	.72	.00	.52	.40	.24
113	1.04	.32	.28	.16	.16	.04
119	1.64	.72	.12	.32	.24	.64
125	1.12	.20	.52	.12	-.04	.08
131	1.44	.60	.48	.44	.00	.24
Mean	1.382	.531	.402	.374	.087	.264

TABLE 30.—SCALE VALUE DIFFERENCES OF ECONOMIC CONSERVATISM ITEMS COMPUTED FOR EVERY SCALE

(Sociology I men; N = 100)

Item	Economic Conserv-atism	Morale	Law	Inferi-ority	Fam-ily	Educa-tion
5	1.68	.28	.56	.00	.24	-.52
11	1.12	.20	.40	.08	.44	-.64
17	1.16	-.16	-.20	.08	.12	-.56
23	.68	-.28	-.12	.16	.40	-.40
29	1.92	.56	.76	.24	.04	-.16
35	1.48	.08	.12	.12	.68	.04
41	.72	.16	.48	.04	.24	-.20
47	1.84	.48	.28	.60	.32	-.12
53	1.84	.20	-.08	.44	.32	-.40
59	1.12	-.08	.52	.32	-.32	.00
65	1.28	1.12	.88	.56	.12	-.04
71	1.04	.08	.88	.24	.44	-.36
77	.88	.48	.40	.60	.20	.24
83	1.32	.36	.88	.16	.20	-.08
89	1.24	.40	.64	.28	.40	-.36
95	2.12	.64	.56	.40	.44	-.52
101	.84	.56	.80	.08	.40	.04
107	1.08	.28	.84	.00	.32	-.20
113	1.08	.48	.60	.00	.52	.32
119	1.92	.48	.08	.24	.08	.32
125	1.56	.36	.20	.40	-.20	-.24
131	1.40	.48	.76	.16	.00	.20
Mean	1.333	.325	.465	.236	.245	-.165

TABLE 31.—SCALE VALUE DIFFERENCES OF MORALE ITEMS COMPUTED FOR EVERY SCALE

(Controlled sample of high school men; N = 100)

Item	Morale	Law	Inferiority	Economic Conservatism	Family	Education
1	.72	.00	.40	-.56	.32	-.12
7	.96	.40	.80	.56	.28	.12
13	.96	.32	.64	.68	.16	.68
19	1.24	.20	.36	.28	.44	.44
25	.64	.44	.48	.00	.28	-.04
31	.80	.32	.20	.28	.28	.60
37	1.20	.16	.56	.36	.52	.68
43	1.08	.52	1.28	-.56	.24	.64
49	.80	.44	.68	-.16	.48	.24
55	.76	-.16	.56	.04	.36	.16
61	.84	.28	.08	.52	.00	.72
67	1.44	.28	1.08	.52	.24	.88
73	1.60	.64	.80	.56	.28	.44
79	1.16	.24	.64	.40	.20	.36
85	.12	.36	-.04	-.16	.68	.04
91	.44	.48	.40	-.64	.76	-.72
97	1.20	.40	.56	.44	.24	.40
103	.80	-.04	.48	-.08	-.16	.08
109	.72	1.12	.28	-.24	.68	.44
115	.60	.08	.32	-.16	.32	.76
121	.60	.92	.60	-.28	.52	.24
127	.52	.24	.32	.32	.52	.44
Mean	.873	.347	.522	.096	.347	.340

TABLE 32.-SCALE VALUE DIFFERENCES OF MORALE ITEMS COMPUTED FOR EVERY SCALE

(Controlled sample of high school women; N = 100)

Item	Morale	Law	Inferi- ority	Economic Conserv- atism	Fam- ily	Educa- tion
1	.92	.16	.96	.36	-.20	.20
7	.96	.48	.64	.24	.16	.68
13	1.60	.60	.88	.84	.48	.88
19	1.76	.60	1.52	.44	.60	.72
25	1.04	.32	.44	-.16	-.12	.56
31	.80	.48	.36	.16	-.04	.68
37	1.44	.20	1.12	.12	.64	1.16
43	1.60	.88	1.08	.56	.52	1.08
49	1.00	.60	.88	.76	1.08	.72
55	.52	.72	.40	.68	.24	.68
61	1.36	.84	1.08	.96	1.24	.96
67	2.12	1.20	1.68	.96	.92	1.36
73	.96	.88	.56	.72	.24	.60
79	1.56	1.00	1.20	.84	.72	.92
85	.56	.52	.32	.44	.72	.68
91	1.00	.52	.44	.20	.48	.76
97	1.48	.88	1.20	.64	1.08	.60
103	1.00	.12	.96	.84	.76	.00
109	.96	.56	.88	.72	.80	.64
115	1.68	1.00	.96	.92	.84	1.44
121	1.20	.64	.68	.48	.40	.88
127	1.00	.64	.64	.68	.60	.48
Mean	1.205	.629	.858	.564	.553	.758

TABLE 33.-SCALE VALUE DIFFERENCES OF LAW ITEMS COMPUTED FOR EVERY SCALE

(Controlled sample of employed men; N = 100)

Item	Law	Morale	Inferi-ority	Economic Conserv-atism	Fam-ily	Educa-tion
4	.88	.52	.12	.48	.64	.52
10	.84	.52	.24	.12	.28	.00
16	.76	.40	.36	-.12	.44	.20
22	1.08	.64	.12	.32	.60	.44
28	1.24	.88	.16	.16	.60	.36
34	1.88	1.20	.44	.76	1.04	.96
40	1.24	.88	.28	-.32	.76	.80
46	1.12	.96	.16	-.04	.72	.80
52	1.76	1.04	.64	.28	.76	1.08
58	1.92	1.00	.72	.64	1.08	.60
64	1.52	.92	.44.	.08	.88	.64
70	1.00	.40	.20	.00	.52	.64
76	.84	.88	.76	.36	.24	.28
82	1.20	.24	.04	.32	.56	.60
88	1.24	.60	.84	.92	.48	.68
94	1.20	.56	.72	.32	.64	.56
100	1.64	1.00	.72	.68	.88	.96
106	1.20	.80	.84	.72	.52	.44
112	1.08	.52	.20	-.16	.52	.36
118	.84	.52	.56	.04	.36	.04
124	.92	.68	.76	.56	.88	.76
130	.48	.36	.04	-.08	.44	.52
Mean	1.176	.705	.425	.274	.629	.556

TABLE 34.–SCALE VALUE DIFFERENCES OF LAW ITEMS COMPUTED FOR EVERY SCALE

(Controlled sample of employed women; N = 100)

Item	Law	Morale	Inferiority	Economic Conservatism	Family	Education
4	-.12	.24	.36	.76	-.20	-.12
10	1.36	.96	.60	.40	.76	.96
16	1.04	.32	-.20	.08	.16	.56
22	.92	.52	.36	.20	.48	1.12
28	.80	.56	.00	-.08	.48	.68
34	.52	.12	.68	.60	.00	.32
40	1.28	.80	.36	.88	.16	.60
46	1.04	.28	-.12	.04	.32	.00
52	.88	.60	.08	.36	.12	.36
58	1.12	.48	.56	.48	.32	.32
64	1.32	.24	-.36	.08	.80	.32
70	1.32	.36	.00	.56	.92	.56
76	.92	.32	.68	.28	.64	.92
82	.84	.52	.20	.12	.72	.72
88	.64	.16	.24	.80	.48	-.28
94	1.20	.32	.24	.16	.76	.12
100	.76	.56	.08	.52	.16	.68
106	.92	.36	-.20	.60	.00	.60
112	.96	.28	-.12	-.20	.56	.48
118	1.60	1.20	.40	.60	.28	1.00
124	.76	.12	-.24	.16	-.12	-.08
130	.80	.60	.08	.12	.36	.64
Mean	.949	.451	.167	.342	.371	.476

TABLE 35.-AVERAGE DISCRIMINATIVE VALUE OF THE 22 ITEMS OF EACH SCALE COMPUTED IN EVERY SCALE

(N = 100 in each group.)

	Men							Women						
	Morale	Inferi-ority	Family	Law	Economic Conserv-atism	Educa-tion	Mean	Morale	Inferi-ority	Family	Law	Economic Conserv-atism	Educa-tion	Mean
Morale Items:														
Sociology I	1.182	.560	.551	.689	.449	.898	.721	.991	.407	.127	.373	.269	.193	.393
Employed (C)#	.984	.571	.493	.524	.194	.507	.545	1.116	.555	.284	.498	.322	.489	.544
Unemployed (C)	1.122	.664	.338	.634	.500	.614	.645	1.120	.709	.380	.485	.360	.662	.619
High school seniors . . .	.873	.522	.347	.347	.096	.340	.421	1.205	.858	.553	.629	.564	.758	.761
Mean	1.040	.579	.432	.548	.310	.590		1.108	.632	.336	.496	.379	.525	
Inferiority Items:														
Sociology I	.542	1.078	.316	.431	.305	.442	.519	.307	1.049	.175	.042	.169	-.027	.286
Employed (C)	.587	.940	.360	.375	.351	.218	.472	.482	1.020	.096	.138	.220	.342	.383
Unemployed (C)	.504	.951	.094	.069	.254	.205	.346	.642	1.125	.480	.254	.214	.385	.517
High school seniors . . .	.613	1.062	.084	.113	.100	.282	.376	.854	1.265	.642	.391	.358	.425	.656
Mean	.561	1.008	.213	.247	.252	.287		.571	1.115	.348	.206	.240	.281	
Family Items:														
Sociology I	.476	.300	1.114	.382	.122	.422	.469	.304	.309	1.294	.307	.325	.205	.457
Employed (C)	.476	.451	1.158	.625	.084	.331	.521	.365	.240	1.435	.647	.069	.304	.510
Unemployed (C)	.447	.309	1.205	.434	.127	.307	.471	.398	.491	1.231	.685	.091	.476	.562
High school seniors . . .	.409	.325	1.149	.534	.094	.471	.497	.684	.578	1.431	.460	.344	.558	.676
Mean	.452	.346	1.156	.494	.107	.383		.438	.404	1.348	.525	.207	.386	
Law Items:														
Sociology I	.547	.302	.220	1.011	.274	.340	.449	.338	-.044	.287	.980	.291	.184	.339
Employed (C)	.705	.425	.629	1.176	.274	.556	.627	.451	.167	.371	.949	.342	.476	.459
Unemployed (C)	.633	.214	.407	1.064	.238	.502	.509	.447	.267	.611	1.004	.298	.604	.538
High school seniors . . .	.387	.209	.445	1.022	.193	.494	.458	.414	.345	.438	1.045	.356	.525	.520
Mean	.568	.287	.425	1.068	.245	.473		.412	.184	.427	.994	.322	.447	
Economic Conservatism Items:														
Sociology I	.531	.374	.087	.402	1.382	.264	.507	.325	.236	.245	.465	1.333	-.165	.406
Employed (C)	.182	.327	.131	.254	1.134	-.024	.334	.258	.154	.040	.258	.929	.065	.284
Unemployed (C)	.407	.203	.276	.504	1.195	.322	.484	.258	.185	.187	.231	.789	.309	.326
High school seniors . . .	.307	.235	-.013	.216	1.293	.089	.354	.436	.220	.042	.354	.984	.276	.385
Mean	.357	.285	.120	.344	1.251	.163		.319	.199	.128	.327	1.009	.121	
Education Items:														
Sociology I	.747	.405	.338	.405	.334	1.094	.554	.234	.078	.125	.207	-.107	.829	.228
Employed (C)	.662	.256	.296	.491	.064	1.016	.464	.476	.351	.142	.569	.084	1.149	.462
Unemployed (C)	.638	.285	.291	.485	.265	1.167	.522	.553	.204	.464	.507	.289	1.018	.506
High school seniors . . .	.429	.222	.145	.425	.067	.998	.381	.654	.262	.576	.585	.316	1.202	.599
Mean	.619	.292	.267	.451	.182	1.069		.479	.224	.327	.467	.145	1.049	

#(C) = controlled sample.

TABLE 36.-NUMBER OF ITEMS WITH GREATER DISCRIMINATIVE VALUES IN SCALES OTHER THAN THE ONE IN WHICH THEY ARE PLACED

(N = 100 in each group)

Group	Morale	Inferiority	Family	Law	Economic Conservatism	Education	Total
			Men				
Sociology I	4	2	3	2	0	1	12
Employed (C)*	2	3	0	1	0	1	7
Unemployed (C)	7	1	0	2	3	0	13
High School Seniors (C)	6	4	1	4	3	1	19
Total	19	10	4	9	6	3	51
			Women				
Sociology I	0	1	1	1	0	3	6
Employed (C)	2	0	1	4	3	1	11
Unemployed (C)	4	5	1	4	4	0	18
High School Seniors (C)	2	0	1	1	2	0	6
Total	8	6	4	10	9	4	41

*C = Controlled sample.

indicating that the item having less discriminative value in the scale in which it occurs than in some other is poorly placed, but merely that it would function more effectively in another scale. It should also be remembered that the items which might function more effectively for one group if they were placed in another scale would not necessarily do so for another group. Considering that the items were assigned to each scale on a subjective basis, except that the morale items were analyzed for the inferiority scale and vice versa in the original standardization group, they are surprisingly well placed. Fifty-one of a possible 528 cases (132 items times 4 groups), or 10 per cent of the items, might be better placed for men; and 41, or about 8 per cent, for women. The number that might be more effectively placed for any one group varies from 7 out of 22 morale items for the controlled sample of unemployed men to no items in four of the six scales for some groups. The survey as a whole shows most items that might be better placed for the controlled samples of unemployed. The morale scale shows most items that could be better placed for men; the family scale for women. The male groups show more items that could be better scored in other scales than do the female. This may well be due to a sex difference in the pervasiveness of the general factor, a problem that will be considered later. These results point clearly to the conclusion that the scales, while influenced by a general factor, measure different continua.

Table 35, as has been noted, summarizes the discriminative values of the items of each scale. It is again evident that the items as a group discriminate best in the scale in which they are placed. The 22 morale items have, for example, a mean discriminative value of 1.040 for men. The highest average discriminative value for the combined groups attained by these items for men in any other scale is .59. This table affords clear evidence of the potency of the general factor. The problem of what discriminative value to use when applying the criterion of internal consistency in the selection of items is complicated by these results. While a discriminative value of .60 gives a D/σ diff. ratio of about 2 for quartiles of 25 each, the items of the morale scale often show mean discriminative values higher than this when considered in the other scales. For example, the average discriminative value of the items of the morale scale is .664 for the controlled sample of unemployed men when placed in the inferiority scale; that of the inferiority items when placed in the morale scale, is .504 for this same group. To be certain that the items in a scale measure more than a general factor the critical discriminative level should certainly be placed at .80 or perhaps even at 1.00. Were the authors constructing these scales again they would attempt to keep the discriminative value of every item higher than 1.00. Inspection of the table will show what will be more quantitatively expressed in a later chapter, that morale is the most generalized trait here measured.

Consider the mean discriminative value of the items in scales other than the morale for the four male groups. The items of every scale except the family discriminate better in the morale scale than in any other scale save their own. The items in the family scale discriminate slightly better in the law scale than they do in the morale scale, which is the next best scale for the family items. The trend is not quite so clear for women, but it is evident. The items in the inferiority and education scales discriminate best (the scale in which they are placed excepted) in the morale scale; items in the family and economic conservatism scale discriminate second best in the morale scales; and law items third best. The evidence suggests a sex difference in the pervasiveness of the general factor.

A comparison of the mean discriminative values of morale items for the four groups also indicates that morale is the most general of the traits here measured. Exclusive of the items in the given scale, morale items discriminate better in every scale than do the items of any other scale, so far as men are concerned. Women again contribute some exceptions. The morale items do not discriminate as well in the family scale as do the inferiority and law items, nor as well in the law scale as do the family items. No entirely consistent group differences in the generality of the morale scale appear, although there is some indication that all scales combined have higher discriminative values for high school girls than for the women of other groups. The Sociology I men appear to be the male group yielding responses most saturated with the general factor. For a complete analysis of these interrelationships, see Chapter VI.

The data analyzed in this chapter lead naturally to the question whether some items discriminate sufficiently well in more than one scale to be scored in more than one. Tables 29 to 34 show that while some items discriminate well in other scales, so few items discriminated consistently for the eight samples (four of each sex) when included in a scale other than the one to which they belonged that it was not considered worth while to attempt double scoring of items. For example, even when the critical point was placed as low as +.60, no morale item was found which when placed in another scale would consistently discriminate to this extent for all eight groups. It seems almost incredible that most of the items have a value exceeding +.60 for all groups for the scale in which they are placed, but that none of the items outside the scale do so. Such, however, is the case. The attempt to increase reliability by scoring items in more than one scale was therefore abandoned. Failure to find many items that could be scored in other scales is further evidence that for the most part the items are placed in the scale in which they belong. This versatility of items is of importance in the interpretation of results obtained from testing in the personality field. Obviously all scales having items with this general scope will correlate. The correlations between scales and with validating data may well be more influenced by a general factor than by the specific factor or factors presumed to be the common element of a particular scale. While it is possible that the weighting of the general factor is enhanced by the fact that all measures were obtained at a single sitting from a single blank upon which the items of each scale were equally spaced, there is evidence in the table themselves that the scales measure different traits to a greater extent than they measure the general factor. For it is noteworthy that on the whole the items discriminate best in the scale in which they are placed.

SUMMARY

Six general findings emerge from this chapter:

1. A general factor permeates the six scales.
2. The scales appear to be applicable to a wide range of groups.
3. For the most part the items are placed in the scale in which they function most effectively.
4. While individual items vary in their effectiveness from group to group, the items of a single scale considered as a unit are about equally effective in any of the groups considered here.

5. Scoring an item in more than one scale will not, so far as these scales are concerned, yield sufficiently better results to justify the additional labor involved in the scoring.

6. Since items of the type used here vary so widely from group to group in their discriminative values, it does not appear worth while to utilize a weighted method of scoring.

Chapter IV

SCORING

The method of selecting the standard samples has been described. The group used for computing standard scores consisted of 1,000 persons, 500 of each sex, drawn from five groups that did not differ strikingly in means or standard deviations. One hundred of each sex were drawn from the General College and Sociology I groups and the controlled samples of employed, unemployed, and high school seniors. This procedure does not distort nor conceal any sex or group difference present in the original data. It was believed that by combining these groups more adequate norms would be obtained than by utilizing any one of the groups alone.

The distribution of the responses of these thousand persons are presented in detail in Tables 37 to 42. It is clear from these tables that individual items vary greatly in the form of their distribution. Some are distinctly bimodal, some markedly skewed, and some nearly symmetrical. Items presenting a bimodal distribution are of particular interest. The bimodality always occurs around 3, the undecided response, as a midpoint; apparently most people have a definite reaction to such items. The extent to which items of the six scales are bimodal varies appreciably. The criterion of bimodality used was an excess of 5 per cent or more in the number of responses, (there are 500 responses, so 5 per cent is 25) at the 2 and at the 4 position over that at the 3 position. The number of bimodal items in each scale is presented in Table 43. Positive and negative items are given separately. A positive item, it will be recalled is one for which agreement represents a favorable attitude, a negative item one for which agreement represents an unfavorable attitude. Although favorable and unfavorable are relative concepts, it will probably be conceded that for all

TABLE 37.-DISTRIBUTION OF 22,000 RESPONSES TO POSITIVE AND NEGATIVE MORALE ITEMS

(N = 500 of each sex)

Response	11 Positive Items											Total	Per Cent
	25	31	37	55	61	79	85	91	103	109	121		
Male:													
1. Strongly agree . . .	22	90	43	162	81	64	28	30	13	34	14	581	10.56
2. Agree	200	258	258	254	255	195	147	175	165	231	122	2260	41.09
3. Undecided	79	109	67	38	106	144	146	61	96	103	115	1064	19.35
4. Disagree	144	27	111	39	47	81	142	191	186	119	208	1295	23.55
5. Strongly disagree .	55	16	21	7	11	16	37	43	40	13	41	300	5.45
												5500	100.00
Female:													
1. Strongly agree . . .	16	51	37	158	73	26	25	28	20	32	13	479	8.71
2. Agree	179	244	227	249	261	150	141	181	146	180	95	2053	37.33
3. Undecided	105	157	76	35	91	179	211	51	69	122	109	1205	21.91
4. Disagree	157	33	139	49	65	125	99	182	229	149	221	1448	26.33
5. Strongly disagree .	43	15	21	9	10	20	24	58	36	17	62	315	5.73
												5500	100.01

Response	11 Negative Items											Total	Per Cent
	1	7	13	19	43	49	67	73	97	115	127		
Male:													
1. Strongly disagree .	49	99	127	73	85	91	66	41	75	97	222	1025	18.64
2. Disagree	158	250	232	260	263	260	212	207	292	271	204	2609	47.44
3. Undecided	106	50	81	49	37	44	67	109	69	77	48	737	13.40
4. Agree	137	79	47	89	91	73	136	117	51	43	19	882	16.04
5. Strongly agree . . .	50	22	13	29	24	32	19	26	13	12	7	247	4.49
												5500	100.01
Female:													
1. Strongly disagree .	61	76	97	78	54	124	58	37	89	109	248	1031	18.75
2. Disagree	189	253	254	225	239	258	178	206	263	254	172	2491	45.29
3. Undecided	90	46	86	50	27	38	56	129	71	72	58	723	13.15
4. Agree	130	109	52	123	131	65	175	100	63	58	16	1022	18.58
5. Strongly agree . . .	30	16	11	24	49	15	33	28	14	7	6	233	4.24
												5500	100.01

TABLE 38.-DISTRIBUTION OF 22,000 RESPONSES TO POSITIVE AND NEGATIVE INFERIORITY ITEMS

(N = 500 of each sex)

Response	11 Positive Items											Total	Per Cent
	8	20	26	32	44	50	56	74	80	104	110		
Male:													
1. Strongly agree . . .	31	30	7	82	19	15	38	40	21	20	17	320	5.82
2. Agree	156	194	81	261	166	99	241	304	130	88	145	1865	33.91
3. Undecided	76	85	89	73	112	45	84	80	110	89	67	910	16.55
4. Disagree	216	178	277	75	188	285	132	71	220	278	254	2174	39.53
5. Strongly disagree .	21	13	46	9	15	56	5	5	19	25	17	231	4.20
												5500	100.01
Female:													
1. Strongly agree . . .	18	21	9	88	16	12	41	49	14	20	15	303	5.51
2. Agree	143	196	74	255	113	51	263	311	73	86	121	1686	30.65
3. Undecided	73	72	74	59	87	47	62	62	86	83	77	782	14.22
4. Disagree	236	197	298	89	263	280	118	65	294	253	265	2358	42.87
5. Strongly disagree .	30	14	45	9	21	110	16	13	33	58	22	371	6.75
												5500	100.00

Response	11 Negative Items											Total	Per Cent
	2	14	38	62	68	86	92	98	116	122	128		
Male:													
1. Strongly disagree .	49	24	86	16	19	25	29	17	13	21	31	330	6.00
2. Disagree	213	222	289	181	159	233	231	144	137	223	172	2204	40.07
3. Undecided	59	84	42	88	47	112	90	77	106	76	96	877	15.95
4. Agree	160	156	73	182	234	113	135	236	217	161	186	1853	33.69
5. Strongly agree . . .	19	14	10	33	41	17	15	26	27	19	15	236	4.29
												5500	100.00
Female:													
1. Strongly disagree .	44	27	101	30	15	35	28	20	17	22	23	362	6.58
2. Disagree	179	213	305	213	111	246	213	150	141	223	136	2130	38.73
3. Undecided	55	81	25	43	25	106	78	55	83	68	64	583	12.42
4. Disagree	196	155	59	190	277	100	160	227	222	158	246	1990	36.18
5. Strongly agree . . .	26	24	10	24	72	13	21	48	37	29	31	335	6.09
												5500	100.00

TABLE 39.-DISTRIBUTION OF 22,000 RESPONSES TO POSITIVE AND NEGATIVE FAMILY ITEMS

(N = 500 of each sex)

Response	11 Positive Items											Total	Per Cent
	3	15	21	27	45	57	75	81	87	93	111		
Male:													
1. Strongly agree . . .	145	117	40	77	86	80	139	47	55	63	67	916	16.65
2. Agree	218	310	150	216	276	224	305	268	284	264	345	2860	52.00
3. Undecided	75	34	109	100	90	87	33	96	81	80	53	838	15.24
4. Disagree	49	29	165	89	44	96	21	82	72	84	32	763	13.87
5. Strongly disagree .	13	10	36	18	4	13	2	7	8	9	3	123	2.24
												5500	100.00
Female:													
1. Strongly agree . . .	128	135	40	44	71	78	140	52	73	78	89	928	16.87
2. Agree	221	281	100	167	217	206	292	237	225	255	322	2523	45.87
3. Undecided	82	38	98	106	108	89	32	82	98	82	52	867	15.76
4. Disagree	62	44	217	160	91	117	32	120	93	78	33	1047	19.04
5. Strongly disagree .	7	2	45	23	13	10	4	9	11	7	4	135	2.45
												5500	99.99

Response	11 Negative Items											Total	Per Cent
	9	33	39	51	63	69	99	105	117	123	129		
Male:													
1. Strongly disagree .	51	13	115	57	84	48	15	15	41	18	42	499	9.07
2. Disagree	248	116	211	264	273	197	177	197	254	220	166	2323	42.24
3. Undecided	95	82	64	61	53	114	80	68	79	103	77	876	15.93
4. Agree	78	241	94	103	79	125	192	184	107	134	175	1512	27.49
5. Strongly agree . . .	28	48	16	15	11	16	36	36	19	25	40	290	5.27
												5500	100.00
Female:													
1. Strongly disagree .	48	14	136	80	98	55	38	31	47	23	38	608	11.05
2. Disagree	254	122	224	239	260	205	203	242	288	187	185	2409	43.80
3. Undecided	81	70	42	60	40	86	71	66	50	107	83	756	13.75
4. Agree	97	235	75	98	87	131	156	134	96	160	148	1417	25.76
5. Strongly agree . . .	20	59	23	23	15	23	32	27	19	23	46	310	5.64
												5500	100.00

TABLE 40.-DISTRIBUTION OF 22,000 RESPONSES TO POSITIVE AND NEGATIVE LAW ITEMS

(N = 500 of each sex)

Response	11 Positive Items											Total	Per Cent
	28	40	46	52	58	64	70	94	112	118	124		
Male:													
1. Strongly agree . . .	53	13	84	23	19	54	88	58	54	14	27	487	8.85
2. Agree	305	221	283	197	76	197	268	223	278	172	187	2407	43.76
3. Undecided	78	102	80	133	85	96	92	83	64	157	50	1020	18.54
4. Disagree	46	128	44	116	178	127	46	117	95	118	195	1210	22.00
5. Strongly disagree .	18	36	9	31	142	26	6	19	9	39	41	376	6.84
												5500	99.99
Female:													
1. Strongly agree . . .	37	21	92	12	20	69	128	93	91	12	19	594	10.80
2. Agree	275	210	281	144	56	193	253	221	272	130	164	2199	39.98
3. Undecided	137	150	82	200	113	100	78	85	67	185	59	1256	22.83
4. Disagree	44	89	41	116	198	117	37	90	60	129	210	1131	20.56
5. Strongly disagree .	7	30	4	28	113	21	4	11	10	44	48	320	5.82
												5500	99.99

Response	11 Negative Items											Total	Per Cent
	4	10	16	22	34	76	82	88	100	106	130		
Male:													
1. Strongly disagree .	46	152	81	77	24	23	85	42	22	16	210	778	14.15
2. Disagree	140	238	224	218	150	144	267	206	168	133	264	2152	39.13
3. Undecided	108	39	91	131	114	100	104	106	136	140	20	1089	19.80
4. Agree	166	56	92	58	147	187	40	108	149	168	5	1176	21.38
5. Strongly agree . . .	40	15	12	16	65	46	4	38	25	43	1	305	5.55
												5500	100.01
Female:													
1. Strongly disagree .	17	128	86	70	28	24	87	56	28	20	258	802	14.58
2. Disagree	131	269	249	223	129	156	256	232	190	110	212	2157	39.22
3. Undecided	181	33	78	141	148	126	113	111	177	125	23	1256	22.84
4. Agree	148	61	83	54	160	165	38	74	91	204	6	1084	19.71
5. Strongly agree . . .	23	9	4	12	35	29	6	27	14	41	1	201	3.65
												5500	100.00

TABLE 41.-DISTRIBUTION OF 22,000 RESPONSES TO POSITIVE AND NEGATIVE ECONOMIC CONSERVATISM ITEMS

(N = 500 of each sex)

Response	11 Positive Items											Total	Per Cent
	17	23	35	41	59	65	71	83	107	119	131		
Male:													
1. Strongly agree . . .	31	31	33	12	79	9	58	13	10	38	27	341	6.20
2. Agree	99	92	131	81	190	96	194	138	114	158	164	1457	26.49
3. Undecided	160	71	82	165	122	118	153	194	121	92	147	1425	25.91
4. Disagree	167	239	159	183	86	173	73	122	194	155	126	1677	30.49
5. Strongly disagree .	43	67	95	59	23	104	22	33	61	57	36	600	10.91
												5500	100.00
Female:													
1. Strongly agree . . .	20	10	20	6	51	11	33	14	9	31	16	221	4.02
2. Agree	85	81	96	58	154	64	171	113	86	155	157	1220	22.18
3. Undecided	262	119	188	244	185	145	222	255	178	116	214	2128	38.69
4. Disagree	116	248	160	158	84	195	62	97	171	154	87	1532	27.85
5. Strongly disagree .	17	42	36	34	26	85	12	21	56	44	26	399	7.25
												5500	99.99

Response	11 Negative Items											Total	Per Cent
	5	11	29	47	53	77	89	95	101	113	125		
Male:													
1. Strongly disagree .	100	33	48	64	29	16	16	72	19	50	53	500	9.09
2. Disagree	172	111	214	137	79	127	72	220	135	213	170	1650	30.00
3. Undecided	78	120	74	140	101	190	75	84	123	132	151	1268	23.05
4. Agree	97	166	101	116	154	127	261	89	182	84	103	1480	26.91
5. Strongly agree . . .	53	70	63	43	137	40	76	35	41	21	23	602	10.95
												5500	100.00
Female:													
1. Strongly disagree .	55	18	56	34	19	4	5	77	12	68	34	382	6.95
2. Disagree	169	84	192	162	77	73	61	244	84	215	167	1528	27.78
3. Undecided	141	168	87	145	139	266	147	104	221	152	157	1727	31.40
4. Agree	106	175	118	127	170	128	238	56	154	56	114	1442	26.22
5. Strongly agree . . .	29	55	47	32	95	29	49	19	29	9	28	421	7.65
												5500	100.00

TABLE 42.-DISTRIBUTION OF 22,000 RESPONSES TO POSITIVE AND NEGATIVE EDUCATION ITEMS

(N = 500 of each sex)

Response	11 Positive Items											Total	Per Cent
	12	18	24	48	54	78	84	102	108	120	126		
Male:													
1. Strongly agree . . .	191	206	59	200	92	41	81	135	139	151	109	1404	25.53
2. Agree	179	250	180	238	251	174	264	308	309	300	306	2759	50.16
3. Undecided	46	26	63	32	56	104	83	39	26	28	44	547	9.95
4. Disagree	67	15	136	24	74	143	58	11	23	19	38	608	11.05
5. Strongly disagree .	17	3	62	6	27	38	14	7	3	2	3	182	3.31
												5500	100.00
Female:													
1. Strongly agree . . .	153	225	56	239	97	43	71	166	158	207	140	1555	28.27
2. Agree	203	244	138	218	257	154	225	276	285	250	279	2529	45.98
3. Undecided	52	11	60	17	46	102	134	38	33	27	49	569	10.35
4. Disagree	86	18	195	20	75	165	60	13	21	14	30	697	12.67
5. Strongly disagree .	6	2	51	6	25	36	10	7	3	2	2	150	2.73
												5500	100.00

Response	11 Negative Items											Total	Per Cent
	6	30	36	42	60	66	72	90	96	114	132		
Male:													
1. Strongly disagree .	153	201	178	162	28	97	103	44	92	157	155	1370	24.91
2. Disagree	201	232	235	257	206	289	269	227	226	283	233	2658	48.33
3. Undecided	68	34	40	40	108	73	56	84	126	24	64	717	13.04
4. Agree	65	26	35	34	133	33	51	113	44	33	37	604	10.98
5. Strongly agree . . .	13	7	12	7	25	8	21	32	12	3	11	151	2.75
												5500	100.01
Female:													
1. Strongly disagree .	105	187	180	178	45	136	116	55	77	190	195	1464	26.62
2. Disagree	226	253	242	273	235	268	265	274	212	263	187	2698	49.05
3. Undecided	77	28	27	22	100	53	49	79	126	23	79	663	12.05
4. Agree	72	23	38	19	96	31	54	80	75	19	29	536	9.75
5. Strongly agree . . .	20	9	13	8	24	12	16	12	10	5	10	139	2.53
												5500	100.00

scales except possibly the economic conservatism scale, the adjectives describe the situation; for favorable refers to high morale, absence of inferiority feelings, a good attitude toward the family, respect for law, acceptance of the prevailing economic order, and a high estimate of the value of education.

Table 43 reveals two facts of major interest. The morale, family, and inferiority scales are clearly differentiated from the other three scales with respect to the proportion of bimodal items. In these three scales more negative than positive items are bimodal; in the other three the reverse tends to be true. There is no consistent sex difference in the number of bimodal items. The significance of the difference between positive and negative items will be considered in detail in a later chapter. The difference between scales will be our concern here.

TABLE 43.-NUMBER OF BIMODAL ITEMS IN EACH SCALE (5 PER CENT OR MORE RESPONSES AT BOTH THE 2 AND 4 POSITIONS THAN AT THE 3 POSITION)

Scale	Positive Items		Negative Items	
	Male	Female	Male	Female
Morale	4	5	6	6
Inferiority	6	6	10	10
Family	1	3	9	10
Law	5	1	3	2
Economic Conservatism . . .	2	1	1	1
Education	2	4	2	0
Total	20	20	31	29

SIGNIFICANCE OF BIMODAL ITEM DISTRIBUTIONS

The most obvious point to consider in evaluating the significance of the difference in frequency of bimodal items is the nature of the traits presumed to be measured. The morale, family, and inferiority scales seem less intellectualized than the other three--education, law, and economic conservatism. The three scales having the largest number of bimodal items are based on more direct personal experience than are the others. They not only are based on more direct personal experience but on more frequent experience. Every day of a person's life he faces situations affecting morale, family adjustment, and feelings of inferiority. Respect for law, attitude toward education, and economic conservatism are traits representing less personal concerns, and problems involving these traits arise less frequently. A consideration of the specific items strengthens this argument. Such items as most people can be trusted, the future looks very black, it is easy to express one's ideas, parents are inclined to be too old-fashioned in their ideas are more immediately significant to an individual and are concerned with situations he meets more frequently than such items as labor should have more voice in deciding government policies, the sentences of judges in courts are determined by their prejudices, and solution of the world's problems will come through education. It may be noted too, that the three scales having the greatest number of bimodal items are those which presumably measure general phases of personality adjustment rather than fairly specific social attitudes.

On items relating to more personal affairs and to situations more frequently met, individuals are least likely to be undecided. Bimodality results. Lack of indecision by itself does not characterize the more personal items but lack of indecision plus bimodality. Table 42 shows that the items of the education scale evoke the undecided response infrequently, but the tendency toward bimodality is small. (See Table 43.) The infrequency of the undecided response for this scale is due to the fact that nearly everyone favors education in the sense that they agree with favorable statements about it; over 75 per cent of the men either agree or strongly agree with positive statements. There has been little adverse criticism of education itself. The emphasis on education as a panacea is so universal that its value is scarcely ever questioned. For the remaining scales it will be noted (See Table 44) that there is the least indecision in the responses for those scales--the morale, inferiority, and family scales--the items of which have the greatest personal connotation, and the most indecision with respect to the law and economic conservatism items, which seemingly have the least personal connotation.

If this analysis is sound, a valuable indication of the degree to which items are measuring reactions based on direct personal experience is at hand, at least in the case of the five-point scale. While many items measuring reactions based on direct personal experience may be found symmetrically distributed about undecided as the central position, the probability that reactions of immediate personal significance are being aroused would seem to be considerably enhanced by the occurrence of a bimodal distribution. The probability of this interpretation being correct is increased by the fact that negative items, as will be demonstrated in Chapter IX, evoke reactions of more fundamental significance to the individual.

Table 44 summarizes for each scale the percentage of responses at each position. The large percentage of responses at the favorable position on the education items and the smaller proportion of undecided responses for the morale, family, and inferiority scales have already been mentioned. Since each percentage is based on 5,500 responses, a very small difference will be of statistical significance. The difference of 2.56 per cent between the proportion of male and female undecided responses for the morale scale positive items is 3.33 times its standard error. Any difference of more than 2 per cent will approximate 3 times its standard error.

Five of the six comparisons for positive statements show a greater proportion of undecided responses for women. Only two comparisons for the negative statements are in this direction. The greatest sex difference is noted for the economic conservatism items, both positive and negative. It will probably be conceded that in general women are less well informed on economic affairs than men. A greater proportion of indecision among women may therefore be expected on the items of this scale. This sex difference in indecision on the economic conservatism scale, the scale appearing to be based least on direct personal experience and yielding the fewest bimodal items, tends to confirm the

TABLE 44.-DISTRIBUTION OF RESPONSES TO POSITIVE (P.) AND NEGATIVE (N.) STATEMENTS FOR EACH SCALE

(Standard sample; N = 500 of each sex)

Response	Morale		Inferiority		Family		Law		Economic Conservatism		Education	
	P.	N.	P.	N.	P.	N.	P.	N.	P.	N.	P.	N.
Male:												
1	10.56	18.64	5.82	6.00	16.65	9.07	8.85	14.15	6.20	9.09	25.53	24.91
2	41.09	47.44	33.91	40.07	52.00	42.24	43.76	39.13	26.49	30.00	50.16	48.33
3	19.35	13.40	16.55	15.95	15.24	15.93	18.54	19.80	25.91	23.05	9.95	13.04
4	23.55	16.04	39.53	33.69	13.87	27.49	22.00	21.38	30.49	26.91	11.05	10.98
5	5.45	4.49	4.20	4.29	2.24	5.27	6.84	5.55	10.91	10.95	3.31	2.75
Total	100.00	100.01	100.01	100.00	100.00	100.00	99.99	100.01	100.00	100.00	100.00	100.01
Female:												
1	8.71	18.75	5.51	6.56	16.87	11.05	10.80	14.58	4.02	6.95	28.27	26.62
2	37.33	45.29	30.65	38.73	45.87	43.80	39.98	39.22	22.18	27.78	45.98	49.05
3	21.91	13.15	14.22	12.42	15.76	13.75	22.83	22.84	38.69	31.40	10.35	12.05
4	26.33	18.58	42.87	36.18	19.04	25.76	20.56	19.71	27.85	26.22	12.67	9.75
5	5.73	4.24	6.75	6.09	2.45	5.64	5.82	3.65	7.25	7.65	2.73	2.53
Total	100.01	100.01	100.00	100.00	99.99	100.00	99.99	100.00	99.99	100.00	100.00	100.00

hypothesis that bimodality indicates that the item is reacted to on the basis of direct personal experience.

An additional difference between positive and negative items may be noted in Table 44. With the exception of the family scale, where the difference is reversed, and the education scale, which shows little difference, there is a definite tendency for the favorable positions to be taken more frequently on negative items and the unfavorable positions to be taken relatively more frequently on positive items. In other words, there is a greater tendency to disagree with negative items than to agree with positive items. The significance of this may also be more profitably considered in connection with the data of a later chapter.

CAN BIMODALITY OF ITEMS BE ACCOUNTED FOR BY THE TECHNIQUE OF SCALE CONSTRUCTION?

The frequency of bimodal items with its implications for scoring is what chiefly concerns us here. Likert (13) assumed a normal distribution of item responses in order to apply the sigma technique. The distributions of total arbitrary scores for the various scales are not bimodal. (See Figures 1 to 6.) They are roughly symmetrical or skewed toward the favorable end (low score) of the scale. This implies that cancellation has occurred when the item scores were summed.

One problem to be considered in connection with bimodal items is whether the bimodality is the result of selecting items on the basis of their discriminative values. That the items are not bimodal in all the scales implies that it is not. Further evidence supporting the contention can be obtained by comparing the percentage of responses at the 3 position for the retained items with that for the excluded items in the second preliminary form of the scales. The inferiority scale was chosen for this comparison because it has the greatest proportion of bimodal statements and because it yields the fewest responses at the 1 and 5 positions. This latter condition permits a consideration of bimodality least complicated by the extreme positions. The percentage of responses at the 3 position for retained and excluded statements for the original standardization group of 72 men and 112 women was as follows:

	Men	Women
Excluded statements (18)	13.6	13.1
Retained statements (22)	14.8	14.5

There is almost no difference in the index of bimodality. It is quite clear that the method of selection of items does not account for the bimodal distributions of the retained items. The excluded items are equally bimodal; in fact, they yield slightly fewer responses at the central 3 position.

To determine whether the bimodality could be considered to be a by-product of the number of steps in the item scale, 16 statements (8 positive and 8 negative) that were bimodal at least to some extent in each of 10 groups (5 of each sex) and 16 statements that were unimodal (the distributions were either symmetrical or skewed) were chosen to be administered under different conditions. These 32 items were given to a group of 150 Sociology I students and a group of 155 sophomores in psychology. For the sociology group instead of the 5 phrases strongly agree, agree, undecided, disagree, and strongly disagree, 7 were used: strongly agree, definitely agree, mildly agree, undecided, mildly disagree, definitely disagree, and strongly disagree. For the psychology group a graphic rating scale was employed. The directions for the 7-point scale were identical with those for the 5-point and need not be given here. They were somewhat modified for the graphic rating scale, where they read as follows:

> The following pages contain a number of statements about which there is no general agreement. People differ widely in the way they feel about each item. There are no right answers. The purpose of the survey is to see how different groups feel about each item. We should like your honest opinion on each of these statements.
>
> Below each item you will find a line representing a scale of opinion running from strongly agree on one end to strongly disagree at the other. A vertical line is drawn through this in order to indicate the central position. Indicate your opinion by

by marking an X at that point on the line which you think best expresses your position on this scale.

Example: THE GOVERNMENT SHOULD TAKE OVER ALL LARGE INDUSTRIES

X______________________ ______________________
Strongly Agree Strongly Disagree

An X at the point above indicates that the person making it agreed to the maximum extent possible. Had the X been placed in this position:

______________________ ______________________X
Strongly Agree Strongly Disagree

it would mean that the person disagreed to the maximum extent possible. Had it been placed in this position:

______________________X______________________
Strongly Agree Strongly Disagree

it would mean that the person had no opinion one way or the other on this item.

Had the X been placed as follows:

______________________ X______________________
Strongly Agree Strongly Disagree

it would mean that the person disagreed with the statement to the smallest possible extent.

It will be noted that the two ends and the midpoints were defined by the graphic rating scales. The graphic rating scale was scored by dividing it into five and into seven equal parts in order to compare the results with the five- and seven-point defined-response scales.

Since the bimodal and unimodal items chosen were consistently bimodal or consistently unimodal for ten groups, it can scarcely be argued that differences found are due to differences in sampling. The comparison between the graphic method and the five-point defined-response scale is madé in Table 45. While there are certain interesting differences between positive and negative items in this table, they are consistent with the general trends for such statements and need not concern us here.

The main point to be noted here from Table 45 is that the graphic rating scale throws no light on the problem that it was intended to solve. For both originally bimodal and unimodal items the graphic scale shows a tendency toward a trimodal distribution. The responses concentrate around the two extremes and the mid-position, the three positions it was deemed essential to define. This finding decidedly limits the utility of the graphic rating method.[1] In fact, there is greater tendency for responses to unimodal items than for responses to bimodal items to concentrate at the favorable extreme (the 1 position), making the distributions of the unimodal items more distinctly trimodal than those of the originally bimodal.

When the seven-point graphic rating scale scored in seven steps is compared with the seven-point defined scale, the results are so similar that it is deemed unnecessary to publish the table.

The comparison between the five and the seven-point defined scales (Table 46) is, however, of considerable interest in connection with the problem of the item distributions. Use of the seven defined-positions scale tends to equalize the responses at all positions on the scale. The items that were originally unimodal, however, for the five-point method tend to remain so for the seven-point method, whereas those items that

---

1. The authors have not made a systematic survey of the literature with respect to this point, but it may be noted that Symonds (17) does not mention it in his Diagnosing Personality and Conduct. The finding is consistent with that of other users of the method. Professor F. L. Goodenough informed the writers that it has been her unvarying experience that ratings on a graphic rating scale tend to concentrate at whatever positions happen to be defined. This is, of course, not true of every individual, but it holds for the majority of cases.

TABLE 45.-RESPONSES ON A FIVE-POINT DEFINED-RESPONSE SCALE COMPARED WITH RESPONSES ON A GRAPHIC SCALE*

Response Position	Male		Female	
	Five-Point Scale (N=500)	Graphic Scale (N=80)	Five-Point Scale (N=75)	Graphic Scale (N=80)
		16 Positive Items		
1 Position				
Unimodal	13.9	25.5	12.0	26.7
Bimodal	5.7	16.3	6.0	16.4
2 Position				
Unimodal	39.8	18.6	34.8	16.2
Bimodal	36.6	15.8	35.3	13.4
3 Position				
Unimodal	24.6	28.6	34.1	37.8
Bimodal	14.7	30.5	13.0	29.2
4 Position				
Unimodal	16.8	12.2	15.7	8.3
Bimodal	36.6	19.7	38.8	19.1
5 Position				
Unimodal	4.8	15.2	3.4	10.9
Bimodal	6.4	17.8	6.9	21.9
Total				
Unimodal	99.9	100.1	100.0	99.9
Bimodal	100.0	100.1	100.0	100.0
		16 Negative Items		
1 Position				
Unimodal	19.8	37.8	22.1	40.6
Bimodal	7.1	20.9	7.6	21.6
2 Position				
Unimodal	44.4	23.1	40.1	17.8
Bimodal	41.7	18.0	39.6	18.4
3 Position				
Unimodal	21.7	23.6	24.7	28.7
Bimodal	13.5	29.5	11.1	33.0
4 Position				
Unimodal	11.0	6.7	10.7	6.6
Bimodal	32.6	18.1	35.2	10.9
5 Position				
Unimodal	3.0	8.7	2.4	6.3
Bimodal	5.3	13.4	6.5	16.1
Total				
Unimodal	99.9	99.9	100.0	100.0
Bimodal	100.2	99.9	100.0	100.0

*Percentages are based on responses to 8 unimodal and 8 bimodal items. Hence, the percentages in each column are based on totals obtained by multiplying N by 8.

yielded bimodal distributions with the five-point defined scale continue to do so with the seven-point scale. Apparently the bimodality brought about by the small proportion of undecided responses is characteristic of certain items to such an extent that changing the number of steps will not induce unimodality. It may be that the distributions could be markedly changed by using the term neutral or a phrase implying alternating agreement and disagreement rather than indecision. The marked differences between scales in the number of bimodal items also indicate that the extent to which indecision exists is due to the nature of the trait measured.

Before considering the implications of these findings for scoring, certain additional comparisons between the results obtained by the two methods should be made. The extreme and middle positions on the five-defined and the seven defined-positions scale can be directly compared, since the phrases are identical under both methods. Further, the 2 and 3 positions on the seven-point scale may be combined for comparison with the 2 position on the five-point scale, and the 5 and 6 positions may be combined for comparison with the 4 position. These comparisons can be made from the data presented in Table 46. Consider first the undecided position, which is 3 on the five-point scale and 4 on the seven-point defined scale. In every instance there is a smaller percentage of responses at the midpoint on the seven-point scale. The originally bimodal statements show the greatest change at this position. In three of four comparisons the percentage of responses at the midpoint of the seven-point scale is less than half of what it was for the five-point scale. The originally unimodal statements show no instance of a 50 per cent reduction. In other words, bimodal items become even more bimodal when a seven-point scale is used.

At what position or positions is there a gain in the percentage of responses at the expense of the midpoint? Not at the intermediate positions. This is apparent when the sum of the responses at the intermediate positions of the five-point scale (positions 2 and 4) are compared with those of the seven-point scale (positions 2, 3, 5, 6). It is better to compare the

TABLE 46.–COMPARISON OF RESPONSES ON A FIVE-POINT DEFINED-RESPONSE SCALE AND ON A SEVEN-POINT DEFINED-RESPONSE SCALE*

Position:												
On five-point scale	1		2		3		4		2+4		5	
On seven-point scale		1		2+3		4		5+6		2+3+5+6		7
						Male						
Type of Statement												
Positive unimodal	13.9	17.0	39.8	36.8	24.6	15.0	16.8	21.5	56.6	58.3	4.8	9.7
Positive bimodal	5.7	7.5	36.6	36.4	14.7	6.7	36.6	36.2	73.2	72.6	6.4	13.3
Negative unimodal	19.8	27.5	44.4	38.1	21.7	12.8	11.0	17.4	55.4	55.5	3.0	4.2
Negative bimodal	7.1	10.8	41.7	36.8	13.5	7.8	32.6	36.9	74.3	73.7	5.3	7.7
						Female						
Type of Statement												
Positive unimodal	12.0	20.3	34.8	30.7	34.1	21.3	15.7	22.6	50.5	53.3	3.4	5.1
Positive bimodal	6.0	9.6	35.3	32.8	13.0	6.1	38.8	38.5	74.1	71.3	6.9	12.8
Negative unimodal	22.1	32.9	40.1	32.4	24.7	13.3	10.7	15.7	50.8	48.1	2.4	5.6
Negative bimodal	7.6	11.1	39.6	35.3	11.1	3.5	35.2	38.8	74.8	74.1	6.5	11.1

*N = 500 males and 500 females for the five-point scale. N = 75 males and 75 females for the seven-point scale. Percentages are based on N multiplied by 8, the number of statements of each type.

intermediate responses on both sides of the midpoint than to compare those on each side singly. Possible group differences are less likely to influence the comparison. Finding the percentage of responses at the intermediate positions unchanged leads to the completely unexpected result that it is at the extreme positions of the seven-point scale that there is a gain in the proportion of responses received. Every possible comparison (there are 8) between the extreme positions (the 1 with the 1 and the 5 with the 7) shows a greater proportion of responses at the extremes for the seven-point scale. If the increase had occurred at but one end of the response scale, it might more readily have been accounted for by differences between the group given one type of item scale and that given the other. Since it occurs at both extremes, it is probably a feature of the method. The determination of the number of points most useful for personality measurement is a matter for further investigation. These results do not indicate whether the five-point or the seven-point defined-response scale is preferable. They do indicate that the bimodality found on the five-point scale on certain items will persist if a seven-point defined-positions scale is used.

THE ARBITRARY VERSUS THE WEIGHTED METHOD OF SCORING

The problem of how to weight item responses in scoring requires attention. The arbitrary method of scoring item responses was adopted on the basis of the evidence now to be presented. It will be recalled that the arbitrary method scores item responses as though the distances between them were equal; these arbitrary weights are uniform from item to item. It is obvious that these distances may not be equal in fact, and that they may vary from item to item. How much distortion in total score results from such a uniform arbitrary method of scoring? Since we do not know the true weights that should be assigned to the item responses, the question in the above form, cannot be answered. The pragmatic form of the question is, will there be any differences in the results yielded by the arbitrary method and methods differing from the arbitrary in that responses are weighted differently? Since evidence has already been presented to indicate that it is not advisable to weight items of this kind in terms of their discriminative values, we must look elsewhere for a weighted method of scoring. The question, as finally investigated, is, How much will total scores be altered by the use of sigma weights instead of arbitrary weights for item responses? Two sigma methods of scoring were tried, one based on the tables for the normal probability curve integral and the second on the standard deviations of the actually obtained distribution for one thousand persons.

Sigma weights based on the first method are obtained by computing the percentage of responses at each position for an item and ascertaining from a table of the normal probability integral the distance in sigma units from the mean which these percentages would represent if the curve were normal. Since the sigma weight desired is the midpoint of a response position, the percentage one must compute is that exceeding a given response position plus one-half the percentage at the given position. McCall's (14) table of equivalent sigma weights for percentages yielded by an actual distribution is based on the normal probability curve, and was chosen because of the simplicity of his method. He has presented the sigma units in terms of a ten-sigma range converted into the convenient scale of 0--100 points, each point representing one-tenth of a sigma.

The use of such a conversion table assumes that the obtained distribution is normal or approximates normality. Deviations from normality are assumed to be largely due to errors in the arbitrary units used. Two situations may be conceived in which this assumption is not warranted. Suppose that the units used are equal and the distribution is truly normal in the universe, but that the sampling is unrepresentative; use of the conversion table will alter the distribution in the direction of normality by changing the units on the base line, since the frequencies on the vertical axis remain fixed. Assume in the second instance that the units are equal and the sampling representative, but that the distribution in the universe is not normal; use of the conversion table will again pull the distribution toward normality by distorting the scoring units.

The second sigma method of scoring derives the sigma weights for the item responses solely from the actually obtained distribution. Use of the standard deviation does not require a normal distribution, (Yule, 23, pages 140ff.) although a representative distribution is desirable for the establishment of scoring norms. By this method the mean and standard deviation of the distribution of the 1,000 responses to an item were computed in terms of the arbitrary five-point scale. The deviations of the five arbitrary weights from the calculated item mean were than computed. These deviations were divided by the obtained standard deviation to express them in terms of standard deviation units. The resulting values were then multiplied by 10 to eliminate the decimal point; 50 was added to these values to obviate the necessity of working with negative signs in scoring and to make them comparable with McCall's scale of 0-100 in tenths of sigma units. It should be noted that this method changes no relationship within the distributions. It does not change the relationship of the arbitrary units but merely expresses them differently. Every arbitrary item weight is divided by a constant--the standard deviation. It is the relationship of units on two or more items that may be changed by this method. This method permits variation in the weight assigned to a given response position from item to item, but maintains a constant difference in weights between the various response positions for a given item. It is different from the first sigma method in that the first permits variations both in the weights assigned to a given response position from item to item and in the distances between the five response positions for a given item. This may be otherwise expressed by saying that the conversion sigma method yields weights for the five alternative response positions for a given item that may not be uniformly proportional to the arbitrary weights. This follows from the facts that the conversion method utilizes only the frequencies at each verbally defined response position, whereas the arbitrary weights enter into the calculations of sigma weights by the direct method.

TABLE 47.-CALCULATION OF SIGMA WEIGHTS FOR RESPONSE POSITIONS ON A SINGLE ITEM*

(N = 1000; 500 of each sex)

Method Utilizing McCall Conversion Table**

Response	Frequency of Response No. (A)	Frequency of Response Per cent (B)	B÷2 (C)	Percentage Giving More Favorable Response (D)	(C) +(D) (E)	McCall Sigma Weight*** (F)
Strongly disagree	110	11.0	5.5	0.0	5.5	66
Disagree	347	34.7	17.35	11.0	28.35	56
Undecided . . .	196	19.6	9.8	45.7	55.5	49
Agree	267	26.7	13.35	65.3	78.65	42
Strongly agree .	80	8.0	4.0	92.0	96.0	32
Total	1,000	100.00				

Method Based Entirely on Obtained Distribution**

Response	Arbitrary Weight (A)	Frequency (B)	(A) x(B) (C)	Mean -(A) (D)	Mean -(A)÷ Sigma of Distribution (E)	Sigma Weights**** (F)
Strongly disagree	1	110	110	1.86	1.6	66
Disagree	2	347	694	.86	.7	57
Undecided	3	196	588	-.14	-.1	49
Agree	4	267	1068	-1.14	-1.0	40
Strongly agree . .	5	80	400	-2.14	-1.8	32
Total		1,000	2,860			
Mean			2.86			
σ of Distribution			1.16			

*"The Future is Too Uncertain for a Person to Plan on Marrying."

**For further description see page 97.

***These weights are read from McCall's conversion table, which provides equivalent sigma values in terms of the normal probability curve for percentages in column (E).

****These values are obtained by multiplying sigma deviations from the mean in column (E) by 10 to eliminate the decimal point, and adding 50 algebraically. Since adding 50 will make all values positive, this practice was adopted to conform with McCall method, which places the mean at 50 (5 sigma steps from either hypothetical extreme).

The upper half of Table 47 illustrates the McCall conversion method of obtaining sigma weights. Column A gives the frequency at each of the five response positions for 1,000 persons. Column B shows the percentage at each position, and column C gives this percentage divided by 2. Column D gives the percentage whose response was more favorable than the response of those at a given position. Column E is the sum of D and E, giving the percentage exceeding plus one-half at the position. The sigma weights in column F are read from the McCall conversion table, the percentages in column E being used.

The lower half of Table 47 illustrates the direct sigma method. It is self-explanatory. The mean and standard deviation are computed by the usual methods on the basis of the arbitrary weights. Each arbitrary score for the response positions is expressed as a deviation from the mean and is divided by the actually obtained sigma.

Using each method the weights for the 22 items were added to obtain a total score for the individual. It is realized that the item distributions are such that the assumption underlying the first method is sometimes violated. The problem of whether the arbitrary and the two sigma methods yield similar or different results remains.

First let us consider the results in terms of correlation. The papers of the hundred General College men were scored by the three methods. In Table 48 are given the correlations between the arbitrary, the direct sigma, and the McCall T-score methods of scoring. It is immediately evident that so far as correlational purposes are concerned the three methods yield substantially the same results--the correlations ranging from .946 to .987. As would be expected, the McCall T-scores tend to yield slightly lower correlations. The inferiority and family scales, the two having the greatest number of bimodal items, yield among the highest correlations between the methods. Whether or not the assumption of normality of distribution is fulfilled, the two sigma methods of scoring yield about the same results as the arbitrary method. Perhaps this result simply indicates the impossibility of escaping from the

TABLE 48.-CORRELATIONS BETWEEN DIRECT SIGMA SCORES, McCALL SIGMA SCORES (T-SCORES), AND ARBITRARY SCORES

Scale	Direct Sigma Correlated with Arbitrary Scores	McCall Sigma Correlated with Arbitrary Scores	McCall Sigma Correlated with Direct Sigma Scores
	100 General College Males		
Morale	.951	.946	.953
Inferiority	.975	.979	.975
Family	.968	.961	.962
Law	.987	.972	.978
Economic Conservatism	.970	.950	.978
Education	.967	.955	.957
	62 Federal-Aid Male Students		
Economic Conservatism		.981	
	100 First-Year Law Male Students		
Law	.990	.973	

original limitations of the measure by statistical manipulation. Likert obtained correlations of approximately .99 between the sigma method, based on the theoretical curve and the arbitrary method, higher than most of the correlations presented here. Some may question his results because he applied the sigma method of scoring to the same group of cases from which he obtained the sigma units. In the last comparison the one hundred cases to which the sigma scoring was applied were only one-tenth of the cases used to derive the sigma units. To completely eliminate the spurious element, the two sigma methods of scoring were applied to the sixty-two federal-aid students and to the hundred law freshmen, neither group having been involved in the standardization group. As may be seen from Table 48, the correlation of the methods runs even higher for these groups. So far as correlational material is concerned, the three methods of scoring will yield substantially the same results. Further, it will be shown that the Smith inferiority inventory (16) correlates with the authors' inferiority scale to the extent of .796 for men and .755 for women when the arbitrary scoring is used. When the McCall T-score is used to weight item responses, the correlations are .784 and .758 respectively--an unappreciable difference.

The argument is frequently met with, however, that a high correlation between the two methods simply indicates that the methods rank the individuals in the same order. This is unquestionably the case if one is dealing with scores that are directly derived and not obtained by combining several items. No matter by what method a single item is scored, the various methods will rank individuals in the same order and hence always correlate 1.00. When items are combined, the problem is entirely different. In a scale of 22 items an individual may obtain his total score by checking positions on all the items that are underweighted, if sigma scoring is taken as the standard. If such a phenomenon occurs with any frequency, the correlation between the arbitrary and sigma method must be considerably lowered. If cancellation takes place so that the irregularities in the value of scale positions from item to item are ironed out, the correlation will approach 1.00 and a correlation approaching 1.00 under these circumstances seems to imply that the total score units, derived by combining the items, are roughly equal within the scale. They are not necessarily equal from scale to scale, nor are they adequate in the sense that they would not be different if the technique were modified, for instance by changing the nature of the phrases or increasing the number of defined positions for each item.

It can be demonstrated that correlations of the magnitude obtained between arbitrary and sigma methods of scoring mean that this cancellation process has taken place. Arbitrary weights can be expressed in such a way as to make them comparable with sigma scores. The average sigma values for the 1 and 5 positions on the economic conservatism items were computed in order to determine their range. The average value was close to 31 for the 1 position and 71 for the 5 position. The arbitrary scores of 1, 2, 3, 4, and 5 were assigned values of 31, 41, 51, 61, and 71, respectively. The process was repeated for the T-scores. Here the range between the 1 and 5 positions was 36 (from 33 to 69)--restricted by 10 per cent when compared with the direct sigma method. Nine was therefore taken as the arbitrary unit and, starting with 1, the positions were given the scores 33, 42, 51, 60, 69. Both these new sets of values are arbitrary in that there is a uniform distance between them and the weights are uniformly applied from item to item. They are merely expressed in numbers that can be compared to sigma scores. The economic conservatism scale for the federal-aid group was scored by the new arbitrary weightings. For example, the 1 response to any of the 22 items received a weighting of 31 for the direct sigma comparison and a value of 33 for the T-score comparison. The total scores and the differences between them were computed. For some individuals there is no difference in the total scores obtained by the direct sigma or T-score method and the arbitrary method. On the average the difference between the arbitrary and the direct sigma totals is 1.08 per cent of the range of the scores in the group. The maximum difference is 2.96 per cent. The T-score method differs from the arbitrary method 0 per cent at the minimum, 1.67 per cent on the average, and 4.32 per cent at the maximum. (See Table 49.)

TABLE 49.-DIFFERENCES BETWEEN TOTAL ARBITRARY SCORES AND TOTAL SCORES DERIVED FROM ITEM SIGMA WEIGHTS FOR ECONOMIC CONSERVATISM SCALE

(Federal-aid students; N = 62)

Difference*	Arbitrary and Direct Sigma Totals**	Arbitrary and McCall T-Score Totals***
Maximum	2.96	4.32
Minimum	0.00	0.00
Average	1.08	1.67

*Differences are expressed in percentages of the actual range of scores in this group.

**Arbitrary weights in direct sigma comparison: 31, 41, 51, 61, 71.

***Arbitrary weights in McCall T-score comparison: 33, 42, 51, 60, 69.

These results appear even closer when we consider the fact that the zero points could not be accurately adjusted in round numbers. For example, the average for the 1 position on the scale for the McCall values was 32.72; 33 was taken to simplify the calculation. The average for the 1 position on the direct sigma values was 31.09; 31 was taken to facilitate the calculations. That the zero point was more closely adjusted for the direct sigma comparison is one reason that this comparison shows less difference from the arbitrary method than did the McCall T-score.

After the computations in Table 49 were made, it was discovered that rescoring with the new arbitrary weights was unnecessary for the comparison of total scores by the arbitrary and sigma methods. Exactly the same total score as was obtained by rescoring with the new arbitrary weights--31, 41, 51, 61, 71--could have always been obtained without the labor of rescoring. The original total arbitrary score from the earlier arbitrary weights--1, 2, 3, 4, 5--could have been multiplied by 10 and 462 added. Multiplying the original weights by 10 would yield the weights 10, 20, 30, 40, 50, as compared with the new arbitrary weights 31, 41, 51, 61, 71. The difference between old and new weights is always 21, and this multiplied by 22 (the number of items) yields 462. If the original scoring method was arbitrary, it remains arbitrary after multiplying total score by a constant and adding a constant.

In the comparison of arbitrary and McCall scores, it was again unnecessary to rescore with the weights 33, 42, 51, 60, 69. Exactly the same result would always have been obtained if the total score derived from the original arbitrary weights had been multiplied by 9 and 528 added. Nine instead of 10 would serve as the multiplying constant, since the conversion sigma method restricted the item range by 10 per cent on the average; 528 was the necessary additive constant, since the constant distance between old and new arbitrary weights is always 24 after the original weights are multiplied by 9.

The conclusion is forced upon us that all three methods yield essentially the same results, not relatively but absolutely. If we know the score based on any one of the methods, the others may be predicted with a negligible margin of error.

These results show clearly that a high correlation between methods of scoring, when the scores are derived by combining items, means that the cancellation process described has taken place. The greater the number of items in a scale, the greater the opportunity for irregularities in the item and response weights to be ironed out. The authors have never met with a correlation between the sigma and arbitrary methods of scoring that has not been high.

It is clear from these data that arbitrary weights are fully as satisfactory as sigma weights in combining the items of the present scales. The data suggest further that the total score units are roughly equal within any scale. Thorndike (19, page 212) quotes Bowley as follows: "Bowley gives a rule that is satisfactory for most cases that occur in practice, namely, to give your attention to eliminating constant errors and not to manipulating weights." A likely source of constant error in the construction of tests is biased sampling. In the light of the results obtained here, this advice might be rephrased as follows: In constructing a personality test, place the emphasis on the adequacy of sampling. The chances appear good that, with scales containing 22 or more items, the units will take care of themselves.

The next problem is to make the scores comparable from scale to scale. This can be done by converting the total scores derived from arbitrary response weights to standard scores either on the basis of the obtained distribution alone or on the basis of the probability curve. Conversion on the basis of the normal probability curve assumes that any departure from normality is caused by inequality of units, and it corrects for this by forcing the distribution in the direction of normality by changing the units on the base line.

The evidence just presented indicates that the units of the six scales dealt with here are roughly equal within scales. The distributions obtained for the six scales (See Figures 1 to 6) were assumed to approximate symmetry closely enough to justify the conversion to standard scores on the basis of actually

FIG. 1.
DISTRIBUTION OF MORALE SCORES.

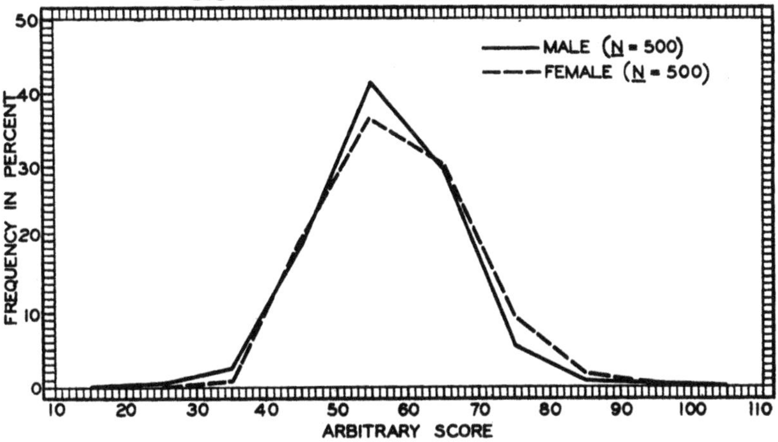

FIG. 2.
DISTRIBUTION OF INFERIORITY SCORES.

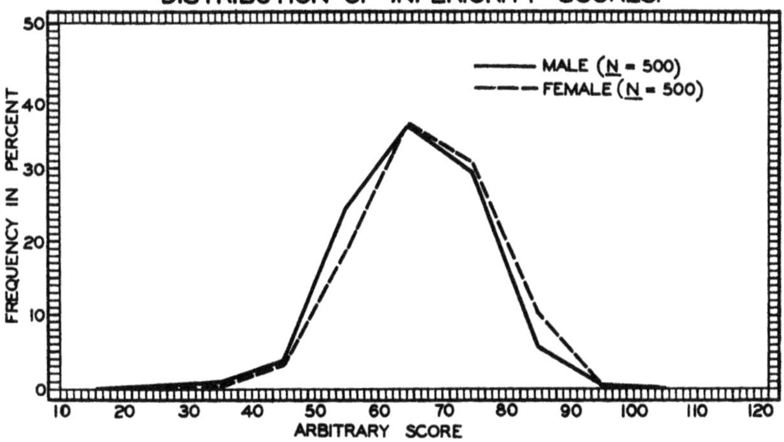

FIG. 3.

DISTRIBUTION OF FAMILY SCORES.

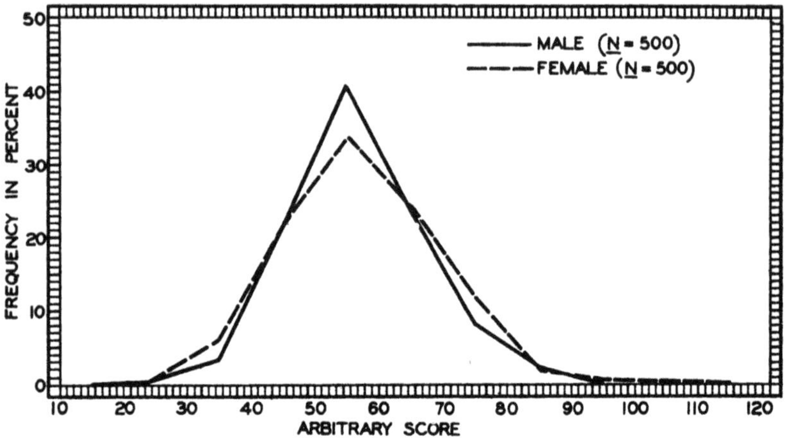

FIG. 4.

DISTRIBUTION OF LAW SCORES.

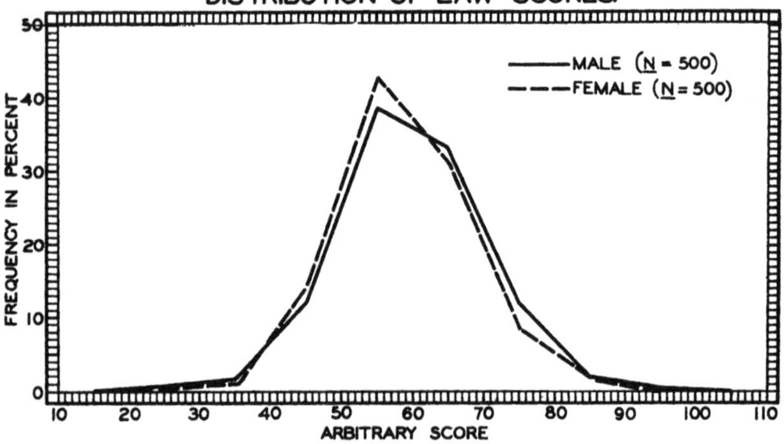

FIG. 5.

DISTRIBUTION OF ECONOMIC CONSERVATISM SCORES.

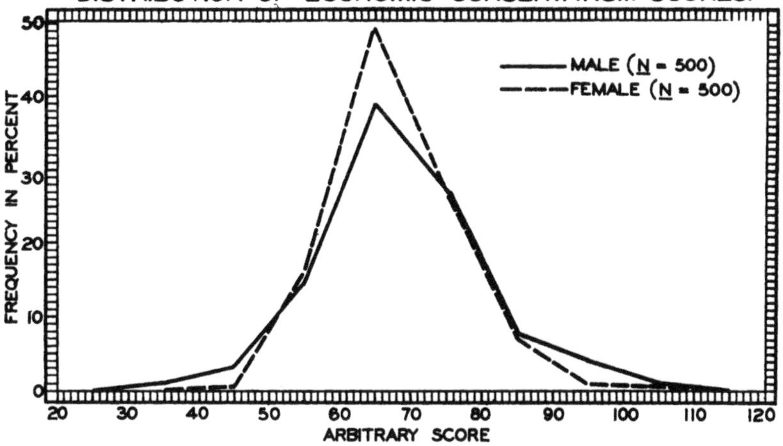

FIG. 6.

DISTRIBUTION OF EDUCATION SCORES.

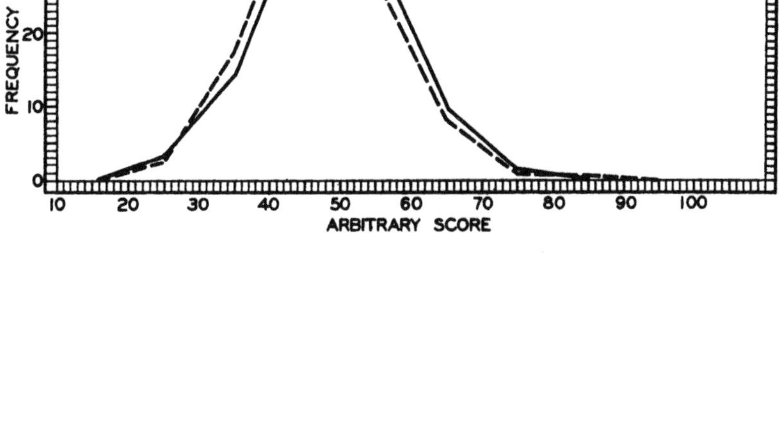

obtained sigmas. This changes no relationship within a scale, since it simply involves dividing each score by a constant. At least the scores from scale to scale are more comparable than without the conversion. The arbitrary scores, together with the corresponding sigma scores for each, are presented in the Appendix.

THE MEAN SCORE AS THE POINT OF ORIGIN IN INTERPRETING PERSONALITY SCORES

Before leaving the data in this chapter, certain of their implications for the theory of personality measurement may be considered. Attitudes and personality traits have been defined by many as "sets" to respond. Likert defines an attitude as "a cluster of habits sufficiently related to be treated as a unit." If such a definition is accepted it becomes difficult to conceive of the persons who make mean scores on certain scales as possessing the trait to be measured at all. Individuals who make mean scores on the inferiority scale appear to lack an integration of the specific traits implied by the single items into a generalized pattern of response. Those at the mean appear to respond to each item independently rather than to the items as a group in a constant way. They possess no "set" or tendency to respond in constant fashion. This analysis points to the mean position rather than to either extreme position on the range as the point of origin. This conception emphasizes organization or pattern of responses as the essential characteristic of the general trait and not the idea that an individual's response to every item is reflecting a single generalized set, regardless of how these responses are integrated.

When a group of items has been selected that meet the criterion of internal consistency, how shall we regard individuals at the mean who exhibit inconsistency from item to item? It is tenable to urge that their responses are not determined by a generalized set which the scale is designed to measure, and that the various traits implied by the items are not organized into a more general pattern.

This conception is particularly applicable to the inferiority scale. The mean total score in arbitrary units is very close to 66, precisely the score that one would obtain if he checked the undecided or 3 position on all 22 items. This is not, however, the way in which individuals who score at or close to the mean obtain their scores. Their scores are obtained rather by checking an equal number of responses weighted 2 and 4, 1 and 5. These individuals usually take definite positions on most of the items, but their responses are not consistent from item to item. It may therefore be argued that they do not possess an average amount of generalized inferiority feeling but rather possess feelings about the specific situations implied by the single items--feelings that are not integrated.

It can be demonstrated that on the average the individual who makes a mean score on the inferiority scale does so as a result of conflicting responses to the items rather than because he has checked the undecided position consistently. In Figure 7 are presented the frequencies with which each of the five response positions are taken by the middle 25 persons in the groups of 100 of each sex in the Sociology I course. It is clear that for each sex the mean scores are obtained primarily by taking the 2 and 4 positions with approximately equal frequency. The concept that the mean position is the point of origin for the trait and that those at the mean simply do not possess the trait in the form of a generalized set seems applicable to the inferiority scale.

The economic conservatism scale also yields a mean for total arbitrary scores close to 66. In this case, however, the mean scores are obtained largely by checking the 3 response consistently, as is also shown in Figure 7. May it not be urged again that the consistent checking of the undecided position implies absence of an attitudinal set? It appears reasonable to maintain that an attitude which can be designated as one of economic conservatism or liberalism emerges as the individual checks with some consistency one of the positions denoting decision. It is, however, possible to maintain that a mean score obtained by checking the undecided position represents a certain amount of the

FIG. 7.

DISTRIBUTIONS OF ITEM RESPONSES FOR MIDDLE 25 CASES IN A SERIES OF 100 FOR THE INFERIORITY AND ECONOMIC CONSERVATISM SCALES.

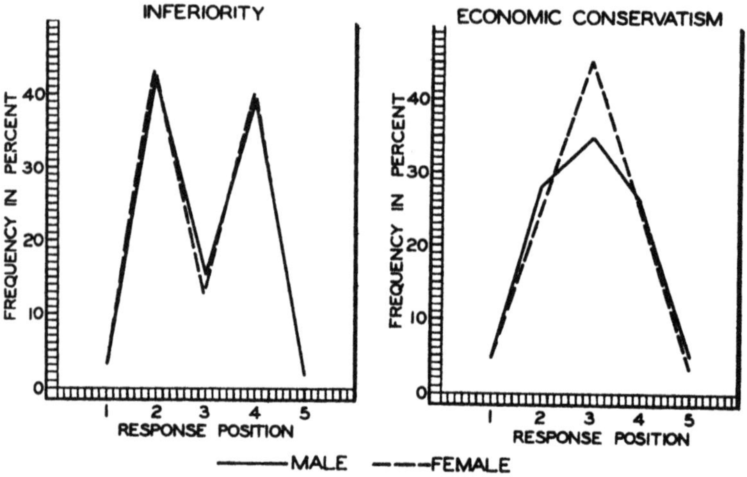

trait. The authors incline toward the former view. This conception can also be applied to the remaining scales even though consistent checking of the undecided position would yield a score which is relatively unfavorable.

SUMMARY

The distributions of the responses to items of the scales showed marked differences in form--some being symmetrical, some skewed, and some clearly bimodal. Bimodality, occurring always around the undecided position as a midpoint, was most characteristic of the morale, inferiority, and family items. In these three scales more negative than positive items are bimodal. The nature of the bimodal items suggests that bimodality may be used as an index of whether items are measuring a trait of direct, immediate, personal significance to the individual. The greater frequency of bimodality among the negative items may also be interpreted in the same light; negative items probably evoke reactions of more personal and fundamental significance to the individual, (See Chapter IX.) The fact that items in the economic conservatism scale, the scale appearing to be least based on direct personal experience, evoke more undecided responses from women also supports this position; women, as a group, are almost certainly less well informed about economic matters.

Proof that bimodality cannot be accounted for by the general technique of scale construction used or by the number of steps of the item scale is presented in detail. Previous evidence that the graphic rating scale has decided limitations is confirmed in this study.

The bimodality of certain items raised scoring problems. The arbitrary method of scoring was compared with the two methods of sigma weighting--that based on the probability curve and that based on the actually obtained distributions of the standard sample of one thousand cases. The three methods were found to yield almost identical results, not only in the relative but in the absolute sense. When dealing with a total score based on a number of items, irregularities of item units are cancelled, so that the final total score units are roughly equal within a scale.

The data point clearly to the conclusion that in the construction of scales of the type dealt with here, the emphasis should be on the adequacy of sampling. If the sampling is adequate, the chances are good that the units will take care of themselves.

Chapter V

RELIABILITY OF THE SCALES

RELIABILITY COEFFICIENTS

Correlations between Form A and Form B for each of the scales are given in Table 50 for the standard samples of 500 of each sex, and for each of the five smaller groups of which they are composed. Correlations are also listed for each scale for a group of 62 federal-aid students, and for 50 unemployed men receiving public relief who were not included in the standard sample. The reliability coefficients, or the Form A-Form B correlations corrected by the Spearman-Brown formula to estimate the reliability for the complete scales, are likewise given in Table 50. Reliability coefficients for the groups of 500 are:

Scale	500 Males	500 Females
Morale	.79[1]	.81
Inferiority	.78	.82
Family	.83	.88
Law	.84	.82
Economic conservatism . .	.85	.82
Education	.82	.83

The range of variation in these coefficients is small. Other research workers who use these scales can anticipate reliability coefficients above .80 for

---

1. O. Milton Hall (9, page 19) obtained a corrected split-half coefficient of .69 for a group of 84 engineering students on his Occupational Morale Scale, and coefficients of .82 and .84 for unemployed and employed engineers. The corrected split-half coefficients for a group of older unemployed men on our morale scale was .87, for a young employed male group, .84.

most groups. However, they may find coefficients as high as .90 in groups that are very heterogeneous with regard to some of the attitudes measured, and in rare instances the reliability coefficients may fall below .70 if a group is very homogeneous. Only one of the 84 reliability coefficients that were computed fell below .70, and this is to be explained by the unusual homogeneity of this group for that variable.

STANDARD ERRORS OF TRUE SCORES

The essential dependence of a reliability coefficient on the range of scores obtained in the group used as the basis for its computation makes direct comparison of reliability coefficients difficult. When a series of scales is given to a group, the scale that yields the highest reliability coefficient may do so solely because the variability in that attitude is greater for that particular group, whereas the test may not be giving as accurate measures as those obtained from another scale yielding a lower reliability coefficient. Truman Kelley (12, page 223) in discussing this point says: "For this reason, the reporting of standard errors of true scores is to be recommended, for these will not change with the range, if the test is equally reliable throughout the range."

By a "true score" is meant the average score that would be obtained from an infinite number of strictly comparable tests. The measure of reliability which is recommended as being of most value is the standard error of estimate of a true score by means of a single score of the same function, for which Kelley gives this formula (page 215):

$$\sigma_{\infty.1} = \sigma_1\sqrt{r_{1I} - r_{1I}^2}$$

σ_1 is the standard deviation of the distribution of scores; r_{1I} is the reliability coefficient. This formula enables us to estimate the extent to which scores obtained from a single giving of the scales will deviate from those that would be secured as average scores on an infinite number of strictly comparable forms of

TABLE 50.-FORM B RELIABILITY COEFFICIENTS FOR VARIOUS GROUPS

(Standard scores.)

Group	N	Morale		Inferiority		Family		Law		Economic Conservatism		Education	
		Raw	Corrected§	Raw	Corrected§	Raw	Corrected§	Raw	Corrected§	Raw	Corrected§	Raw	Corrected§
STANDARD SAMPLE													
Male													
All males	500	.65	.79	.64	.78	.71	.83	.72	.84	.74	.85	.69	.82
Sociology I	100	.75	.86	.68	.81	.61	.76	.73	.84	.79	.88	.70	.82
General College	100	.57	.73	.76	.86	.71	.83	.74	.85	.71	.83	.85	.79
High school seniors (C)#	100	.48	.65	.62	.77	.69	.82	.64	.79	.78	.88	.60	.75
Employed (C)	100	.72	.84	.55	.71	.76	.86	.75	.86	.66	.79	.68	.81
Unemployed (C)	100	.68	.81	.68	.81	.77	.87	.72	.84	.68	.81	.81	.90
Female													
All females	500	.68	.81	.69	.82	.79	.88	.70	.82	.69	.82	.71	.83
Sociology I	100	.79	.88	.65	.79	.79	.88	.71	.83	.85	.92	.64	.78
General College	100	.63	.77	.68	.81	.76	.86	.68	.81	.59	.74	.72	.84
High school seniors (C)#	100	.63	.77	.72	.84	.81	.90	.72	.84	.74	.85	.78	.88
Employed (C)	100	.71	.83	.71	.83	.82	.90	.74	.85	.60	.75	.75	.86
Unemployed (C)	100	.67	.80	.59	.74	.74	.85	.67	.80	.54	.70	.65	.79
FEDERAL-AID STUDENTS													
Male	62	.64	.78	.77	.87	.75	.86	.76	.87	.81	.90	.60	.75
PUBLIC RELIEF GROUP													
Male	50	.77	.87	.74	.85	.62	.77	.83	.91	.75	.86	.76	.86

§Corrected by the Spearman-Brown formula.
#(C) = controlled sample.

the same scales. In two-thirds of the cases the error between true score and score obtained from a single test should lie within the range $\pm\sigma_{\infty.1}$. The standard errors of estimate of true scores for the groups of 500 males and 500 females on the various scales are as follows:

Scale	500 Males	500 Females
Morale	3.82	4.01
Inferiority	4.06	3.82
Family	3.50	3.44
Law	3.76	3.74
Economic conservatism . .	3.94	2.66
Education	3.88	3.71

These standard errors, ranging from 2.66 to 4.06 points, are eminently satisfactory, if one considers the length of the measuring instruments. Although it would be possible to reduce these errors substantially by lengthening the measuring instruments, it was not deemed feasible to do this. In lengthening the scales the gain in reliability is subject to the law of diminishing returns. A battery of scales much longer than that developed would make unreasonable demands on the time of the subject given the scales without yielding improvement in measurement commensurate with the increased time demanded.

The variation in the reliability coefficients reported in Table 50 is chiefly due to more or less restriction of range in scores from group to group. The lowest reliability coefficient obtained for any group on any scale was .65 for high school boys on the morale scale. The standard deviation of scores (8.25) for this group on this scale was the lowest of 36 computed for males. The standard error of estimate (of "true scores") for this group is only 3.94 points. The standard error of estimate for high school boys on morale scores is identical with the standard error of estimate for the group of 500 males on the economic conservatism scale, although the reliability coefficients (.65 and .85) would lead one to infer that the reliability was greater for the 500 group.

INTERNAL CONSISTENCY AND STANDARD DEVIATIONS

The relationship between range and the magnitude of the reliability coefficient has been discussed in the usual manner. True differences in the variability of the trait measured have been assumed to account for the variation in standard deviations from group to group. There is, however, another way of viewing the differences in standard deviations. Standard deviations as well as reliability coefficients may be conceived as a function of internal consistency of responses. This conception is not applicable where a variable is measured by a single measure, as height by inches, but only when measurement is by instruments composed of many items, each of which contributes to the total score. In this case range is affected by the extent to which items yield internally consistent responses.

A scale given to a group for which it is not appropriate will not yield internally consistent responses. For such a group the items are not homogeneous in the sense that they are consistently significant as measures of a common variable. Other factors than the degree to which the variable is present are the determinants of response. These other factors will reduce the average item discriminative values and the standard deviations on total scores. If there is no consistency in the responses of any individual from item to item, the split-half reliability coefficient, the range, and the standard deviation will deviate from zero only within the limits of chance fluctuation. If all individuals were to check the responses weighted 1, 2, 3, 4, and 5 with equal frequency all scores would be identical. As scales to measure a variable elicit increasing consistency of responses, total scores of individuals will diverge from the mean, and standard deviations will become larger, assuming, of course, that heterogeneity on the trait measured actually exists in the group.[2]

2. John E. Anderson (2) recently studied the range and reliability of responses yielded by retained and rejected items in an

Standard deviations may therefore be low because items do not discriminate on a homogeneous basis. This in turn means inadaptability of the scale. When a scale is not adaptable to a particular group, the effect upon standard deviation is the same as that resulting from true homogeneity within the group upon the variable to be measured.

TEST-RETEST COEFFICIENTS

A second measure of the reliability of the measuring instruments can be obtained by retesting a group after a time interval. Retesting with the same instrument involves some error because of the factor of recall of previous response and because attitudes are dynamic--they may not remain constant during the interval. The longer the interval the less error there may be due to recall, but the greater will be the difference due to change in attitudes. Assuming that test conditions are held relatively constant, wide changes in attitude scores over an interval of a few months would indicate either excessive unreliability of the tests or marked instability in the attitudes measured. To provide a fairly stringent test of the reliability of the scales and of the stability of the attitudes it was decided to retest one group after a two-month interval.

Working with 100 original test papers of each sex, 70 retest papers of men and 75 of women could be matched with the originals by means of face sheet data. The matching was done by each of the investigators independently, and only those pairs were retained which both agreed had been filled out by the same person. There is a large enough number of items of information on the face sheet to make error in matching only a remote possibility. If such errors did occur, they would be almost certain to result in a lowering of the test-retest correlations. During the course of two months

(Footnote cont'd.) objective psychology examination. Items were rejected for the reason that they did not discriminate well between the upper and lower thirds in the distribution of total scores. The rejected items yielded small standard deviations and almost a zero split-half reliability coefficient.

some of the subjects had dropped from the course and some were absent on the retest date. These circumstances probably account almost entirely for the fact that thirty of the original tests for males and twenty-five of those for females could not be matched with retests.

Table 51 gives the correlations between first and second scores and comparisons with the reliability coefficients.

TABLE 51.-TEST-RETEST CORRELATIONS

	70 Males		75 Females	
	60-day Test-Retest r*	Reliability Coefficient (First Test)	60-day Test-Retest r*	Reliability Coefficient (First Test)
Morale	.72	.75	.61	.70
Inferiority . . .	.81	.87	.77	.84
Family	.83	.84	.78	.86
Law	.78	.87	.78	.73
Economic conservatism	.86	.84	.82	.75
Education	.84	.81	.85	.84

*The relatively low retest coefficients on morale scores are in accord with Hall's results for his Occupational Morale Scale. His 30-day retest coefficient was .63 for 84 engineering students. Op. cit., page 19.

Rosenthal's Survey of Socio-Economic Attitudes (15, page 20), containing 47 statements, yielded a retest coefficient of .77 after a one-month interval. This is a slightly lower coefficient than those yielded by the present Economic Conservatism Scale after a two month interval.

Inspection of the data shows that the Spearman-Brown formula applied to the Form A-Form B correlation coefficients calculated on the basis of test scores usually predicted the test-retest coefficients of the complete scales with a small range of error. The test-retest correlations exceeded the reliability coefficients in about half the instances--five times out of twelve. The size of the retest coefficients indicates a marked degree of stability in these attitudes. They indicate the degree of consistency that may be expected in practice. It is of some interest from the viewpoint of degree of stability of the traits measured to correct the reliability coefficients for attenuation. Hull (11, p. 243) gives the following formula for correction for attenuation:

$$\text{True } r_{01} = \frac{r_{(0+0)(1+1)}}{\sqrt{\frac{2r_{00}}{1+r_{00}}}\sqrt{\frac{2r_{11}}{1+r_{11}}}}$$

The observed *r* in the numerator is to be computed on the basis of two combined measures of each variable correlated. In the application of the formula we are treating each form of a scale as a single measure, and the sum of the scores on the two forms at each giving of a scale is treated as a combined measure. The correlation between the total scores at the first and second administrations of a scale is substituted in the formula as the "observed *r*." The raw correlation between Form A and Form B scores at the first giving of a scale is substituted in the formula for r_{00} and the raw coefficient between Form A and Form B scores at the second giving of a scale is substituted for r_{11}. We are treating test scores and retest scores as two variables. This involves some error because retest score is not strictly independent of test score, and there is likelihood that some errors of measurement will be correlated from test to retest. However, the formula will enable us to gain a rough approximation of the retest coefficients that would be yielded over a two-month period between scores on two perfectly reliable and perfectly comparable measuring instruments. Judgment as to the relative stability of the various aspects of personality measured should be fairly reliable, since the errors involved in retesting with the same instrument should be relatively constant from scale to scale. The coefficients corrected for attenuation by this formula range from .782 for women on the morale scale to 1.03 for women on the economic conservatism scale. The latter coefficient is of course absurd. The excess over 1.00 is, however, probably within the limits of the probable error of the coefficient. The lowest coefficient for males is .903

on the morale scale, and the highest is 1.00 on the education scale. These data indicate that morale changed most from test to retest for both sexes, and that the other aspects of personality measured are highly stable. It seems probable on others than the morale scale, that perfectly reliable and comparable instruments would yield correlation coefficients exceeding .90 over a two-month period. Readers are cautioned that such coefficients are estimates of the stability of attitudes, and that coefficients corrected for attenuation have no reference to the practical reliability or consistency that may be anticipated from the scales in their present form.

SCALES COMPARED AS TO RELIABILITY

Three available criteria for judging the relative reliability of the various scales are:

1. The reliability coefficients for the groups of 500.
2. The standard errors of estimate of true score.
3. The test-retest coefficients.

Judged on the basis of these criteria, the scales do not vary greatly in reliability. However, the range of variation is sufficient to justify the following conclusions:

1. The family and economic conservatism scales are the most reliable for men. Judged on the basis of standard error of estimate, the family scale is most reliable. However, on the basis of reliability coefficients for the groups of 500 males, and on the basis of test-retest coefficient, the economic conservatism scale is most reliable. In every group for which standard deviations were computed, the range of scores was wider on the economic conservatism scale. This probably means that our groups are in reality more heterogeneous in their economic than in their family attitudes, although this may be merely a temporary phenomenon associated with the present period of economic distress.

2. The inferiority scale is the least reliable of the six scales for men. The reliability coefficient was lowest for the group of 500 males, and the

standard error of estimate of true scores was greatest. The scale was fourth in terms of test-retest coefficient, but the standard deviation for the group used in the test-retest comparison is larger on this scale than on any other, and larger on this scale for this group than it is on this scale for any other male group.

3. The family and economic conservatism scales are also the most reliable for women. Judged on the basis of standard error of estimate of true scores, the economic conservatism scale is most reliable, but the family scale is most reliable on the basis of the reliability coefficients. The standard deviation of scores is larger for four or five female groups on the family scale than on the economic conservatism scale. Assuming that this condition prevails in most groups that may be given the scales in the future, investigators may anticipate highest reliability coefficients for women on the family scale.

4. The morale scale is the least reliable of the six for women. This scale yielded the lowest reliability coefficient for the group of 500 females, the largest standard error of estimate of true scores, and the lowest test-retest coefficient.

It may be argued that lower reliability for certain scales is a consequence of the nature of the traits measured rather than a result of the way in which the methods of scale construction are applied. It is entirely possible that the morale and inferiority scales evoke responses that create greater emotional disturbance in the subject than do the other scales, and that this emotional disturbance is accompanied by more evasion. Even though the scales are given anonymously, individuals may be unwilling to reveal their true attitudes in their responses to some scales because the act of revelation brings to the surface feelings that the subject finds unpleasant.

IDENTICAL RESPONSES, COMPENSATING CHANGES, AND RETEST COEFFICIENTS

To determine whether the retest reliability of the various scales is primarily a result of identical responses to the various items or of changes in response which are compensating, the percentage of identical responses and the percentage of changes of more than one position are compared in Table 52 with the retest coefficients for total score. There is a slight but consistent sex difference in this table. Women show a greater proportion of identical responses and fewer shifts of more than one position on five of the six scales, but the retest coefficients for women are not consistently higher. In fact, they are lower for total score on four of the six scales. Compensating shifts appear to be less frequent than for men.

TABLE 52.-COMPARISON OF TEST-RETEST r WITH PERCENTAGE OF IDENTICAL RESPONSES AND PERCENTAGE OF RESPONSE SHIFTS OF MORE THAN ONE POSITION

(General College; N = 50 of each sex.)

Scale	Test-Retest r		Percentage of Identical Responses		Percentage of Shifts of More Than 1 Position	
	Male	Female	Male	Female	Male	Female
Morale	.72	.61	54.6	55.6	15.18	14.09
Inferiority	.81	.77	57.5	57.6	16.27	18.18
Family	.83	.78	56.4	59.6	14.36	13.27
Law	.78	.78	62.6	55.6	17.18	12.18
Economic conservatism	.86	.82	50.2	50.7	16.27	13.00
Education	.84	.85	58.4	60.4	11.45	9.09

Item response shifts which cancel so that the score remains unchanged are undoubtedly operative on all of the scales. The scales differ in the extent to which shifts are compensating. The morale scale is particularly noteworthy. It yields the lowest test-retest coefficients for both sexes, but does not yield fewest identical responses or the greatest number of shifts of more than one position. Shifts on this scale are more often directional and less often of the cancelling type than on other scales.

The economic conservatism scale is the best example of a scale that yields stable total scores in spite of a considerable number of changes in response. It yields fewest identical responses for both sexes and yet total scores have the highest test-retest coefficient for males and the second highest for females. Shifts in response are more often compensating on this than on other scales.

The education scale is typical of those that gain their reliability by means of a high proportion of identical responses and few shifts of more than one position. On this scale there are fewest changes of more than one position and the greatest proportion of identical responses. This marked stability of response is reflected in the retest coefficients for total score. Retest coefficient is highest for females and second highest for males among the six scales. Such changes in response as occur do not lower the retest coefficient by failing to compensate as was true of the morale scale.

STABILITY OF SCORES ANALYZED BY QUARTILES

In order to scrutinize the reliability of the scales in greater detail the average changes in scores from test to retest are presented in Table 53; the changes were obtained by summing the individual changes without regard to sign and dividing by the number of cases. The morale scale, judged to be the least reliable for women, yielded scores which, on the average, changed most from test to retest. Likewise, the inferiority scale, judged least reliable for men, yielded scores that changed most from test to retest.

The least change in scores for women in Q_1 occurred on the economic conservatism scale; the greatest change occurred on the morale scale. For men in Q_1 the least change occurred in scores on the family scale, the greatest change on the morale scale. Average scores for women in Q_4, the quartile containing scores indicative of most favorable attitudes, changed most on the morale and law scales, and least on the economic conservatism and education scales. Average scores for men in Q_4 changed least on the law scale and most on the inferiority scale.

TABLE 53.-AVERAGE CHANGES IN INDIVIDUAL SCORES BY QUARTILES FROM TEST TO RETEST

(General College group; N = 68 of each sex.)

Quartile	Morale		Inferiority		Family		Law		Economic Conservatism		Education	
	M.*	F.**	M.	F.	M.	F.	M.	F.	M.	F.	M.	F.
Arithmetic Changes:												
Q_1	8.0	9.2	5.6	4.7	4.0	5.3	8.5	5.4	5.4	3.8	4.7	4.9
Q_2	6.0	4.8	7.7	5.4	4.1	4.7	6.1	5.7	3.7	3.1	3.6	3.3
Q_3	3.1	4.0	6.7	5.3	5.4	4.4	6.4	4.9	4.1	4.2	4.9	4.8
Q_4	4.2	5.1	6.6	6.0	4.8	5.0	4.2	6.4	5.4	3.9	4.5	3.0
Mean	5.3	5.8	6.7	5.4	4.6	4.9	6.3	5.6	4.7	3.8	4.4	4.0
Directional Changes:												
Q_1	-2.8	-2.5	-3.0	-2.7	-1.7	+.8	+1.2	-1.4	-2.7	-2.0	-3.1	-2.1
Q_2	-.9	-3.2	-6.2	-1.1	-.8	+.8	-2.9	+3.8	-.5	-.2	+.1	-1.3
Q_3	+.9	+.9	-3.4	-4.2	-2.0	-.2	+2.3	-.5	+.3	+1.5	+2.9	-2.9
Q_4	+.8	+1.5	-2.6	-.7	+1.4	+2.1	+3.0	+3.9	-1.2	+1.0	+.1	+1.1

*M = male.
**F = female.

Table 53 also indicates the average directional shift in scores for individuals from quartile to quartile. These quantities were obtained by subtracting the sum of the positive differences in scores from test to retest for individuals in a quartile from the sum of the negative differences, and dividing by the number of cases. The trend of these directional shifts exhibits the well-known phenomenon of regression. The tendency for scores to regress toward the mean on the second giving of the scales is evident in the number of instances in which the sign for the average directional shift is positive and the number of instances in which it is negative from quartile to quartile.

There are twelve measures of directional shift for each quartile (six scales and two sexes). The relative frequency with which the average change is in the direction of higher or lower scores for each quartile is shown below:

	Average Score Lower at Retest	Average Score Higher at Retest
Q_1	10	2
Q_2	9	3
Q_3	6	6
Q_4	3	9

There was a slightly greater tendency for scores in Q_1 and Q_2 to be lower at the retest than there was for scores in Q_3 and Q_4 to be higher. Moreover, in nine of twelve possible comparisons, the size of the directional shift in total score toward the mean was greater for Q_1 than for Q_4.

CHANGES AT THE VARIOUS RESPONSE POSITIONS

To provide further data concerning the reliability of these scales, the changes in response position from test to retest were tabulated separately for positive and negative items. These data for males are given in Table 54 and for females in Table 55. The following explanation will clarify these tables. A segment of Table 55 is reprinted on page 126.

TABLE 54.-PERCENTAGE CHANGES IN ITEM RESPONSE FROM TEST TO RETEST

(General College Men; N = 50.)

Response Change	Morale		Inferiority		Family		Law		Economic Conserv-atism		Education	
	P.*	N.**	P.	N.	P.	N.	P.	N.	P.	N.	P.	N.
1 POSITION:												
1-1 . .	43.1	48.7	48.5	55.5	45.6	42.9	42.5	38.2	41.9	52.5	58.9	50.0
1-2 . .	46.6	41.7	42.4	18.5	50.0	35.7	30.0	42.1	30.2	35.0	35.6	40.1
1-3 . .	6.9	5.2	3.0	7.4	2.2	10.7	15.0	9.2	16.3	6.2	2.1	6.6
1-4 . .	1.7	3.5	3.0	11.1	2.2	8.9	2.5	6.6	7.0	6.2	2.7	3.3
1-5 . .	1.7	1.0	3.0	7.4	0.0	1.8	10.0	4.0	4.6	0.0	.7	0.0
Total .	100.0	100.1	99.9	99.9	100.0	100.0	100.0	100.1	100.0	99.9	100.0	100.0
2 POSITION:												
2-2 . .	68.2	69.3	70.9	73.7	71.6	68.6	67.9	61.8	53.1	60.0	71.6	71.5
2-1 . .	8.3	11.5	9.2	5.4	12.2	6.1	6.2	9.2	8.8	12.0	14.6	12.9
2-3 . .	12.0	9.4	9.7	5.8	8.1	12.1	9.2	13.0	14.1	17.5	5.8	9.0
2-4 . .	11.1	9.1	9.2	14.0	7.7	12.1	15.4	15.4	20.8	9.5	8.0	5.0
2-5 . .	.5	.7	1.0	1.2	.4	1.1	1.2	.5	3.1	1.0	0.0	1.6
Total .	100.1	100.0	100.0	100.1	100.0	100.0	99.9	99.9	99.9	100.0	100.0	100.0
3 POSITION:												
3-3 . .	37.4	25.0	28.8	30.9	42.7	23.3	35.2	38.6	46.0	46.9	34.7	32.9
3-1 . .	6.1	7.7	3.8	2.9	3.4	8.2	3.3	4.0	5.3	5.3	0.0	12.3
3-2 . .	31.3	42.3	50.0	50.0	34.8	38.4	30.8	31.7	26.5	26.5	46.9	41.1
3-4 . .	23.2	21.2	17.5	16.2	18.0	28.8	26.4	21.8	19.5	20.4	14.3	12.3
3-5 . .	2.0	3.8	0.0	0.0	1.1	1.4	4.4	4.0	2.6	.9	4.1	1.4
Total .	100.0	100.0	100.1	100.0	100.0	100.1	100.1	100.1	99.9	100.0	100.0	100.0
4 POSITION:												
4-4 . .	51.3	43.0	56.1	53.7	48.4	51.8	50.0	58.0	51.2	49.2	42.6	41.7
4-1 . .	4.0	2.5	1.8	0.5	2.2	2.9	1.4	1.4	3.0	1.6	1.5	1.7
4-2 . .	28.0	29.1	19.5	27.4	23.7	27.3	22.5	16.7	12.6	21.0	36.8	28.3
4-3 . .	13.3	12.7	17.2	14.9	22.6	10.8	14.1	18.1	26.5	18.5	17.6	13.3
4-5 . .	3.3	12.7	5.4	3.5	3.2	7.2	12.0	5.8	6.6	9.7	1.5	15.0
Total .	99.9	100.0	100.0	100.0	100.1	100.0	100.0	100.0	99.9	99.9	100.0	100.0
5 POSITION:												
5-5 . .	23.1	35.3	25.0	18.2	14.3	44.4	46.0	42.9	27.8	27.3	33.3	11.1
5-1 . .	0.0	17.6	0.0	0.0	0.0	0.0	2.7	7.1	5.6	3.0	16.7	11.1
5-2 . .	15.4	5.9	5.0	18.2	14.3	5.6	13.5	3.6	2.8	12.1	8.3	33.3
5-3 . .	3.8	5.9	5.0	0.0	42.9	16.7	8.1	14.3	13.9	21.2	0.0	11.1
5-4 . .	57.7	35.3	65.0	63.4	28.6	33.3	29.7	32.1	50.0	36.4	41.7	33.3
Total .	100.0	100.0	100.0	100.0	100.1	100.0	100.0	100.0	100.1	100.0	100.0	99.9

* P. = positive.
** N. = negative.

TABLE 55.-PERCENTAGE CHANGE IN ITEM RESPONSE FROM TEST TO RETEST

(General College Women; N = 50.)

Response Change	Morale		Inferiority		Family		Law		Economic Conserv-atism		Education	
	P.*	N.**	P.	N.	P.	N.	P.	N.	P.	N.	P.	N.
1 POSITION:												
1-1 . .	56.0	52.8	34.6	34.4	49.4	52.0	34.5	55.3	33.3	42.1	62.0	63.5
1-2 . .	26.8	31.4	50.0	46.9	40.7	34.3	51.7	60.3	40.7	42.1	37.2	31.8
1-3 . .	7.3	2.1	3.8	3.1	7.7	9.6	8.6	9.2	11.1	10.5	0.0	2.7
1-4 . .	7.3	2.1	7.7	15.6	1.1	4.1	3.4	5.3	14.8	2.6	0.7	1.4
1-5 . .	2.4	1.4	3.8	0.0	1.1	0.0	1.7	0.0	0.0	2.6	0.0	0.7
Total .	99.8	99.8	99.9	100.0	100.0	100.0	99.9	100.1	99.9	99.9	99.9	100.1
2 POSITION:												
2-2 . .	67.3	70.0	70.2	71.6	68.8	67.9	63.8	61.3	54.8	55.9	69.1	74.1
2-1 . .	10.6	13.0	8.3	6.5	11.5	11.1	7.0	12.9	4.3	6.8	22.0	17.8
2-3 . .	12.4	8.2	7.2	8.8	11.1	7.1	16.9	16.5	20.9	17.5	4.2	4.4
2-4 . .	7.5	7.4	12.2	12.6	7.5	12.9	11.9	8.5	19.1	16.4	4.2	3.7
2-5 . .	2.2	1.5	2.2	0.4	1.2	1.1	0.4	0.8	0.9	3.4	0.4	0.0
Total .	100.0	100.1	100.1	99.9	100.1	100.1	100.0	100.0	100.0	100.0	99.9	100.0
3 POSITION:												
3-3 . .	36.7	40.8	38.7	40.8	41.7	45.2	41.2	53.0	52.7	51.2	20.4	25.4
3-1 . .	2.5	8.2	1.3	2.0	1.2	4.8	4.1	2.0	1.8	2.9	12.2	14.9
3-2 . .	38.3	22.4	36.0	36.7	34.5	27.4	39.2	20.0	23.6	21.8	40.8	46.3
3-4 . .	21.7	26.5	24.0	18.4	22.6	22.6	13.4	24.0	20.4	23.8	22.4	13.4
3-5 . .	.8	2.0	0.0	2.0	0.0	0.0	2.0	1.0	1.4	0.6	4.1	0.0
Total .	100.0	99.9	100.0	99.9	100.0	100.0	99.9	100.0	99.9	100.3	99.9	100.0
4 POSITION:												
4-4 . .	44.2	48.1	55.1	59.4	57.1	65.0	52.9	56.4	51.9	45.0	56.2	35.0
4-1 . .	2.9	1.2	1.3	2.3	3.6	0.0	3.6	1.8	0.0	0.0	3.4	1.7
4-2 . .	30.4	29.6	23.5	21.7	24.1	20.5	15.2	18.2	15.2	12.8	20.2	38.3
4-3 . .	17.4	13.6	15.4	12.6	14.3	9.4	16.7	17.3	24.7	35.0	12.4	20.0
4-5 . .	5.1	7.4	4.7	4.0	0.9	5.1	11.6	6.3	8.2	7.1	7.9	5.0
Total .	100.0	99.9	100.0	100.0	100.0	100.0	100.0	100.0	100.0	99.9	100.1	100.0
5 POSITION:												
5-5 . .	25.0	33.3	17.6	31.3	10.0	20.0	57.1	37.5	40.0	44.0	37.5	40.0
5-1 . .	12.5	8.3	2.9	3.1	0.0	5.0	0.0	6.2	0.0	4.0	0.0	20.0
5-2 . .	8.3	25.0	11.8	15.6	10.0	15.0	0.0	6.2	13.3	12.0	25.0	40.0
5-3 . .	16.7	8.3	8.8	6.3	20.0	0.0	7.1	12.5	16.7	16.0	0.0	0.0
5-4 . .	37.5	25.0	58.9	43.6	60.0	60.0	35.7	37.5	30.0	24.0	37.5	0.0
Total .	100.0	99.9	100.0	99.9	100.0	100.0	99.9	99.9	100.0	100.0	100.0	100.0

*P. = positive.
**N. = negative.

MORALE SCALE

1 Position

Response Change	Positive
1 - 1	56.0
1 - 2	26.8
1 - 3	7.3
1 - 4	7.3
1 - 5	2.4
Total	99.8

This segment shows that of the original responses in the 1 position on positive items (the strongly agree position), 56.0 per cent remained identical on retest; 26.8 per cent shifted to the 2 position (agree response); 7.3 per cent shifted to the 3 position (undecided); 7.3 per cent shifted to the 4 position (disagree); and 2.4 per cent shifted to the 5 position (strongly disagree).

The frequency of responses in each position at the first giving of each scale is shown in Table 56 in percentages of the total number of each sex, data for positive and negative statements being tabulated separately. The number of responses made by either sex can be obtained, for either type of statement in a given scale, by multiplying 550 by the percentage in the appropriate column and row, since percentages in each column are based on 550 responses (50 persons; 11 items). Certain shifts in response that appear especially large or small in Tables 54 and 55 as compared with other scales will be found by inspection of Table 56 to be based on too small an N to be reliable.

Inspection of Tables 54 and 55 indicates that the 2 position (agree on positive items; disagree on negative items) is most stable. This holds true for both positive and negative items, both sexes, and every scale. The other positions are more variable, but the average rank of the positions in terms of stability is uniformly consistent for both sexes and both types of statement. The positions given in order of proportion of identical response from test to retest, are 2, 4, 1,

TABLE 56.-RESPONSES TO POSITIVE (P.) AND NEGATIVE (N.) STATEMENTS FOR EACH SCALE

(General College group; N = 50 of each sex.*)

	Morale		Inferiority		Family		Law		Conservatism		Education	
	P.	N.	P.	N.	P.	N.	P.	N.	P.	N.	P.	N.
Male:												
1 . . .	10.5	20.9	6.0	5.0	16.4	10.2	7.3	13.8	7.8	14.5	26.6	27.6
2 . . .	39.5	52.2	35.6	44.2	49.3	48.0	43.6	37.6	34.9	36.4	50.0	46.6
3 . . .	18.0	9.5	14.6	12.4	16.2	13.3	16.5	18.4	20.5	20.5	8.9	13.3
4 . . .	27.3	14.4	40.2	36.6	16.9	25.3	25.8	25.1	30.2	22.5	12.4	10.9
5 . . .	4.7	3.1	3.6	2.0	1.3	3.3	6.7	5.1	6.5	6.0	2.2	1.6
Total .	100.0	100.1	100.0	100.2	100.1	100.1	99.9	100.0	99.9	99.9	100.1	100.0
Female:												
1 . . .	7.5	25.5	5.8	4.8	16.5	13.3	10.5	13.8	4.9	6.9	24.9	26.9
2 . . .	41.1	48.9	33.0	47.6	46.0	50.9	44.2	45.1	20.9	32.2	47.1	49.1
3 . . .	21.8	8.9	13.6	9.0	15.3	11.3	17.6	18.2	40.0	30.9	8.9	12.2
4 . . .	25.1	14.7	42.6	31.8	20.4	21.3	25.1	20.0	28.7	25.4	16.2	10.9
5 . . .	4.4	2.2	6.2	5.8	1.8	3.6	2.5	2.9	5.4	4.5	2.9	0.9
Total .	99.9	100.2	100.2	100.0	100.0	100.4	99.9	100.0	99.9	99.9	100.0	100.0

*Since there are 11 items of each type in each scale, the percentage base is always 550 responses.

3, 5. It is surprising to find that the 5 position, which denotes the most unfavorable reaction, yields a lower proportion of identical responses than does the 3 position, which indicates indecision. The instability of the most unfavorable response position is consistent with our previous finding that unfavorable total scores tend to be the least stable. These findings indicate that scales which call for merely an agree or disagree response can be expected to yield a greater proportion of identical responses than will be obtained on a five-point alternate-response scale such as we used. This gain in identity of response through use of a two-point scale is accompanied by a loss in the discriminative value of the scale, particularly if the scale is short.

The data in Tables 54 and 55 not only permit judgment as to the relative stability of the various response positions but also show the relative frequency with which each response was chosen when responses were not identical from test to retest. For each position, the shift most commonly made is given below.

Position	Most Common Shift
1	2
2	3
3	2
4	2
5	4

The shift most commonly made was determined by ranking the positions according to the percentage of persons shifting to it from another position for each scale, and computing the average rank order of each position for the six scales combined. The most common shifts indicated above were consistent for positive and negative items and for both sexes, but are not consistent on every scale.

The most common shift from the 2 position is less certain than those for other positions. The proportions shifting to 1 and 4 are almost equal to the proportion shifting to 3. The fact that the 4 responses shifted more often to 2 than to the 3, or undecided, position is interesting. We observed earlier that the extreme unfavorable scores regressed more toward the mean than did extreme favorable scores, and also that the 5 position, although eliciting the fewest responses, changed in a larger proportion of instances. The mean position in terms of a five-point scale for the group of 1,000 lay between 2 and 3 for four of the six scales, the scales for economic conservatism and inferiority being the exceptions. Those who respond in the 4 position are thus further from the mean than are those who respond in the 2 position, and may therefore be expected to shift somewhat further on retest toward the favorable end of the scale. This suggests that the distance from 2 to 4 may be greater for those whose attitudes are favorable than is the distance from 4 to 2 for those whose attitudes are unfavorable. However, of those who respond in any given position, there is undoubtedly a range in the degree to which they agree, disagree, or are undecided. The distribution of those who respond in the 3 or 4 positions is probably skewed in such a way that there is a bunching of cases toward the favorable end of the hypothetical range within each position. Since the mean on the five-point scale is not at 3 on most of the items but lies somewhere between 2 and 3, one may reasonably assume that such skewness exists. In the light of these assumptions, the greater shift for the variable responses in the 4 position is to be expected.

The percentage of shifts from the 5 position to the 1 and 2 positions on the negative items of the education scale is deceptively high. There were few responses at the 5 position on this scale, so chance had a maximum opportunity to distort the percentages.

Sex differences in the tables just discussed require some attention. Of the responses in the 1 position on the inferiority scale, those of the men were more often identical on retest than were those of the women. Perhaps men who feel superior are more certain of it.

There are no appreciable sex differences on any scale so far as changes at the 2 Position are concerned. This fact, together with the greater number of responses at this position make one rather wary of attaching great significance to other sex differences where the number of cases is smaller.

There was a greater tendency for men than for women who were undecided on the education scale to remain so on retest. Our subjects were first and second-year university students, among whom the proportion of men undecided as to future vocations was doubtless larger than the proportion of women. Women have few vocations to choose from, and "housekeeper" probably describes the future vocation of the majority. The proportion of men who were undecided on negative family items and remained so on retest was twice as large as that among women who were originally undecided. Perhaps women's thinking centers so much more on family affairs that judgments are facilitated.

TEST-RETEST COEFFICIENTS FOR ITEMS

The analysis of reliability and stability of total scores for each sex and each scale, the analysis of change in score by quartile, and the analysis of stability of item response for the five alternative positions should provide a fairly intimate knowledge of how the scales function in use. To complete the analysis of reliability, retest correlation coefficients were computed for each item in every scale. Fifty men and fifty women served as the subject group; the retest group was reduced to this number to facilitate computation. Scattergrams were made for each of the 132 items, and these provide the most useful means for evaluating the reliability of items, and for perceiving the range of responses which they evoke. Since reproduction of all these scattergrams would not be feasible, it was decided to compute the correlation coefficients to provide concise data concerning each item. (See Table 57.) The size of these coefficients reflects both the stability and range of responses which an item yields.

Publication of data concerning the discriminative value of each item (Chapter III) and an index of individual item reliability is designed to facilitate the construction of better scales, as well as to give

TABLE 57.-TEST-RETEST ITEM CORRELATIONS

(General College group; N = 100, 50 of each sex.)

Morale		Inferior-ity		Family		Law		Economic Conserv-atism		Education	
Item	r	Item	r	Item	r	Item	r	Item	r	Item	r
1	.674	2	.553	3	.647	4	.452	5	.615	6	.875
7	.635	8	.358	9	.492	10	.515	11	.453	12	.695
13	.864	14	.587	15	.385	16	.447	17	.501	18	.730
19	.683	20	.485	21	.670	22	.495	23	.492	24	.704
25	.745	26	.595	27	.547	28	.695	29	.525	30	.492
31	.419	32	.515	33	.543	34	.572	35	.593	36	.579
37	.538	38	.586	39	.773	40	.524	41	.014	42	.519
43	.425	44	.530	45	.582	46	.301	47	.628	48	.530
49	.763	50	.359	51	.686	52	.524	53	.668	54	.603
55	.213	56	.710	57	.564	58	.536	59	.376	60	.403
61	.695	62	.508	63	.609	64	.303	65	.514	66	.517
67	.460	68	.577	69	.529	70	.520	71	.295	72	.400
73	.505	74	.584	75	.575	76	.449	77	.448	78	.499
79	.600	80	.538	81	.566	82	.577	83	.708	84	.611
85	.377	86	.633	87	.565	88	.721	89	.527	90	.573
91	.397	92	.322	93	.541	94	.566	95	.369	96	.902
97	.671	98	.518	99	.654	100	.368	101	.422	102	.265
103	.829	104	.624	105	.578	106	.584	107	.383	108	.583
109	.699	110	.551	111	.608	112	.446	113	.515	114	.427
115	.362	116	.503	117	.599	118	.627	119	.655	120	.594
121	.543	122	.572	123	.330	124	.441	125	.751	126	.717
127	.916	128	.600	129	.574	130	.510	131	.570	132	.468
Average r*	.623		.544		.578		.515		.523		.604

*r of items converted to Fisher's z values, and average z reconverted to r.

the reader a more intimate knowledge of the present battery of scales. If such data are made available by research workers, future investigators should be materially aided in the selection of items that are likely to prove discriminative and reliable.

The range in the size of the test-retest coefficients for the items in the various scales is apparent in the following statistics:

Scale	Highest r	Lowest r	Average r
Morale	.916	.213	.623
Inferiority	.710	.322	.544
Family	.773	.330	.578
Law	.721	.301	.515
Economic conservatism .	.751	.014	.523
Education	.902	.265	.604

To make the individual coefficients more comparable for averaging, they were converted into Fisher's z values, summed, and the computed average z value was then converted back into its equivalent r.

The most reliable items for the morale, inferiority, family, law, economic conservatism, and education scale, respectively, are:

127. THERE IS REALLY NO POINT IN LIVING.
56. IT IS EASY TO ACT NATURALLY IN A GROUP.
39. ONE CANNOT FIND AS MUCH UNDERSTANDING AT HOME AS ELSEWHERE.
88. A HUNGRY MAN HAS A RIGHT TO STEAL.
125. MONEY SHOULD BE TAKEN FROM THE RICH AND GIVEN TO THE POOR DURING HARD TIMES.
96. A MAN IS FOOLISH TO KEEP ON GOING TO SCHOOL IF HE CAN GET A JOB.

The least reliable items are:

55. ANY MAN WITH ABILITY AND WILLINGNESS TO WORK HARD HAS A GOOD CHANCE OF BEING SUCCESSFUL.
92. SO MANY PEOPLE DO THINGS WELL THAT IT IS EASY TO BECOME DISCOURAGED.
123. OBLIGATIONS TO ONE'S FAMILY ARE A GREAT HANDICAP TO A YOUNG MAN TODAY.
46. A PERSON SHOULD OBEY THE LAWS NO MATTER HOW MUCH THEY INTERFERE WITH HIS PERSONAL AMBITIONS.
41. THE MORE A MAN LEARNS ABOUT OUR ECONOMIC SYSTEM. THE LESS WILLING HE IS TO SEE CHANGES MADE.
102. SAVINGS SPENT ON EDUCATION ARE WISELY INVESTED.

The two morale items that yielded the lowest test-retest coefficients, 55 and 115, were from Hall's Scale for Measuring Occupational Morale, which had been retained after the test of discriminating value was applied to all five. These least reliable morale items are:

55. ANY MAN WITH ABILITY AND WILLINGNESS TO WORK HARD HAS A GOOD CHANCE OF BEING SUCCESSFUL.
115. SUCCESS IS MORE DEPENDENT ON LUCK THAN ON REAL ABILITY.

That these items yielded lowest retest coefficients for our group may mean merely that they are less applicable to a young student group than to the older professional group Hall worked with. It is possible that these items are extremely sensitive measures of morale, and measure portions of the continuum that are less stable than those aspects of morale that are measured by our items. It may be, too, that placing these items in a different context has reduced their reliability.

Although the average item retest coefficient was higher for the morale scale than for the other scales, we recall that the morale scale was least reliable for women and about average for men. This probably means that changes in the responses of individuals do not cancel out from item to item to so great an extent on the morale scale as on other scales. It will be shown that the morale items are the most general in the sense that scores on this scale correlate highest with concomitant variation in scores on other scales. This interdependence may make morale a more variable phase of personality. Elsewhere it has been shown that items placed in one scale frequently discriminate well in other scales also--that an item which measures a single aspect of personality and that one alone may not be capable of formulation. Individual scores may be relatively less stable on the morale scale because morale is more closely related to other attitudes, and morale score is probably more responsive to changes in other attitudes. Correction of the retest coefficients for attenuation indicated that greatest change occurred in morale over a two-month period.

In order to discover whether a close relationship exists between item scale value differences (the differences between Q_1 and Q_4 means) and item retest coefficient, the average retest coefficients for the 11 most discriminating and the 11 least discriminating items in each scale were computed. The findings are presented in Table 58. The average item correlations were obtained as before by obtaining the average of Fisher's z equivalents for the correlation coefficients, and converting the average z value back into r. Allocation of items into the most or least discriminating dichotomy was done on the basis of calculations for groups including 400 of each sex. The values obtained for these larger groups were used in preference to those that could be computed for groups of 50 of each sex because they are less affected by random errors of sampling.

Although the average item retest coefficients are higher on five of the six scales for the 11 most discriminating items, the differences are always small. It is to be remembered that the range of item scale value differences is narrow, because items were rarely retained that yielded discriminating values of less than .90. Even so, the range is sufficient to warrant the conclusion that the relationship between item retest reliability and item discriminating value is not close.

It is interesting to observe that the 11 least discriminating items in the morale scale yielded a slightly higher average item correlation than did the 11 most discriminating items. The fact that the average item retest coefficients were higher for the morale scale than for other scales in spite of lower retest coefficients for total score has been discussed, and the hypothesis advanced that changes in item response tended to be cancelled out in total score to a lesser extent on the morale scale than on other scales. If changes in response to items are a consequence of random error, the cancellation process may result in bringing about stability in total score. The correction of test-retest coefficients on total scores for attenuation showed greater change for each sex on this scale than on other scales during the time interval between test and retest. Assuming that the most discriminating items reflect this change to a more marked degree, the lower

TABLE 58.-AVERAGE TEST-RETEST ITEM CORRELATIONS FOR THE 11 ITEMS WITH HIGHEST AND THE 11 ITEMS WITH LOWEST SCALE VALUE DIFFERENCES

(General College group; N = 50 of each sex for correlations; N = 400 of each sex for scale value differences.)

Scale	Average Scale Value Difference		Average Item Correlation	
	Highest 11	Lowest 11	Highest 11	Lowest 11
Morale	1.271	.877	.55	.69
Inferiority	1.256	.866	.56	.53
Family	1.475	1.021	.61	.55
Law	1.195	.868	.55	.48
Economic conservatism	1.403	.856	.58	.44
Education	1.195	.926	.61	.60

average item retest coefficients for the most discriminating morale items is explained. However, the difference between the average item retest coefficients for the 11 most discriminating and the 11 least discriminating items is not sufficient to warrant the conclusion that chance is not the true explanation.

RELIABILITY OF SCALES WHEN TAKEN OUT OF CONTEXT

It is obvious that removing a given scale from a battery of scales for separate use may result in change in its reliability coefficient. In the present battery of scales, the aspects of personality being measured are not apparent to the subject, nor is he usually aware that anything other than his opinions on a considerable number of statements is desired. A few of the factors that might change reliability when a scale is taken from its original context are the following:

1. There may be a greater striving for consistency when a scale is given separately because inconsistencies are more obvious to the subject.

2. There may be more evasion when a scale is

given separately because of greater awareness that not isolated opinions but generalized measures are being sought.

3. There may be more "carry over" from one item to the next when items in a single scale are immediately adjacent to each other. Regarding each item as a sample of a larger universe, the samples are probably more independent of each other when spaced.

4. Assuming that some emotional disturbance is aroused by scales that inquire into such intimate phases of self as do the inferiority and morale scales, the resulting disturbance may be greater when the items are not spaced.

5. Reliability may be related to the time required of the subject in the testing period.

Two scales, the morale and the economic conservatism, were taken from the battery and given separately to a group of university students in the Introduction to Sociology course. These two scales were chosen because they stand at opposite extremes with respect to reliability. In mimeographed form they were given to 100 women and 50 men. The students were in several class sections, and the order in which the two scales were given was varied from section to section. The Form A-Form B correlation for the morale scale, corrected by the Spearman-Brown formula to give the reliability coefficient for the complete scale, was .70 for men and .74 for women. The reliability coefficient for the economic conservatism scale was .93 for men and .87 for women. During the preceding school term, the battery of scales had been given to a different group of introductory sociology classes and the reliability coefficient obtained on the morale scale was .86 for males and .92 for females in contrast to .70 for males and .74 for females when the morale scale was given separately. On the economic conservatism scale, coefficients of .88 for males and .92 for females had been obtained from the battery. We can be fairly certain that the economic conservatism scale will yield excellent reliability if given separately. Although the differences in the morale reliability coefficients of the battery results and the results from the scale given separately may be due to chance, we are inclined to believe that giving this scale separately will lower its reliability coefficient. Time did not permit giving other scales separately, but it seems probable that reliability coefficients of .80 or better would usually result from the family, law, economic conservatism, and education scales in any fairly heterogeneous group if these scales were to be given separately. The morale scale and the inferiority scale would probably yield least reliable results if used separately, although final judgment on this point must be deferred until further experimental evidence is available.

SUMMARY

The six scales yielded split-half reliability coefficients corrected by the Spearman-Brown formula ranging from .78 to .88 for the standard samples of 500 of each sex. The retest coefficients were of approximately the same magnitude as the corrected coefficients between forms, except those for the morale scale. The lower retest coefficient for this scale probably means that morale changed most during the two-month interval. The standard errors of estimate of true score are small, ranging from 2.66 to 4.06 points for the standard groups of 500.

While the variation in the reliability of the scales is small, the family and economic conservatism scales appear to be the most reliable. The inferiority scale was found to be least reliable for men and the morale scale for women.

The high retest coefficient for the economic conservatism scale was found to be a consequence not of an unusually high proportion of identical responses but of compensating shifts. The morale scale, which yielded lower retest coefficients than the other scales, lost in reliability through non-compensating shifts in response rather than through a lower proportion of identical responses. The high retest coefficients for the education scale were a consequence of the fact that it yielded a high proportion of identical responses and few shifts of more than one position.

The response positions in order of stability

of response were 2, 4, 1, 3, 5. The tendency for the extreme unfavorable response position to be less stable is also shown in greater arithmetical and directional shifts of the most unfavorable total scores.

The relationship between item retest coefficient and item discriminative value was found to be small.

Chapter VI

RELATIONSHIPS BETWEEN THE SCALES

The battery of scales used in this study provides an excellent opportunity for the study of personality interrelationships. It is important to learn, for example, whether economic conservatism is associated with inferiority feelings, or whether low morale is associated with unfavorable attitudes toward law and legal institutions. The wide variation in the composition of social groups tested and the considerable differences in the experiential background of individuals who comprise them may be reflected in personality integrations. The groups studied ranged from boys and girls in high school who had not encountered the necessity of self-support to older men who had found it impossible to support their families without dependence on public relief agencies.

Major attention will be focussed on the interrelationships between attitudes that were found to exist in the standard samples, which contained 500 persons of each sex. Data for certain other groups will be presented to indicate something of the range of variability of these relationships in less heterogeneous groups than the standard samples.

A study of these interrelationships may be made either by subclassification of data or by means of correlational techniques. The first method has the advantage of simplicity, but the extent to which subclassification of data can be profitably carried is limited decidedly by the small frequencies that result when more than a very few variables are held constant by subclassification.

INTERCORRELATIONS

The zero order intercorrelations between standard scores on the six attitudes scales are presented in

Table 59 for the standard groups of 500, and for certain smaller groups that comprise parts of the standard groups. The intercorrelations for men dependent on public relief are included to show something of the range of variability in these relationships. Of all the groups tested, the men receiving public relief are most unlike the groups that comprise the standard samples. They are unlike the standard sample, for example, in terms of marital status and age.

The highest intercorrelations for the male standard group are those between morale scores and scores on the inferiority, family, law, and education scales. The intercorrelation between morale score and score on the economic conservatism scale is low (.235). Of the fifteen intercorrelations between the scores of the standard group, the five lowest are those for economic conservatism. This indicates that morale is most closely associated with other variables measured, and economic conservatism least closely associated. The fourth order partial coefficients between economic conservatism score and score on each of the other scales were computed for 500 men. Their size ranged from -.041 (economic conservatism vs. family) to .119 (economic conservatism vs. morale). These are obviously not significantly different from zero. The intercorrelations between economic conservatism score and other scores are consistently higher for men on public relief than for the group of 500 males, and almost always higher for the relief group than for the controlled sample of younger unemployed. The intercorrelations for the latter group, in turn, are higher than those for the standard group of 500 with one exception. The exception is the intercorrelation between economic conservatism score and inferiority score. That the intercorrelations for the unemployed group are higher than those for the standard group on the economic conservatism scale is probably a result of closer integration of economic attitudes with other personality traits as a consequence of unemployment experience.

Scores on the inferiority scale correlate more closely with morale scores than with any of the other measures. It is to be noted that scores on the inferiority scale also correlate more closely with those on each of the other scales for the men on public relief than for other groups. However, the differences between these intercorrelations for the relief group and for the standard sample of 500 men are not

TABLE 59.-INTERCORRELATIONS BETWEEN STANDARD SCORES

Scales	Male Standard Group (N=500)	Male Sociology I (N=100)	Male Unemployed (C)* (N=100)	Male High School Seniors(C) (N=100)	Male Public Relief Group (N=50)	Female Standard Group (N=500)	Female Sociology I (N=100)	Female Unemployed (C) (N=100)	Female High School Seniors(C) (N=100)
Morale correlated with:									
Inferiority	.511	.471	.537	.512	.626	.509	.240	.588	.656
Family	.420	.409	.368	.408	.377	.348	.179	.358	.447
Law	.518	.539	.582	.390	.572	.437	.359	.481	.465
Economic conservatism . .	.235	.329	.330	.145	.379	.329	.334	.335	.468
Education	.534	.587	.502	.430	.552	.441	.256	.561	.524
Inferiority correlated with:									
Family	.248	.248	.212	.177	.478	.319	.192	.406	.436
Law	.262	.314	.113	.198	.342	.200	-.017	.238	.341
Economic conservatism . .	.205	.218	.183	.197	.316	.201	.152	.209	.237
Education	.234	.296	.148	.226	.407	.216	.054	.259	.251
Family correlated with:									
Law	.388	.276	.336	.452	.366	.419	.296	.532	.408
Economic conservatism . .	.081	.096	.110	.009	.089	.122	.174	.092	.174
Education	.303	.259	.259	.316	.243	.269	.123	.420	.371
Law correlated with:									
Economic conservatism . .	.191	.217	.328	.181	.564	.299	.328	.241	.374
Education	.369	.187	.403	.444	.563	.431	.115	.575	.480
Economic conservatism correlated with:									
Education	.087	.097	.132	.051	.098	.093	-.184	.265	.201

*(C) = Controlled sample.

statistically significant when taken individually--i.e., the difference between the correlation coefficients does not exceed twice the standard error of the difference. In applying the test for significance, Fisher's (5, page 170) technique for small samples was used.[1]

None of the differences between the intercorrelations for male and female standard groups of 500 are large enough to be statistically significant. However, in ten of the fifteen possible comparisons between groups, the family correlations are higher for females than for males. Of particular interest is the definite relationship between attitude toward family and attitude toward law and legal institutions. It is likely that attitude toward law and attitude toward parental control may together represent attitude toward authority.

It is to be further noted that the intercorrelations for high school girls are higher in fourteen of fifteen instances than those for the standard sample of 500 females, and are higher in the same frequency than the intercorrelations for high school boys. There are statistically significant differences between high school boys and girls on the morale-economic conservatism, and inferiority-law associations, the association being closer for females.

The same tendency for intercorrelations to be higher for females than for males is evident in the controlled sample of unemployed, where eleven of the fifteen intercorrelations are higher. Although no one of the intercorrelations for the controlled sample of unemployed and controlled sample of high school women differ significantly from those for the standard sample of 500 females, the consistency of the positive differences appears significant. The evidence is not sufficient to support a claim for the existence of a general sex difference, since most of the intercorrelations are lower for university women in the Sociology I course than for men. In fact, the probability is greater than 95 in 100 that the morale-education, and inferiority-law

1. The test of significance throughout this chapter, unless otherwise stated, is a difference between coefficients of at least twice the standard error of the difference. The chances of significance for such a difference are approximately 95 in 100.

associations are closer for males than for females in the Sociology I course.

Since the interrelationships between attitude scores may be brought into sharper relief by the use of partial and multiple correlation techniques, these methods of analysis have been applied. To simplify the presentation of the data, the scales will be discussed singly, and attention drawn to some of the outstanding differences between scales.

PARTIAL AND MULTIPLE CORRELATIONS

THE MORALE SCALE

The extent to which the scores on the morale scale are associated with scores on the other five scales can be shown by the multiple correlation coefficient. This is .735 for the standard sample of 500 men and .795 for the 100 men in the controlled sample of unemployed. The standard error of estimate for 500 men can be derived from the following formula:

$$S.E.^2_{1.23\ldots n} = \sigma_1^2 \left(1-R^2_{1.23\ldots n}\right).$$

Applying this formula to the standard group of 500 men yields a standard error of estimate 6.84, and of 6.25 for the controlled sample of unemployed men. By use of the multiple regression equation, it should be possible to estimate the actual morale score in two thirds of the cases with the error not exceeding 6.84 points (the standard error of estimate).

The multiple regression equations computed in score form for these two groups are as follows:

500 Males

Morale = -3.8070 + .3125 inferiority + .1453 family + .2293 law + .3015 education + .0727 economic conservatism.

100 Males in Controlled Sample of Unemployed

Morale = -13.5215 + .4959 inferiority + .0788 family + .3810 law + .2441 education + .0844 economic conservatism.

The estimated morale score is obtained by multiplying the individual's standard score on each of the other scales by the coefficient that precedes the scale name in the above equation, and adding the sum of these products to the first expression in the equation, which is known as the additive constant. To clarify the meaning of the multiple correlation coefficient and the multiple regression equation for those who are unfamiliar with their use, the scores for 100 men in the controlled sample of unemployed were predicted from the equation above and are given in Table 60 along with their actual scores and the differences between actual and predicted scores.

It will be recalled that the multiple correlation coefficient for the men in the controlled sample of unemployed was .795.[2] If there are no errors in the calculation of this coefficient, it is possible to obtain almost exactly the same value by means of a zero order correlation between actual scores and scores predicted by use of the multiple regression equation. These actual scores and predicted scores were correlated and yielded an r of .796. This demonstrates that the multiple correlation coefficient does give an exceedingly accurate measure of the degree of association between morale scores and scores predicted from a knowledge of the individual's scores on other scales in this group used as a basis for the computations.

It is also possible to obtain the standard error of estimate directly from the residuals (z) or difference between actual and predicted scores. This may be computed by the formula:

$$S.E.^2 = \frac{\Sigma z^2}{N-1}$$

When computed for the men in the standard sample of unemployed by this formula, the standard error of estimate is 6.25--the identical value obtained for this group by the earlier formula. This means that in approximately two-thirds of the cases the predicted scores should be

2. It will be seen in Table 61 that this value is .791 after economic conservatism scores are omitted from the calculation.

TABLE 60.-DIFFERENCE BETWEEN ACTUAL MORALE STANDARD SCORES AND SCORES PREDICTED BY THE MULTIPLE REGRESSION EQUATION

(Controlled sample of Unemployed Men; N = 100.)

Actual Score	Predicted Score	Difference (z)	Actual Score	Predicted Score	Difference (z)	Actual Score	Predicted Score	Difference (z)
26	30.71	4.71	45	52.53	7.53	53	50.81	-2.19
27	32.06	5.06	46	52.11	6.11	54	52.46	-1.54
31	27.34	-3.66	46	41.52	-4.48	54	59.40	5.40
33	40.21	7.21	46	42.38	-3.62	54	58.48	4.48
35	45.69	10.69	46	44.90	-1.10	54	52.61	-1.39
35	38.24	3.24	46	42.71	-3.29	55	59.94	4.94
36	40.20	4.20	46	47.61	1.61	57	50.73	-6.27
37	34.78	-2.22	47	42.44	-4.56	57	56.96	-0.04
37	36.80	-0.20	47	49.56	2.56	57	44.37	-12.63
37	48.97	11.97	48	50.96	2.96	58	54.68	-3.32
37	43.35	6.35	48	45.21	-2.79	58	49.18	-8.82
38	44.22	6.22	48	41.12	-6.88	58	56.26	-1.74
39	47.84	8.84	48	43.43	-4.57	58	62.15	4.15
40	44.44	4.44	48	53.44	5.44	59	59.49	.49
41	36.49	-4.51	48	56.13	8.13	59	51.21	-7.79
41	48.20	7.20	48	46.33	-1.67	59	58.05	-0.95
41	42.10	1.10	48	48.61	.61	60	65.41	5.41
41	46.95	5.95	49	48.12	-.88	60	56.86	-3.14
42	50.97	8.97	49	55.37	6.37	61	60.32	-.68
42	42.83	.83	49	53.61	4.61	61	52.28	-8.72
42	41.87	-0.13	49	39.80	-9.20	61	50.21	-10.79
42	37.79	-4.21	50	48.30	-1.70	61	57.35	-3.65
42	46.56	4.56	50	45.15	-4.85	61	58.90	-2.10
43	44.30	1.30	51	39.31	-11.69	62	63.85	1.85
43	50.73	7.73	51	53.49	2.49	66	55.11	-10.89
43	46.84	3.84	51	50.47	-.53	68	59.85	-8.15
43	43.72	.72	51	46.68	-4.32	68	61.42	-6.58
43	53.14	10.14	51	46.97	-4.03	69	62.00	-7.00
43	50.78	7.78	51	49.21	-1.79	70	63.43	-6.57
43	47.38	4.38	52	67.22	15.22	72	57.26	-14.74
45	45.82	.82	52	51.58	-.42	73	66.20	-6.80
45	51.68	6.68	53	51.70	-1.30	75	67.61	-7.39
45	56.99	11.99	53	54.44	1.44	79	60.88	-18.12
			53	52.43	-.57			

in error not more than 6.25 points. The actual percentage of cases in which the error is within these limits is 66 per cent, as can be seen by counting in Table 60 the number of times the error is within these limits. The average error of prediction is five points in a range of 53 points for the controlled sample of unemployed, or about 10 per cent of the range.

Since there was ample evidence to indicate that scores on the economic conservatism scale are not appreciably correlated with other scores, the economic conservatism score was included in the multiple regression equations and multiple correlation coefficients for two groups only--the 500 men in the standard group and the 100 men in the controlled sample of unemployed. However, multiple correlation coefficients were computed on all variables except economic conservatism for the controlled samples of high school males and females, for the male and female standard samples of 500, and for 100 of each sex in the controlled sample of unemployed. All the multiple correlation coefficients of the fourth order are presented for the six scales in Table 61. The multiple correlations between morale score and other scores range from .658 for the controlled sample of high school males to .791 for the men in the controlled sample of unemployed. Little importance should be attached to the variations, since they may be easily dependent on such factors as variation in the range of scores from one group to another or slight differences in the reliability of the scales from group to group. The multiple coefficient .731 for the standard group of 500 males and .654 for the standard group of 500 females are conservative estimates of the degree of association between morale score and the totality of variation on the inferiority, family, law, and education scales associated with morale scores.

The square of the multiple correlation coefficient yields a measure of the proportion of the total variation in the dependent variable that has been mathematically accounted for.[3] This measure indicates that with a multiple correlation of .73 for 500 men,

3. Mordecai Ezekiel calls this the "coefficient of multiple determination." (4, page 178.)

approximately half of the total variation in morale scores has been accounted for on the basis of scores on other scales. Although this indicates a high degree of interdependence between morale score and scores on other scales, it also indicates that approximately half of the variation in morale score is dependent on other factors than those that enter into or are adequately measured in the inferiority, family, law, and education scales.

The multiple correlation coefficients based on five attitude scores were found to be consistently higher for the morale scale than for any of the other scales, and this holds true for each of the six groups for which such coefficients were computed. This is sufficient evidence to justify the statement that the association between morale scores and the totality of concomitant variation in other scores is undoubtedly higher than the association between any of the other scores and the totality of concomitant variation in the remaining scales.

In studying the interrelationships between scales, a knowledge of the association between scores on a single scale and the totality of variation in other scores is not sufficient. It is also necessary to determine what the association is between scores on any two scales when variation in these scores which is associated with variation in scores on other scales has been held constant. This can be accomplished by the use of partial correlation.

The partial correlations for 500 men and 500 women between morale and each of the other attitude scores are:

Scores Correlated	Scores Partialled Out	Male	Female
Morale-inferiority	Law, family, education	.420	.436
Morale-family	Inferiority, law, education	.181	.073
Morale-law	Inferiority, family, education	.314	.246
Morale-education	Inferiority, family, law	.389	.274

Before discussing these coefficients, it is pertinent to inquire to what extent the partials have been affected by the exclusion of the economic conservatism scale from the computations. To show of how little importance the economic conservatism score is in affecting the coefficients, the partial coefficients with economic conservatism score partialled out are given below for 500 males.

Scores Correlated	All Other Scores Partialled Out	Economic Conservatism Not Partialled Out
Morale-Inferiority	.403	.420
Morale-Family	.184	.181
Morale-Law	.299	.314
Morale-Education	.392	.389

The partial correlation coefficients already presented indicate that there are significant associations between morale scores and scores on the inferiority, law, and education scales. That feelings of inferiority and low morale are rather closely associated is an important, although not surprising, finding. The size of the correlations between morale and inferiority may lead one to wonder whether we are really measuring two different aspects of personality in these scales. There is abundant evidence in the data to prove that the scales do measure different aspects of personality. A few of the differences between the correlations of these two scales with other personality measures may be pointed out. For example, the partial correlation coefficient between morale and law, other scores being held constant, is .314 for 500 men. For the same group the inferiority-law partial coefficient, other variables being held constant, is -.008. Again for the same group, the morale-education partial coefficient is .389, inferiority, family, and education scores being held constant. The equivalent inferiority-education association is -.057. For the controlled sample of unemployed women the morale-family partial, three variables being held constant, is -.122; the equivalent inferiority-family partial is .333. In Chapter VII there is additional evidence to show that these scales correlate differently with outside criteria.

There is also a definite association between morale and attitude toward law and legal institutions. Although the third order partial coefficient is only .314 for 500 men and .246 for 500 women, the size of the coefficients varies widely from group to group. In the group of high school boys, the third order partial coefficient between morale and law is low (.126); this association reaches the magnitude of .506 for the men in the controlled sample of unemployed. This is evidence of the necessity of maintaining the morale of unemployed men if favorable attitudes toward law and legal institutions are to be maintained. Further evidence to indicate that unemployment brings morale and attitudes toward law into closer association is found in the intercorrelation between morale and law for the older men in the relief group, for whom the intercorrelation is .572.

The partial correlation coefficients between morale and education, three variables being held constant, are higher in five of six possible comparisons than those between morale and law. The only group in which the association between morale and law exceeds that between morale and education is the controlled sample of unemployed males. In a society where the importance of education in securing advancement and economic security is stressed, and where education is usually regarded as a panacea for social ills, it would be astonishing indeed if morale and attitude toward education were not associated. It is entirely reasonable to expect that the individuals who are most discouraged, as indicated by their morale scores, should place a lower value on education than those who still feel confident that the future will bring realization of desired goals. In these trying times when millions of young people find that high school graduation or academic degrees are of little avail in securing employment, it is surprising that the unemployed who have been tested still approve so generally of education. To be sure, the young unemployed persons tested were probably to some extent a selected group as regards attitude toward education, since those who place little value on it would probably not enroll in educational classes for the unemployed.

Table 62 shows that the partial correlation coefficients between morale and education are lower for the high school controlled sample and the controlled sample of unemployed males than for the 500 males, while the partial correlation coefficients for the high school controlled sample and the controlled sample of unemployed females are higher than for the 500 females. This probably indicates a less close association between morale and attitude toward education among college women than among college men, since college students comprise the bulk of those individuals in the 500 groups who are not included in the high school controlled sample and the controlled sample of unemployed. It will be recalled that there was a statistically significant difference between the morale-education intercorrelations for men and women in the Sociology I course.

The partial coefficients between morale and family attitudes are slightly higher for males than for females. Although singly none of the differences is statistically significant, the difference exists for the high school controlled sample and the controlled sample of unemployed as well as for the 500 groups. The intercorrelations for the Sociology I male and female groups indicate the existence of the same difference. Although the evidence is not at all conclusive, it suggests the possibility that discouragement is more readily reflected in family attitudes for males than for females.

THE INFERIORITY SCALE

The fourth order multiple correlations ($R_{2.1345}$) for certain groups are:

500 males	.515	500 females	.536
Controlled sample of high school males	.513	Controlled sample of high school females	.691
Controlled sample of unemployed males	.602	Controlled sample of unemployed females	.652

TABLE 61.—MULTIPLE CORRELATION COEFFICIENTS

Variables Correlated*	500 Males		High School Senior Men (C)**		Unemployed Men (C)		500 Females		High School Senior Women (C)		Unemployed Women (C)	
	R	±	R	±	R	±	R	±	R	±	R	±
$R_{1.2345}$	.731	.021	.658	.058	.791	.038	.654	.026	.763	.043	.743	.046
$R_{2.1345}$	.515	.033	.513	.076	.602	.065	.536	.032	.691	.054	.652	.059
$R_{3.1245}$	.471	.035	.521	.075	.408	.086	.491	.034	.547	.072	.620	.063
$R_{4.1235}$	.558	.031	.566	.070	.648	.059	.573	.030	.572	.069	.682	.055
$R_{5.1234}$	.551	.031	.527	.074	.536	.073	.516	.033	.615	.064	.674	.056

*X_1 Morale X_2 Inferiority X_3 Family X_4 Law X_5 Education
**(C) = Controlled sample.

TABLE 62.-PARTIAL CORRELATION COEFFICIENTS

Variables Correlated*	500 Males		High School Senior Men (C)**		Unemployed Men (C)		500 Females		High School Senior Women (C)		Unemployed Women (C)	
	r	±	r	±	r	±	r	±	r	±	r	±
$r_{12.345}$	.420	.037	.457	.081	.571	.069	.436	.036	.572	.069	.551	.071
$r_{13.245}$	.181	.043	.244	.096	.108	.101	.073	.044	.077	.102	-.122	.101
$r_{14.235}$	.314	.040	.126	.101	.506	.076	.246	.042	.143	.100	.237	.097
$r_{15.234}$	.389	.038	.249	.096	.352	.090	.274	.041	.389	.087	.390	.087
$r_{23.145}$	.049	.045	-.046	.102	.079	.102	.195	.043	.227	.097	.333	.091
$r_{24.135}$	-.008	.045	.009	.103	-.280	.094	-.084	.044	.057	.102	-.149	.100
$r_{25.134}$	-.057	.044	.012	.103	-.133	.101	-.012	.045	-.197	.099	-.135	.101
$r_{34.125}$	.209	.043	.314	.092	.165	.100	.302	.041	.192	.099	.393	.087
$r_{35.124}$	.080	.044	.062	.102	.078	.102	.049	.045	.149	.100	.159	.100
$r_{45.123}$	.108	.044	.295	.094	.101	.102	.266	.042	.287	.094	.315	.092

*X_1 Morale; X_2 Inferiority; X_3 Family; X_4 Law; X_5 Education

**(C) = Controlled sample.

These correlations indicate that there is a definite association between variation on inferiority scale scores and variation in scores on other scales. The standard error of estimate for the group of 500 males is 7.21, that for the group of 500 females, 7.09. The multiple correlation coefficients of approximately .50 leave almost three-fourths of the total variation in inferiority scores unaccounted for on the basis of concomitant variation in other scores.

The multiple regression equations for the six groups are:

500 Males:	Inferiority = 23.1709 + .5404 morale +.0501 family -.0079 law - .0568 education
Controlled sample of high school males:	Inferiority = 20.6197 +.6193 morale -.0462 family +.0098 law +.0128 education
Controlled sample of unemployed males:	Inferiority = 31.2942 +.6370 morale +.0615 family -.2533 law -.1027 education
500 females:	Inferiority = 23.1798 +.4719 morale +.1761 family -.0884 law -.0119 education
Controlled sample of high school females:	Inferiority = 16.4080 +.6504 morale +.1894 family +.0572 law -.1827 education
Controlled sample of unemployed females:	Inferiority = 18.3410 +.6017 morale +.3354 family -.1648 law -.1503 education

These multiple equations have the merit of indicating briefly the extent to which scores on the scale under consideration are associated with scores on other scales. For our data these equations usually indicate the principal relationships that are apparent in the partial coefficients, and do so in a form that is often more readily comprehended.

Any given multiplying coefficient in a regression equation will be identical with the corresponding partial correlation coefficient, if the standard deviations for the predicted variable and the other variable in the primary subscript are of the same magnitude for the same order of the partial correlations. This follows from the equation for obtaining the multiplying coefficient:

$$b_{12.34\ldots n} = r_{12.34\ldots n} \frac{\sigma_{1.23\ldots n}}{\sigma_{2.13\ldots n}}$$

Since the standard deviations are frequently of about the same magnitude, the multiplying coefficients are usually very similar to the partial correlation coefficients. To illustrate, the multiplying coefficients for the inferiority regression equation are compared below with the third-order partial coefficients for three groups.

Association between Inferiority and:	Partial Correlation Coefficient	Corresponding Multiplying Coefficient
Morale	.420	.540
Family	.049	.050
Law	-.008	-.008
Education	-.057	-.057
Controlled Sample of High School Males		
Morale	.457	.619
Family	-.046	-.046
Law	.009	.010
Education	.012	.013
Controlled Sample of Unemployed Males		
Morale	.571	.637
Family	.079	.062
Law	-.280	-.253
Education	-.133	-.103

The largest difference between partial coefficient and multiplying coefficient is that for the high school controlled sample on the morale scale score. The difference between .457 and .619 is accounted for by the fact that the standard deviation for the inferiority scale ($\sigma_{2.1345}$ = 8.4223) is larger than that for the morale scale ($\sigma_{1.234}$ = 6.2148) in the ratio of 1.354 to 1.

Since the standard deviations on the original distributions of these two series of scores were almost identical, the difference in standard deviations for the third order partial coefficients just cited is to be ascribed to the fact that a substantially smaller proportion of the variation in inferiority scores than in morale scores can be accounted for on the basis of other scores. The multiple correlation coefficients show this same fact.

The regression equations presented indicate that inferiority scores are most closely related to scores on the morale scale. The multiplying coefficients for the family score are higher for each of the female groups than for the male groups. Although none of the differences is statistically significant, their consistency indicates the probable existence of a real difference. The association between inferiority score and family score is statistically significant for the controlled sample of unemployed females. This means that for the controlled sample of unemployed females at least, and probably for other female groups, there is a definite relationship between the extent to which inferiority feelings exist and the degree to which unfavorable family attitudes are held as measured by the scores on these scales.

The multiplying coefficients and partial correlations indicate that there is very little relationship between inferiority feelings and attitude toward law for the groups of 500. The chances are greater than 98 in 100, however, that an inverse relationship does exist between inferiority score and law score for the young unemployed men. Moreover, the multiplying coefficient for the law scale is somewhat higher for the controlled sample of unemployed females than for other female groups, which is in accord with the findings for the controlled sample of unemployed males.

It is surprising to find that the presence of inferiority feelings is associated with more favorable scores on the law scale for the controlled sample of unemployed men, especially when we recall that poor morale is definitely associated with unfavorable law score for that group, and that morale and inferiority scores are positively correlated. This means that the interrelationship between morale and law and that between inferiority and law must have been obscured in the intercorrelations presented in Table 59 by the relationship that exists between morale and inferiority scores.

Turning to the partial correlations, we find confirmation of this assumption. The intercorrelation (zero order correlation) between morale and law scores for the controlled sample of unemployed men is .582; when the law score is held constant by partial analysis, the morale-law coefficient ($r_{14.3}$) becomes .622. The morale-law coefficient was only slightly reduced by the fact that variation in inferiority scores is associated inversely with law scores. The intercorrelation between inferiority and law is +.113; when morale is held constant by partial analysis ($r_{24.1}$), the coefficient becomes -.291. Obviously the relationship between inferiority score and law score was seriously distorted in the intercorrelation coefficient by the morale-inferiority association. This illustrates the utility of partial correlation analysis in isolating the relationship between two variables when that relationship is obscured by their associations with a third variable.

The negative signs for the multiplying coefficients on the education score in the inferiority multiple regression equations are interesting. Neither the size of the multiplying regression equations nor that of the partial correlation coefficients shown in Table 72 demonstrate the existence of a statistically significant association between inferiority and education scores. But the negative character of the signs in five of six instances probably means that a slight inverse relationship really exists between these variables--i.e., that presence of inferiority feelings is associated with more favorable attitude toward the value of education.[4] It is strange that the inverse

4. In Table 92 are presented data for another group which indicates the existence of a similar relationship between Bernreuter's Neurotic Tendency Index and our education scale.

association is not greater, since one might suppose on a priori grounds that those who feel inferior would attach most value to education as a means for surmounting imagined or real shortcomings.

THE FAMILY SCALE

The multiple correlation coefficients of the fourth order ($R_{3.1245}$) for the various groups are as follows:

500 males	.471	500 females	.491
Controlled sample of high school males	.521	Controlled sample of high school females	.547
Controlled sample of unemployed males	.408	Controlled sample of unemployed females	.620

The multiple correlation coefficients for the groups of 500 are lower than those found to exist on any other scale except the economic conservatism. For five of the six groups, the multiple correlation coefficients are lower than those for morale, inferiority, law, and education scales.

The standard errors of estimate for the group of 500 males and that of 500 females are 8.23 and 9.29, respectively. They indicate that the error of prediction from a multiple regression equation will be large; the multiple correlation coefficients for the two groups indicate that less than one-fourth of the variability in scores on the family scale can be mathematically accounted for on the basis of associated variation in scores on other scales. The larger multiple coefficients for the controlled sample of unemployed females (.620) can be accounted for on the basis of fourth order partial correlations, which are always of greater magnitude for this group than for the high school females and the standard sample of 500. These differences, however, are never large enough to be demonstrably significant when the statistical test is applied.

The multiple regression equations for the six groups are given below:

FAMILY SCORE

500 males	= 22.1250 +.2279 morale +.0479 inferiority +.2022 law +.0780 education
Controlled sample of high school males	= 16.9988 +31.50 morale -.0419 inferiority +.3245 law +.0628 education
Controlled sample of unemployed males	= 25.3710 +.1537 morale +.1008 inferiority +.1904 law +.0768 education
500 females	= 14.7111 +.0875 morale +.2159 inferiority +.3518 law +.0537 education
Controlled sample of high school females	= 10.6388 +.1050 morale +.2721 inferiority +.2309 law +.1657 education
Controlled sample of unemployed females	= 10.6999 - .1330 morale +.3346 inferiority +.4342 law +.1767 education

It is interesting to observe that family score is more closely allied with the law score than with morale score, especially for women. The fourth order partial correlations between law and morale ($r_{31.245}$) are compared below with the fourth order partials between family and law scores ($r_{34.125}$).

Group	$r_{31.245}$	$r_{34.125}$
500 males	.181	.209
Controlled sample of high school males	.244	.314
Controlled sample of unemployed males	.108	.165
500 females	.073	.302
Controlled sample of high school females	.077	.192
Controlled sample of unemployed females	-.122	.393

The difference between $r_{31.245}$ and $r_{34.125}$ for the controlled sample of unemployed females is statistically significant; the difference between the coefficients exceeds three times the standard error of their difference. The fact that the family-law fourth order partials are always larger than the family-morale partials indicates the probability that the family-law association is closer; this probability is greater for females. A possible explanation of the association lies in a transfer of attitudes. Both scales may be reflecting impatience with restraints, whether they be those imposed by parents or those imposed by law. The association may also mean that attitudes toward parental authority conditioned in childhood are somehow transferred into attitudes toward law as the maturing individual becomes decreasingly subject to parental control and increasingly conscious of the controls exercised by law.

It has already been pointed out that the family-morale partial coefficients are uniformly higher, and the family-inferiority partial coefficients are uniformly lower for males than for females. The fourth order partial coefficients between family score and education ($r_{35.124}$) are small and do not indicate the existence of a sex difference in this association.

THE LAW SCALE

The multiple correlations of the fourth order ($R_{4.1235}$) are as follows:

500 males	.558	500 females	.573
Controlled sample of high school males	.566	Controlled sample of high school females	.572
Controlled sample of unemployed males	.648	Controlled sample of unemployed females	.682

There is little evidence in these coefficients to indicate the existence of a sex difference in the extent to which law scores are associated with the totality of variation in other scales. The standard errors of estimate for the 500 males and 500 females are 8.50 and 7.97, respectively. The size of the multiple correlation coefficients indicates that about one-third of the variation in the scores on the law scale can be accounted for in the multiple regression equations for the groups of 500, and that the proportion is higher for the controlled samples of unemployed, for which slightly more than two-fifths of the variation can be accounted for on the basis of other scores. The multiple correlation coefficients for five of the six groups are larger for the law scale than for any other scale except morale.

The multiple regression equations for the six groups are as follows:

LAW SCORE

500 males	= 14.6838+.4086 morale -.0081 inferiority +.2160 family +.1088 education
Controlled sample of high school males	= 12.8158+.1574 morale +.0083 inferiority +.3038 family +.2892 education
Controlled sample of unemployed males	= 21.4163+.6241 morale -.3096 inferiority +.1430 family +.0862 education
500 females	= 15.1643+.2530 morale -.0798 inferiority +.2592 family +.2501 education
Controlled sample of high school females	= 15.8493 +.1621 morale +.0568 inferiority +.1597 family +.2654 education
Controlled sample of unemployed females	= 8.0254 +.2339 morale -.1347 inferiority +.3557 family +.3170 education

The associations between law scores and morale, inferiority, and family scores have already been discussed. The size of the coefficients indicates that the association between attitude toward law and morale is probably not as pronounced among high school students as among other groups in the standard samples. The inverse relationship between attitude toward law and presence of inferiority feelings among the controlled samples of unemployed has been pointed out. The partial correlation coefficients between law score and score on the education scale ($r_{45.123}$) are as follows:

500 males	.108	500 females	.266
Controlled sample of high school males	.295	Controlled sample of high school females	.287
Controlled sample of unemployed males	.101	Controlled sample of unemployed females	.315

It will be observed that the association between law and education scores is closer for the 500 female group than for the 500 males. This relationship holds for the controlled sample of unemployed females, but not for the high school groups. It cannot be demonstrated that the sex difference is statistically significant. The test of the reality of associations of this kind which are not of sufficient magnitude to meet the test of significant difference must be whether the same relationship is found by other research workers who use this or similar instruments. Although such differences may be due to chance errors in sampling, many of them are more likely to be reflections of genuine relationships.

THE EDUCATION SCALE

The multiple correlation coefficients measuring the association between education scores and the totality of associated variation in other scores ($R_{5.1234}$) are as follows:

500 males	.551	500 females	.516
Controlled sample of high school males	.527	Controlled sample of high school females	.615
Controlled sample of unemployed males	.536	Controlled sample of unemployed females	.674

The standard errors of estimate for the groups of 500 males and 500 females are 8.12 and 8.36, respectively. The moderate size of the multiple correlation coefficients indicates that about two-thirds of the variability in education scores cannot be accounted for on the basis of co-variation in other scales.

The multiple regression equations for various groups are as follows:

EDUCATION SCORE

500 males	= 18.8960 +.5025 morale -.0572 inferiority +.0821 family +.1072 law
Controlled sample of high school males	= 14.2899 +.3172 morale +.0112 inferiority +.0621 family +.3009 law
Controlled sample of unemployed males	= 22.5260 +.5087 morale -.1723 inferiority +.0792 family +.1183 law
500 females	= 18.7932 +.2997 morale -.0572 inferiority +.0821 family +.2829 law
Controlled sample of high school females	= -9.6817 +.4769 morale +.2124 inferiority +.1340 family +.3103 law
Controlled sample of unemployed females	= 15.2061 +.3826 morale -.1213 inferiority +.1430 family +.3131 law

The associations of greatest interest revealed in these regressions equations are those between education and morale score. The pronounced difference between the male and female groups of 500 in the size of the morale regression coefficient, and the reversal of this sex difference for high school groups, is interesting. The explanation of this difference lies in the fact that the education score is more closely related to the morale score for men in the university groups and for men in the unemployed group than for females in the same groups. The university and unemployed groups constitute the bulk of the groups of 500. It seems probable then that attitude toward the value of education is more closely related to morale among university men than among university women, and that the inverse is true for the general run of high school students. A much greater proportion of first and second-year university men than of university women are preparing for entrance into professional schools, and completion of certain specified courses is the major requirement for attainment of that goal. Hence their estimates of the value of education, varying as they probably do with the extent of their success in meeting these requirements, will be closely related to their future plans.

Discouragement concerning the probability of reaching desired goals should be reflected in morale scores, since this is essentially what the morale scale is designed to measure. If this thesis is correct, the same tendency for the education score to vary more closely with the morale score among men than among women should be apparent in high schools, which are almost exclusively college preparatory institutions and in which scholastic requirements are fairly rigid. In the University of Minnesota High School, where these conditions are met, morale scores are much more closely related to school achievement among boys than among girls.

The higher association between education score and law score among the female group of 500 and the controlled sample of unemployed females than among corresponding male groups is worth noting. The sex difference among high school students is negligible.

A second important fact is evident when the multiplying coefficient for morale score in the education regression equation is compared for males with the multiplying coefficient for education score in the morale regression equation. Multiplying coefficient for:

	Education Score in Morale Regression Equation	Morale Score in Education Regression Equation
500 males	.3011	.5025
Controlled sample of high school males . . .	.1955	.3172
Controlled sample of unemployed males . . .	.2436	.5087

This indicates that the morale score is much more important in predicting the education score than is the education score in predicting morale score. The score of major importance in predicting morale is that on the inferiority scale; the inferiority score is of secondary importance in predicting education score, and the sign in the multiplying coefficient is negative for two of the male groups. This association of morale score with education score made the inferiority-education intercorrelation coefficients deceptive, because these intercorrelations were reflecting primarily the association between morale and inferiority, together with the association of morale with education score. Let us compare the intercorrelation between education and inferiority scores (r_{52}) with the first order partial coefficient in which morale is held constant ($r_{52.1}$).

	r_{52}	$r_{52.1}$
500 males	.234	-.053
Controlled sample of high school males	.226	.008
Controlled sample of unemployed males .	.148	-.167
500 females	.216	-.011
Controlled sample of high school females	.251	-.144
Controlled sample of unemployed females	.259	-.106

The change in magnitude and sign for the correlation when morale score is held constant reflects the effects of the morale-inferiority interdependence, together with the morale-education interdependence.

The partial correlation coefficient of the fourth order between morale and education ($r_{15.234}$) cannot reveal the difference between the dependence of education score on morale score and the dependence of morale score on education score. The values of the partial coefficients occupy mid-positions between the values of the multiplying coefficients for education score in the morale regression equation and the values of the multiplying coefficient for morale score in the education regression equation.

SUMMARY

The morale scale yields highest intercorrelations with other scales. The partial coefficients of the fourth order, the multiple correlation coefficients, and the regression equations all indicate morale to be the most generalized of the traits measured. The economic conservatism scale yields lowest intercorrelations, and the fourth order partial coefficients were found not to differ significantly from zero for the standard group of 500 males. Morale and economic conservatism scores were more closely associated in the two unemployed groups than in other groups. The morale-law association was also found to be closer among the unemployed.

Inferiority scores correlated higher with morale scores than with scores on any other scale. The relationship is also revealed in the regression equations and in the fourth order partial coefficients. The inferiority-family score association was found to be closer for females than for males by the same criteria. Although the intercorrelations indicated the possibility of a slight positive relationship between inferiority and law scores, the fourth order partial coefficients and the regression equations indicate that the true relationship is a slight negative one.

The family-morale association was found to be consistently higher, and the family-law association was found to be consistently lower among males than among females.

Education scores were found to be more closely related to morale scores among university men than among university women. This relationship did not prevail in other groups. Education scores varied inversely with inferiority scores.

Chapter VII

SCALES RELATED TO OTHER VARIABLES HAVING SOME BEARING UPON THEIR VALIDITY

It appears from the evidence presented that the method of internal consistency, as applied in this study, has produced short scales of reasonable reliability. According to some, the test of internal consistency produces scales in which the items are _ipso facto_ valid, although it cannot be determined just what trait the scale is measuring.

In an effort to validate the scales in the more usual sense of the term, the authors have collected two types of information: the information on the face sheet (see the appendix), and the scores on tests devised by others and given similar names.

The interpretations of the relationships on the basis of the face sheet information is inevitably rendered difficult by possible factors of selection which affect the composition of the various groups. These factors are particularly difficult to evaluate for the day and evening classes. While these groups do not differ strikingly from the general population with respect to father's occupation, intelligence, or size of family, their interest in education is in itself a selective factor, the influence of which cannot be determined for these groups as well as it can be for typical high school and university populations. To avoid being misled by possible selective effects, most comparisons will be made within groups, and reliance will be chiefly placed on consistency of relations from group to group. The statistical labor involved in relating six scales to the many items on the face sheet also influenced the decision to rely on consistency of mean trends, a procedure that has ample justification when as many groups are involved as are in this study.

The groups analyzed in this chapter are the high school seniors, the university sophomores, the day classes, and the evening classes. The last-mentioned group has been divided into three subgroups on the basis of employment status, not only for a better evaluation of trends but also for the purpose of observing whether unemployment may have particularly adverse effects when other unfavorable factors are present. Some items will be observed to be inapplicable to the high school and university groups; hence these groups will not appear in certain tables.

It will be observed that in many of the comparisons the number of cases in certain categories is small. This is inevitable from the nature of many of the factors considered, i.e., separation of the parents and over-ageness. While the matching technique is usually a preferable means of detecting relationships, the use of this method would have reduced the number too much in most instances to prove practicable. Prior to the analysis it was unknown which factors needed to be controlled, and a much larger number of cases would have been necessary to make it possible to control them by matching after they were detected.

The authors' primary purpose in the investigation discussed in this chapter was to detect broad, general trends. A more exact, quantitative statement of the extent of these relationships must await research designed more specifically to meet these particular problems.

Scores on each of the six personality scales were related to each of the variables on the face sheet. This analysis yielded more tables than can be included in this chapter. Every relationship was carefully studied, but only those are presented here that were consistent from group to group or that presented a consistent trend within a group. No tables showing consistent trends within a group or between groups have been omitted. The tables omitted show no relationship between the variable and scores on the personality scales.

Variables showing no consistent relationship were: parental occupation (with the exception of the farming group), most experienced occupation, size of sibship, and special type of education. A fact that increased the authors' faith in the relationships uncovered was the rarity of unfavorable mean scores in the unpublished tables as high as 55, even when N was so small that chance had a maximum opportunity to operate. When scores of 55 or larger appear for variables in retained tables and are consistently unfavorable from group to group, the probability of a chance explanation is exceedingly remote.

CERTAINTY OF MAINTAINING OR OBTAINING EMPLOYMENT

Item 23: If you are employed, how certain are you that your employment will last through the coming year?

Very certain   Certain   Uncertain   Very uncertain

Item 24: If you are unemployed, how certain are you that you will find a position this year?

Very certain   Certain   Uncertain   Very uncertain

Items 23 and 24 were included primarily to relate them to scores on the morale scale. The relationship for men of the various degrees of certainty to morale scores is shown in Table 63. The morale scale validates itself well against this criterion. Not only is there no exception to the fact that the *very uncertain* position yields more unfavorable (higher) scores than the *very certain* position but the scores for most groups tend to increase steadily from *very certain* to *certain* to *uncertain* to *very uncertain*. The major exceptions to the trend within each group are provided by the part-time employed in evening classes and the unemployed day classes. While the part-time group is considered in evaluating the data given in this chapter, it will be evident that they constitute a peculiar group, sometimes following the trend of the employed, sometimes of the unemployed, sometimes being more affected than the unemployed. In some instances full-time employment is desired, and certainty of continuing on a part-time basis may well produce feelings of discouragement and insecurity; in other instances part-time employment may be exactly what is desired at the moment. Such heterogeneity within a group will tend to reduce differences. The differences which are slight here between the unemployed of the evening and day classes also run through the data. A possible explanation for this is that the unemployed of the evening classes are somewhat older on the average, and a smaller proportion are residing at home. Such a group will be more liable to possess feelings of insecurity.

The variation of morale with feelings of occupational security is convincing evidence of the validity of the morale scale. Table 63 well exemplifies the tendency of scores on all scales to vary together in relation to outside criteria. The differences are not as large and consistent for other scales as for morale, but they are clearly present. For all scales there are 96 mean scores (4 groups, 4 degrees of certainty, and 6 scales) in Table 63. Since there are 6 scales and 4 groups, there are 24 most favorable and 24 least favorable scores distributed among the four categories of certainty. In the very uncertain category there are 16 of the least favorable scores and only one of the most favorable--the mean inferiority score for the part-time group. In the very certain category there are 9 of the most favorable and none of the least favorable scores.

If the very certain and certain categories in Table 63 are combined, there are 18 of the most favorable and 4 of the least favorable mean scores. As usual, the principal exceptions (3 of 4) are provided by the part-time employed group. Among the full-time employed and unemployed evening school groups, all the most favorable and none of the least favorable mean scores were associated with the two certain categories. There was only one exception for the day school unemployed for whom the family score was poorest for those who expressed certainty of finding employment.

Combining the very uncertain and uncertain categories, we find 20 of the poorest scores and 6 of the best in these categories. Of the 6 most favorable scores, 3 were made by the part-time employed and 3 by the day school unemployed.

TABLE 63.—MEAN ATTITUDE SCORES AND CERTAINTY OF MAINTAINING OR OBTAINING EMPLOYMENT WITHIN A YEAR FOR SINGLE MALES

Certainty of Employment	N	Morale	Inferiority	Family	Law	Economic Conservatism	Education
			EVENING CLASSES				
Employed Full Time							
Very certain	41	44.63	45.32	49.46	49.07	50.98	43.05
Certain	67	47.99	49.82	49.61	50.24	49.93	43.34
Uncertain	37	53.84	54.38	51.14	54.32	52.73	47.57
Very uncertain	6	53.67	50.50	55.00	61.00	58.50	46.50
Employed Part Time							
Very certain	4	53.50	53.00	48.50	51.00	54.25	53.00
Certain	4	47.25	57.50	47.75	54.25	61.00	44.00
Uncertain	20	48.55	53.95	51.10	49.30	53.90	50.40
Very uncertain	11	63.09	50.45	51.45	54.45	59.27	52.45
Unemployed							
Very certain	2	40.50	46.50	49.00	48.00	50.50	37.50
Certain	15	45.60	45.87	43.87	45.00	51.67	49.20
Uncertain	34	53.97	51.06	51.35	48.00	57.50	48.03
Very uncertain	18	57.39	50.44	54.78	57.28	58.06	53.28
			DAY CLASSES (UNEMPLOYED)				
Unemployed							
Very certain	8	48.00	49.50	55.63	51.50	53.00	47.50
Certain	7	46.29	46.71	54.14	50.14	53.14	47.57
Uncertain	77	49.84	49.47	49.36	46.69	51.49	50.14
Very uncertain	20	58.30	50.35	51.70	53.70	55.75	55.80

Table 64 presents similar data for females. The same trends are present but the best discrimination often appears between the certain and uncertain rather than between the extreme categories. Combining the very certain and certain categories, we find that the most favorable scores are associated with one of the two certain categories in 21 instances and the least favorable scores in 9 instances. The least favorable scores are associated with one of the two uncertain categories in 15 instances, while the most favorable scores are so associated in 3 instances. None of the exceptions to complete consistency as between the certain and uncertain categories occurs on the morale or inferiority scales and only one on the family scale.

These findings indicate that there is a general factor running through the six scales which is more generalized and pervasive for men. This general factor may be morale or something closely related, since the uncorrected multiple R of four scales (excluding the economic conservatism) with morale is .73 for men, .65 for women. That the general factor is more effective for men than for women is indicated by both methods of analysis. These results do more than illustrate the potency of the general factor. They raise again the problem of what accounts for the co-variation in relationships. While the hypothesis which we are presenting was not derived until the remaining data given in this chapter had been studied, it will be presented at this point in order to facilitate the integration of this material. In brief, the data rather strongly suggest that the general factor is the adjustment of the individual to his particular circumstances. In practically every instance where one is entitled to assume that a certain group is maladjusted, there the scores on all or nearly all the scales tend to deviate in the unfavorable direction. Since occupational insecurity is symptomatic of poor adjustment, the data just discussed are good evidence for this hypothesis.

TABLE 64.-MEAN ATTITUDE SCORES AND TO CERTAINTY OF MAINTAINING OR OBTAINING EMPLOYMENT WITHIN A YEAR FOR SINGLE FEMALES

Certainty of Employment	N	Morale	Inferiority	Family	Law	Economic Conservatism	Education
			EVENING CLASSES				
Employed Full Time							
Very certain	63	47.48	51.21	51.79	48.87	51.89	48.63
Certain	133	48.90	50.92	50.79	47.57	49.24	48.22
Uncertain	67	51.54	52.33	51.06	48.09	50.40	49.70
Very uncertain	31	54.52	54.26	56.23	51.81	50.71	48.03
Employed Part Time							
Very certain	6	48.33	50.33	50.33	52.33	53.50	52.83
Certain	8	45.00	45.25	51.25	47.38	44.00	46.75
Uncertain	35	53.83	55.80	52.29	50.11	52.94	50.31
Very uncertain	14	51.86	57.64	50.93	46.93	50.86	45.07
Unemployed							
Very certain	9	53.33	46.56	54.00	52.56	46.44	55.89
Certain	22	45.55	47.36	50.36	44.73	50.59	47.93
Uncertain	121	54.91	52.36	51.66	49.33	51.46	50.80
Very uncertain	56	54.16	53.21	52.59	51.11	49.95	49.27
			DAY CLASSES (UNEMPLOYED)				
Unemployed							
Very certain	6	47.17	45.50	49.83	44.83	51.50	53.00
Certain	17	49.59	48.35	46.35	48.47	49.41	50.47
Uncertain	122	51.65	51.36	50.34	46.26	51.38	50.71
Very uncertain	36	53.83	53.08	50.00	46.31	52.75	49.53

OVER-AGENESS

In the school system over-ageness is almost synonymous with retardation and is generally accepted as evidence of educational maladjustment, if not of more generalized maladjustment. Tables 65 to 70 give the

TABLE 65.-MORALE SCORES AND AGE

(Single males only.)*

Age	Evening Classes								Day Classes			University Group			High School Seniors		
	Employed Full Time		Employed Part Time		Unem-ployed		All Cases		Unemployed								
	Mean	N	Mean	N	Mean	N	Mean	N	Age	Mean	N	Age	Mean	N	Age	Mean	N
15-19	46.97	31	52.85	14	50.79	33	49.64	78	15-19...	50.87	63	17-18	49.11	38	16.....	45.96	25
20-24	48.46	94	51.71	17	51.88	33	49.63	144	20-24...	50.26	54	19-20	49.39	105	17.....	49.70	171
25-29	48.25	24	53.25	8	54.73	11	50.84	43	25-29...	46.17	6	21-22	47.19	42	18.....	49.24	129
30-39	56.40	10	52.25	4	65.00	4	57.40	18	30-39...	65.33	3	23-24	51.00	9	19.....	52.40	25
												25 and over	61.00	5	20 and over	55.00	5

*Note the higher scores in the oldest age category. Data for women show no relationship to age.

TABLE 66.-INFERIORITY SCORES AND AGE

(Single persons only.)

	Evening Classes								Day Classes								
	Employed Full Time		Employed Part Time		Unem- ployed		All Cases		Unemployed			University Group			High School Seniors		
Age	Mean	N	Mean	N	Mean	N	Mean	N	Age	Mean	N	Age	Mean	N	Age	Mean	N
Men:*									Men:			Men:			Men:		
15-19	45.77	31	58.43	14	50.15	33	49.90	78	15-19	49.51	63	17-18	49.92	38	16	51.28	25
20-24	50.23	94	48.12	17	47.97	33	49.47	144	20-24	48.83	54	19-20	47.68	105	17	51.04	171
25-29	49.63	24	52.13	8	53.64	11	51.12	43	25-29	47.67	6	21-22	45.50	42	18	50.54	129
30-39	53.80	10	54.75	4	59.00	4	55.17	18	30-39	45.33	3	23-24	47.78	9	19	48.44	25
												25 and over	55.20	5	20 and over	50.60	5
Women:									Women:			Women:			Women:		
15-19	51.94	47	52.87	30	51.18	117	51.62	194	15-19	51.73	128	15-16	35.00	1	15	62.50	2
20-24	51.02	143	54.86	25	50.89	76	51.36	244	20-24	51.01	74	17-18	47.81	58	16	52.25	51
25-29	51.53	72	55.88	8	53.37	19	52.23	99	25-29	48.53	17	19-20	49.43	104	17	52.39	243
30-39	51.67	35	53.60	5	54.69	13	54.04	53	30-39	47.11	9	21-22	48.81	21	18	51.22	69
40 and over	53.11	9	59.67	3	51.00	4	53.81	16	40 and over	54.00	2	23-24	53.40	5	19	53.06	16
												25 and over	54.10	10	20	37.50	2

*Note the higher scores older age category.

TABLE 67.-FAMILY SCORES AND AGE

(Single males only.)*

	Evening Classes								Day Classes								
	Employed Full Time		Employed Part Time		Unem-ployed		All Cases		Unemployed			University Group			High School Seniors		
Age	Mean	N	Mean	N	Mean	N	Mean	N	Age	Mean	N	Age	Mean	N	Age	Mean	N
15-19	49.65	31	52.86	14	50.33	33	50.51	78	15-19	50.43	63	17-18	47.79	38	16	51.04	25
20-24	50.46	94	48.06	17	50.03	33	50.08	144	20-24	50.43	54	19-20	50.48	105	17	50.87	171
25-29	49.58	24	53.13	8	50.82	11	50.56	43	25-29	52.83	6	21-22	47.36	42	18	49.98	129
30-39	50.80	10	49.50	4	60.75	4	52.72	18	30-39	50.67	3	23-24	50.44	9	19	47.52	25
												25 and over	54.00	5	20 and over	55.20	5

*Date for women show no relationship to age.

TABLE 68.-LAW SCORES AND AGE

(Single males only.)*

	Evening Classes								Day Classes								
	Employed Full Time		Employed Part Time		Unem-ployed		All Cases		Unemployed			University Group			High School Seniors		
Age	Mean	N	Mean	N	Mean	N	Mean	N	Age	Mean	N	Age	Mean	N	Age	Mean	N
15-19	50.03	31	49.86	14	49.00	33	49.56	78	15-19	48.08	63	17-18	49.34	38	16	46.36	25
20-24	51.19	94	49.24	17	52.61	33	51.29	144	20-24	48.63	54	19-20	52.10	105	17	51.51	171
25-29	52.78	24	52.63	8	47.27	11	51.12	43	25-29	47.17	6	21-22	52.14	42	18	50.55	129
30-39	53.80	10	57.50	4	58.50	4	55.67	18	30-39	52.00	3	23-24	51.78	9	19	51.96	25
												25 and over	56.20	5	20 and over	55.80	5

*Note the higher scores in the oldest age category. Data for women show no relationship to age.

TABLE 69.-ECONOMIC CONSERVATISM SCORES AND AGE

(Single males only.)*

	Evening Classes								Day Classes								
	Employed Full Time		Employed Part Time		Unem-ployed		All Cases		Unemployed			University Group			High School Seniors		
Age	Mean	N	Mean	N	Mean	N	Mean	N	Age	Mean	N	Age	Mean	N	Age	Mean	N
15-19	48.81	31	53.86	14	52.33	33	51.21	78	15-19	51.78	63	17-18	46.32	38	16	53.64	25
20-24	50.49	94	52.88	17	58.18	33	52.54	144	20-24	52.89	54	19-20	47.57	105	17	51.77	171
25-29	51.12	24	60.88	8	54.18	11	53.72	43	25-29	47.83	6	21-22	48.43	42	18	50.12	129
30-39	62.80	10	60.00	4	72.75	4	64.39	18	30-39	57.00	3	23-24	49.56	9	19	47.72	25
												25 and over	59.80	5	20 and over	48.80	5

*Note the high scores in the oldest age category. Data for women show no relationship to age.

TABLE 70.-EDUCATION SCORES AND AGE

(Single males only.)*

	Evening Classes								Day Classes								
	Employed Full Time		Employed Part Time		Unem-ployed		All Cases		Unemployed			University Group			High School Seniors		
Age	Mean	N	Mean	N	Mean	N	Mean	N	Age	Mean	N	Age	Mean	N	Age	Mean	N
15-19	38.39	31	53.93	14	51.42	33	46.69	78	15-19	50.68	63	17-18	51.87	38	16	46.16	25
20-24	44.24	94	47.53	17	48.36	33	45.58	144	20-24	49.72	54	19-20	52.87	105	17	49.00	171
25-29	47.58	24	51.63	8	51.64	11	49.37	43	25-29	49.67	6	21-22	48.88	42	18	48.13	129
30-39	54.50	10	52.25	4	51.50	4	53.33	18	30-39	60.00	3	23-24	52.67	9	19	49.84	25
												25 and over	60.00	5	20 and over	55.00	5

*Note the higher scores in the oldest age category. Data for women show no relationship to age.

personality scale scores by the age groupings appropriate for each group. It will be noted that as soon as the age which is characteristic of a group is exceeded, the morale scores of the men begin to deviate in the unfavorable direction. (Table 65) The scores of those in the evening and day classes increase after the age of 30 is reached. Not only does the mere fact of over-ageness suggest poor adjustment, but it is highly probable that, on the average, men over 30 who find it necessary to continue their formal education are not occupationally adjusted. University sophomore men of 23 and over tend to possess poorer morale as do high school seniors over 18. Among both these groups there can be little argument that over-ageness contributes to poor adjustment. Since morale is most heavily loaded for the general factor of adjustment, the scores on other scales cannot be expected to show the trend to the same extent. Morale and economic conservatism scores show the most pronounced relationships in conjunction with unemployment. For men it is not so pronounced on the inferiority scale; for women it is more pronounced than on the other scales. The trend is nearly absent from the family scale, but the law and economic conservatism scales exhibit it clearly, so far as men are concerned, the high school seniors being the only exception on the law scale. The attitude toward education of over-age men is quite clearly unfavorable. The trend is again absent among women.

The sex difference noted above is so consistent throughout the data that it can scarcely be attributed to chance. Apparently, within limits, over-ageness is not a factor in women's adjustment to the educational situation at the levels dealt with here. It may well be that women's adjustment is more closely related to social success, and that over-ageness, within limits, is apt to be an advantage, if anything, in social situations.

PREVIOUS EDUCATION

Previous education was analyzed in relation to scores on the various scales. The most consistent associations were evident for males on the morale, law, and economic conservatism scales. The data for these three scales are presented in Table 71. In every group the mean score for men with from 13 to 16 years of education is more favorable than that for men with eighth-grade education or less. The differences are particularly marked on the law scale, but are striking on the economic conservatism scale also. The morale scores show the same trend, but the differences are of much smaller magnitude. Presumably those with less education find themselves under a handicap when they compete for employment with those who are better trained, and to that extent are maladjusted. That they are usually handicapped in the school situation is fairly certain. The data, therefore, may be interpreted as favoring the adjustment hypothesis.

PARENTAL OCCUPATION

The only consistently appreciable relation detected between parental occupation and scores on the scales was a tendency for farmers' sons to score unfavorably, particularly in the evening and day classes, where such men are probably compelled to rely chiefly on their own financial resources (See Table 72). This tendency is least evident among high school seniors, for whom the conservatism and education scales are the only ones to reveal higher scores for farmers sons. University men score unfavorably on three scales--law, economic conservatism, and education. Unemployed farmers' sons in the day classes deviate in the unfavorable direction on the morale, law, conservatism, and education scales, the unemployed of the evening classes on all scales except education, the part-time employed on all scales and the full-time employed on the morale, law, and economic conservatism scales. These differences are generally most pronounced in the unemployed and part-time groups, where transition from a rural to an urban environment in conjunction with unemployment will raise many problems of adjustment for the individual. Dissatisfaction with the present economic system manifest among farmers' sons in all groups is of particular interest in the light of present efforts to

TABLE 71.—MORALE, LAW, AND ECONOMIC CONSERVATISM SCORES AND PREVIOUS EDUCATION

(Single males only.)

Previous Education	Morale	Law	Economic Conserv-atism	N
	EVENING CLASSES			
	Employed Full Time			
8th grade or less	53.12	58.77	57.29	17
9-12	47.55	50.40	50.34	120
13-16	48.41	45.47	49.41	17
	Employed Part Time			
8th grade or less	54.25	63.38	56.50	8
9-12	52.18	54.36	49.39	28
13-16	50.50	48.50	47.00	6
	Unemployed			
8th grade or less	51.50	61.25	55.28	4
9-12	52.52	54.70	50.18	66
13-16	49.67	57.83	50.33	6
	DAY CLASSES (UNEMPLOYED)			
8th grade or less	66.00	66.00	60.00	1
9-12	50.49	52.81	48.58	106
13-16	51.42	47.95	46.16	19
	ALL CASES			
8th grade or less	53.63	60.57	56.90	30
9-12	49.95	52.43	49.64	320
13-16	50.02	48.38	47.94	48

alleviate agricultural distress. These data for farmers' sons are given in Table 72, where the scores are to be evaluated by relating them to the standard mean of 50 on all scales.

TABLE 72.-ATTITUDE SCORES IN THE VARIOUS GROUPS FOR FARMERS' SONS

N	Morale	Inferi-ority	Family	Law	Economic Conserv-atism	Educa-tion
			EVENING CLASSES			
			Employed Full Time			
18	53.44	49.67	51.78	53.39	56.56	39.50
			Employed Part Time			
5	57.60	55.80	53.80	59.40	62.80	55.00
			Unemployed			
2	62.50	63.00	55.50	58.50	62.00	43.00
			DAY CLASSES (UNEMPLOYED)			
3	55.00	48.00	51.67	59.00	54.33	55.33
			UNIVERSITY			
8	51.00	51.25	49.37	56.25	55.25	56.38
			HIGH SCHOOL			
4	46.75	48.50	49.75	49.50	59.75	52.50

HOME CONDITIONS

The remaining face sheet data to be presented in this chapter relate to parental or home conditions, and their associations with scores on the various scales. Does the individual live at home? Are the parents living together or separated? Is the father deceased, retired, employed, or unemployed? Is the mother deceased, a housewife, employed, or unemployed? How are marriage, the possession of children, and divorce related to scores among the evening and day school unemployed groups? Frequent sex differences made it advisable to present the data for the sexes separately. Group differences also are evident.

Nonresidence at home raises certain problems of adjustment for a young person. Table 73 shows that

TABLE 73.-ATTITUDE SCORES AND HOME RESIDENCE FOR SINGLE MALES

Residence	N	Morale	Inferi-ority	Fam-ily	Law	Economic Conserv-atism	Educa-tion
			EVENING CLASSES Employed Full Time				
At home	115	48.37	49.26	49.78	50.94	49.84	44.70
Not at home	32	51.09	50.03	51.63	54.44	55.34	42.69
			Employed Part Time				
At home	31	52.64	53.61	50.26	49.90	53.94	50.48
Not at home	8	55.38	51.75	53.25	55.88	62.00	55.00
			Unemployed				
At home	70	51.11	49.60	50.17	49.49	50.01	49.79
Not at home	7	61.43	50.14	56.00	58.29	67.14	54.00
			DAY CLASSES (UNEMPLOYED)				
At home	52	52.13	50.13	51.33	49.04	50.54	52.37
Not at home	2	59.00	57.50	73.00	52.00	48.50	42.00
			UNIVERSITY				
At home	37	52.24	47.97	51.46	52.24	50.05	55.65
Not at home	18	54.72	51.44	50.89	53.00	52.39	53.56

TABLE 74.-ATTITUDE SCORES AND HOME RESIDENCE FOR SINGLE FEMALES

Residence	N	Morale	Inferi-ority	Fam-ily	Law	Economic Conserv-atism	Educa-tion
			EVENING CLASSES Employed Full Time				
At home	188	50.21	51.91	51.43	49.07	49.94	48.43
Not at home	94	48.55	50.84	51.96	47.52	50.59	48.40
			Employed Part Time				
At home	46	52.15	53.22	51.65	49.57	51.74	49.46
Not at home	19	53.37	56.26	53.11	50.53	51.42	51.58
			Unemployed				
At home	188	53.76	51.56	51.45	49.68	51.00	50.71
Not at home	30	49.63	48.90	51.87	45.90	48.30	44.50
			DAY CLASSES (UNEMPLOYED)				
At home	41	51.54	49.90	52.07	47.17	52.59	52.95
Not at home	2	54.00	43.50	46.00	39.50	56.50	40.50
			UNIVERSITY				
At home	44	50.32	51.95	48.82	51.50	50.50	50.18
Not at home	13	48.08	48.07	51.07	58.00	52.08	46.54

in every group the morale and law mean scores were consistently higher for males not residing at home. Note also the general increase in the difference from the employed to the unemployed groups. Family, inferiority, and economic conservatism scores were higher in four of the five groups for men not residing at home. The economic conservatism scores average almost one a half sigmas above the standard mean for the 15 cases in the part-time and unemployed evening groups not residing at home. Group differences but no general difference appear on the education scale in association with home residence.

In Table 74 similar data are presented for women. Favorable scores are as frequent for females not living at home as for those at home, considering all groups and scales. For four of the five groups, inferiority and education scores are actually better for those not at home, but on the family scale the trend is consistent with that for men, four of the five groups yielding less favorable scores for those not at home. University women not residing at home made a distinctly unfavorable mean score on the law scale (58.00 N 13), but employed and unemployed women residing elsewhere than at home made slightly better mean scores on the law scale.

The fact that for men over-ageness, non-home residence, and the difficulty of adjusting to urban life on the part of farmers' sons affect personality adversely raises the problem of whether any one of the factors is primarily responsible for the differences noted, since all three may be associated. Consider the relationship of home residence and personality scores. None of the 7 unemployed cases (Table 73) is a farmer's son. Among this group age is not a factor in producing unfavorable scores until 30 is reached; and only 2 of the 7 cases reach this level. Non-home residence plus unemployment, the two factors implying that the individual is thrown on his own resources, definitely produce unfavorable personality effects.

Nor is age a factor in the comparisons of the part-time and full-time employed. Only 4 of the 32 full-time employed are not living at home. Only one of the 8 part-time employed is 30 years of age. Both the

TABLE 75.-ATTITUDE SCORES AND HOME RESIDENCE FOR SINGLE MALES IN EVENING CLASSES

	N	Morale	Inferiority	Family	Law	Economic Conservation	Education
		Employed Full Time					
Non-farmers' sons not residing at home	18	48.28	49.39	51.11	53.89	52.78	43.33
Farmers' sons not residing at home	14	54.71	50.86	52.29	55.14	58.64	41.86
		Employed Part Time					
Non-farmers' sons not residing at home	4	52.75	48.75	50.00	49.00	61.25	54.50
Farmers' sons not residing at home	4	58.00	54.75	56.50	62.75	62.75	55.50

part-time employed and the full-time employed groups include farmers' and non-farmers' sons in about equal numbers. Table 75 shows the relationship for each of these groups. It is clear that the association between unfavorable scores and non-home residence noted in Table 73 for these groups is largely due to the presence of farmers' sons. This is particularly the case with the employed group. In other words, when circumstances are relatively favorable, as when an individual is employed, it takes a combination of two factors--non-home residence and the difficulty of making an adjustment from rural to urban environment--to produce a generally poor adjustment. Non-home residence, in itself, does not appear to condition personality unfavorably. Since scores for women showed no relationship here, it was not considered necessary to analyze them further.

The frequent lack of relationship between home residence and scores for women and the very frequent association between unfavorable scores and non-home residence for men may reflect a double standard in home supervision and discipline. The daughter living at home is often restricted in her freedom to entertain, to determine when she shall return from social engagements, to choose her friends, to be free from interrogation concerning her social activities. Such freedom is more commonly denied daughters than sons, and may account for the more frequent unfavorable scores among those residing at home.

TABLE 76.-ATTITUDE SCORES AND SEPARATION OF PARENTS FOR SINGLE FEMALES

Status of Parents	N	Morale	Inferiority	Family	Law	Economic Conservatism	Education
			EVENING CLASSES				
			Employed Full Time				
Together	179	50.88	52.16	51.92	48.99	50.17	49.28
Separated	12	50.83	48.75	49.17	55.08	51.75	51.67
			Employed Part Time				
Together	43	51.21	54.19	50.56	50.33	52.65	49.47
Separated	2	52.50	47.00	59.60	51.50	49.00	52.00
			Unemployed				
Together	163	53.67	51.76	51.54	48.89	50.97	50.95
Separated	12	58.42	54.67	54.17	52.42	52.17	53.08
			DAY CLASSES (UNEMPLOYED)				
Together	165	51.55	51.19	51.02	47.23	51.76	51.78
Separated	12	58.17	53.83	52.00	48.33	52.42	50.75
			UNIVERSITY				
Together	158	48.82	48.71	48.18	50.67	49.08	49.80
Separated	5	52.80	53.00	60.60	54.20	50.60	59.40
			HIGH SCHOOL				
Together	281	50.02	52.42	49.57	47.26	50.21	47.38
Separated	16	59.38	57.25	55.06	51.13	47.81	55.13

TABLE 77.-ATTITUDE SCORES AND SEPARATION OF THE PARENTS

(Males only.)

Status of Parents	N	Morale	Inferi-ority	Fam-ily	Law	Economic Conserv-atism	Educa-tion
			EVENING CLASSES				
			Employed Full Time				
Together	106	48.76	49.84	48.95	50.98	51.37	45.64
Separated	3	55.00	48.00	50.33	51.33	51.67	49.67
			Employed Part Time				
Together	27	54.19	49.18	50.52	50.52	55.22	52.41
Separated	1	68.00	50.86	65.00	66.00	63.00	43.00
			Unemployed				
Together	55	51.31	50.17	49.89	49.82	55.23	50.55
Separated	3	59.33	51.14	47.33	55.83	49.86	58.67
			DAY CLASSES (UNEMPLOYED)				
Together	100	50.18	49.07	49.73	48.09	52.56	50.04
Separated	4	42.50	46.50	49.75	46.75	44.00	49.50
			UNIVERSITY				
Together	139	48.85	47.66	49.73	50.93	48.60	50.06
Separated	8	53.50	46.50	51.14	57.88	42.88	54.38
			HIGH SCHOOL				
Together	266	49.38	50.41	49.92	50.88	50.82	48.42
Separated	16	47.56	50.88	51.88	50.94	48.38	47.81

How is separation of the parents related to scores on the various scales? Tables 76 and 77 give the mean scores of those whose parents are separated in comparison with the scores of those whose parents are living together.[1] Inspection of the tables shows a marked sex difference. Separation of the parents is much more closely associated with unfavorable scores among females. Of 36 mean scores for women in 6 groups, 29 are less favorable when parents were separated than when parents were together. Five of the 7 exceptions are furnished by the two employed groups. In 5 groups the morale scores are poorer for women whose parents were separated, and are particularly bad in the two unemployed groups and in the high school group, the mean morale score exceeding 58 in each of the three instances. For all 6 female groups, the law scores are also higher among those whose parents were separated. Family, inferiority, law, education, and conservatism scores also suffer; on each scale the scores of those whose parents were separated are higher in 4 or 5 female groups.

Considering all male groups and all scales, separation of the parents does not seem to have pronounced effects; in 22 cases where parents were separated and in 14 where parents were living together, the score is higher. Three scales, however—morale, family and law--do show rather pronounced and consistent differences. In 4 of the 6 groups the group whose parents were separated had the most unfavorable score on the morale scale, and in 5 of the 6 on the family and law scales.

The association among both sexes of poorer family scores with separation of the parents is a partial validation of the family scale. The equally close association among both sexes of law scores with separation of the parents suggests a possible extension of attitude concerning parental authority to legal authority. Both scales may be measuring a fairly generalized attitude toward authority.

Our evidence indicates that separation of the parents is decidedly more closely associated with

1. Both parents living; persons reporting parents separated because of the death of one were excluded from the tabulation.

TABLE 78.-ATTITUDE SCORES AND STATUS OF FATHER FOR SINGLE MALES

Status of Father	N	Morale	Inferiority	Family	Law	Economic Conservatism	Education
			EVENING CLASSES				
			Employed Full Time				
Deceased . .	32	47.28	48.75	52.34	50.13	50.72	40.47
Retired . . .	18	50.61	50.56	50.39	52.56	51.00	45.61
Employed . .	86	48.19	49.62	49.80	51.21	50.85	46.14
Unemployed .	18	49.33	49.06	47.78	51.11	53.22	39.28
			Employed Part Time				
Deceased . .	7	50.57	53.43	45.71	46.00	53.71	45.86
Retired . . .	5	53.20	53.80	56.60	61.60	57.20	52.20
Employed . .	23	54.86	53.52	50.35	51.09	56.52	51.61
Unemployed .	6	48.83	52.00	55.00	49.17	53.50	54.83
			Unemployed				
Deceased . .	14	52.00	52.57	50.50	48.13	56.14	49.00
Retired . . .	6	57.67	53.83	54.00	57.67	64.17	46.00
Employed . .	48	51.06	48.44	49.06	48.65	54.17	49.72
Unemployed .	12	54.50	52.83	54.42	56.42	57.08	55.17
			DAY CLASSES (UNEMPLOYED)				
Deceased . .	14	56.50	51.29	52.43	50.50	53.14	54.29
Retired . . .	1	47.00	44.00	51.00	59.00	39.00	47.00
Employed . .	99	50.11	48.95	50.17	48.06	52.23	50.34
Unemployed .	11	49.73	50.45	50.55	47.09	51.27	47.37
			UNIVERSITY				
Deceased . .	34	50.35	49.74	50.82	54.91	48.65	50.94
Retired . . .	7	55.00	49.71	50.57	49.14	49.57	48.57
Employed . .	144	48.72	47.42	48.92	51.21	47.83	51.43
Unemployed .	8	52.13	51.63	51.62	51.50	52.75	56.13
			HIGH SCHOOL				
Deceased . .	39	49.23	50.97	48.54	49.38	51.38	47.28
Retired . . .	10	52.20	56.50	50.90	54.70	48.50	48.80
Employed . .	259	48.95	50.53	49.98	50.88	50.52	48.29
Unemployed .	32	52.50	51.13	50.41	51.09	54.66	50.06

TABLE 79.-ATTITUDE SCORES AND STATUS OF FATHER FOR SINGLE FEMALES

Status of Father	N	Morale	Inferiority	Family	Law	Economic Conservatism	Education
			EVENING CLASSES				
			Employed Full Time				
Deceased . .	83	47.57	51.01	49.73	46.76	50.01	46.69
Retired . . .	32	50.88	52.66	51.91	46.69	50.03	48.53
Employed . .	123	49.16	51.24	53.14	48.91	50.23	49.27
Unemployed .	60	54.08	53.28	51.08	50.53	50.12	50.13
			Employed Part Time				
Deceased . .	17	47.76	54.18	51.41	43.41	47.00	46.76
Retired . . .	7	49.71	54.57	52.29	49.29	52.57	48.57
Employed . .	33	52.88	55.27	50.21	50.85	52.18	51.70
Unemployed .	8	53.50	49.50	52.50	51.13	56.63	43.38
			Unemployed				
Deceased . .	39	52.23	50.33	51.05	47.79	48.97	47.28
Retired . . .	13	47.00	46.62	49.85	48.08	50.46	45.92
Employed . .	134	51.94	50.78	49.60	48.28	49.72	49.80
Unemployed .	32	58.50	54.91	55.94	50.81	52.94	51.31
			DAY CLASSES (UNEMPLOYED)				
Deceased . .	43	50.35	48.84	49.93	45.37	51.21	50.98
Retired . . .	6	55.33	50.83	53.83	51.33	55.17	56.00
Employed . .	135	51.53	51.24	51.30	47.70	51.63	51.27
Unemployed .	41	54.00	52.39	50.49	46.07	51.44	52.44
			UNIVERSITY				
Deceased . .	18	50.28	47.83	48.83	48.92	50.56	47.44
Retired . . .	17	50.53	49.53	50.94	52.35	46.82	49.29
Employed . .	156	48.90	48.88	48.69	50.96	49.47	50.56
Unemployed .	6	53.83	55.83	54.33	51.50	56.83	49.33
			HIGH SCHOOL				
Deceased . .	43	50.19	52.56	51.70	49.19	50.53	47.05
Retired . . .	8	49.75	52.25	49.13	47.50	51.13	50.63
Employed . .	277	49.93	51.97	50.16	47.23	49.88	47.77
Unemployed .	38	53.82	55.16	50.18	49.32	52.13	48.61

unfavorable scores among females than among males. This is especially true for females who are economically dependent rather than self-supporting through employment.

Tables 78 and 79 show the relationship between father's status (deceased, retired, employed, or unemployed) and scores on the various scales. For males in the evening unemployed, high school, and university groups the scores of those whose fathers were employed were uniformly better than the scores of those whose fathers were unemployed. In only 2 of the 36 comparisons of score in relation to father's status is the score of men whose fathers are employed least favorable, while in 11 instances it is most favorable. The relationship between unemployment of the father and unfavorable scores is much less marked than was anticipated, the closest association being evident among the unemployed of the evening classes. Unfavorable scores were appreciably more frequent among the group who reported the father as retired than among those who reported the father as unemployed. Unfavorable scores among those whose fathers were retired were most frequent in the part-time employed and unemployed of the evening classes. The law scale scores were least favorable in 5 of 6 groups and particularly so for the part-time and unemployed groups. When the father is retired or unemployed and the son is unemployed, the situation presents many opportunities for conflict. The data may thus be interpreted as favoring the adjustment hypothesis.

The employed full-time men in the evening classes whose fathers are unemployed or deceased make unusually favorable scores on the education scale. The mean score for the unemployed men in the evening classes whose fathers are retired was unusually high, 64.17, on the economic conservatism scale. Men in the unemployed day classes whose fathers were deceased scored unfavorably on the morale scale, and all scores are above the standard mean for them. For the sons of retired fathers in the university group the morale score is unfavorable but other scores are not. Sons of unemployed fathers in the university group score least favorably on the education scale. In the high school group those whose fathers are retired score unfavorably on the inferiority and law scales.

Unfavorable scores are more clearly related to unemployment of the father among women than among men. Table 79 shows that 30 of 36 mean scores for women whose fathers were unemployed are above the standard mean. Scores on the morale scale appear to be most affected, particularly for the unemployed with unemployed fathers. Inferiority scores exhibit the same trend for all groups except the part-time employed, and inferiority feelings seem particularly prevalent among high school and university women under these conditions. Unfavorable family scores are related to unemployment of the father most clearly in the evening unemployed and university groups. Law and education scores appear to suffer least. The least favorable scores on the economic conservatism scale for the part-time employed and university groups are the scores of those whose fathers were unemployed.

Scores made by women whose fathers were deceased can be compared in 36 instances with scores made by women whose fathers were unemployed. In 33 of these 36 instances the scores are more favorable for women whose fathers were deceased.

Scores made by women whose fathers were retired or employed were usually more favorable than the scores made by women whose fathers were unemployed. In 29 of 36 instances the scores of those whose fathers were employed, and in 26 instances the scores of those whose fathers were retired, are more favorable than the scores of those whose fathers were unemployed.

TABLE 80.-ATTITUDE SCORES OF MEN WHOSE FATHERS WERE RETIRED

(Single men of evening classes living at home.)

Employment Status	N	Morale	Inferiority	Family	Law	Economic Conservation	Education
Employed full time	12	47.33	49.17	50.50	49.50	45.17	44.67
Employed part time	2	42.00	50.00	54.00	52.50	49.50	43.50
Unemployed	4	61.00	56.50	59.75	57.50	67.75	45.25

Here again the influence upon the men of age, home residence, and farming as the occupation of the father must be considered. The effects of the first and third factors, particularly, might tend to be concealed in the scores of men whose fathers were retired. The group whose fathers were retired does not contain a disproportionate number of individuals over 30. Age is therefore not the primary factor in these differences. Of the full-time employed group three are 30 or over; of the part-time employed group, two; and of the unemployed group, one. To estimate the effect of home residence and of the farming occupation of the father on these results, all individuals not living at home and all reporting farming as the parental occupation were removed. (See Table 80.) This leaves 12 full-time employed, 2 part-time employed, and 4 unemployed. The slight differences which existed between the employed and part-time employed groups whose fathers were retired tend to disappear. This is not at all the case with the unemployed; their scores tend to become even more unfavorable. When it is considered that unemployment had practically no effect on the scores of individuals living at home (See Table 73), these differences become more significant. Since the opportunities and reasons for conflict between father and son are increased when both are in the home and the son is unemployed, these results are completely consistent with the hypothesis that the general factor running through the scales is adjustment.

How do scores vary when the groups are analyzed with reference to whether the mother is deceased, a housewife, employed, or unemployed? Table 81 indicates that unemployed young men in homes where the mother is deceased have particularly unfavorable attitudes. This difference is not influenced by age. Six of the 8 in the evening group were living at home. None of these was over 30. The mean scores of these 6 on the morale, inferiority, family, law, economic conservatism, and education scales were, respectively, 60.00, 53.67, 60.50, 59.67, 59.50, and 52.67. Of the fathers of these six men, three were employed, one was retired, one was dead (had been a farmer), and one was unemployed. For the three living at home whose fathers are employed,

TABLE 81.-ATTITUDE SCORES AND STATUS OF MOTHER FOR SINGLE MALES

Status of Mother	N	Morale	Inferiority	Family	Law	Economic Conservatism	Education
			EVENING CLASSES				
			Employed Full Time				
Deceased . .	23	47.65	48.61	52.00	53.26	51.04	39.17
Housewife .	119	48.21	49.21	49.27	51.08	50.92	45.50
Employed . .	10	52.30	53.00	55.90	49.70	51.90	39.50
Unemployed .	2	53.00	49.50	58.50	48.50	61.00	30.25
			Employed Part Time				
Deceased . .	9	46.67	50.56	52.56	52.89	55.78	50.78
Housewife .	31	54.06	53.48	50.81	50.87	55.42	51.84
Employed . .	1	57.00	53.00	47.00	44.00	44.00	47.00
Unemployed .	1	47.00	60.00	33.00	42.00	62.00	28.00
			Unemployed				
Deceased . .	8	62.00	54.50	60.75	58.88	62.63	49.38
Housewife .	64	51.91	50.03	49.81	49.47	55.42	51.08
Employed . .	7	46.14	47.71	46.71	50.43	51.14	42.71
Unemployed .	0						
			DAY CLASSES (UNEMPLOYED)				
Deceased . .	9	54.78	53.33	58.22	51.56	53.67	53.00
Housewife .	109	50.38	48.75	49.58	49.98	52.15	51.67
Employed . .	6	48.83	50.83	52.00	50.83	49.33	43.50
Unemployed .	1	50.00	62.00	55.00	37.00	54.00	48.00
			UNIVERSITY				
Deceased . .	20	50.60	50.05	52.55	52.45	46.05	45.55
Housewife .	153	49.14	47.73	49.22	51.64	48.34	52.08
Employed . .	18	50.05	49.06	47.61	54.00	47.44	50.50
Unemployed .	2	54.50	44.50	52.00	44.00	60.00	54.50
			HIGH SCHOOL				
Deceased . .	15	49.07	53.13	52.20	53.60	50.47	50.86
Housewife .	276	49.76	50.61	49.96	51.04	51.22	49.08
Employed . .	43	46.77	50.88	48.93	48.79	48.79	48.98
Unemployed .	6	53.17	47.83	46.67	53.50	51.67	48.67

the scores on the respective scales, listed in the previous order, are: 46.67, 54.67, 58.67, 53.00, 56.67, 44.33. Four of the six scores still tend in the unfavorable direction. Attitude toward the family is poorest. This is reasonable, since it is family equilibrium that is most upset by the death of the mother, particularly when the individual is living at home. Decease of the mother does appear to affect men's personalities, particularly when they are unemployed.

The family scores, 60.75 for the unemployed in the evening classes and 58.22 for the unemployed in the day classes, suggest that the factor of unemployment is a potent source of family discord when the mother is deceased. While the family scores for the employed full-time and employed part-time groups and the university and high school groups deviate in the unfavorable direction among those whose mothers were deceased, they are slight deviations in comparison with those for the unemployed. That family scores in all groups deviate in the unfavorable direction from the standard mean of 50 for men whose mothers are deceased, as well as for those whose parents are separated, strengthens the argument for validity of the family scale.

The mean law scores of the men whose mothers were deceased are also above the standard mean in every group. The least favorable scores were again made by the unemployed in the evening classes. It will be recalled that separation of the parents was also associated with poorer law scores. None of the individuals in the "parents separated" category were included in the group of men in the "mother deceased" category.

Unfavorable morale scores were associated with the "mother deceased" category in the two unemployed groups, the scores being particularly high for the unemployed of the evening classes. Most unfavorable economic conservatism scores were made in the two unemployed groups and in the part-time employed group. Education scores show no appreciable relationship to decease of the mother; in fact, the scores for the men employed full time are excellent on this scale.

Men reporting their mothers to be unemployed were so few in any group that the relationships are not

TABLE 82.-ATTITUDE SCORES AND STATUS OF MOTHER FOR SINGLE FEMALES

Status of Mother	N	Morale	Inferiority	Family	Law	Economic Conservatism	Education
			EVENING CLASSES				
			Employed Full Time				
Deceased . .	55	49.96	51.98	53.44	46.44	49.49	48.56
Housewife . .	219	49.80	51.61	51.10	48.41	49.62	48.60
Employed . .	19	45.53	48.68	52.47	50.21	51.00	49.16
Unemployed .	12	56.17	55.83	52.42	54.42	60.75	46.67
			Employed Part Time				
Deceased . .	11	57.91	54.91	55.00	48.27	52.27	50.18
Housewife . .	50	49.98	53.84	50.72	48.98	51.48	49.28
Employed . .	5	51.20	52.40	51.20	46.40	46.40	42.60
Unemployed .	1	54.00	58.00	58.00	49.00	54.00	53.00
			Unemployed				
Deceased . .	28	46.46	48.14	50.68	44.68	47.93	45.79
Housewife . .	168	53.55	51.49	50.76	49.18	50.77	50.29
Employed . .	15	55.13	50.53	56.87	55.20	50.73	53.33
Unemployed .	6	59.67	56.00	53.00	55.00	57.58	57.17
			DAY CLASSES (UNEMPLOYED)				
Deceased . .	13	53.08	50.92	55.08	39.15	51.23	51.69
Housewife . .	185	51.68	51.33	50.74	46.75	51.55	50.75
Employed . .	21	51.95	48.05	50.24	48.81	51.71	54.62
Unemployed .	4	54.25	56.25	56.00	47.50	53.25	64.00
			UNIVERSITY				
Deceased . .	16	50.13	52.19	52.81	53.69	52.38	50.94
Housewife . .	170	48.77	48.55	48.53	50.62	49.05	49.91
Employed . .	11	55.18	52.18	49.36	49.82	52.00	48.73
Unemployed .	2	53.50	51.50	63.50	56.50	52.60	62.50
			HIGH SCHOOL				
Deceased . .	22	49.77	51.36	54.45	48.50	49.14	49.27
Housewife . .	304	50.46	52.46	49.59	47.49	50.44	47.58
Employed . .	37	49.46	51.78	55.19	48.59	49.59	48.32
Unemployed .	4	58.25	56.50	54.75	49.00	48.00	53.00

reliably measured. There is a distinct tendency, however, in the direction of economic radicalism for these cases, all groups yielding scores above the standard mean.

Table 82 presents similar data for females. Among the women whose mothers were deceased unfavorable scores were made most often in the part-time employed and day school unemployed groups. Family scores are higher than the standard mean for all groups, the part-time and day class unemployed again scoring least favorably. Scores on other scales show little tendency in the unfavorable direction among those whose mothers are deceased. A clear sex difference is present in the extent to which unfavorable scores are associated with this status of the mother. In both the day and evening classes unemployed men scored less favorably on every scale than did unemployed women whose mothers were deceased. This sex difference may be of significance for psychoanalytic theory. On the basis of the greater rivalry between mother and daughter it is understandable that the mother's death would produce less unfavorable results on women than on men. Evidence from father's status is not consistent with this interpretation, for no sex difference appears with respect to the effect of the decease of the father.

The most striking relationship in Table 82 is that between unfavorable scores and unemployment of the mother. This is particularly evident for the morale, inferiority, and family scales. The unfavorable economic conservatism score for women of this group is worthy of note, for women tend to remain conservative under most of the circumstances studied in this chapter.

Information concerning marital status and employment status is given in Tables 83 and 84. While it might be contended that the fact of divorce is indicative of an underlying maladjustment, it may also be pointed out that a divorce from an undesired husband (the divorced were all women in the group studied) might do much to facilitate adjustment. The only scale on which the married group consistently exceeds the single group is the economic conservatism scale. Married people have more responsibilities, and those who are not yet sufficiently secure to discontinue their formal education may be expected to be more unfavorably inclined

TABLE 83.-ATTITUDE SCORES AND MARITAL STATUS

Marital Status	N	Morale	Inferiority	Family	Law	Economic Conservatism	Education
			MALES				
			Evening Classes				
Single . . .	283	50.31	50.20	50.44	51.06	53.10	46.95
Married . .	56	47.71	47.48	47.79	48.75	56.46	47.34
			Day Classes				
Single . . .	145	49.70	48.30	50.49	48.17	52.13	50.48
Married . .	5	52.40	48.20	52.20	56.80	56.00	57.40
			FEMALES				
			Evening Classes				
Single . . .	606	51.32	51.88	51.67	48.78	50.44	49.21
Married . .	58	50.71	51.28	52.36	49.91	52.78	48.53
Divorced . .	12	50.75	51.25	55.00	48.75	49.18	49.67
			Day Classes				
Single . . .	231	51.88	51.16	51.02	47.09	51.60	51.63
Married . .	26	48.85	50.27	48.58	47.69	53.81	49.12

toward the prevailing economic organization. The divorced group differs appreciably from the married and single groups on only one scale, the family scale. Since it is wholly reasonable that their attitude toward the family should be unfavorable, this difference may be considered as evidence in validation of the family scale. It is of considerable interest to note that married and single persons do not differ strikingly on the family scale. Although the scale was constructed with single persons in mind, it may well work for married people because the items express an underlying attitude, and because the word family can be interpreted either as the parental family or as one's own. Unemployment is most closely related to morale scores among the married group; For the divorced women unemployment seems to affect morale, inferiority, and economic conservatism. The family scale reveals rather high scores for both the employed and unemployed. It is of interest, too, that

TABLE 84.-ATTITUDE SCORES AND EMPLOYMENT STATUS FOR MARRIED AND DIVORCED PERSONS IN EVENING CLASSES

Marital Status	N	Morale	Inferiority	Family	Law	Economic Conservatism	Education
			Married Men				
Employed Full Time	43	47.28	47.58	47.63	48.94	56.12	47.16
Employed Part Time	7	48.14	46.71	45.71	51.57	61.43	51.43
Unemployed	6	50.33	47.61	51.33	44.83	57.33	43.83
			Married Women				
Employed Full Time	26	48.65	51.19	49.85	49.77	52.08	48.03
Employed Part Time	5	49.60	52.20	55.00	53.20	57.60	52.60
Unemployed	25	53.96	50.88	54.40	50.16	52.36	48.68
			Divorced Women				
Employed Full Time	8	48.00	48.37	55.50	49.25	46.38	50.13
Unemployed	4	56.26	57.00	54.00	47.75	54.75	48.75

unemployment among the divorced group produces the widest swing in attitude. Possession of children shows a large swing for men only on the economic conservatism scale, the reason being clear from the nature of the group with which we are dealing. Fathers in this group also score slightly less favorably on the family and law scales. The scores in relation to possession of children are as follows:

	Men		Women	
	No Children (N=19)	1 or more Children (N=28)	No Children (N=23)	1 or more Children (N=27)
Morale	48.68	48.36	50.65	51.48
Inferiority . . .	46.69	49.04	50.61	53.30
Family	45.16	49.04	52.56	51.59
Law	45.69	52.18	51.35	49.37
Economic Conservatism	51.37	59.71	54.83	50.89
Education	47.11	47.36	49.39	48.22

A finding that has frequently appeared in the various analyses of this chapter is that the differences noted are most pronounced for the unemployed group. In some groups--for instance, those not living at home and those whose fathers are retired--the differences disappear for the employed group when additional factors are controlled. It may be objected, therefore, that all the differences noted are caused solely by unemployment. This is clearly not the case, since the farmers' sons who were employed made poor scores. Conclusive evidence that unemployment alone is not reponsible for the differences is found in Tables 85-90. It will be noted there that unemployment has little effect on the personality scores so far as the group as a whole is concerned. The economic conservatism scale is the only one that shows considerable association with employment status. Length of unemployment shows little relationship to any of the scales. It is only when additional factors are introduced that differences become really striking. The data provide an excellent illustration of the multiple causation of personality traits. One unfavorable factor alone may not measurably affect a person. As the number of unfavorable factors are increased; however, adverse effects become more and more clear. The data further suggest that unemployment affects young people in proportion to the number of other adverse factors that have previously been present. In other words, the effect of one strain on the individual may become evident only when another strain is imposed. Some such hypothesis as this is needed to explain the relatively small effect of unemployment that is apparent for the group as a whole and the marked effects that are evident when certain additional factors are studied in conjunction with unemployment.

If this hypothesis is correct, it follows that in personality work the control of all factors except one may yield negative results, whereas the same factor studied in conjunction with another will yield positive results.

TABLE 85.-MORALE SCORES AND EMPLOYMENT STATUS

(Single persons only.)

Employment Status	Evening Classes				Day Classes			
	Men		Women		Men		Women	
	Mean	N	Mean	N	Mean	N	Mean	N
Employed full time	48.64	159	49.85	306	.....	..	.....	..
Employed part time	52.42	43	52.17	71	41.88	18	.....	..
Unemployed 1 year or less	53.97	33	53.44	85	50.79	61	52.23	64
Unemployed more than 1 year	51.09	23	53.52	44	53.61	23	50.20	35
Unemployed time unspecified	51.76	25	52.50	100	49.32	43	52.14	131
All unemployed	52.47	81	53.09	229	50.80	127	51.87	230

TABLE 86.-INFERIORITY SCORES AND EMPLOYMENT STATUS

(Single persons only.)

Employment Status	Evening Classes				Day Classes			
	Men		Women		Men		Women	
	Mean	N	Mean	N	Mean	N	Mean	N
Employed full time	49.50	159	51.67	306	.....	..	.....	..
Employed part time	52.84	43	54.21	71	41.61	18	.....	..
Unemployed 1 year or less	50.21	33	51.73	85	49.15	61	51.48	64
Unemployed more than 1 year	51.52	23	51.32	44	49.43	23	49.40	35
Unemployed time unspecified	48.88	25	51.30	100	49.30	43	51.31	131
All unemployed	50.17	81	51.46	229	49.25	127	51.10	230

TABLE 87.-FAMILY SCORES AND EMPLOYMENT STATUS

(Single persons only.)

Employment Status	Evening Classes				Day Classes			
	Men		Women		Men		Women	
	Mean	N	Mean	N	Mean	N	Mean	N
Employed full time	50.19	159	51.67	306	.....	..	.....	..
Employed part time	50.70	43	52.03	71	51.22	18	.....	..
Unemployed 1 year or less	52.54	33	51.65	85	51.18	61	48.75	64
Unemployed more than 1 year	50.00	23	52.43	44	52.17	23	49.83	35
Unemployed time unspecified	49.20	25	51.13	100	48.30	43	52.41	131
All unemployed	50.79	81	51.57	229	50.38	127	51.00	230

TABLE 88.-LAW SCORES AND EMPLOYMENT STATUS

(Single persons only.)

Employment Status	Evening Classes				Day Classes			
	Men		Women		Men		Women	
	Mean	N	Mean	N	Mean	N	Mean	N
Employed full time	51.31	159	48.40	306	.....	..	.....	..
Employed part time	50.84	43	49.16	71	46.61	18	.....	..
Unemployed 1 year or less	52.09	33	49.93	85	47.64	61	46.58	64
Unemployed more than 1 year	49.91	23	48.70	44	50.26	23	46.06	35
Unemployed time unspecified	49.60	25	48.78	100	48.46	43	47.54	131
All unemployed	50.70	81	49.19	229	48.39	127	47.05	230

TABLE 89.-ECONOMIC CONSERVATISM SCORES AND EMPLOYMENT STATUS

(Single persons only.)

Employment Status	Evening Classes				Day Classes			
	Men		Women		Men		Women	
	Mean	N	Mean	N	Mean	N	Mean	N
Employed full time	51.03	159	50.12	306	.....	..	.....	..
Employed part time	55.35	43	51.50	71	51.50	18	.....	..
Unemployed 1 year or less	57.97	33	50.95	85	51.90	61	53.09	64
Unemployed more than 1 year	57.09	23	51.95	44	53.26	23	50.74	35
Unemployed time unspecified	52.32	25	49.57	100	52.12	43	51.06	131
All unemployed	55.98	81	50.23	229	52.22	127	51.58	230

TABLE 90.-EDUCATION SCORES AND EMPLOYMENT STATUS

(Single persons only.)

Employment Status	Evening Classes				Day Classes			
	Men		Women		Men		Women	
	Mean	N	Mean	N	Mean	N	Mean	N
Employed full time	44.25	159	48.56	306	.....	..	.....	..
Employed part time	50.81	43	49.39	71	51.50	18	.....	..
Unemployed 1 year or less	51.52	33	50.35	85	51.23	61	52.22	64
Unemployed more than 1 year	47.39	23	50.34	44	53.09	23	50.26	35
Unemployed time unspecified	51.08	25	49.64	100	48.16	43	51.69	131
All unemployed	50.21	81	50.04	229	50.53	127	51.62	230

VALIDITY OF THE SINGLE SCALES

Though the evidence is conclusive that a general factor permeates the six scales, it does not follow that the magnitude of the relationships found in this chapter are wholly the result of this factor. In fact, there is evidence that it is not. If the general factor were solely responsible, one would expect the scales to be related to the outside variables in proportion to their intercorrelations. Such is not the case. The economic conservatism scale is negligibly related to the other scales, and yet in its relationship with those outside variables with which the scales tended to vary as a unit, it is one of the best. Secondly, there is considerable variation in the scales which are related to a variable. In one comparison the morale, law, and economic conservatism scale vary together; in another the morale, family, and law scales. In one comparison the inferiority scale follows the trend; in the next it is an exception.

To future research must be left the problem of disentangling the effect of the general and specific factors of each scale in their relationship to the factors studied. Here we are concerned with the problem of the validity of the total score of each scale. It is scarcely necessary to point out that the logical continuity of the items of a scale is preliminary evidence of its validity.

THE MORALE SCALE

Morale is by definition an exceedingly generalized trait. The word connotes zeal, hope, confidence in oneself and in what the future will bring. It might be defined as confidence in one's ability to cope with the future. In addition there are symptoms that are commonly assumed to be present when one's morale is poor; distrust of people, the feeling that no one is friendly, and the belief that life is not worth living. All these are tapped by the present scale. Some items have a very specific reference to the future--i.e., the future looks very black. Others directly imply discouragement--i.e., there is really no point in living. Still others approach the problem indirectly--i.e., most people can be trusted. Such items were culled from a study of case histories of those whose morale was presumed to have been shattered by depression effects.

That something akin to morale as defined is being measured is suggested by at least two lines of evidence: 1. It is the most general of the six scales measured. Both the multiple correlation analysis and the analysis of the power of the items of a scale to discriminate in a scale other than its own show this. 2. Morale is related to more factors on the face sheet than any of the other scales. These factors (only the more conspicuous are mentioned) are:

Men	Women
Occupational security[2]	Separation of parents
Over-ageness	Unemployment of father
Previous education	Unemployment of mother
Farmers' sons in urban environment score unfavorably	Divorced who are unemployed score unfavorably
Non-home residence	Unemployment
Separation of parents	
Retirement of father	
Unemployment	

The wide range of factors to which this scale is related is rather convincing evidence that it is tapping a trait of fundamental importance, one closely akin to morale in the usual sense of the word.

A sex difference, both in the number and in the kind of factors with which the scale is related, is evident from the above tabulation, fewer relationships existing for women.

Another method of validating a scale is to correlate it with other scales designed to measure the

2. Hall likewise found a close relationship between his occupational morale scale and occupational security.

same or closely related traits. Hall's Scale for Measuring Occupational Morale is the only other morale scale the authors know of. It consists of 5 items:

THERE IS LITTLE CHANCE FOR ADVANCEMENT IN INDUSTRY AND BUSINESS UNLESS A MAN HAS UNFAIR PULL.

"AMBITION" IS ALL RIGHT FOR YOUNGSTERS, BUT A MAN GETS TO REALIZE THAT IT IS ALL THE BUNK.

ANY MAN WITH ABILITY AND WILLINGNESS TO WORK HARD HAS A GOOD CHANCE OF BEING SUCCESSFUL.

SUCCESS IS MORE DEPENDENT ON LUCK THAN ON REAL ABILITY.

THERE IS NOT MUCH SENSE IN TRYING VERY HARD TO MAKE GOOD.

It will be recalled that our purpose was to construct a more generalized morale scale. It will also be recalled that we followed Hall in his choice of the alternative response phrases. His scale is scored exactly as the present one. All 5 of Hall's items were tried out in the present scale, 3 of them (the first, third, and fourth above) meeting the criterion for incorporation into the present scale.

TABLE 91.-INTERCORRELATIONS BETWEEN HALL'S MORALE ITEMS AND ATTITUDE SCALES

Attitude Scale	3 Hall Items: Sociology I Males (N=100)	3 Hall Items: Public Relief Group (N=50)
Morale (excluding 3 Hall items)	.652*	.593
Inferiority	.364	.450
Family	.275	.361
Law	.465**	.608
Economic Conservatism	.434	.504***
Education	.530	.453

*Authors' Morale Scale (including 3 Hall items) vs. 3 Hall items: .775.

**Authors' Morale Scale (excluding 3 Hall items) vs. Economic Conservatism: .278.

***Authors' Morale Scale (including 3 Hall items) vs. Economic Conservatism: .268.

Table 91 shows the correlation that exists between the scores on the total scale of 22 items and the total score on Hall's 3 items contained therein, and the correlation between total score on 19 items in the scale and the total score on Hall's 3 items. Correlations between Hall's 3 items and the remaining scales are included for comparative purposes. The spurious element involved in correlating total score on 22 items with total score on 3 items contained therein is obvious; this correlation, however, indicates the extent to which the scales are interchangeable. For 100 male university students in the Sociology I course, the correlation between total score on 22 items and score on the 3 Hall items contained therein was +.775. The correlation coefficient was reduced to +.652 when the spurious element was removed by correlating total score on our 19 items and total score on Hall's 3 items. The score on Hall's 3 items correlated with 19 other items was +.593 for 50 men receiving public relief.

It is evident that the use of 3 of Hall's 5 items as the basis of computations may have produced substantial changes in the results obtained. Inasmuch as all 5 items were included in a preliminary form of the morale scale, the correlation coefficients between total score on all 5 items and total score on the authors' 19 items retained in the final scale were computed. This computation yielded a coefficient of .480 for males and .406 for females. In this group of 72 males enrolled in advanced sociology classes, the coefficient between total score on Hall's 3 items retained in the final scale and total score on the other 19 items was higher than it was between total score on all 5 items and total score on 19 items. This suggests that the 2 items in Hall's scale that were not retained are less similar to our 19 items than the 3 retained, and this same fact is indicated by their exclusion on the basis of insufficient discriminative value. The data may be interpreted as tentative validation of the morale scale, for the two morale scales correlate more consistently than do Hall's 3 items and any of the other 5 scales.

Table 91 also shows that the 3 Hall items retained yielded substantial correlation coefficients with total scores on the inferiority, law, economic conservatism, and education scales for both the Sociology I and the unemployed group. For the group of men on public relief, scores on Hall's 3 items correlated as high with score on the law scale as with morale score (excluding Hall's items). These 3 items also appear to be measuring economic conservatism to a greater degree than do our morale items, since the correlation coefficient with scores on that scale is .504, whereas the coefficient between total score on our 19 items and economic conservatism score was only .278.

Hall's scale was designed to measure occupational morale, whereas we sought to develop a more generalized measure of morale. Undoubtedly the true correlation between the scales is well in excess of .50 for men, and yet the scales do not appear to be interchangeable. That all scales correlate with Hall's 3 items illustrates the difficulty of determining precisely what is being measured by any given scale. The operation of a general factor is against suggested.

In a further effort to validate the morale scale it was correlated against three Bernreuter scores: dominance-submission, self-sufficiency, and neurotic tendencies. The correlations between these indices and all six scales are presented in Table 92.

TABLE 92.-ATTITUDE SCORES CORRELATED WITH BERNREUTER SCORES*

(University High School group; N = 37 males, 34 females.)

Scale	Dominance-Submission		Self-Sufficiency		Neurotic Tendencies	
	Male	Female	Male	Female	Male	Female
Morale	+.329	+.308	+.510	-.162	-.202	-.361
Inferiority . . .	+.612	+.462	+.389	+.042	-.562	-.487
Family	+.056	+.095	+.311	+.042	-.147	-.150
Law	+.182	+.016	+.245	+.004	-.109	+.018
Economic Conservatism	+.220	+.114	+.057	-.062	-.326	-.165
Education	-.025	+.052	+.008	-.084	+.268	-.043

*A positive correlation indicates a direct relationship between dominance, self-sufficiency, or presence of neurotic tendencies and favorable attitude as defined in the text.

The Bernreuter Personality Inventory was given to a group of 37 third-year high school boys and 34 third-year high school girls nine months before they were given our battery of scales. Although this interval has probably somewhat reduced the correlations, the test-retest reliability of the scales makes it unlikely that the major relationships differ substantially from what would be obtained if they were given simultaneously.

While the number of cases involved here is small, the probability that the results are adequate for this group, if not for others, is enhanced by the fact that Smith's scale correlated three years ago against the Bernreuter yielded substantially the same results as our inferiority scale does at the present time. This group differs from most high school juniors in that it is selected more on the basis of intelligence than is usually the case.

The morale scale behaves in common-sense fashion in its relationship to the Bernreuter scores. As was expected, those whose morale is good tend to be more self-reliant or self-sufficient. This, however, is only true for men (r +.510). The correlation, though small (-.162), is in the reverse direction for women. While this particular finding is unexpected, it is in line with the numerous sex differences already noted for the morale scale in its relationship to other variables. Hence the sex difference cannot well be interpreted as showing the chance nature of these correlations--the position one would usually take in view of the small size of the groups involved. Good morale is also related to dominance and absence of neurotic tendencies, but not to the degree that it is related to self-sufficiency among men. A comparison of the morale and inferiority relationships to the Bernreuter scores is suggestive of the difference between the two traits. Morale is most closely related to self-sufficiency, or confidence in oneself, whereas inferiority is more closely related to neurotic tendencies and dominance-submission.

Scores on the six personality scales were also correlated with I.Q. and honor-point ratio for this school group.[3] (See Table 93.) The measures of intelligence and scholastic achievement, as well as the Bernreuter scores, were kindly made available by Dr. F. H. Finch, staff member of the College of Education. The measure of intelligence is unusually reliable, being based on five group tests, the scores on each being converted into comparable units, and the median being used as a measure. Honor-point ratio is based solely on academic subjects taken during the year preceding the testing.

TABLE 93.-ATTITUDE SCORES CORRELATED WITH I.Q. AND HONOR POINTS*

(University High School group; N = 37 males, 34 females.)

Scale	Male		Female	
	I.Q.**	Honor Points	I.Q.**	Honor Points
Morale	+.296	+.506	-.192	-.194
Inferiority	+.201	+.237	+.053	-.242
Family	-.380	-.013	-.383	-.116
Law	+.177	+.297	-.141	-.353
Economic Conservatism . .	-.247	-.270	-.125	-.171
Education	+.242	+.191	-.400	-.289

*A positive correlation indicates a direct relationship between high I.Q. (or high honor point ratio) and the possession of favorable attitude as defined in text.

**Correlation between I.Q. and honor points; male, +.471; female, +.561.

While the groups are small and the finding may be atypical, the correlation between morale and honor-point ratio is so striking that it deserves mention. It is +.506 for men and -.194 for women--again the sex difference. Holding I.Q. constant slightly reduces the correlation for boys, to +.435. In fact the raw correlation for boys is higher than that between

3. The scales were given anonymously, but the papers were identified by means of the birth date, a simple matter in a small high school.

I.Q. and honor points for this same group (+.471). Correlations between personality scales and scholastic achievement of the magnitude of .50 are exceedingly rare in the literature. It may be a chance finding or may be typical only of the present group, which is composed largely of individuals planning professional careers. Failure to meet academic requirements is a serious matter for them. Little weight can be placed on this surprisingly high correlation until it is confirmed with a more adequate sampling. If it is confirmed, the morale scale is, indeed, a useful instrument.

To sum up, the morale scale appears to be a valid measure of a very general trait akin to its name. It will be a useful member of any battery of personality scales.

THE INFERIORITY SCALE

The concept of inferiority is so familiar to psychologists that no definition need be offered. The authors, guided by the work of earlier investigators, have emphasized social as opposed to physical and intellectual inferiority.

The inferiority scale correlates most closely with the morale scale; yet the two do not vary together in their relations to other variables. It is not related to as many factors, and the sex difference is reversed, the scale being related to more variables for women than for men. The most conspicuous are:

Men	Women
Over-ageness	Occupational security
Farmer's sons score unfavorably	Over-ageness
Unemployment when father is retired	Separation of parents for women not employed
	Unemployment of father
	Divorced who are unemployed
	Possession of children

How does it correlate with similar instruments? Randolph Smith's (16) scale for measuring inferiority feelings at the high school level was given to the University High School group at the same time that our battery was administered. Our survey preceded Smith's in the administration. Sections 3 and 4 of form PN, containing 100 items, were used. The correlations between the two scales are .796 for boys and .755 for girls. Taking .95, the reliability reported by Smith for sections 3 and 4, and the reliability coefficients for the groups of 500, .78 for men and .82 for women, as the best estimates of the reliability of the present scales and correcting for attenuation, the correlations became .92 and .85.

These results validate the present scale in the sense that they demonstrate that Smith's and this scale are measuring essentially the same aspect of personality. So far as group comparisons are concerned, the two scales will reveal the same trends. For individual diagnosis of inferiority feelings Smith's scale, because of its greater reliability, is to be preferred. It should be noted, however, that Smith's scale yields only one measure and the 200-item form will take longer to administer than the present six scales. In practice it is often preferable to obtain six reasonably reliable measures of somewhat different aspects of personality than to obtain one more reliable measure of one aspect. Which scale is to be preferred depends largely on the particular interest of the investigator.

The correlations with Bernreuter's index of neurotic tendencies also point in the direction of the validity of the scale. (See Table 92.)

THE FAMILY SCALE

In constructing this scale the authors had in mind parent-child relationships and family tensions. The latter had to be measured indirectly by such statements as <u>one becomes nervous at home</u> and <u>people in the family can be trusted completely</u>.

The only evidence, aside from the ideational content of the items, available to validate this scale comes from the information elicited on the face sheet. The major relationships follow:

Men	Women
Occupational security	Separation of parents
Over-ageness	Mother deceased
Separation of parents	Mother employed
Retired father	Divorce
Mother deceased	Unemployed who are married

The variables showing relationships here do tend to suggest family tension. The evidence is not as convincing as one would like it to be, but it points in the expected direction.

THE LAW SCALE

This scale was intended to measure attitudes toward legal institutions and willingness to evade the law. The face sheet information is the only validating material available. The more pronounced relationships are these:

Men	Women
Occupational security	Separation of parents
Over-ageness	Mother unemployed
Previous education	
Farmers' sons in urban environment score unfavorably	
Non-home residence	
Separation of parents	
Father retired	
Mother deceased	
Possession of children for married	

This scale shows the most conspicuous sex difference in the number of variables related to it. There are only two relationships for women as compared with nine for men. The preponderance of variables implying family relationships suggests that this scale may be measuring an extension of parental authority--attitude toward authority in general. For men, every factor related to the family scale is also related to the law scale.

THE ECONOMIC CONSERVATISM SCALE

Radicalism is relatively so intellectualized a trait that the ideational continuity is almost validation enough. Among the problems over which the radical and the conservative have disputed for years are the distribution of wealth, government ownership, the importance of the profit motive, the relationship of social problems to the economic structure, taxation of wealth, and the rights of labor. Additional validation is desirable, but the authors were unable to undertake the task. Its relationships to the face sheet data are:

Men	Women
Occupational security	Father unemployed
Over-ageness	Mother unemployed
Previous education	Divorced who are unemployed score unfavorably
Farmers' sons in urban environment score unfavorably	
Non-home residence	
Unemployment when father is retired	
Married score unfavorably[4]	
Married who have children score unfavorably[4]	
Unemployment (slight relationship here but a fundamental one as will be shown later)	

4. It is likely that these relationships are confined to married persons subject to economic pressure.

Again, men show more relationships than women. The relationship to unemployment of self or a member of the family is of considerable interest. This will be discussed more fully in a later chapter. It is also of interest to note that the slight inverse relationship between conservatism in economic views and I.Q. found to exist in this study (-.247 for men and -.125 for women, Table 93) is very similar to that found by Rosenthal (15), who used a scale which differs considerably from the present one.

THE EDUCATION SCALE

The validating evidence is slight. It relates itself to very few of the face sheet variables:

Men	Women
Over-ageness	Separation of parents
Farmers' sons score unfavorably (except among the employed full-time and unemployed)	Unemployment of mother
Separation of parents	
Unemployment of father	
Favorable scores for full-time employed	

The relationship with over-ageness might be interpreted as validating this scale. Over-ageness in the school situation implies school maladjustment. It will be shown in Chapter XII that a statistically significant difference exists between the scores of men receiving public relief in favor of those who have more education.

SUMMARY

One fact clearly emerges from the analysis in this chapter--the widespread effect of the general factor running through the scales. This factor is so general that it often overshadows any relationships that might be characteristic of a single scale. While obtaining all six measures from an omnibus survey may have enhanced the effect of this general factor, the analysis of the discriminative values (see Chapter III), which revealed that each item was placed in the scale for which it discriminates best, plus the scale differences in the relationships to outside criteria noted in this chapter, make it improbable that any spurious effect is markedly present. It would be interesting to give the scales separately, or even by sections of the survey, and compare the relationships of the scales to each other and to outside variables with what has been obtained under the conditions of this experiment.

The evidence strongly suggests that the factor influencing all the scales is in the nature of general adjustment. When all scales tend to be related to the same variable, logic itself suggests that the scales, considered as a unit, are measuring general adjustment. Any individual who possesses poor morale, feelings of inferiority, a poor attitude toward the family, law, the economic organization, and the value of education cannot well be considered an adjusted person. It may be weakness in the individual himself (the implications of over-ageness) or an accumulation of such factors as unemployment, a broken home, and a considerable change in environment (the transition from rural to urban life); but whenever the information we possess suggests maladjustment, just there do we find unfavorable scores on several or all of the scales. Occupational insecurity, separation of parents, over-ageness, residence away from home, transition from a rural to an urban environment, unemployment when the father has been sufficiently successful to retire--all these factors tend to produce unfavorable scores on most of the scales. All suggest maladjustment. These statements hold true chiefly for men. Among women only three factors seem to be related to the general factor: occupational security (certainty of obtaining or maintaining a position), separation of parents, and unemployment of either parent. Over-ageness, transition from rural to urban life, and previous education do not seem to affect these aspects of personality so far as women are concerned.

When we list the factors that show a rather clear relationship to the individual scales, the sex difference is even more conspicuous. Fewer factors are related to every scale for women except the inferiority scale. The difference is particularly evident in the case of the law scale.

There are several possible reasons for this sex difference. Differential selective factors may be responsible for bringing together the educational groups. That trends are frequently noticeable within the high school and university groups as well as in special classes for the unemployed does not favor this argument.

It may well be that the adjustment of women is conditioned by strictly social factors to a greater extent than is the case among men. Information concerning such factors is lacking in this study. The fact that the inferiority scale, which emphasizes social inferiority, is related to a greater number of factors for women than for men favors this hypothesis. Most of the sex differences noted could be explained on this basis. Over-ageness, within limits, need not be a handicap in the social situation. Living away from home permits social contacts, particularly with the opposite sex, to proceed with greater freedom. Any disturbance of family income, as implied by such factors as unemployment of the father or mother, can be interpreted as interfering with the usual social contacts.

Another explanation for this sex difference should be mentioned. The scales may not be as well suited to women. They were constructed by men, although feminine responses were given equal weight in the final selection of items. Another possibility is that the feminine personality may not be as generally organized as the masculine. Evidence favoring this hypothesis will be presented in a later chapter.

Throughout this chapter it has been apparent under adverse circumstances women are more conservative in their economic views than are men. In fact, the only variable that tended to produce strikingly radical scores is unemployment of a parent. Men, however, usually show radical tendencies whenever they show unfavorable attitudes on the other scales. This sex difference is of particular interest in view of the fact that the average scores of men and women show virtually no differences. Lack of sex differences in mean scores is clearly no justification for combining the sexes in relating such scores to outside factors. This is an obvious point, but it is often overlooked.

The data in this chapter provide a clear illustration of the multiple causation of personality traits. Considered singly, some factors appear to have no effect on personality score. Definite relationships appear when this factor is combined with another which likewise shows no appreciable effect when considered by itself. While the influence of a general factor is unmistakable, evidence has been presented to indicate that it is not solely responsible for the relationships noted.

Are the scales valid? Morale, being by definition a very general trait--it may, in fact, be the factor responsible for the co-variation of the six scales--the evidence that it is the most generalized of the six scales may be considered as evidence for its validity. Morale has the highest multiple R against scores on the remaining scales, the morale items discriminate best in scales other than their own, and the scale is related to the largest number of outside variables. The morale scale also appears valid in that it correlates well with Hall's scale, which was designed to measure a more specific aspect of morale. Further, the morale scale behaves in the expected manner in its correlation with three Bernreuter scores.

The inferiority scale is valid in the sense that it correlates well with another instrument designed to measure the same trait. Both inferiority scales behave in a similar manner in their relationships with outside variables.

Clear-cut validating evidence for the remaining scales is lacking. The nature of radicalism makes it highly probable that the economic conservatism scale will prove to be valid. The evidence points in the correct direction for the family scale, but it is not completely convincing. The law scale, the scale which shows the greatest sex difference in the number of face sheet factors to which it is related, has no experimental support for its name. There is a suggestion that this scale measures attitude toward authority in general. Precisely what the education scale is measuring is not indicated by anything except the apparent ideational content of the items.

Chapter VIII

THE SCALE OF GENERAL ADJUSTMENT

In the last chapter it was discovered that in their relationships to such variables as home residence, separation of parents, or over-ageness, all six scales tended to vary in the same manner. The relationships were, to be sure, of varying magnitude, but the tendency toward unit behavior of the scales was unmistakable. Such evidence points directly to the operation of a general factor. An attempt was therefore made to define this factor more specifically in terms of the items most directly related to it.

PROBLEMS IN SELECTING THE ITEMS

There were at least two methods available for ascertaining the items most reponsible for the unit behavior of the six scales in their relationship to the information contained on the face sheet. The method of factor analysis, as developed by Thurstone, could have been used. The statistical labor involved when dealing with 132 variables ($\frac{N(N-1)}{2}$ or 8,646 basic correlations would be required) is one reason for rejecting this method. Since our primary interest was in isolating the items most heavily loaded for the most general factor and not in determining the number of factors involved in the six scales, another method, which has the advantage of being exceedingly simple in its application, was chosen. The logic of the method of internal consistency was simply extended to total score on the 132 items considered as an entity. This method should isolate the items most heavily loaded for the most general factor.

An additional problem arose in attempting to construct a scale measuring the general factor. The behavior of the six scales as a unit was most conspicuous for men. Since the general factor is not so clearly operative for women, it seemed best not to utilize their responses in the selection of the items for this scale.

Earlier analysis has also demonstrated the fluctuations in the discriminative value of an item from group to group. To increase the probability of obtaining items that would yield more stable discriminative values and hence insure the general applicability of the scale, two groups differing considerably in composition were utilized in the selection of the items.[1] The two groups chosen for this purpose were the Sociology I and the controlled sample of unemployed men. Since these groups are samplings of two rather dissimilar populations, items meeting the criteria of selection will presumably be more generally applicable. The two groups are similar in age and in the fact that both are continuing their education, albeit at different levels.

The scores of the six scales for these groups were therefore summed and the quartile test of internal consistency applied. The analysis of the discriminative values in scales other than that in which the items were placed has shown the necessity for discriminative values in the neighborhood of 1.00 as a minimum value. The criterion for retention of an item for the general scale thus became a discriminative value of 1.00 or better in each of the two groups.

The distribution of the discriminative values of the 132 items for each group is given in Table 94. No great difference is noted in these distributions. An approximately equal number of items discriminate at each level. But are they the same ones? Figure 8 shows that many are not. While a positive relation between the discriminative values in the two groups is evident, more conspicuous is the variation. Fifteen items do discriminate 1.00 or better in both groups. To

1. This is a more rigorous criterion than is the selection of items on the basis of the two groups combined.

balance odd and even forms, a sixteenth was added, the average discriminative value of which was over 1.00. According to the theory underlying the construction of these scales, these 16 items should be most heavily loaded for the general factor that permeates the six scales. On the basis of the evidence of the preceding chapter, it is assumed that this factor is in the nature of adjustment, and the scale is called a general adjustment scale.

FIG. 8.

DISTRIBUTION OF ITEM DISCRIMINATIVE VALUES IN RELATION TO TOTAL SCORE ON ALL SCALES.

MALE RESPONSES ONLY

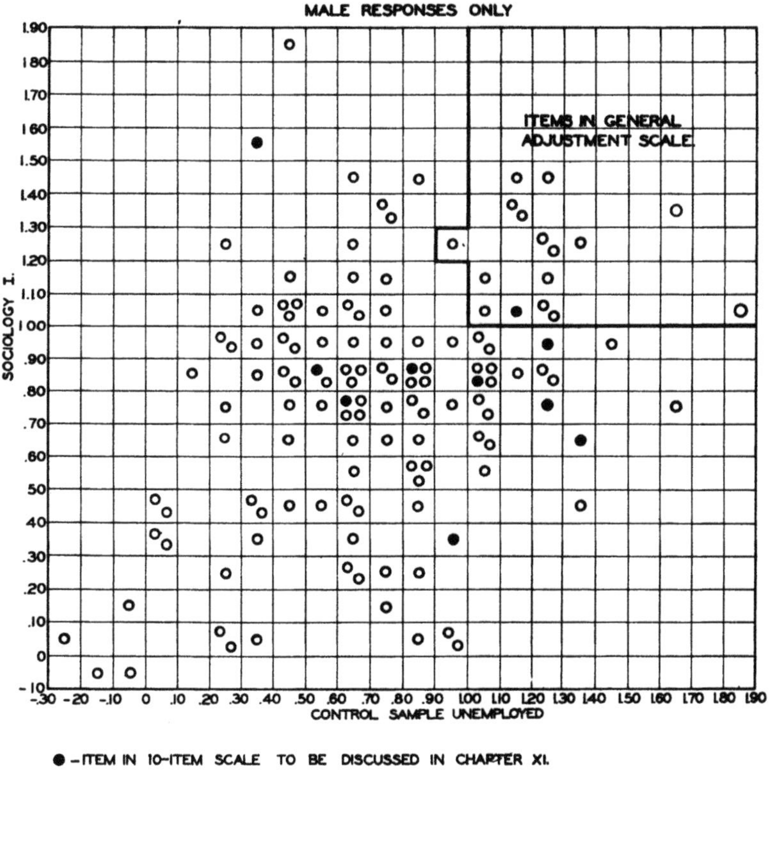

● – ITEM IN 10-ITEM SCALE TO BE DISCUSSED IN CHAPTER XI.

TABLE 94.—SCALE VALUE DIFFERENCES FOR THE 132 ITEMS IN TERMS OF QUARTILES FOR TOTAL COMBINED SCORES ON SIX SCALES

(N = 100 males in each group.)

Scale Value Difference Level	Morale	Inferi-ority	Family	Law	Economic Conserv-atism	Educa-tion	Total
			Sociology I				
1.00+ . . .	11	3	2	4	7	8	35
.60-.99	9	9	12	9	11	11	61
.20-.59	1	9	6	6	1	2	25
.20- . . .	1	1	2	3	3	1	11
			Controlled Sample of Unemployed				
1.00+ . . .	10	3	3	6	8	5	35
.60-.99	6	9	13	10	8	8	54
.20-.59	5	7	4	6	3	9	34
.20- . . .	1	3	2	0	3	0	9

ITEMS CHOSEN FOR THE SCALE

These 16 items were arbitrarily divided into two forms which are given here. The numbers refer to the position of the item in the survey of opinions.

ITEMS IN THE GENERAL ADJUSTMENT SCALE

Even Form

13. THE FUTURE LOOKS VERY BLACK.
Strongly agree⁵ Agree⁴ Undecided³ Disagree² Strongly disagree¹

19. LIFE IS JUST ONE WORRY AFTER ANOTHER.
Strongly agree⁵ Agree⁴ Undecided³ Disagree² Strongly disagree¹

31. TIMES ARE GETTING BETTER.
Strongly agree¹ Agree² Undecided³ Disagree⁴ Strongly disagree⁵

39. ONE CANNOT FIND AS MUCH UNDERSTANDING AT HOME AS ELSEWHERE.
Strongly agree⁵ Agree⁴ Undecided³ Disagree² Strongly disagree¹

73. THERE IS LITTLE CHANCE FOR ADVANCEMENT IN INDUSTRY AND BUSINESS UNLESS A MAN HAS UNFAIR PULL.
Strongly agree^5 Agree^4 Undecided^3 Disagree^2 Strongly disagree^1

86. MOST PEOPLE JUST PRETEND THAT THEY LIKE YOU.
Strongly agree^5 Agree^4 Undecided^3 Disagree^2 Strongly disagree^1

90. HIGH SCHOOL COURSES ARE TOO IMPRACTICAL.
Strongly agree^5 Agree^4 Undecided^3 Disagree^2 Strongly disagree^1

101. IF OUR ECONOMIC SYSTEM WERE JUST, THERE WOULD BE MUCH LESS CRIME.
Strongly agree^5 Agree^4 Undecided^3 Disagree^2 Strongly disagree^1

Odd Form

6. A MAN CAN LEARN MORE BY WORKING FOUR YEARS THAN BY GOING TO HIGH SCHOOL.
Strongly agree^5 Agree^4 Undecided^3 Disagree^2 Strongly disagree^1

14. IT IS DIFFICULT TO SAY THE RIGHT THING AT THE RIGHT TIME.
Strongly agree^5 Agree^4 Undecided^3 Disagree^2 Strongly disagree^1

29. POVERTY IS CHIEFLY A RESULT OF INJUSTICE IN THE DISTRIBUTION OF WEALTH.
Strongly agree^5 Agree^4 Undecided^3 Disagree^2 Strongly disagree^1

36. EDUCATION IS OF NO HELP IN GETTING A JOB TODAY.
Strongly agree^5 Agree^4 Undecided^3 Disagree^2 Strongly disagree^1

49. NO ONE CARES MUCH WHAT HAPPENS TO YOU.
Strongly agree^5 Agree^4 Undecided^3 Disagree^2 Strongly disagree^1

79. THE YOUNG MAN OF TODAY CAN EXPECT MUCH OF THE FUTURE.
Strongly agree^1 Agree^2 Undecided^3 Disagree^4 Strongly disagree^5

97. LIFE IS JUST A SERIES OF DISAPPOINTMENTS.
Strongly agree^5 Agree^4 Undecided^3 Disagree^2 Strongly disagree^1

100. LAWS ARE SO OFTEN MADE FOR THE BENEFIT OF SMALL SELFISH GROUPS THAT A MAN CANNOT RESPECT THE LAW.
Strongly agree^5 Agree^4 Undecided^3 Disagree^2 Strongly disagree^1

Two points are rather clear from an inspection of these items: (1) all are very general statements and (2) several items are included which a priori would probably never have been considered as belonging to the same scale. Seven of the items were originally placed in the morale, two in the inferiority, one in the family, one in the law, two in the conservatism, and three in the education scale. The advantage of the completely inductive nature of the method as applied here needs no emphasis. Again, the morale scale appears the most heavily loaded for the general factor. Almost half the items are derived from this scale.

PREPONDERANCE OF NEGATIVE ITEMS

The most significant feature of these items, however, is their preponderately negative character. Fourteen of the 16 are negatively stated. Is this a function of their ideational content or of the fact that they are negatively stated? This problem will be considered in detail in the next chapter. Here it need only be noted that this phenomenon provides a practical reason for not relaxing the criteria of item selection to obtain more items and presumably increase the reliability of the scale. Now if it can be demonstrated that the scale of general adjustment containing 16 items actually measures some such general factor as is implied by its title, the scale becomes an exceedingly valuable instrument to score or administer independently of the remaining 116 items in the survey. Since it is highly probable that the difference between positively and negatively stated items noted in the next chapter will be characteristic of this scale administered separately, some positive items may have to be added to balance the scale. The items added need not, of course, be scored, save as they are determined to yield an independent measure of some value. It would take 12 positive items to balance the scale, 26 items in all.[2] It could be administered in fifteen or twenty

2. Evidence presented in the next chapter suggests that the addition of the positively stated morale items would add to the usefulness of such a scale. See the Appendix for a short form of the survey.

minutes. Development of short instruments of such general significance would be of infinite aid in personality study.

TABLE 95.—MEAN STANDARD SCORES AND STANDARD DEVIATIONS ON GENERAL ADJUSTMENT SCALE

(Standard groups; N = 500 of each sex.)

Group	Males		Females	
	Mean	σ	Mean	σ
500 of each sex	50.10	10.11	49.95	9.86
Sociology I	49.96	10.79	49.49	7.88
General College	48.73	8.93	47.64	10.04
Controlled sample of high school seniors	50.59	8.64	50.73	10.23
Controlled sample of employed . .	49.15	9.65	49.62	10.28
Controlled sample of unemployed .	52.06	11.90	52.29	9.99

SCORING

The procedure for scoring the general scale was identical with that described for the six original scales of the survey. The arbitrary scores were added, and on the basis of the actual distribution of the standard group of 1,000, each score was converted into a standard score according to the method described in Chapter IV. The arbitrary scores and the standard score equivalents are given in the Appendix. Table 95 gives the means and standard deviations of each of the subgroups of the standard group of 1,000. The similarities between the groups are much more striking than the differences. It is of interest to note that the unemployed group has the most unfavorable score. This point will be considered later. No marked sex differences are evident from this table nor from Figure 9, which gives the distribution of arbitrary scores of the standard group. This distribution is symmetrical, and it is clear that the scale discriminates very sharply.

FIG. 9.

DISTRIBUTION OF GENERAL ADJUSTMENT SCORES.

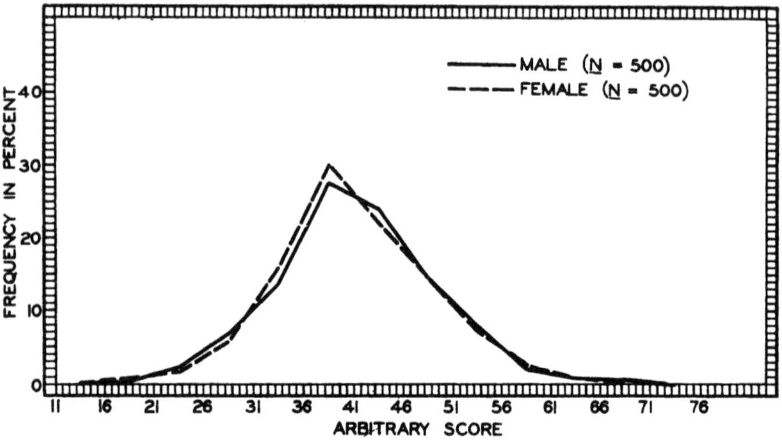

TABLE 96.-SPLIT-HALF RELIABILITY COEFFICIENTS FOR THE GENERAL ADJUSTMENT SCALE

(Standard samples.)

Group	N	Reliability Coefficient Raw	Reliability Coefficient Corrected*
		Male	
All males	500	.696	.821
Sociology I	100	.682	.811
General College	100	.567	.724
Controlled sample of high school seniors	100	.507	.673
Controlled sample of employed	100	.690	.816
Controlled sample of unemployed	100	.745	.854
		Female	
All females	500	.664	.798
Sociology I	100	.522	.686
General College	100	.718	.836
Controlled sample of high school seniors	100	.689	.816
Controlled sample of employed	100	.717	.835
Controlled sample of unemployed	100	.620	.765
		60-Day Test--Retest Correlations	
		Male	
General College	70	.793	
		Female	
General College	70	.668	

*By the Spearman-Brown formula.

RELIABILITY

Do the 16 items yield satisfactory reliability? The split-half coefficients for the various subgroups and for the standard group as a whole are given in Table 96. The r's range from .673 for high school males to .854 for the controlled sample of unemployed males. The reliability for the group of 500 is approximately .80 for each sex. Considering the number of items in the scale, these coefficients are an encouraging indication of the value of the method. The fluctuation in the size of the coefficients is in good part owing to variations in the range of scores from group to group. Reference to Table 95 will show that the lowest reliability is obtained for those groups whose standard deviations are smallest. Computation of the standard error of estimate is an additional method of indicating reliability. Should they be similar for the various groups, it would be additional evidence that range is responsible for the fluctuation in the magnitude of the reliability coefficients.[3] The standard error of estimate of true score for the high school males is 4.06; for the controlled sample of unemployed men, 4.20 points. For 500 males, it is 3.88, and for 500 females, 3.96 points, on the basis of standard scores. The standard errors of estimate are very similar for the groups yielding the highest and the lowest reliability coefficients. Four-tenths of a standard deviation (for the standard group of 1,000) seems like a small error of estimate of true score. The range of standard scores of the standardizing group is from 16 to 89 points, or 7.3 standard deviations. The standard error of estimate is, therefore, approximately 6 per cent of the range.

When deviation of actual scores from test to retest is considered as a measure of reliability, similar results are obtained, Sixty days elapsed between test and retest, so the memory factor is not likely to be affecting this comparison decidedly. The average change for 68 General College men is 4.03; for 68 General College women, 5.03. Analysis of change by quartiles shows the characteristic regression phenomenon.

---

3. See Chapter V for additional ways of interpreting variation in the split-half reliability coefficient.

From highest to lowest quartiles the men change on the average -2.24, -.59, -.71, and +.24; women, -3.12, -.82, -.92, and +4.41. The average arithmetical change by quartiles for men is 4.12, 4.71, 4.12, and 4.88; for women, 8.06, 3.53, 3.29, and 5.24. The relatively large arithmetical change for women who make most unfavorable scores may mean that evasion is operative among the women who are least well adjusted. The fact that the most unfavorable quartile for women shows the largest average change may be, it should also be remembered, a consequence of change in the trait measured instead of an indication of the greater unreliability of the measure. These data, as well as the test-retest r's of .793 for men and .668 for women, indicate that the scale yields less stable measures for women. A conservative conclusion from these data is that the scale is quite satisfactory for group purposes, and that it will differentiate the extremes well enough for most practical purposes.

VALIDITY OF THE SCALE

The general adjustment scale may be validated by two general methods: (1) relating it to those outside variables that imply maladjustment and (2) relating it to scores on the other six scales. Relationships with outside·variables will first be considered

It will be recalled that over-ageness, separation of parents, home residence, being a farmer's son, status of father, status of mother, and certainty of maintaining or obtaining employment were the factors with which the six scales tended to vary as a unit. This was true for the most part only for men. These variables were, therefore, related to score on the general adjustment scale. Table 97 gives the relationship of this score to certainty of maintaining or obtaining employment. Those who are most uncertain almost invariably show the highest (most unfavorable) scores. The relationship is clearer for men than for women. The unemployed of the day classes and the part-time employed of the evening classes furnish exceptions to absolute consistency from <u>very certain</u> to <u>very uncertain</u>.

As was pointed out in the previous chapter, the part-time employed group may well be expected to deviate from the trend. These results are quite consistent with those in the previous chapter. If anything, they are clearer, and suggest that the general adjustment scale does contain items that are most influential in determining the behavior of the six scales as a unit.

TABLE 97.-GENERAL ADJUSTMENT SCORE AND CERTAINTY OF MAINTAINING OR OBTAINING EMPLOYMENT WITHIN A YEAR

(Single persons only.)

Certainty of Employment	Evening Classes								Day Classes	
	Employed Full Time		Employed Part Time		All Employed		Un-employed		Un-employed	
	Mean	N	Mean	N	Mean	N	Mean	N	Mean	N
Men:										
Very certain	47.39	41	57.50	4	48.29	45	46.00	2	51.63	8
Certain . . .	49.85	67	51.50	4	49.94	71	47.40	15	45.71	7
Uncertain . .	53.70	37	52.00	20	53.11	57	54.15	34	51.12	77
Very uncertain	55.67	6	62.09	11	59.82	17	60.50	18	61.20	20
Women:										
Very certain	48.29	63	47.20	6	48.21	69	50.22	9	49.86	6
Certain . . .	48.19	133	46.38	8	48.09	141	44.48	22	50.86	17
Uncertain . .	50.99	67	52.49	35	51.50	102	53.03	121	52.04	122
Very uncertain	53.81	31	52.13	14	53.26	45	52.96	56	51.90	36

In Tables 97 to 104 mean scores are presented in relation to those factors with which the six scales tended to vary as a unit--factors that are assumed to imply maladjustment. In general, the relationships noted in the last chapter are confirmed. In many instances they are more pronounced, a fact which argues strongly for the validity of the relationships uncovered in Chapter VII. The tendency for the relationships to be more pronounced among the unemployed groups is again present, as is the tendency of women's scores to be unrelated to many of the factors.

TABLE 98.—GENERAL ADJUSTMENT SCORE AND AGE

(Single men only.)*

	Evening Classes								Day Classes								
	Employed Full Time		Employed Part Time		Un-employed		All Cases		Unemployed			University Group			High School Seniors		
Age	Mean	N	Mean	N	Mean	N	Mean	N	Age	Mean	N	Age	Mean	N	Age	Mean	N
15-19	48.94	31	56.21	14	53.09	33	52.01	78	15-19	52.46	63	17-18	47.03	38	16	47.56	25
20-24	50.26	94	50.82	17	53.45	33	51.06	144	20-24	51.13	54	19-20	50.17	105	17	51.82	171
25-29	49.00	24	56.25	8	52.73	11	51.30	43	25-29	47.17	6	21-22	47.38	42	18	51.12	129
30-39	56.20	10	58.00	4	72.00	4	60.11	18	30-39	63.33	3	23-24	52.11	9	19	53.65	25
												25 and over	61.00	5	20 and over	54.40	5

*Data for women omitted, since no relationship is apparent between over-ageness and score. The mean standard score for 18 women over 40 in the evening and day classes was 51.0.

TABLE 99.-GENERAL ADJUSTMENT SCORE AND HOME RESIDENCE

(Single men only.)

Residence	Mean	N
	EVENING CLASSES	
	Employed Full Time	
At home	49.77	115
Not at home	52.13	32
	Employed Part Time	
At home	53.50	31
Not at home	59.20	8
	Unemployed	
At home	52.56	70
Not at home	66.86	7
	All Cases	
At home	51.23	216
Not at home	55.46	47
	UNIVERSITY GROUP	
At home	52.78	37
Not at home	53.39	18

*Date for women omitted for the reason that no relationship is evident. The mean score for 422 women in the evening class who were at home was 49.73; for 143 women not at home, it was 50.88.

TABLE 100.-GENERAL ADJUSTMENT SCORE AND NON-RESIDENCE AT HOME

(Single men, evening classes.)

Residence	Mean	N
Employed Full Time		
Non-farmers' sons not residing at home	49.72	18
Farmers' sons not residing at home	55.21	14
Employed Part Time		
Non-farmers' sons not residing at home	59.00	3
Farmers' sons not residing at home	59.50	4

TABLE 101.-GENERAL ADJUSTMENT SCORE AND SEPARATION OF PARENTS

Status of Parents	Evening Classes								Day Classes		University Group		High School Seniors	
	Employed Full Time		Employed Part Time		Unemployed		All Cases		Unemployed					
	Mean	N	Mean	N	Mean	N	Mean	N	Mean	N	Mean	N	Mean	N
Men:														
Together	50.23	106	54.70	27	53.07	55	51.75	188	51.86	100	49.34	139	51.38	266
Separated	58.33	3	60.00	1	59.00	3	58.86	7	44.33	4	52.57	8	49.50	16
Women:														
Together	48.17	179	52.98	43	52.20	153	51.40	375	51.81	165	48.25	158	49.67	281
Separated	49.82	12	52.00	2	55.92	12	52.92	26	53.83	12	49.80	5	55.13	16

TABLE 102.-GENERAL ADJUSTMENT SCORE AND STATUS OF FATHER

(Single persons only.)

Status of Father	Evening Classes								Day Classes		University Group		High School Seniors	
	Employed Full Time		Employed Part Time		Unemployed		All Cases		Unemployed					
	Mean	N	Mean	N	Mean	N	Mean	N	Mean	N	Mean	N	Mean	N
Men:														
Deceased	49.19	32	51.57	7	53.64	14	50.68	53	56.29	14	50.35	34	50.46	39
Retired	49.78	18	55.40	5	58.17	6	52.48	29	53.00	1	49.14	7	52.50	10
Employed	50.03	86	55.35	23	51.55	48	51.28	157	51.48	99	49.05	144	51.05	259
Unemployed	51.83	18	55.67	6	61.42	12	55.67	36	49.73	11	55.00	8	55.69	32
Women:														
Deceased	47.22	83	46.82	17	50.53	39	48.08	139	51.26	43	47.56	18	49.30	43
Retired	51.16	32	49.00	7	46.00	13	49.58	52	55.00	6	49.94	17	50.50	8
Employed	48.89	123	54.48	33	51.00	134	50.50	290	51.70	135	48.24	156	49.47	277
Unemployed	53.37	60	51.38	8	55.88	32	54.01	100	53.10	41	56.00	6	53.37	38

TABLE 103.-GENERAL ADJUSTMENT SCORES FOR FARMERS' CHILDREN

Employed Full Time		Evening Classes: Employed Part Time		Evening Classes: Unemployed		Evening Classes: All Cases		Day Classes: Unemployed		University Group		High School Seniors	
Mean	N	Mean	N	Mean	N	Mean	N	Mean	N	Mean	N	Mean	N
Men:													
53.67	18	59.20	5	63.00	2	55.22	25	45.00	3	53.12	8	52.00	4
Women:													
50.75	56	50.75	8	50.24	16	50.65	80	51.25	12	47.55	18	54.66	16

TABLE 104.-GENERAL ADJUSTMENT SCORE AND STATUS OF MOTHER

(Single persons only.)

Status of Mother	Evening Classes								Day Classes		University Group		High School Seniors	
	Employed Full Time		Employed Part Time		Unemployed		All Cases		Unemployed					
	Mean	N	Mean	N	Mean	N	Mean	N	Mean	N	Mean	N	Mean	N
Men														
Deceased	49.48	23	51.78	9	63.25	8	52.75	40	52.00	9	48.26	20	53.33	15
Housewife	50.20	119	55.45	31	53.69	64	51.84	214	51.58	109	49.76	153	51.57	276
Employed	50.90	10	53.50	1	47.50	7	49.63	18	54.40	6	48.44	18	49.05	43
Unemployed	46.00	2	41.00	1		..	44.33	3	53.00	1	56.00	2	57.17	6
Women:														
Deceased	50.42	55	52.64	11	47.46	28	49.80	94	52.54	13	50.88	16	49.09	22
Housewife	49.30	219	51.38	50	51.93	168	50.55	437	51.63	185	48.01	170	50.00	304
Employed	46.16	19	46.00	5	52.29	15	48.39	39	50.71	21	52.82	11	48.19	37
Unemployed	53.67	12	52.00	1	57.00	6	54.50	19	64.00	4	49.50	2	60.00	4

TABLE 105.—NUMBER OF UNFAVORABLE FACTORS FOR THE EXTREME ADJUSTMENT QUARTILES

(Evening class unemployed males; N = 80.)

Unfavorable Factor	Q_1 (N=20)	Q_4 (N=20)
1. Not at home	4	0
2. Parents separated	1	0
3. Father dead	3	4
4. Father unemployed	3	1
5. Father retired	2	0
6. Mother deceased	3	1
7. Rural[a]-urban migrant	1	0
8. Overage	3	0
Factors present	20	6
Individuals involved	11	5

The score on the adjustment scale varies with certainty of employment. (See Table 97.) The relationship between over-ageness and maladjustment is clearly evident for men in Table 98. The oldest age category in the various groups averages well over a standard deviation above the standard mean score. Non-home residence likewise shows a convincing relationship. (See Table 99.) The children of separated parents yield less favorable scores (see Table 101), as do those from homes where the father is unemployed. (See Table 102.). The relationship between unemployment of the father and unfavorable score is one of the few which holds for the women. That farmers' sons, even those who are employed, score less favorably is shown in Table 103. Table 104 reveals few wide departures from the standard mean associated with status of the mother. The mean score for unemployed men in the evening classes whose mothers are deceased (63.25) is the most striking. The scores of women whose mothers are unemployed are definitely more unfavorable than those of women whose mothers are housewives, are employed, or are deceased.

A further analysis in terms of quartiles on general adjustment scale score in relation to unfavorable face sheet factors is presented in Table 105.

Eighty unemployed men in the evening classes were separated into quartiles on the basis of adjustment scale score. For the 20 men in the most unfavorable quartile, Q_1, 20 unfavorable factors were reported, involving 11 individuals. In Q_4 only 6 unfavorable factors were reported, and these involved only 5 individuals. In other words, over half of the individuals in Q_1 reported one of the unfavorable factors to be present, while only one-fourth of the individuals in Q_4 so reported. Apparently Q_1 men are those who are placed in particularly unfavorable circumstances. The nine persons in Q_1 who did not report the presence of one of the unfavorable factors may well be those whose maladjustment is associated with other unfavorable factors than those inquired about on the face sheet.

The father being retired had seemed from the previous analysis to affect the scores more unfavorably than unemployment of the father. So far as the general scale is concerned, unemployment appears to be the more influential factor. The tendency of retirement of the father to be related to unfavorable score is, however, still apparent.

In general, the data point to the conclusion that certain specific factors were operative, in addition to the adjustment factor, in the relationships noted in the last chapter. The data in these tables help validate the adjustment scale and the method of construction. That items most heavily loaded for the general factor were selected by the method is indicated by the data in the tables.

While it does not provide good validating data for the scale, it is of interest to consider the relationship of the adjustment scale to honor point ratio, I.Q. and Bernreuter scores. These data, available only for the university high juniors, are presented in Table 106. Most of the correlations do not vary from zero sufficiently to be considered significant for a group of this size. The highest correlation of -.452 between favorable adjustment and the possession of neurotic tendencies points in the direction of validating the scale. The data imply that, even though the morale scale is most heavily loaded for the adjustment factor, the morale and adjustment scales measure different traits. For self-sufficiency correlates to the extent of +.510 with morale for men (Table 92), while it correlates only -.23 with favorable adjustment score for these same cases. The adjustment scale correlates better with neurotic tendencies than does any scale except the inferiority scale. (See Table 92.) The sex difference is more pronounced for the adjustment scale than for the inferiority scale.

TABLE 106.-GENERAL ADJUSTMENT SCORES CORRELATED WITH BERNREUTER SCORES, I.Q., AND HONOR POINTS*

(University High School juniors; N = 37 males, 34 females.)

General Adjustment Score Correlated with:	Male	Female
Bernreuter scores:		
B I N (neurotic tendencies)	-.452	-.184
B 2 S (self-sufficiency)	-.230	-.030
B 4 D (dominance-submission)	+.249	+.043
I.Q.	+.051	+.248
Honor point ratio	-.160	+.284

*Negative correlations indicate that neurotic tendencies and self-sufficiency are inversely associated with favorable adjustment scores.

It is also of interest to note the low correlation that exists between adjustment score and honor-point ratio, whereas the morale scale correlated +.506 for men. It will later be shown that this correlation is carried entirely by the positive items of the morale scale. Since the adjustment scale is a negative item scale, it is understandable why no correlation appears. Now if the findings for the university high school group can be confirmed on a larger group so that we may be sure that the results obtained are not due to chance or to a group idiosyncrasy, these relationships suggest that the positive items in the morale scale should be included with the adjustment scale to make the instrument of maximum value.[4]

4. See the Appendix for a short form which includes the adjustment scale.

As an additional means of validating the adjustment scale, the mean scores on the original six scales for the quartiles of the adjustment scale were tabulated. These are given in Table 107. If the adjustment scale is measuring a factor common to all scales, the scores for each should vary with the adjustment score. This is indeed the case. Only two exceptions to absolute consistency of trends occur within the four groups. Both occur on the economic conservatism scale. It should be noted, however, that in the individual case even a highly unfavorable score on the adjustment scale does not necessitate unfavorable scores on all six scales. Upon what scale a maladjusted individual will score most unfavorably depends on his own particular experience. An analysis of the relationship between the adjustment score and the other six scores may help to locate the personality area in which the greatest difficulty lies. Considered as a group, however, maladjusted persons have unfavorable scores on all the traits measured. As a matter of fact, 23 of the 25 men in the least favorable adjustment scale quartile for the controlled sample of unemployed men scored above the standard mean of 50 on four or more of the six scales. At the other extreme quartile, 21 of 25 men scored below the standard mean on four or more scales.

To bring out more clearly the differences in degree of relationship of each scale to the adjustment scale, the tabulation was reversed--the adjustment score was computed for the quartiles of each of the six scales. Table 108 is to be interpreted as follows: The highest (most unfavorable in score) quartile for men on the family scale gained a mean adjustment score of 56.36, the lowest quartile on the family scale gained an adjustment score of 45.28; when separated into quartiles on the basis of the education score, the highest quartile gained a mean adjustment score of 62.24, the lowest, 43.92.

One point is clear from an inspection of the two last mentioned tables. They show that the present data provide no exception to the dictum that favorable traits are correlated. They go further and suggest that the central factor responsible for this correlation

TABLE 107.-RELATIONSHIP OF THE SCALE OF GENERAL ADJUSTMENT TO THE SIX LESS GENERAL SCALES

(N = 25 in each quartile.)

Scale of General Adjustment	Mean Scores: General Adjustment	Morale	Inferiority	Family	Law	Economic Conservatism	Education
Controlled Sample of Unemployed Men							
Q_1 (highest)	68.48	61.96	54.92	57.12	58.12	60.44	55.80
Q_2	54.60	50.36	49.20	51.16	50.04	54.44	54.20
Q_3	47.00	47.68	48.36	48.80	46.68	50.96	48.08
Q_4 (lowest)	38.16	40.12	42.60	47.28	41.72	47.44	39.40
Q_1-Q_4 . . .	30.32	21.84	12.26	9.84	16.40	13.00	16.40
Controlled Sample of Unemployed Women							
Q_1	64.72	63.96	57.88	56.04	53.48	53.48	58.12
Q_2	55.88	55.80	54.64	52.36	49.04	51.16	53.80
Q_3	49.04	50.96	49.36	47.96	46.00	48.88	49.72
Q_4	39.52	42.20	45.24	47.16	43.20	47.28	44.68
Q_1-Q_4 . . .	25.20	21.76	12.64	8.88	10.28	6.20	13.44
General College Men							
Q_1	58.88	57.20	52.16	54.80	60.56	48.80	55.64
Q_2	51.84	48.96	51.08	51.44	52.32	51.48	51.28
Q_3	47.16	47.12	48.52	47.92	50.40	46.04	49.12
Q_4	37.04	41.28	41.28	43.08	45.92	40.60	43.56
Q_1-Q_4 . . .	21.84	15.92	10.88	11.72	14.64	8.20	12.08
General College Women							
Q_1	59.96	57.84	54.28	53.28	58.12	48.24	58.20
Q_2	50.84	50.28	51.20	52.52	52.56	49.52	53.12
Q_3	44.76	46.28	45.12	47.28	44.16	48.12	45.88
Q_4	36.12	39.20	43.24	40.24	42.52	45.32	43.88
Q_1-Q_4 . . .	23.84	18.64	11.04	13.04	15.60	2.92	14.30

TABLE 108.-GENERAL ADJUSTMENT SCORES BY QUARTILES OF THE OTHER SIX SCALES

(Controlled sample of unemployed; N=25 in each quartile.)

Quartile	General Adjustment Score For:					
	Morale	Inferi-ority	Family	Law	Economic Conserv-atism	Educa-tion
Men:						
Q_1	66.24	59.92	56.36	60.88	59.68	62.24
Q_2	52.60	53.24	55.84	56.12	53.24	54.48
Q_3	47.96	52.04	50.72	47.88	50.72	47.16
Q_4	41.44	43.04	45.28	43.36	44.96	43.92
Q_1-Q_4 . . .	24.80	16.88	11.08	17.52	14.72	18.32
Women:						
Q_1	61.84	59.64	56.68	58.44	55.60	59.76
Q_2	55.52	51.96	54.16	53.88	54.12	53.56
Q_3	51.04	52.20	51.92	49.32	51.52	51.48
Q_4	40.80	45.36	46.32	47.52	47.44	43.80
Q_1-Q_4 . . .	21.04	14.28	10.36	10.92	8.16	15.96

so far as personality scales are concerned is the general adjustment of the individual.

Utilizing the Q_1 minus Q_4 differences in Table 107 as a measure of the degree of relationship that exists between a single scale and the general adjustment scale, the scales arrange themselves in the following order when tabulated in terms of the adjustment quartiles (the largest difference is given the rank of 1, Table 107):

	Controlled Sample of Unemployed		General College Group	
	Men	Women	Men	Women
1.	Morale	Morale	Morale	Morale
2.	Education	Education	Law	Law
3.	Law	Inferiority	Education	Education
4.	Economic conservatism	Law	Family	Family
5.	Inferiority	Family	Inferiority	Inferiority
6.	Family	Economic conservatism	Economic conservatism	Economic conservatism

The general order of degree of relationship to the adjustment score does not exactly follow the order expected on the basis of the number of items contributed to the adjustment scale. The morale scale contributed 7 items to the adjustment scale and invariably shows the largest Q_1 minus Q_4 difference. The education scale, which contributed 3 items, is always among the first three scales in the magnitude of the Q_1 minus Q_4 difference in relation to adjustment quartiles. The inferiority and economic conservatism scales, which contribute 2 items each, and the law and family scales, which contribute one item, do not arrange themselves according to the number of items they contributed. The economic conservatism scale is the most notable exception. In 3 of 4 comparisons it is the scale that is least related to the adjustment scale. It ranks fourth for the controlled sample of unemployed men; the common-sense interpretation is that discontent with the prevailing economic order (radicalism) is more closely related to the adjustment of men when unemployed.

The only sex difference that is consistent for both groups occurs on the economic conservatism scale. Economic matters seem to affect the adjustment of women less than that of men. It should be remembered, however, that unemployment of parents affects women's adjustment, and in particular that unemployment of the mother is a significant factor.

The absence of conspicuous sex differences here implies that the adjustment scale is at least partially valid for women. This point will be considered in detail in a later chapter.

SUMMARY

The construction of a scale for which there is evidence to warrant the name general adjustment scale has been described in this chapter. This scale was constructed on the basis of male responses, and found to be at least partially valid for women. In addition to being valid from a logical standpoint, the scale validated itself against scores on the six original scales and by relating itself to those variables with which the six scales tended to vary as a unit. The sex differences with respect to the relation of the adjustment scale to these outside factors seem to mean that the variables on the face sheet are not highly significant for women's adjustment or that the general adjustment items are not sufficiently diagnostic of adjustment for women.

A feature of the method used in the construction of this scale is its completely inductive character. The concept that it is measuring adjustment was derived primarily from the data. The method selected items that are not likely to be grouped together on a priori grounds, and the data go a long way toward validating the scale. They also indicate that favorable personality scores are correlated because each is related to the general adjustment of the individual.

Group differences in the applicability of individual items were again striking and serve to emphasize the conclusion previously drawn that, to insure general significance of the items and to secure adequate group comparisons, items should be selected on the basis of their ability to discriminate well in dissimilar groups. The difficulty in obtaining items for a scale that are specific in their implications for the individual, a point also noted earlier, is again illustrated by the number of items that discriminate in the adjustment scale. A problem of particular importance has been brought into focus by the fact that the items selected for the adjustment scale are predominately negative in form of statement. This problem will be considered next.

Chapter IX

THE SIGNIFICANCE OF THE FORM OF STATEMENT

Smith (16) in a study designed to evaluate positively and negatively stated inferiority statements, paired positive and negative statements for content and found that the greatest differences existed between the two types when each was administered separately. When both types were arranged at random within a single form, these differences were reduced.

On the basis of this finding, 11 items of each type were retained in each of the present scales. During our analysis, differences between positive and negative statements appeared so persistently that a reexamination of the problem was necessary, particularly since Smith's analysis left unanswered so many questions that concern differences between the two types of item when administered in a single form.

The full import of the differences did not become clear until late in the study, after much statistical work had been completed. Had the findings here presented been available, the analyses would often have been different.

Since the limits of the study precluded a complete analysis of the problem of differences yielded by the two types of item, the authors' aim has been to determine general trends by the use of the simplest statistical procedures. Exceptions for single scales and groups are only incidentally considered. Because of the fundamental significance of the results for personality measurement, it seems better to make available the general findings of this study rather than to delay publication for a more exhaustive analysis which the present authors could not undertake at this time.

REDEFINITION OF THE TERMS "POSITIVE" AND "NEGATIVE"

Smith's (16, page 33) closest approach to a definition is as follows: "The connotation of the positive items was predominately one of personality asset, that of the negative items predominately one of personality liability." He illustrates with a typical pair of his items: feels he's succeeded at most everything he ever tried and feels he's failed at most everything he ever tried. The first item is positively, the second negatively, stated. One point is immediately clear from an inspection of these items. The terms positive and negative are not used in their grammatical sense. The verb of the negatively stated item is not negative. This leads to confusion of thought. In discussing these data with others the authors have constantly encountered this confusion. Nearly everyone interpreted the terms positive and negative in their grammatical sense. For this reason and because the terms are not descriptive of the essential difference between the two types of items, it is suggested that their use be discontinued.

What is the essèntial difference between the two statements used by Smith as his illustrative definition? This difference is definitely implied by Smith's statements, but the use of the phrases agree and disagree in the present study makes the discussion of the present scales more understandable. Consider first how the scoring weights were assigned to all items of the six scales. The five phrases, constituting the scale of agreement and disagreement with each item were so weighted that a low score implied the possession of the favorable aspect of the trait; while a high score implied the possession of the unfavorable aspect. Favorable and unfavorable, however, have meaning solely as they refer to some standard. In this case the standard is general social approval on the part of the standardizing group. Low numerical weights were consistently assigned to that response which, in the authors' opinion, implied the possession of the socially desirable aspect of the trait. The objective test of internal consistency, earlier described, demonstrated that complete consistency existed in these decisions as to which extreme response to items should be given the highest or the lowest weight. It is almost self-evident that high morale, scarcity of inferiority feelings, lack of antagonistic attitude toward the family, respect for law, economic conservatism, and an appreciation of the value of education are the ends of the traits presumed to be measured here that will command general social approval.

Certain evidence is available to suggest that these are the aspects of the traits measured which do command social approval. The phrases strongly agree, agree, undecided, disagree, and strongly disagree which constitute the scale for the individual item imply a definite position with respect to the trait, apart from their relative position in the actually obtained series of scores. Weights of 1, 2, 3, 4, and 5 were assigned to the phrases in such a way that the low scores represent the aspect of the trait which the authors considered socially approved. While it is not certain whether a mean that represents the uhdecided position can be considered to indicate that the trait has no socially approved aspect, means deviating toward 2 or 4 will indicate whether a definite position is taken by the group as a whole on any trait or traits. The average item means for the standardization group of 1,000 follow:

Morale	2.59
Inferiority	3.00
Family	2.54
Law	2.68
Economic conservatism	3.04
Education	2.16
General adjustment	2.56

The tendency for the group as a whole to deviate from the undecided position of 3 toward the end of the scales the authors have termed socially approved is unmistakable. Five of the seven means are well below 3. Our contention is strengthened by the fact that the mean for the education scale is the lowest, for the virtues of education have been emphasized constantly with scarcely a dissenting voice.

A redefinition of positive and negative items in terms of the socially approved and socially disapproved aspects of the trait points to the essential difference between the two types of item. Positive items have, in fact, been defined earlier in this study as those items to which agreement implied the possession of the favorable aspect of the trait.

This reasoning points to the essential difference between positive and negative items: positive items are those stated in conformity with socially accepted views; negative items are those stated in opposition to socially accepted views.

If this argument is sound, negative items should yield lower mean scores than positive, and the group as a whole should deviate more toward the favorable aspect of the trait on negative than on positive items. In general this is the case. In four of the six scales for men and five of the six for women, negative items yield lower mean scores. The mean scores are given in Tables 115 and 116, where they are discussed in greater detail.

Socially acceptable and socially unacceptable, then, are the terms that actually describe the difference between the two types of item. Their use will avoid the confusion of thought resulting from the grammatical implications of the terms positive and negative. For these reasons socially acceptable and socially unacceptable will be used in the following discussions, rather than positive and negative.[1] For brevity acceptable and unacceptable will be used alone.

THE IMPORTANCE OF THE FORM OF STATEMENT

The fundamental importance of the form of statement is plain from Table 109, which gives the interrelations of the six scales when either or both types of items are scored. Striking differences exist which do not disappear when the coefficients are corrected for attenuation, the magnitude of the

1. The terms favorable and unfavorable are alternative terms which may be more suitable in some research.

relationships between any two scales depending to a considerable degree upon which type of item is scored. To illustrate, the inferiority-family relationship may be expressed by coefficients ranging from +.401 to -.046. Certain trends are evident from this table and will be referred to later. Here it is only necessary to note the wide range in the degree of relationship between two scales, a relationship that is markedly influenced by the type of item scored. Factor analyses based on total scores of several scales are certainly hazardous. For, with the present state of knowledge, who can say which of these coefficients represents the true relationship between any two of these scales? If the method of factor analysis is to be applied to personality data, it would seem best to apply it to the items and not to total score, at least until it can be determined which total score is the most valid--one based solely on either type of item or one based on the sum of an equal number of both types.

It is apparent, too, that correlations between personality scales need to be interpreted with care, if they can be interpreted at all, until we come to a greater understanding of the nature of the items of the scales themselves.

THE SCALE OF GENERAL ADJUSTMENT IN ITS RELATION TO THE PROBLEM OF ACCEPTABLE AND UNACCEPTABLE ITEMS

The most significant finding with respect to the problem of acceptable and unacceptable items is that the items that emerged as the best measures of general adjustment were predominately unacceptable. Although each type of item was equally represented--there were 66 of each--14 of the 16 adjustment items are unacceptably stated. That the preponderance of unacceptable items meeting the criterion of the adjustment scale is not due solely to the ideational content of these items but is a result of their form of statement is shown by the fact that the 66 unacceptable items as a group discriminate better in the adjustment scale than do the 66 acceptable ones. In Table 110 two trends are

TABLE 109.-INTERCORRELATIONS OF VARIOUS TYPES BETWEEN SCALES

(Controlled sample of unemployed men; N = 100)

Scales Correlated	r(1)* +vs.+	r(2)* -vs.-	r(3)* +vs.-	r(4)* -vs.+	r(5)* T.vs.T.
Morale—Inferiority	.568	.500	.331	.159	.537
Morale—Family	.319	.426	.198	.128	.368
Morale—Law	.491	.593	.325	.346	.582
Morale—Economic conservatism	.236	.400	.091	.194	.330
Morale—Education	.245	.585	.294	.383	.502
Inferiority—Family	.118	.401	.117	-.046	.212
Inferiority—Law	.094	.354	-.156	.048	.113
Inferiority—Economic conservatism	.113	.382	-.010	-.004	.183
Inferiority—Education . . .	.053	.295	-.061	.095	.148
Family—Law	.310	.286	.159	.191	.336
Family—Economic conservatism	.045	.294	-.011	.062	.110
Family—Education	.222	.178	.158	.126	.259
Law—Economic conservatism .	.344	.322	.241	.014	.328
Law—Education	.333	.450	.234	.263	.403
Economic conservatism—education	.156	.219	-.040	.084	.132

*r(1) Scores on acceptable items in first scale against scores on acceptable items in second.

r(2) Scores on unacceptable items in first scale against scores on unacceptable items in second.

r(3) Scores on acceptable items in first scale against scores on unacceptable items in second.

r(4) Scores on unacceptable items in first scale against scores on acceptable items in second.

r(5) Total scores on first scale against total scores on second scale.

conspicuous. There is a group difference with which we are not concerned here. The most significant finding is the tendency for the unacceptable items to be more frequent throughout the upper range of discriminative values and not only above 1.00, the critical level used in the selection of the 16 adjustment items. This tendency is more pronounced for the controlled sample of unemployed. In fact, the item yielding the greatest discriminative value for the Sociology I group is acceptably stated. The trend for this group reverses quickly to conform to that of the controlled sample of unemployed, since for discriminative values of 1.20 or better there are 10 unacceptable items and 7 acceptable ones. For the controlled sample of unemployed there are 33 acceptable and 56 unacceptable items discriminating .60 or better, whereas for the Sociology I group at this discriminative level there are 44 acceptable and 52 unacceptable items. These results definitely indicate that the preponderance of unacceptable items in the adjustment scale is in good part a function of the form of statement and is not attributable solely to the ideational content, a problem that was raised in the last chapter.

TABLE 110.-CUMULATIVE FREQUENCY FOR ACCEPTABLE (A.) AND UNACCEPTABLE (U.) STATEMENTS AT VARIOUS LEVELS OF DISCRIMINATIVE VALUE IN THE GENERAL ADJUSTMENT SCALE

(N = 100 in each group.)

Discriminative Value	Controlled Sample of Unemployed		Sociology I	
	A.	U.	A.	U.
1.80 - 1.99 . .	0	1	1	0
1.60 - 1.79 . .	1	2	1	0
1.40 - 1.59 . .	1	3	3	3
1.20 - 1.39 . .	4	13	7	10
1.00 - 1.19 . .	8	27	14	21
.80 - .99 . .	13	43	35	38
.60 - .79 . .	33	56	44	52
.40 - .59 . .	46	61	50	61
.20 - .39 . .	58	65	58	63
.0 - .19 . .	62	66	64	66
Less than 0 . .	66	66	66	66

In itself the preponderance of unacceptable items in the adjustment scale strongly suggests that such items are more generalized in their significance for the individual. This does not necessarily imply that they are more generalized in their logical meaning.

A second line of evidence indicating the greater generality of unacceptable items is found in Table 109, which shows that the unacceptable items of the six scales intercorrelate more highly than do the scores on the acceptable items. The average of the 15 correlations between acceptable items is .243; of the correlations between unacceptable items, .379. If all the r's in Table 109 are corrected for attenuation, the average becomes .368 for acceptable and .518 for unacceptable items. Controlling the factor of reliability statistically actually enhances the difference.

A third fact that points to the greater generality of unacceptable items is the close relation of the morale and adjustment scales. For the morale scale has been shown in terms of intercorrelation to be the most generalized of the six original scales of the survey.

A fourth and probably the most convincing line of evidence for the greater generality of unacceptable items is at hand. Since the adjustment scale is virtually an unacceptable-item scale, on the basis of the argument, it should be more closely related to the remaining unacceptable than to the acceptable items. Table 111, in which the two types of item are independently related to the adjustment scale, shows that this is indeed the case.

The difference on acceptable items between the extreme adjustment quartiles is less than one-half that on the unacceptable items for the 66 items combined, and the unacceptable items of each scale also show a more consistent association with the unacceptable-item adjustment scale throughout its range. For the single scales unacceptable item scores show no reversal of the trend to become greater as the adjustment score increases, whereas the direction of the trend reverses on several scales for acceptable item quartiles 2 and 3. Acceptable items do, in every case, however, show differences between the extreme adjustment quartiles. This difference is consistently small for the economic conservatism scale. Table 112, which gives similar data for a group of 52 men who were receiving public relief amply confirms the trends discussed. Again the economic conservatism acceptable-item scores

TABLE 111.-RELATIONSHIP OF THE ADJUSTMENT SCALE TO TOTAL ACCEPTABLE AND TOTAL UNACCEPTABLE SCORE ON ALL SCALES

(N = 100 in each group, 25 in each quartile.)

General Adjustment Quartiles	General Adjustment#	Mean Unacceptable Scores§							Mean Acceptable Scores§						
		Morale	Inferiority	Family	Law	Economic Conservatism	Education	Total	Morale	Inferiority	Family	Law	Economic Conservatism	Education	Total
Controlled Sample of Unemployed Men															
Q_1	68.48	35.56	36.96	37.48	34.04	40.64	28.96	213.64	33.24	33.92	26.52	32.20	36.68	24.48	187.04
Q_2	54.60	28.24	33.28	31.48	30.04	36.60	26.32	185.96	28.72	32.28	26.92	28.56	35.80	24.64	176.92
Q_3	47.00	25.64	30.08	30.16	26.92	33.44	23.16	169.40	29.28	34.32	24.92	28.32	34.82	22.96	174.62
Q_4	38.16	21.52	28.20	28.60	25.20	30.84	19.28	153.64	26.36	30.64	24.64	25.92	33.76	18.12	159.44
Q_1-Q_4		14.04	8.76	8.88	8.84	9.80	9.68	60.76	6.88	3.28	1.88	6.28	2.92	6.36	27.60
Controlled Sample of Unemployed Women															
Q_1	64.72	34.44	37.96	34.44	31.04	36.68	29.40	203.96	35.80	36.28	29.12	30.96	35.12	25.92	193.20
Q_2	55.88	31.20	35.44	32.60	28.52	34.04	26.76	188.56	31.72	34.68	26.28	29.56	32.80	24.56	179.60
Q_3	49.04	27.68	32.00	29.04	28.16	33.20	23.64	173.72	30.36	33.72	25.60	26.96	32.76	23.60	173.00
Q_4	39.52	21.44	29.84	27.48	24.64	29.76	19.76	152.92	28.48	31.64	25.80	27.84	34.68	22.68	171.12
Q_1-Q_4		13.00	8.12	6.96	6.40	6.92	9.64	51.04	7.32	4.64	3.32	3.12	0.44	3.24	22.08
General College Men															
Q_1	58.88	30.76	34.16	33.80	34.36	33.24	28.08	194.40	33.40	33.76	27.16	33.84	33.36	25.36	186.88
Q_2	51.84	25.88	33.16	31.16	30.24	33.08	23.80	177.32	30.44	34.52	26.28	31.24	35.64	23.08	181.20
Q_3	47.16	24.64	31.44	29.36	28.40	30.08	23.40	167.32	29.48	32.24	25.80	29.88	32.28	24.56	174.24
Q_4	37.04	20.36	26.32	24.16	25.68	25.68	19.72	141.92	28.60	32.24	24.52	30.00	32.28	21.36	169.00
Q_1-Q_4		10.40	7.84	9.64	8.68	7.56	8.36	52.48	4.80	1.52	2.64	3.84	1.08	4.00	17.88
General College Women															
Q_1	59.96	31.20	35.08	31.84	33.92	32.44	27.28	191.76	34.08	35.04	28.72	32.32	33.04	27.72	190.92
Q_2	50.84	26.36	32.48	30.24	29.44	32.56	25.16	176.24	30.72	34.64	27.96	31.48	34.20	26.16	185.16
Q_3	44.76	23.32	29.28	27.04	26.76	31.32	21.32	159.04	29.52	32.28	26.92	27.32	33.20	21.48	170.72
Q_4	36.12	19.56	27.16	22.00	24.12	29.56	20.08	142.48	28.04	31.96	24.16	27.28	32.60	21.84	165.88
Q_1-Q_4		11.64	7.92	9.84	9.80	2.88	7.20	49.28	6.04	3.08	4.56	5.04	0.44	5.88	25.04

#Standard score.
§Acceptable and unacceptable scores are in arbitrary units.

are among those that show only a slight relationship to the adjustment scale. For this group the scores on the acceptable items of the family scale actually tend to discriminate in the reverse direction. Again we note that acceptable-item scores are generally not completely unrelated to the unacceptable-item adjustment scale. Those for the morale and law scales show relationships of considerable strength. Thus both the nature of the group and the kind of scale are factors causing variation in the tendency for unacceptable items to be more generalized in their significance than acceptable ones. In other words, the ideational content plays some part. From Tables 111 and 112 the consistently close relation of acceptable morale items to the adjustment scale may be observed. The more generalized nature of the morale statements and the contribution this makes to the argument that unacceptable items are more generalized in their significance has already been noted.

TABLE 112.-RELATIONSHIP OF THE ADJUSTMENT SCALE TO TOTAL ACCEPTABLE AND TOTAL UNACCEPTABLE SCORES ON ALL SCALES

(Public relief group; N = 52.)

General Adjustment Quartiles	Morale	Inferiority	Family	Law	Economic Conservatism	Education	Total
			Mean Unacceptable Scores				
Q_1 (highest)	38.38	36.46	34.77	38.00	45.31	34.70	227.62
Q_2	34.00	34.31	32.54	31.31	41.54	27.08	200.78
Q_3	27.31	30.08	30.92	29.69	38.62	24.15	180.77
Q_4	21.31	27.54	25.77	25.15	34.31	19.46	153.54
Q_1-Q_4 . . .	17.07	8.92	9.00	12.85	11.00	15.24	74.08
			Mean Acceptable Scores				
Q_1	33.54	31.85	21.23	34.31	38.15	26.08	185.16
Q_2	32.00	28.69	21.92	29.15	35.92	23.92	171.60
Q_3	31.92	31.54	24.38	30.15	37.00	23.00	177.99
Q_4	23.85	28.15	21.69	23.77	35.62	22.77	155.85
Q_1-Q_4 . . .	9.69	3.70	0.46*	10.54	2.53	3.31	29.31

*Difference in the reverse direction, i.e., Q_4 has a higher score than Q_1.

It is of interest to compare the adjustment quartile differences between the two types of item for the three male groups discussed here. The means and standard deviations on the adjustment scale and the differences between extreme adjustment quartiles on acceptable and unacceptable items follow:

Group	Adjustment Score		Adjustment Quartiles	
	Mean	σ	Q_1-Q_4 Acceptable Items	Q_1-Q_4 Unacceptable Items
General College (N=100)	48.73	8.93	17.88	52.48
Controlled sample of Unemployed (N=100) . . .	52.06	11.90	27.60	60.76
Public relief group (N=52)	57.98	13.47	29.77	74.08

The characteristically closer relation of the unacceptable items to the adjustment scale is striking. In every case the difference between the adjustment quartiles for unacceptable items is more than twice that for acceptable items. Since the standard deviations of the unacceptable-item adjustment scale increase from group to group, it is reasonable that the differences between the extreme adjustment quartiles for unacceptable items will also increase. It is evident, too, that while the Q_1-Q_4 differences increase for acceptable items, their relationship to the unacceptable-item adjustment scale is considerably more tenuous than is the relationship for unacceptable items.

It may be objected that these differences are spurious because the 14 unacceptable items in the adjustment scale are included in the unacceptable item scores of the single scales. A moment's consideration will show that this factor is negligible. The family scale, which contributes only one item to the adjustment scale, shows the characteristic relationship as well as scales contributing more items. Even more convincing is the size of the difference between the extreme adjustment quartiles. The maximum difference obtainable on any single item is 4 (5-1). There are 14 unacceptable items in the adjustment scale, giving a maximum difference of 56 points that could be accounted for on the basis of these 14 items. The difference for the public relief group is 74.08. Further, the maximum theoretical difference between extreme adjustment quartiles is not found for this group. The actual total difference between the extreme adjustment quartiles on these 14 items is 23.62 points as compared with the difference of 74.08 actually found. To summarize:

1. Unacceptable items predominate in the adjustment scale.
2. Unacceptable items as a group discriminate better in the adjustment scale than do acceptable items.
3. The morale scale, known to be the most general of the six original scales, is most closely related to the predominately unacceptable-item adjustment scale.
4. Unacceptable-item scores of the scales intercorrelate more highly than do acceptable-item scores.
5. Unacceptable items as a group are more closely related to the adjustment scale than are acceptable items.

All these facts point to the greater generality in significance to the individual of unacceptable items as one of the most characteristic and profound differences between the two types of statement. With this understanding it is profitable to consider other differences in the results yielded by the two types of item.

FURTHER DIFFERENCES ATTRIBUTABLE TO THE FORM OF STATEMENT

How universal are the findings with respect to form of statement? An answer to this question can only come from the analysis of the many personality scales containing both types of statement. Smith's study, however, shows that the differences noted for the six scales considered here are not confined solely to them.

His study is of importance not only because it supplements the findings of the present study but also because he was the first to investigate specifically the influence of form of statement and suggest its importance. He used a three-point scale for each item, the individual indicating whether he possessed the feelings implied by the frequently, occasionally, or rarely --which responses were respectively termed the F, O, and R responses. The previously quoted pair of Smith's items may again be considered: feels he's failed at most everything he ever tried, and feels he's succeeded at most everything he ever tried. The first item is unacceptably stated and the F response indicates the possession of inferiority feelings, whereas the second item is acceptably stated and the R response implies the possession of such feelings. An F response to the first of the above items then, is comparable with the strongly agree response to unacceptable items in the present study, and his R response to the second is similar to the strongly disagree response to acceptable items.

During the course of his study Smith developed three forms of an inventory for the measurement of inferiority feelings, two preliminary forms and a final form. One of the preliminary forms (Form P) contained 284 acceptably stated items, the other (Form N), 284 unacceptably stated items. Each acceptable item was paired with an unacceptable, as in the example given, and an effort was made to state the essential content of the item both acceptably and unacceptably. The final form of the inventory (Form PN) contains 100 items of each type, arranged, except for slight modifications, at random.

Smith's study differs from the present one in an important respect. It was his intention to investigate specifically the influence of form of statement. Hence he attempted to state the same idea both positively and negatively or, to use our terms, acceptably and unacceptably. At the outset of the present study the effect and significance of form of statement was not considered a major purpose of the investigation. The items were not paired for content. If the results are consistent from study to study, they have more significance than if the two studies had not differed in this respect; for if differences appear both when the items are paired for content and when they are not, form of statement must be an exceedingly important factor. Concerning the possibility that differences in content might account for the differences found, Smith comments as follows (16, page 51):

> Even assuming there was no attempt at pairing at all [as was the case in the present study] if one accepts each set of items as a reasonably valid and random sampling of indices of inferiority, one would scarcely expect the same number of items, scored by exactly the same weights, to produce such large significant differences except as those differences were due to a general difference in the emotional attitude created in the subject by the two kinds of items. By the operation of the laws of chance, responses to two randomly selected groups of indices of the same condition should give approximately the same means and standard deviations. It seems to the writer, therefore, that the basic factor operating here is not differences in pairing even if one were to assume for the moment that those differences were large, but rather basic differences in the type of emotional response called forth.

Ignoring for the moment the problem of whether socially approved and socially disapproved items are measuring the same trait, it seems unreasonable that the specific ideational content of the 66 negative items is sufficiently different from that of the 66 positive items to account for the consistent differences noted in Smith's study or in the present scales. Acceptable and unacceptable items of each scale are identified in Chapter I. The authors can detect no differences in intensity of statement or any other difference running through the six scales.

Smith's data are conclusive in demonstrating that the two types of item elicit markedly different reactions when forms containing but a single type are administered. These differences are minimized but do not disappear when the two types of item, arranged at random, are administered in a single scale. Smith did not appreciate the significance of the lesser differences which persist when both types are administered in a single form; neither did the authors until certain facts emerged from the present study. Smith's most general conclusion is that positive items are to be preferred as a research technique on practically every count (page 103). As will be seen this conclusion is not warranted, even from his own data.

THE ITEM DISTRIBUTIONS

The item distributions of Smith's Form P and Form N differ markedly, the unacceptably stated items eliciting responses that tend to concentrate at the "favorable" end of the scale. The percentage distribution (based on more than 284,000 responses, i.e., responses to 284 items by more than 1,000 persons) are as follows:

Response:	R	O	F
Form N . . .	56	33	11
Form P . . .	23	46	31

The tendency for responses to unacceptable items to pile up at the favorable end of the distribution is clear, as is the greater skewness of the distribution derived from unacceptable items.

Smith does not present the distributions of the two types of item when administered in a single form. Considering his other evidence that differences become less under these circumstances, the present data are consistent. Tables 113 and 114 summarize the distribution of the two types of items for the six scales here studied. Unacceptable items do tend to show distributions of response more heavily weighted at the 1 and 2 responses (the favorable end of the scale) than do socially acceptable items. The differences are not as large as those reported by Smith for the two types of items administered singly, but they are in the same direction. The family scale is the only striking exception to the trend for socially unacceptable items to yield more 1 and 2 responses and fewer 4 and 5. The

TABLE 113.-PERCENTAGE AT EACH RESPONSE POSITION FOR ACCEPTABLE AND UNACCEPTABLE ITEMS OF EACH SCALE

(Standard group; percentages based on 5,500 responses.)*

Response	Morale	Inferi-ority	Family	Law	Economic Conserv-atism	Educa-tion
			MEN			
			Unacceptable Items			
1. Strongly disagree	18.64	6.00	9.07	14.15	9.09	24.91
2. Disagree	47.44	40.07	42.24	39.13	30.00	48.33
3. Undecided . . .	13.40	15.95	15.93	19.80	23.05	13.04
4. Agree	16.04	33.69	27.49	21.38	26.91	10.98
5. Strongly agree .	4.49	4.29	5.27	5.55	10.95	2.75
Total	100.01	100.00	100.00	100.01	100.00	100.01
			Acceptable Items			
1. Strongly agree .	10.56	5.82	16.65	8.85	6.20	25.53
2. Agree	41.09	33.91	52.00	43.76	26.49	50.16
3. Undecided . . .	19.35	16.55	15.24	18.54	25.91	9.95
4. Disagree	23.55	39.53	13.87	22.00	30.49	11.05
5. Strongly disagree	5.45	4.20	2.24	6.34	10.91	3.31
Total	100.00	100.01	100.00	99.99	100.01	100.00
			WOMEN			
			Unacceptable Items			
1. Strongly disagree	18.75	6.58	11.05	14.58	6.95	26.62
2. Disagree	45.29	38.73	43.80	39.22	27.78	49.05
3. Undecided . . .	13.15	12.42	13.75	22.84	31.40	12.05
4. Agree	18.58	36.18	25.76	19.71	26.22	9.75
5. Strongly agree .	4.24	6.09	5.64	3.65	7.65	2.53
Total	100.01	100.00	100.00	100.00	100.00	100.00
			Acceptable Items			
1. Strongly agree .	8.71	5.51	16.87	10.80	4.02	28.27
2. Agree	37.33	30.65	45.87	39.98	22.18	45.98
3. Undecided . . .	21.91	14.22	15.76	22.83	38.69	10.35
4. Disagree	26.33	42.87	19.04	20.56	27.85	12.67
5. Strongly disagree	5.73	6.75	2.45	5.82	7.25	2.73
Total	100.01	100.00	99.99	99.99	99.99	100.00

*5500 = 11 times 500 individuals.

TABLE 114.-PERCENTAGE AT THE 1 AND 2 AND THE 4 AND 5 POSITIONS FOR ACCEPTABLE AND UNACCEPTABLE ITEMS OF EACH SCALE

(Percentages based on 5500 responses.)

Scale	Positions 1 and 2		Positions 4 and 5	
	Acceptable Items	Unacceptable Items	Acceptable Items	Unacceptable Items
Men:				
Morale	51.65	66.08	29.00	20.53
Inferiority	39.73	46.07	43.73	49.68
Family	68.65	51.31	16.11	32.76
Law	52.61	53.28	28.84	26.93
Economic conservatism .	32.69	39.09	41.40	37.86
Education	75.69	73.24	14.36	13.73
Women:				
Morale	46.04	64.04	32.06	22.82
Inferiority	36.16	45.31	49.62	48.60
Family	62.74	54.85	21.49	31.40
Law	50.78	53.80	26.38	23.36
Economic conservatism .	26.20	34.73	35.10	33.87
Education	74.25	75.67	15.40	12.28

general tendency, so far as five of the scales are concerned, is for the socially unacceptable items to yield distributions weighted at the favorable end. That the family scale is so striking an exception shows that the differences between stating an item in its socially approved form and in the socially disapproved form need to be evaluated for each scale separately. For the nature of the trait measured can make a considerable difference in the reaction to the two types of items contained in the scale. The meaning of the reversal in trend for the family scale is not clear. The general tendency for socially unacceptable items to yield distributions skewed toward the favorable end is evident and consistent with Smith's findings.

Smith, in commenting on his finding, says (page 41)."It is apparent that the Form N (socially unacceptable) items make much poorer use of the three degrees of response than do the Form P items, and consequently are much less discriminating as measuring elements." This certainly does not follow. While use of all scale positions may increase the utility of an item which is valid, no conclusion concerning the discriminating power of an item as a measuring element can be drawn from its gross distribution. The test of the discriminating power of an item lies wholly in the success with which it meets whatever criterion of validity is used in a particular study. This point will be further considered when the criterion of validity used in the two studies is discussed.

MEAN SCORES BASED ON THE TWO TYPES OF ITEM

A corollary of the above finding is that the means of socially unacceptable items are lower than those based on socially acceptable items. Smith's general finding on this count may be illustrated by the means of his Form P and Form N, when one was given before the comparable form of the other type. Form P yielded a mean of 534.83 (N = 514) and Form N one of 443.66 (N = 490). The differences between these means is 19.07 times its standard error. Again the present data are consistent (see Tables 115 and 116) and illustrate the tendency for differences between the two types of item to be reduced when both are administered in the same form. Again scale exceptions are evident. Smith does not present the means for the two types of item when administered in a single form, so direct comparisons cannot be made.

For men, four of the means for socially unacceptable items are smaller; for women, five. (See Table 115.) Since there is a correlation between acceptable and unacceptable items, the significance of the difference between the means in Table 115 cannot be computed, as correlations for the total groups are not available. The correlations between acceptable and unacceptable items were computed for the 70 General College men and women for whom retest scores are available. In Table 116 the means and standard deviations for this group are presented. A comparison of Tables 115 and

TABLE 115.-MEANS AND STANDARD DEVIATIONS FOR ACCEPTABLE AND UNACCEPTABLE ITEMS FOR THE COMPLETE STANDARDIZING GROUP

(N = 500 of each sex.)

Scale	Male				Female			
	Acceptable		Unacceptable		Acceptable		Unacceptable	
	Mean	σ	Mean	σ	Mean	σ	Mean	σ
Morale	29.94	4.92	26.43	5.81	31.13	5.35	26.92	6.24
Inferiority . . .	33.21	5.72	31.89	5.58	34.56	5.60	32.57	5.89
Family	25.65	5.43	30.54	6.44	26.87	6.23	29.81	7.24
Law	30.18	5.85	29.15	5.31	29.80	5.61	28.42	4.93
Economic conservatism	34.45	5.67	33.06	7.08	34.31	4.97	32.94	5.79
Education	23.79	5.54	24.02	5.49	23.79	5.22	23.40	5.47

TABLE 116.-MEANS AND STANDARD DEVIATIONS FOR ACCEPTABLE AND UNACCEPTABLE ITEMS

(General College group; N = 70 of each sex.)

Scale	Male				Female			
	Acceptable		Unacceptable		Acceptable		Unacceptable	
	Mean	σ	Mean	σ	Mean	σ	Mean	σ
Morale	30.28	4.56	25.96	5.49	31.16	4.80	25.03	5.37
Inferiority . . .	33.46	6.45	32.30	6.36	34.37	4.65	31.33	5.04
Family	26.23	5.76	29.93	6.75	27.09	5.55	28.37	6.93
Law	31.51	5.85	30.14	6.00	29.79	5.10	28.93	4.62
Economic conservatism	33.19	5.55	30.87	6.45	34.16	4.68	31.84	4.65
Education	23.71	5.04	24.14	5.34	25.03	5.10	23.96	4.80

116 shows that the trends are the same. As an orientation to the significance of these differences, D/σ diff. ratios were computed for the law, morale and family scales for men. The first is 1.97, the second 6.57, and the third 4.29 times its standard error.

The significance of the fact that the unacceptable items yield lower means for the contention that so-called negative items are socially unacceptable, has already been mentioned. That some scales do not follow this tendency suggests that the mean score cannot be infallibly relied upon as an index of social approval or disapproval. Evidence will be presented to show that the family items termed unacceptable follow the general pattern of the socially unacceptable items of the other scales, even though they depart from the pattern so far as mean score is concerned.

THE TEST OF INTERNAL CONSISTENCY AND THE TWO TYPES OF ITEM

Smith concluded that the skewed distributions and lower means of the unacceptable items were indices of their lesser value as measuring elements. The utility of an item as a discriminating element depends largely on its ability to meet a criterion of validity. In both studies a form of the test of internal consistency was employed. Is either type of item superior in this respect?

Smith's test of internal consistency consisted of calculating the ability of an item to differentiate between the upper and lower 27 per cent of the distribution in terms of regression weights determined from the Boas-Yulean Φ. The larger the weight the better the differentiation of the item. The items of Form P showed weights ranging from +7 to +37, those for Form N from +10 to +67 (page 57). Since Smith presents only the range of the differentiating or discriminating power of the items, the problem of which kind of item discriminates better cannot be directly evaluated. What evidence he presents does not demonstrate that the acceptable items differentiate better than the unacceptable.

Smith, finding certain Form N papers on which the R response was almost exclusively checked, calls them "unreliable", and explains the greater discriminative weights on this basis. He remarks (page 40): "Cases where this occurred almost certainly indicate general unreliability of response, for it is impossible to believe that an individual could honestly answer 284 items covering as wide a range of experience as do the items of this scale without having to acknowledge the presence of a fair number of such feelings at least occasionally."

According to Smith, such misrepresentation is not general among Form N papers but is largely concentrated in a few papers (4 of 30 for one particular class). Inclusion of such papers in the lower 27 per cent of the distribution will certainly tend to enhance the discriminating capacity of the Form N items, but whether the presence of these papers is the sole cause of the greater discriminating weights of the Form N items cannot be directly determined from the data Smith presents. There is some evidence that such is not the case. When the items of the PN form of the inventory are weighted in the scoring according to their discriminative weights, acceptable items correlate with total score .73 for boys and .78 for girls, while unacceptable items correlate .92 for boys and .92 for girls. This certainly does not suggest that the seemingly greater discriminative power of unacceptable items is due solely to the presence of "unreliable" papers.

Further, Smith reports that the unacceptable items yield larger standard deviations. In these groups for which the means were presented, the sigma for Form P is 63.18; for Form N, 85.97. Unacceptable items could not yield a greater sigma unless they were more consistent internally. To illustrate, if there is no consistency in any individual's responses--that is, if he checked the response at either end of the item scale with equal frequency, the total scores for every individual would be identical and the sigma would be zero. As an individual responds consistently from item to item his total score will increase or decrease, in either case becoming further removed from the mean. The standard deviation will inevitably become larger.

Such evidence from Smith's own study does not support his contention that unacceptable items are less useful as measuring elements; nor does it support his general conclusion that acceptable items are to be preferred.

Our data concerning internal consistency are in harmony with Smith's. For the morale, inferiority, family, law, economic conservatism, and education scales, the average discriminative values for the 11 items of each type are as follows:

Scale	Acceptable Items	Unacceptable Items
Morale	0.960	1.188
Inferiority	1.042	1.080
Family	1.160	1.344
Law	1.125	0.938
Economic conservatism	0.962	1.298
Education	1.026	1.093

In general, unacceptable items have slightly higher average discriminative values, the law scale being the only exception. The differences here are not large and hence lend support to Smith's finding that differences between the two types of item are reduced when they are presented at random within a single scale.

As expected, the standard deviations of unacceptable statements are, in general, larger. This is the case for 3 of the 6 scales for men and 5 of the 6 for women in the larger group (see Table 115); for 5 of the 6 for men, and for 3 of the 6 for women in the smaller group (see Table 116).

Again the differences are not large when the two types of item are administered in a single form. It is noteworthy that the family scale, which provided the most marked exception to the trend in the case of item distributions and mean scores, is one of the scales to conform to the general trend here. Since unacceptable items are more generalized in their significance than are acceptable items, their greater internal consistency within a given scale is understandable.

Smith presents some facts which he discusses under "reliability", using the term in the sense of evasion, but which are pertinent to the present discussion. In demonstrating that such "unreliability" is not general but is confined to specific papers, Smith compares the distributions of contiguous items of Form N and of Form P on the assumption that if the unreliability is general, the distributions of contiguous items should be similar. Taking as his measure 3 item sequences which showed a difference of at least 25 per cent of R responses on the middle item from the items on either side, he finds that there are 59 such sequences in Form P and 23 in Form N and, interpreting the differences in item distribution as evidence that the acceptable item is responded to on the bases of its specific ideational content, concludes that these items are more reliable. While the argument appears cogent, Smith points out that the sex differences expected from the nature of certain items are not obscured for either type of item. This supports his contention that unreliability is not general, but his conclusion that acceptable items are more reliable than unacceptable items and that this is further evidence that acceptable items are to be generally preferred does not necessarily follow.

The data do show that acceptable items are responded to less consistently than are unacceptable items. This tendency can be expected on the basis that unacceptable items are more generalized in their significance, i.e., that they are responded to on the same basis to a greater extent than are acceptable items. It is true, as Smith points out, that this evidence points to the fact that acceptable items are responded to more on the basis of the meaning or ideational content of the item. This suggests that the response to these items contains a more intellectual element than the response to unacceptable items. This point will be considered in detail later.

It should be noted, too, that Smith finds that these differences between the two types of items are reduced when both are included in the same form. The mean percentage of completely consistent responses for the 100 pairs of items before inclusion in Form PN was 42.93; after inclusion in Form PN, 54.06.

RELIABILITY OF THE TWO TYPES OF ITEM

When the usual measures of reliability are considered, Smith's evidence does not support his contention that the acceptable form of statement is to be preferred as a research technique. No marked differences appear from his data. The two-week retest r for Form P is .82, for Form N, .79, not a large difference. When the percentage of identical responses from test to retest is considered, the evidence favors the unacceptable items as being the more reliable, the mean percentage of identical responses from test to retest being 62.25 for Form P and 66.52 for Form N. The data on reliability cannot well be interpreted as favoring definitely either kind of item.

The retest coefficients (60 days) for the present scales are given in Table 117. Four of the six coefficients for socially unacceptable items are higher for both sexes. While the present coefficients cannot be exactly compared with Smith's since his are derived from scales containing only one kind of item, it is of interest to note that the present socially acceptable inferiority items yield slightly higher retest coefficients just as Smith's did. In both studies the difference is small, and in this study the finding holds for men only.[2] The general tendency for the scores on socially unacceptable items to be more consistent over a two-month period is, however, clear and is additional evidence against Smith's conclusion that positive items are to be "preferred on practically every count."

The greater magnitude of the reliability coefficients for scores on unacceptable items is associated with the greater range of scores yielded by them. Reference to Table 116 will show that in virtually every case where the standard deviation is larger for acceptable or unacceptable items the test-retest r is higher. Evidence will shortly be presented to show that range is not the sole factor.

The test-retest r's for the single items of both types are presented in Table 118. In obtaining the average item correlation for each scale, the individual r's were converted into z by means of Fisher's logarithmic transformation, the z's averaged, and the result reconverted to r. The same tendency for unacceptable items to be more reliable is present. The education scale furnishes the only exception to the

2. Smith did not treat the sexes separately in this computation.

TABLE 117.-IDENTICAL RESPONSES, CHANGES OF MORE THAN ONE POSITION, AND TEST-RETEST (60 DAYS) CORRELATIONS FOR ACCEPTABLE (A.) AND UNACCEPTABLE (U.) ITEMS

(General College; N = 50 of each sex; 550 responses to each kind of item.)

	Morale		Inferiority		Family		Law		Economic Conserv-atism		Education	
	A.	U.	A.	U.	A.	U.	A.	U.	A.	U.	A.	U.
Men:												
Number of identical responses	293	308	307	325	319	302	300	288	267	285	333	309
Percentage of identical responses	53.3	56.0	55.8	59.1	58.0	54.9	54.5	52.4	48.5	51.8	60.5	56.2
Number changing more than 1 position	92	75	75	95	58	100	101	87	101	78	61	65
Percentage changing more than 1 position	16.7	13.6	13.6	17.3	10.5	18.2	18.3	15.8	18.4	14.2	11.1	11.8
Test-retest r's total A. and U. scores	.553	.691	.822	.651	.774	.797	.616	.739	.657	.853	.737	.722
Women:												
Number of identical responses	286	325	300	333	319	336	296	315	282	276	330	334
Percentage of identical responses	52.0	59.1	54.5	60.5	58.0	61.1	53.8	57.3	51.3	50.2	60.0	60.7
Number changing more than 1 position	88	67	97	92	66	80	71	63	70	73	46	54
Percentage changing more than 1 position	16.0	12.2	17.6	16.7	12.0	14.5	12.9	11.5	12.7	13.3	8.4	9.8
Test-retest r's total A. and U. scores	.533	.641	.648	.688	.664	.807	.762	.749	.731	.744	.823	.762

trend. The difference is most evident in the case of the morale scale.

The reliability of acceptable and unacceptable items may be investigated from an additional view point--namely, by considering the stability of the response to items from test to retest. Table 117 also gives the percentage of identical responses to items of each type from test to retest (60 days), the percentage changing more than one step, and the test-retest reliability coefficients for total score.

That range is not the only factor causing higher reliability coefficients for unacceptable items is evident from Table 117. Consider the morale scale for men. Such items show a greater proportion of identical responses and a smaller proportion changing more than one step. This is quite consistent with the fact that the total score on unacceptable items yielded a higher test-retest $\underline{r}$ than did the total score on acceptable items (.691 to .553). The percentage differences are not large, but many shifts of more than one point on an item can seriously disturb the reliability coefficient.

In the case of the inferiority scale for men the test-retest r for acceptable items is .822 and for unacceptable .651. The inferiority scale has more identical responses for unacceptable items, but it also shows more large shifts in position. The number of marked changes in response on the unacceptable items does not seem sufficiently greater to cause the considerable difference noted in test-retest r's. The difference in standard deviations, while favoring the acceptable items, is very slight. The only remaining explanation for the higher test-retest r for acceptable inferiority items is that compensating shifts occurred more frequently for them than they did for unacceptable items. It is quite evident that the same total score may be obtained with markedly different series of item responses.

It would serve little purpose to consider the data for the remaining scales for men and those for women in such detail. The five factors--range, test-retest r's for total acceptable and total unacceptable score, percentage of identical responses, percentage of marked changes in position, and the probability of compensating shifts--can be considered by examining

TABLE 118.-ITEM TEST-RETEST CORRELATION COEFFICIENTS FOR ACCEPTABLE AND UNACCEPTABLE ITEMS

(General College group; N=50 of each sex.)

Acceptable Items

Morale		Inferiority		Family		Law		Economic Conservatism		Education	
Item	r	Item	r	Item	r	Item	r	Item	r	Item	r
25	.745	8	.358	3	.647	28	.695	17	.501	12	.695
31	.419	20	.485	15	.385	40	.524	23	.492	18	.730
37	.538	26	.595	21	.670	46	.301	35	.593	24	.704
55	.213	32	.515	27	.547	52	.524	41	.014	48	.530
61	.695	44	.530	45	.582	58	.536	59	.376	54	.603
79	.600	50	.359	57	.564	64	.303	65	.514	78	.499
85	.377	56	.710	75	.575	70	.520	71	.295	84	.611
91	.397	74	.584	81	.566	94	.566	83	.708	102	.265
103	.829	80	.538	87	.565	112	.446	107	.383	108	.583
109	.699	104	.624	93	.541	118	.627	119	.655	120	.594
121	.543	110	.551	111	.608	124	.441	131	.570	126	.717
Mean*	.578		.537		.572		.508		.478		.604

Unacceptable Items

Morale		Inferiority		Family		Law		Economic Conservatism		Education	
Item	r	Item	r	Item	r	Item	r	Item	r	Item	r
1	.674	2	.553	9	.492	4	.452	5	.615	6	.875
7	.635	14	.587	33	.543	10	.515	11	.453	30	.492
13	.864	38	.586	39	.773	16	.447	29	.525	36	.579
19	.683	62	.508	51	.686	22	.495	47	.628	42	.519
43	.425	68	.577	63	.609	34	.572	53	.668	60	.403
49	.763	86	.633	69	.529	76	.449	77	.448	66	.517
67	.460	92	.322	99	.654	82	.577	89	.527	72	.400
73	.505	98	.518	105	.578	88	.721	95	.369	90	.573
97	.671	116	.503	117	.599	100	.368	101	.422	96	.902
115	.362	122	.572	123	.330	106	.584	113	.515	114	.427
127	.916	128	.600	129	.574	130	.510	125	.751	132	.468
Mean*	.670		.544		.585		.523		.558		.598

*r converted to Fisher's z values, summed, and the mean reconverted to r.

Table 117. More detailed analysis is presented in Tables 54 and 55 in Chapter V.

So many factors are involved in the reliability of the two types of item that interpretation is difficult. Considering the test-retest *r*'s for total score and for items, and the stability of item responses, it appears that unacceptable items tend to evoke slightly more decided and more consistent responses. This finding also casts doubt on Smith's conclusion that acceptable items are "to be preferred."

CORRELATION OF EACH TYPE OF ITEM WITH TOTAL SCORE AND WITH ONE ANOTHER

Smith reported that both types of item correlate almost equally well with total score; the acceptable, .86 for boys and .87 for girls; the unacceptable, .88 for boys and .89 for girls. In the present study this is also the case. (See Table 119.) What slight differences there are favor the acceptable items. The spurious factor owing to the fact that total score is simply the sum of the acceptable and the unacceptable item score makes sizable correlations inevitable.

TABLE 119.-CORRELATION OF SCORES ON ACCEPTABLE ITEMS AND SCORES ON UNACCEPTABLE ITEMS WITH TOTAL SCORE

(General College group; N = 100 of each sex.)

	Male		Female	
Scale	Acceptable Correlation	Unacceptable Correlation	Acceptable Correlation	Unacceptable Correlation
Morale	.871	.806	.824	.774
Inferiority	.825	.831	.860	.834
Family	.850	.786	.873	.794
Law	.873	.866	.835	.867
Economic conservatism . .	.907	.872	.839	.841
Education	.916	.904	.895	.903

Scores on acceptable and unacceptable items may correlate equally well with total score, but this constitutes no guarantee that they intercorrelate to the same extent. When the two types of item were administered separately, Smith found an r between them of .36 when Form P was given first and one of .24 when Form N was given first. When both types were included in the same form (Form PN) the correlation for boys became .60 and for girls .53. The smaller difference between the two types of item when administered in the same form is again evident.

Many of the correlations between the two types of item found in the present study are even lower than those found by Smith for Form PN. (See Table 120.) The correlations are, in 11 of 12 instances, lower than the uncorrected split-half reliability coefficients, which are given in the same table. The discrepancy between the uncorrected reliability coefficients and the correlations between acceptable and unacceptable scores is even more evident in Table 121, which contains the data for a group dissimilar in many respects to the college group considered. It is composed of 52 married men, mostly over 30 years of age, virtually all of whom have dependent children, and all of whom were receiving public relief.[3] For one scale, the family scale, the correlation between the acceptable and unacceptable items is practically zero (.08). In this instance every correlation between acceptable and unacceptable items is lower than the corresponding raw split-half reliability coefficient. If form of statement had no influence, these coefficients should be of approximately the same magnitude as the uncorrected split-half r's. These results confirm Smith's and eminently justify his conclusion that form of statement is a potent factor.

Evidence that the differences between acceptable and unacceptable items are not confined to Smith's and the present study is found in the correlations reported by Bell (3) between the various sections of his Adjustment Inventory. Four sections of his inventory refer to home adjustment, health adjustment, social

3. This group will be referred to as the public relief group.

TABLE 120.-CORRELATIONS BETWEEN TOTAL SCORES ON ACCEPTABLE ITEMS (A.) AND UNACCEPTABLE ITEMS (U.) COMPARED WITH RAW RELIABILITY COEFFICIENTS

(General College group; N = 100 of each sex.)

	Men		Women	
	rA.U.	Relia-bility	rA.U.	Relia-bility
Morale	.41	.57	.28	.63
Inferiority	.37	.76	.44	.68
Family	.34	.71	.40	.76
Law	.51	.74	.45	.68
Economic conservatism .	.58	.71	.41	.59
Education	.66	.65	.62	.72

TABLE 121.-CORRELATIONS BETWEEN TOTAL SCORES ON ACCEPTABLE ITEMS (A.) AND UNACCEPTABLE ITEMS (U.) COMPARED WITH RAW RELIABILITY COEFFICIENTS

(Public relief group; N = 52.)

Scale	r A.U.	Reliability
Morale	.58	.77
Inferiority	.21	.74
Family	.08	.62
Law	.51	.83
Economic conservatism	.47	.75
Education	.49	.76

adjustment, and emotional adjustment, respectively. The intercorrelations are:

Home and health . . .	.43	Health and social . .	.24
Home and social . . .	.04	Health and emotional .	.53
Home and emotional .	.38	Social and emotional .	.47

Each section contains 35 items. A study of these items reveals that 31 of the home adjustment items, all the health adjustment items, 21 of the social adjustment items, and all the emotional adjustment items are unacceptably stated. The social section is the only one to possess an appreciable number of acceptably stated items. Inspection of the table of intercorrelations shows that the two lowest r's involve the social section as a variable. Home and social is .04 and health and social, .24. Further, the highest correlation is that between health and emotional adjustment, the two sections that contain only unacceptable items. Such results clearly point to form of statement as a factor in these correlations.

The surprisingly low correlations in our study between the two types of item, both of which met the criterion for inclusion in the scale in which they are placed, raise problems of fundamental importance. How can they be considered to be measuring the same thing? What are the causes of this phenomenon? What are the implications for the criterion of internal consistency? Before considering these problems the facts concerning the two types of item and the inferences from these facts may be summarized. Only the general trends will be considered.

The terms socially acceptable and socially unacceptable are descriptive of the essential difference between the two types of item. That socially unacceptable items yield distributions more heavily weighted at the favorable end of the scale and lower means is evidence for this contention.

The most striking finding is that unacceptable items are more generalized in their significance to the individual. Or, to state it another way, they are more diagnostic of adjustment, the general factor permeating the six scales. Another general finding is that differences between the acceptable and unacceptable items are lessened, but do not disappear when the items are administered in a single form. The more specific facts are these:

1. Unacceptable items yield distributions more heavily weighted at the favorable end of the scale. Hence means are lower.

2. Responses to unacceptable items tend to be more internally consistent and therefore yield larger standard deviations.

3. Unacceptable items tend to yield more consistent responses from test to retest.

4. The two types of item correlate low within a single scale while correlating equally well with total score.

The skewed distributions and lower means of unacceptable items can be rationalized by the concept that they are the unacceptable items. The fact that unacceptable items are responded to partially on the basis of the adjustment factor and hence are responded to more on the same basis would account for their greater internal consistency and larger standard deviations. In addition, it is reasonable to infer that there is a more intellectual element involved in the response to acceptable items. It should be noted that Smith, on the basis of entirely different evidence, concludes that the unacceptable item arouses more emotion in the subject. Since unacceptable items are more generalized, more diagnostic of adjustment, they may be considered to measure traits more fundamental to the individual. On this basis it can be expected that responses from test to retest will be more consistent for these items.

DIFFERENCE BETWEEN THE SCORE ON ACCEPTABLE AND ON UNACCEPTABLE ITEMS AS A SCORING METHOD AND ITS RELATION TO THE LOW CORRELATIONS BETWEEN THE TWO TYPES OF ITEM

It has been shown that unacceptable items are, as a group, more closely related to the adjustment factor than are acceptable items. When the unacceptable items of one scale are correlated with the acceptable items of another, and vice versa, the correlations are lower than when either of the two types of item are correlated. (See Table 109.) The average intercorrelation of the acceptable items of the first scale with the unacceptable items of the second is .125; corrected for attenuation, .189; the intercorrelation of the unacceptable items of the first with the acceptable items of the second is, .136; corrected for attenuation, .192. These coefficients are lower than when either type of item is correlated with its own type in another scale. Both forms of statement carry the general factor, the unacceptable form to the greater extent. That some sort of conflict between the two types of items is present is suggested by the fact that the correlations between the dissimilar types are lower than those between items of a single type. What is the nature of this conflict? A restatement of the general facts provides a clue.

Both acceptable and unacceptable items measure specific traits plus the more general factor which in this work is called a general adjustment factor. This plus factor is more pronounced for unacceptable items as is shown by their greater intercorrelation.

Now it seems probable that there might often be a conflict between the measurement of the specific and the general factor by the same set of items. For example, on what basis is the individual who is generally poorly adjusted but possess a "good" attitude toward education going to respond to the unacceptable education items? He may believe that more education will solve his problems. Obviously there will be a conflict in the measurement of his attitude toward education and the measurement of his adjustment. The chances are that either his adjustment score, his education score, or both will be distorted. Since the unacceptable items imply the general factor to a greater degree than do the acceptable items, the conflict between the measurement of the more and the less general traits will be evident from differences in reactions to the acceptable and the unacceptable items within a given scale.

Whether or not this explanation is sound, the very fact that unacceptable items are more closely related to the adjustment factor than are acceptable items makes low correlations between the two inevitable. The greater increase in the score on unacceptable than on acceptable items as an individual's adjustment score increases is bound to change the relative position of individuals from the acceptable to the unacceptable series. Consider these two individuals. One has an adjustment score well above the mean, standard score, 76; the other has an adjustment score below the mean, standard score, 41. The former gained an arbitrary score of 78 on the inferiority scale, 46 points of which were obtained on unacceptable items and 32 on acceptable. The latter scored 55 arbitrary points on the inferiority scale, 23 points of which were obtained on unacceptable and 33 on acceptable items. In the first case the unacceptable excess is 14, and in the second the acceptable excess is 10. In addition, there is some variation due either to chance or some other factor, which occurs for individuals with the same adjustment score. Two individuals with identical scores of 43 on the adjustment scale scored 64 and 66 on the inferiority scale. The first obtained 8 points more on unacçeptable items, the second 10 points more on acceptable items.

These two factors--the greater increase in score on unacceptable items as the adjustment score increases, and the variation between scores on the two types of item that is due to chance or some unknown factor--account for the low correlations between the two types of item. That the first factor is more potent than the second is implied by the data already presented and will be shown clearly in a moment.

The low correlations can be envisaged as an automatic product of the greater relation of unacceptable items to the adjustment factor. Consider the hypothetical situation where acceptable items are completely unrelated to this general factor. If, then, individuals were divided into quartiles on the basis of their adjustment scores, score on the unacceptable items will vary with the adjustment score, whereas each adjustment quartile will have the same score on the acceptable items. This hypothetical case may be set up as follows:

Adjustment Quartiles	Unacceptable Score	Acceptable Score
Q_1 (highest)	60	45
Q_2	50	45
Q_3	40	45
Q_4	30	45

Such a relationship inevitably changes the individuals position from the acceptable to the unacceptable series, and low correlations between the two types of item will result. It is evident that those with the lowest adjustment scores will have an excess of acceptable over unacceptable score, and those with the highest adjustment score will have an excess of unacceptable over acceptable score.

Unacceptable scores minus acceptable scores in relation to the adjustment scale for the three groups considered in this chapter are given in Table 122. Where the unacceptable score exceeds the acceptable, the values are preceded by a negative sign. The tendencies for poorly adjusted individuals (Q_1) to make higher scores on unacceptable items and for welladjusted individuals (Q_4) to make higher scores on acceptable items are clear. The data are remarkably conclusive. Acceptable-unacceptable differences cumulate and do not cancel when they are combined algebraically for the six scales. To be sure, the ranges covered by the acceptable-unacceptable differences vary from group to group and from scale to scale, even being almost entirely on the positive side for the six scales combined so far as General College women are concerned. Invariably, however, favorable mean-adjustment score is accompanied by a greater excess in the mean acceptable item score.

For the family scale the excess is always on the unacceptable side, but in amount it varies directly with the adjustment score. From the fact that the responses to the family items provided the chief exception to the tendency for unacceptable item responses to concentrate at the favorable end of the item distributions to a greater extent than acceptable, the consistent unacceptable excess of the family scale is readily understood. Since the family unacceptable items follow the trend here, one must avoid placing too great reliance on the differences between mean scores yielded by the two types of item as an index of which type of item is socially acceptable and which socially unacceptable. (It will be recalled that the acceptable items of the family scale yielded the lower mean score.)

Further evidence of the fundamental nature of the acceptable-unacceptable difference is indicated by the finding that on all except the family scale unacceptable excess, for high or unfavorable scores, is not expected from the nature of the item distributions. The 4 and 5 positions are checked more frequently on acceptable items. Hence one would expect that, as a group,

TABLE 122.-RELATIONSHIP OF GENERAL ADJUSTMENT SCALE TO THE DIFFERENCES BETWEEN ACCEPTABLE AND UNACCEPTABLE SCORES

(N = 100 in each group.)

Scale of General Adjustment	Mean Acceptable Score Minus Mean Unacceptable Score*						
	Morale	Inferiority	Family	Law	Economic Conservatism	Education	Total
Controlled Sample of Unemployed Men (N=25 in each quartile)							
Q_1 (highest) . .	-2.32	-3.04	-10.96	-1.84	-3.96	-4.48	-26.60
Q_2	+.48	-1.00	-4.56	-1.48	-.80	-1.68	-9.04
Q_3	+3.64	+4.24	-5.24	+1.40	+1.38	-.20	+5.22
Q_4	+4.84	+2.44	-3.96	+.72	+2.92	-1.16	+5.80
Q_1-Q_4	7.16	5.48	7.00	2.56	6.88	3.32	32.40
Controlled Sample of Unemployed Women (N=25 in each quartile)							
Q_1	+1.36	-1.68	-5.32	-.08	-1.56	-3.48	-10.76
Q_2	+.52	-.76	-6.32	+1.04	-1.24	-2.20	-8.96
Q_3	+2.68	+1.72	-3.44	-1.20	-.44	-.04	-.72
Q_4	+7.04	+1.80	-1.68	+3.20	+4.92	+2.92	+18.20
Q_1-Q_4	5.68	3.48	3.64	3.28	6.48	6.40	28.96
General College Men (N=25 in each quartile)							
Q_1	+2.64	-.40	-6.64	-.52	+.12	-2.72	-7.52
Q_2	+4.56	+1.36	-4.88	+1.00	+2.56	-.72	+4.60
Q_3	+4.84	+.80	-3.56	+1.48	+2.20	+1.16	+6.92
Q_4	+8.24	+5.92	+.36	+4.32	+6.60	+1.64	+27.08
Q_1-Q_4	5.60	6.32	7.00	4.84	6.48	4.36	34.60
General College Women (N=25 in each quartile)							
Q_1	+2.88	-.04	-3.12	-1.60	+.60	+.44	-.84
Q_2	+4.36	+2.16	-2.28	+2.04	+1.64	+1.00	+8.92
Q_3	+6.20	+3.00	-.12	+.56	+1.88	+.16	+11.68
Q_4	+8.48	+4.80	+2.16	+3.16	+3.04	+1.76	+23.40
Q_1-Q_4	5.60	4.84	5.28	4.76	2.44	1.32	24.24
Public Relief Group (N=13 in each quartile)							
Q_1	-4.84	-4.61	-13.54	-3.69	-7.16	-8.62	-42.46
Q_2	-2.00	-5.62	-10.62	-2.16	-5.62	-3.16	-29.18
Q_3	+4.61	+1.46	-6.54	+.46	-1.62	-1.15	-2.78
Q_4	+2.54	+0.61	-4.08	-1.38	+1.31	+3.31	+2.31
Q_1-Q_4	7.38	5.22	9.46	2.31	8.47	11.93	44.77

*Negative sign indicates that mean unacceptable score exceeds mean acceptable score.

acceptable items would yield higher scores. That they do not can only mean that they are less internally consistent than unacceptable items, i.e., that particular individuals are likely to vary more in checking positions on the acceptable items than on the unacceptable. This is illustrated by the tendency for acceptable items to yield smaller discriminative values.

The results in Table 122 show clearly that the variation in acceptable and unacceptable score for individuals with the same adjustment score is a minor factor in producing low correlations between the two types of item within a single scale.

It is noteworthy that acceptable-unacceptable differences on the morale scale are less closely related to the adjustment scale than are morale total score, morale unacceptable score, and morale acceptable score. This follows almost inevitably from the fact that acceptable morale items are rather closely related to the adjustment scale, and hence unacceptable score must increase much more rapidly than in the case of the other scales for the negative excess to appear.

The relation of unacceptable score, acceptable score, and acceptable-unacceptable differences to the adjustment scale again confirms the fact that the selection of preponderately unacceptable items for the adjustment scale was no accident of content. If it had been, the acceptable-unacceptable differences for the individual scales should be directly related to the number of items each contributes to the adjustment scale. The family scale, which contributes only one item to the adjustment scale, compares more favorably with the morale scale, which contributes seven items to the adjustment scale, than could possibly be expected on the basis of the weight of its one item.

For the rest, the acceptable-unacceptable tabulation reveals much the same facts as the tabulation of the acceptable and unacceptable scores singly. The greater relation of unacceptable items to adjustment score for men is evident in the acceptable-unacceptable difference table. The significance of this will be considered in a later chapter.

The group difference is again conspicuous, the public relief group showing greatest unacceptable excess. The group difference is in good part a function of the difference in mean adjustment score. The fact that unacceptable excess for Q_1 is most characteristic of the controlled samples of unemployed and the public relief group is further evidence of the true nature of the relationship. The General College groups are better adjusted (mean score 48.73 for men and 47.64 for women) than the controlled sample of unemployed (mean score 52.06 for men and 52.29 for women), which shows a greater negative excess for the most unfavorable quartile. The public relief group, which has the most unfavorable adjustment score (57.98) has the greatest unacceptable excess. The difference in mean adjustment score would lead one to expect the group difference noted in acceptable-unacceptable score. This group difference was less apparent in the total scores on the six scales, suggesting that the unacceptable score, and perhaps as a sole consequence the acceptable-unacceptable difference is more sensitive to changes in adjustment than is the sum of acceptable and unacceptable scores on the individual scales.

Scale differences in acceptable-unacceptable excess are evident from group to group. These can be determined from a study of the tables. In the present state of our knowledge it seems futile to discuss them in detail.

Now if the low correlations between acceptable and unacceptable item scores of a single scale were solely the result of the closer relationship of the unacceptable items to the general adjustment factor, one would expect the acceptable-unacceptable correlations to decrease as the acceptable-unacceptable difference increased. The relationship of the correlations between acceptable and unacceptable items and the difference between acceptable and unacceptable scores are given in Table 123 for the groups for which both were computed. The scales are ranked from smallest to largest acceptable-unacceptable correlation and from greatest to least acceptable-unacceptable Q_1-Q_4 difference in relation to the unacceptable-item adjustment scale.

The order of the scales is identical for the General College men. For women, as might be expected from the consistent sex differences that have appeared

TABLE 123.-SCALES RANKED ACCORDING TO CORRELATIONS BETWEEN ACCEPTABLE (A.) AND UNACCEPTABLE (U.) ITEMS AND ACCORDING TO DIFFERENCES BETWEEN SCORES ON THESE ITEMS

Scale	General College Men		General College Women		Men on Public Relief Group	
	A.U. r	A.-U. Score	A.U. r	A.-U. Score	A.U. r	A.-U. Score
Morale	3	3	1	1	6	4
Inferiority	2	2	4	3	2	5
Family	1	1	2	4	1	2
Law	4	4	5	2	5	6
Economic conservatism	5	5	3	5	3	3
Education	6	6	6	6	4	1

in this analysis, the agreement is less close, but the tendency is perceptible, particularly in view of the fact that where discrepancies appear the differences in acceptable-unacceptable r's or in acceptable-unacceptable scores are not large. The relationship does not hold at all well for the public relief group. Some factors must be operating in addition to the purely automatic one implied by the closer relationship of unacceptable items to the adjustment score. Taken as a whole, in connection with the data previously discussed, the evidence points to this factor as potent in causing the low acceptable-unacceptable correlations within a single scale.

Since the acceptable-unacceptable difference varies with the adjustment score, the possibility arises that this difference can be used to detect group and individual differences in adjustment. Such a measure will be especially useful when no other measurement of the adjustment factor is available.

To determine the validity of the acceptable-unacceptable difference as a measure of adjustment, the mean difference score for each of the three male groups considered here was computed to ascertain whether this difference arranged the groups in the same order as the adjustment score itself. The difference score was obtained by subtracting the score on the 66 unacceptable items from the score on the 66 acceptable items.

Group	Mean Adjustment Score	Mean Acceptable-Unacceptable Difference
General College Group . .	48.73	7.59
Controlled sample of unemployed	52.06	-6.38
Public relief group . . .	57.98	-19.01

The difference between the scores on 66 acceptable and 66 unacceptable items arranges the groups in the same order, then, as the unacceptable item adjustment scale. This tendency holds for the single scales, as may be seen from the following tabulation of the mean acceptable score minus the mean unacceptable score for three male groups:

	Morale	Inferiority	Family	Law	Economic Conservatism	Education
General College . .	5.07	1.92	-3.68	1.57	2.87	-0.16
Controlled sample of unemployed . .	1.66	0.59	-6.32	-0.24	-0.09	-1.98
Public relief group	0.08	-2.61	-8.69	-1.69	-3.27	-2.83

Can the acceptable-unacceptable difference be used as an index of an individual's adjustment as well as of group adjustment? Table 124, which gives the number of individuals in each adjustment quartile who had an excess of more than 5 or more than 10[4] points on unacceptable items in any single scale, gives an affirmative answer to this question. The table is to be read as follows: of the 25 men in the least adjusted quartile (Q_1) three had an unacceptable excess of more than 10 points on the morale scale, while no one in the remaining three quartiles had so large an excess. Seven individuals in the most poorly adjusted quartile had an unacceptable excess of more than 5 points, 4 individuals in Q_2, 1 in Q_3 and 1 in Q_4. It is evident that the two

4. Since there are only 11 items of each type in a scale, a 10-point excess is, indeed, a large one.

measures do not completely agree. Some of the individuals at the extremes of the adjustment scale appear to be fairly well differentiated if the critical point is well chosen for each scale. Future research may in fact show that the acceptable-unacceptable difference is the preferable measure for some purposes.

TABLE 124.-NUMBER OF INDIVIDUALS IN THE ADJUSTMENT QUARTILES WHO HAD MORE THAN 5-POINT EXCESS AND NUMBER WHO HAD MORE THAN 10-POINT EXCESS ON THE UNACCEPTABLE ITEMS OF ANY SINGLE SCALE

(Controlled sample of unemployed; N = 25 in each quartile.)

Scale	10-Point Excess				5-Point Excess			
	Adjustment Quartiles				Adjustment Quartiles			
	Q_1	Q_2	Q_3	Q_4	Q_1	Q_2	Q_3	Q_4
Men:								
Morale	3	0	0	0	7	4	1	1
Inferiority	5	1	0	0	9	4	0	4
Family	13	1	4	3	19	10	8	7
Law	2	1	0	1	3	7	2	2
Economic conservatism	5	0	0	0	4	2	2	2
Education	3	0	0	1	10	4	2	3
Women:								
Morale	2	1	1	0	4	2	3	1
Inferiority	3	1	1	2	6	4	3	2
Family	7	4	1	2	12	12	6	6
Law	1	2	1	0	3	4	5	1
Economic conservatism	1	3	1	0	10	6	4	1
Education	3	1	0	0	6	5	2	0

In evaluating the possibility that acceptable-unacceptable differences may be useful as a diagnostic index of adjustment its reliability must be considered. While the limits of the study precluded an adequate analysis of this question, test-retest reliability (60 days) was computed for the acceptable-unacceptable difference for 70 general college men. It is .62. The test-retest r for the adjustment scale for this same group is .79. Since, however, it is possible that the difference score is a more sensitive measure of adjustment and detects the real changes more effectively, this result cannot be taken as final. It merely points the problem.

Whatever else these results may mean, they do illustrate, in even more striking fashion than the data on discriminative values and the adjustment scale, the difficulties of obtaining a measure of a specific aspect of personality apart from a consideration of the whole. The conflict between the measurement of more and less general phases of personality, it seems from our data, can scarcely be avoided with the present techniques as generally applied.

It has been noted that the reaction to acceptable items involves a more intellectual response. Can the acceptable-unacceptable difference be used as a clue to the basis on which the items of a particular scale are yielding responses? A partial answer to this question can be obtained by comparing the difference scores on the economic conservatism scale for two groups for which there is reason to assume different bases of reaction. The two groups are the public relief group and the high school teachers. Both are on the left: the mean conservatism score for the public relief group is 59.10; for the high school teachers, 60.20 for men and 60.45 for women. The public relief group is a poorly adjusted group (adjustment score, 57.98), whereas the teachers score slightly below the mean on the adjustment scale (47.30 for men and 49.91 for women). It would seem a priori that the radicalism of the two groups has a markedly different basis. Those in the public relief group are more likely to be radical on an emotional basis because of their unfavorable experience with the workings of the economic order. The employed teachers, on the other hand, are more likely to be intellectual liberals. Both groups make about equal scores. A comparison of the difference score on the conservatism scale should give some clue as to whether the difference score will detect the difference in the kind of radicalism that very probably exists. There are 52 public relief men and 21 teachers (10 men and 11 women). The mean acceptable-unacceptable difference on the 22 economic conservatism items for the public relief group is -3.27, for the teaching group +4.00.[4] These differences may appear small, and data are not at hand to evaluate them statistically; nevertheless they are in the expected direction. The excess on acceptable items of the economic conservatism scale on the part of the employed teachers assumes greater significance when it is recalled that high scores (Q_1) on the economic conservatism scale are usually accompanied by unacceptable excess. The acceptable-unacceptable difference score, then, has great potential significance. Further research is urgently needed to determine just how useful it will be and what is to be its exact interpretation.

One further point concerning the acceptable-unacceptable difference score should be mentioned. It has been pointed out that acceptable-unacceptable differences can be considered as an automatic consequence of the closer relation of unacceptable items to the adjustment factor. Is it possible that the difference may measure directly the degree of some kind of psychological conflict?

That such a factor is present is suggested by the fact that while unacceptable items arrange the General College group, the controlled sample of unemployed, and the men receiving public relief in the same order as does the adjustment scale, acceptable items arrange them in the reverse order.

Group	Mean Adjustment Score	Mean Acceptable Score[5]	Mean Unacceptable Score[5]
General College	48.73	177.83	170.24
Controlled sample of unemployed	52.06	174.25	180.63
Public relief group	57.98	171.95	190.96

It is quite understandable why the acceptable minus the unacceptable scores on the 66 items of each type

4. This holds for each sex considered independently.

5. Total score on 66 items, using arbitrary response weights.

yielded such nice differentiation of the three groups. There is a tendency for the group most poorly adjusted not only to score higher on unacceptable items but also to score lower on acceptable items. This seems to imply a conflict different from that between the measurement of more and less general traits.

These results are completely unexpected. For we have the anomalous situation in which acceptable and unacceptable items tend to vary together within any single group and inversely in group comparisons. The importance of the problem of acceptable-unacceptable differences is pointed with a vengeance. The significance of this finding for the group differences found on the scales as originally standardized will be considered in the next chapter. Here we are concerned only with the attempt to interpret such differences. About all that can be said from the data presented thus far is that acceptable-unacceptable differences which result from the more generalized significance of unacceptable items, are one factor in producing the low acceptable-unacceptable correlations. In addition, the difference score appears to express directly some kind of psychological conflict. Since conflict is one characteristic of maladjustment, the association between the difference score and the adjustment scale is a reasonable finding.

Certain difficulties, however, arise in attempting to interpret acceptable-unacceptable differences in terms of psychological conflict. One is baffled by the fact that the direction of the difference tends to reverse as scores become unfavorable in their significance. Lack of mental conflict is presumed to be characteristic of the well adjusted, but here the well adjusted group shows an excess on the acceptable side. If one accepts the difference score as a direct measure of psychological conflict, he must necessarily admit that it is not the fact of conflict but the "direction", so to speak, of that conflict which is important.

A possible interpretation is suggested by the nature of the maladjusted group. This group, those dependent on public relief, is made up of older men. Speech reactions indicative of conventional ways of thinking have had a longer time in which to become stereotyped. The acceptable items, being stated in accordance with conventional thinking, may be reacted to on this basis more than on the basis of the individual's own feelings and attitudes.

ACCEPTABLE-UNACCEPTABLE DIFFERENCES IN RELATION TO THE SINGLE SCALES

It has been shown that acceptable and unacceptable items correlate about equally well with total score. It follows that differences between score on acceptable and on unacceptable items will be less in relation to total score on any single scale than in relation to the adjustment scale. Acceptable-unacceptable differences in relation to total score on single scales are presented in Table 125. Individuals making the most unfavorable scores on any single scale (Q_1) do tend to make a slightly higher score on unacceptable items, and those who score at the favorable end (Q_4) tend to obtain more points on the acceptable items. The trend, however, is not nearly so marked as it was in relation to the adjustment scale. The Q_1-Q_4 difference is reversed on the inferiority scale for men; and on three scales for women: inferiority, family, and law. Furthermore, when the difference does exist, it is small for the six individual scales, as Table 126 will show. This tabulation, it should be noted, does not involve a spurious factor; for it is not the absolute magnitude of the scores that is considered, but the differences between them.

The table is to be interpreted as follows: for the men, the 11 unacceptable-morale-item score exceeds the 11 acceptable-morale-item score by 2.32 points in relation to the unfavorable (Q_1) adjustment quartile; the acceptable-item score exceeds the unacceptable by 4.84 in relation to the favorable adjustment quartile (Q_4), giving an algebraic difference between the quartiles of 7.16. In relation to total score on the morale scale, however, the unacceptable-morale-item score exceeds the acceptable by 1.64 for Q_1 of the morale scale; the acceptable exceeds the unacceptable by 2.64 for Q_4, giving an algebraic difference of 4.28.

Compare first the algebraic difference

TABLE 125.-ACCEPTABLE (A.) SCORES, UNACCEPTABLE (U.) SCORES, AND ACCEPTABLE-UNACCEPTABLE DIFFERENCES FOR SINGLE SCALES IN RELATION TO TOTAL SCORE ON THAT SCALE

(N = 100 of each sex, 25 in each quartile.)

Total Score Quartiles	Morale		Inferiority		Family		Law		Economic Conserv-atism		Education	
	A.	U.	A.	U.	A.	U.	A.	U.	A.	U.	A.	U.
Controlled Sample of Unemployed Men												
Q_1 (highest)	34.36	36.00	38.40	37.24	32.24	38.80	34.92	35.04	41.08	44.08	27.72	31.68
Q_2	30.68	28.44	32.88	34.24	26.64	33.96	29.84	31.04	36.56	36.24	23.76	26.32
Q_3	28.28	24.88	31.60	30.44	23.60	30.28	27.08	27.00	33.32	32.80	22.44	21.96
Q_4	24.28	21.64	28.00	26.60	20.04	24.68	23.40	23.00	30.20	28.40	15.88	17.76
Q_1-Q_4 . . .	10.08	14.36	10.40	10.64	12.20	14.12	11.52	12.04	10.88	15.68	11.84	13.92
Controlled Sample of Unemployed Women												
Q_1	37.36	35.56	40.64	39.40	33.76	37.20	34.40	33.72	37.96	38.56	29.52	31.24
Q_2	33.76	30.04	36.48	35.16	28.12	32.88	30.76	29.00	35.36	34.24	25.44	26.20
Q_3	29.24	27.72	31.84	33.04	25.12	28.68	27.52	26.24	33.28	32.12	22.40	23.44
Q_4	26.00	21.48	27.40	27.64	19.40	24.36	22.64	23.40	29.88	28.44	19.40	18.68
Q_1-Q_4 . . .	11.36	14.08	13.24	11.76	14.36	12.84	11.76	10.32	8.08	10.12	10.12	12.56

MEAN ACCEPTABLE SCORE MINUS MEAN UNACCEPTABLE SCORE

	Men						Women					
	Morale	Inferi-ority	Family	Law	Economic Conserv-atism	Educa-tion	Morale	Inferi-ority	Family	Law	Economic Conserv-ation	Educa-tion
Q_1	-1.64	1.16	-6.25	-0.12	-3.00	-3.96	1.80	1.24	-3.44	0.68	-0.60	-1.72
Q_2	2.24	-1.36	-7.32	-1.20	0.32	-2.56	3.72	1.32	-4.76	1.76	1.12	-0.76
Q_3	3.40	1.16	-5.60	0.08	0.52	0.48	1.52	-1.20	-3.56	1.28	1.16	-1.04
Q_4	2.64	1.40	-4.68	0.40	1.80	-1.88	4.52	-0.24	-4.96	-0.76	1.44	0.72
Q_1-Q_4	4.28	.24	1.57	0.52	4.80	2.08	2.72	-1.48	-1.52	-1.44	2.04	2.44

TABLE 126.-THE ACCEPTABLE-UNACCEPTABLE DIFFERENCE IN RELATION TO ADJUSTMENT SCALE QUARTILES AND QUARTILES OF OTHER SCALES

Scale	Controlled Sample of Unemployed Men						Controlled Sample of Unemployed Women					
	Adjustment Scale Quartiles			Own Scale Quartiles			Adjustment Scale Quartiles			Own Scale Quartiles		
	Q_1	Q_4	Q_1-Q_4	Q_1	Q_4	Q_1-Q_4	Q_1	Q_4	Q_1-Q_4	Q_1	Q_4	Q_1-Q_4
Morale	-2.32	4.84	7.16	-1.64	2.64	4.28	1.36	7.04	5.68	1.80	4.52	2.72
Inferiority	-3.04	2.44	5.48	1.16	1.40	0.24*	-1.68	1.80	3.48	1.24	0.24	1.48*
Family	-10.96	-3.96	7.00	-6.25	-4.68	1.57	-5.32	1.68	3.64	-3.44	-4.96	1.52*
Law	-1.84	0.72	2.56	-0.12	0.40	0.52	-0.08	3.20	3.28	0.68	-0.76	1.44*
Economic conservatism	-3.96	2.92	6.88	-3.00	1.80	4.80	-1.56	4.92	6.48	-0.60	1.44	2.04
Education	-4.48	-1.16	3.32	-3.96	-1.88	2.08	-3.48	2.92	6.40	-1.72	0.72	2.44

*Starred numbers in the Q_1-Q_4 columns signify that the difference is reversed, i.e., the most favorable quartile shows less unacceptable excess or greater acceptable excess as the case may be. The minus signs in the other columns, of course, signify that unacceptable score exceeds acceptable score.

between Q_1 and Q_4 in relation to the adjustment scale and in relation to the single scales. In every case the difference is larger in relation to the adjustment scale. Also, the trend for unacceptable excess to be present in Q_1 and acceptable excess in Q_4 is, in general, more marked in relation to the adjustment scale.

Since the acceptable-unacceptable differences are smaller in relation to total score on single scales, it is clear that they cannot be fully accounted for by a difference in reaction to the two types of item, characteristic of all individuals. It seems, rather, that the differences are due to the presence of two kinds of individuals, one reacting to the scales on an adjustment basis, the other on a more specific basis. It is when the items are reacted to on an adjustment basis that the acceptable-unacceptable difference is characteristic, largely as an automatic result of the fact that unacceptable items are more diagnostic of adjustment than are acceptable items.

Considered as a group, the items in each scale discriminate better in the scale in which they are placed than they would in the adjustment scale.[6]

TABLE 127.-DISCRIMINATIVE VALUE OF ACCEPTABLE AND UNACCEPTABLE ITEMS IN OWN SCALE AND IN GENERAL ADJUSTMENT SCALE

Scale	Acceptable Items		Unacceptable Items	
	Q_1-Q_4 Own Scale	Q_1-Q_4 General Adjustment	Q_1-Q_4 Own Scale	Q_1-Q_4 General Adjustment
Morale	10.08	6.88	14.36	14.04
Inferiority	10.40	3.22	10.64	8.76
Family	12.20	1.88	14.12	8.88
Law	11.52	6.28	12.04	8.84
Economic conservatism	10.88	2.92	15.68	9.80
Education	11.84	6.36	13.92	9.68

Table 127 is to be interpreted as follows: The 11 acceptable morale items as a group discriminate between the upper and lower morale quartiles by 10.08

6. Data for men in controlled sample of unemployed.

points, whereas they discriminate between the upper and lower adjustment quartiles by 6.88 points. In every instance the items as a group discriminate better in their own scale than in the adjustment scale. As is to be expected, the difference in discriminative power in their own and in the adjustment scale is less for the unacceptable items. It seems reasonable to conclude that the specific items of any single scale measure the specific trait or traits implied by the items better than they measure the adjustment factor. Each scale measures both the general and the specific traits.

FORM VERSUS CONTENT OF STATEMENT

Thus far the evidence points to the conclusion that both acceptable and unacceptable items are reacted to on the basis of their form of statement as well as on their content. Acceptable items, however, appear to be reacted to more largely on the basis of their content. One cannot infer from the evidence that either form or content of the unacceptable statement is the more influential factor. The data do show clearly that both are involved. The evidence of the influence of form has been presented in detail. That content is also influential is shown by the differences in the discriminative values of unacceptable items in the general adjustment scale and by the fact that each item tends to discriminate best in the scale in which it is placed. A third line of evidence showing the influence of content is available. Compare the correlations of the acceptable items of one scale with the unacceptable items of another, and vice versa (Table 109) with the correlations between acceptable and unacceptable items within a single scale (Tables 120 and 121). The latter are, in general, higher. The similarity in content of items of a single scale causes the two types of items to correlate more highly than they would if their content were different. One would, on common sense grounds, expect just such a result.

IMPLICATIONS OF ACCEPTABLE-UNACCEPTABLE DIFFERENCES FOR SCORING

The results thus far presented leave little doubt that acceptable and unacceptable items should be score separately for the information that is yielded by them. This procedure gives three scores for each scale. Which is the more valid for which purpose? What differences in results are yielded by the three scores?

In individual cases, extreme discrepancies are encountered. One of the men receiving public relief gained an adjustment score one and one-half sigmas above the standard mean. His total arbitrary score on the family scale was 57 (which is .1 sigma above the standard mean for this scale). Forty-three points of this score were gained on unacceptable items and only 14 on acceptable items. If unacceptable items were considered, this individual would be among the quartile having the most unfavorable attitude toward the family; if acceptable items were considered, he would be credited with having one of the most favorable attitudes. Combining both types gives him a mean position. Which score best represents his true "attitude" toward the family? The large excess in unacceptable items is a consequence of his general maladjustment. But does his score on the acceptable items indicate his true position on the family continuum? Or does the combination of both types of items best measure his position? Following the logic of the finding that acceptable items are more specific in their connotation, one is tempted to conclude that the acceptable items yield the best measure of his specific attitude toward the family and that the high score on unacceptable items is entirely a result of his poor general adjustment, i.e., that he responded as he did to the unacceptable items primarily because of their form. It may be argued, however, that an individual's specific attitudes or feelings cannot be considered apart from his general adjustment. If this is the case, the combined score would give the best index of his actual reaction in the family situation.

Before examining the clinical aspects of the

question further, it is well to consider the research implications. Effects of acceptable-unacceptable item differences on group means will be analyzed in the chapter on group differences. Here relationships of the correlation type will be discussed. By the use of acceptable score, unacceptable score, and total score, five different correlations between each two scales may be obtained. These are given in Table 109. In general, correlations between unlike items are the lowest and those between like items higher; those based on unacceptable items are of the greatest magnitude, and those based on total score fall between those based on like items.

Which of these coefficients expresses the true relationship? No categorical answer can be given, but it will clarify the issue to consider the possibilities.

Correlations between unlike items almost certainly are not valid. For they may be low even though a marked relationship between the traits exists, since unacceptable items, in addition to measuring the specific factor, are much more closely related to the adjustment factor. The resultant correlations are lowered as a result of the unequal relationship of the two item series to a third variable and not necessarily because of an absence of relationship to each other.

Correlations between acceptable items have the advantage of expressing the relationship between relatively specific measures. But can the specific trait be considered apart from general adjustment?

Correlations between unacceptable items would, in part, take account of the general as well as the specific factor. There is, however, the danger that the general adjustment factor will overshadow the effects of the specific factor.

A total score seems at first glance to overcome the objections to the use of either type alone. Both the general and specific factors would be weighted. When an equal number of each type of item is used, such a procedure seems reasonable.

But there is still another factor to be considered. Even though an equal number of each type of item is used in each scale, their relationship to each other will vary from scale to scale. Acceptable items of one scale may measure the adjustment factor to a greater extent than those of the other. So may unacceptable items. This is actually the case. For example, the acceptable morale items are more heavily loaded for the adjustment factor than are like items of any one of the remaining scales. Further, the correlations between the two types of item vary from scale to scale. Other evidence on this point is contained in many of the tables in this chapter.

Since both types of item will be unequally loaded for the adjustment factor from scale to scale, any correlations between two scales will be lowered to some extent by the same factors which produce low correlations between the two types of item within a single scale.

Any one of the possible methods of expressing the relationship between two personality scales is open to criticism. The problem of the true relationship can only be settled after more information is available concerning the exact meaning of each score; in the meantime all types of relationship should be computed. One thing is reasonably certain: correlations between unlike items will be low, not only because of a possible absence of a relationship between two traits but also because the two types of item are unequally related to a third variable--general adjustment. It may well be that many of the low correlations reported between personality scales are more influenced by the latter than by the former factor. This will be particularly true when the two scales contain the two types of item in unequal proportions. Whenever correlations between two personality scales are reported, they should be accompanied by an analysis of the type of item in each scale.

Since the problem of which score is best in correlational relationships has no completely satisfactory theoretical solution, the problem must be attacked on pragmatic grounds. How much difference does it make in the practical situation? Table 109 shows that in some instances the three scores yield similar results, whereas in others the results are strikingly dissimilar.

To make it possible to consider more fully the differences in degree of relationship shown by the three scores in a practical situation, each has been independently related to certain variables outside the scales.

It will be recalled (see Table 92) that the only correlations between the six original scales of this survey and Bernreuter scores on which much reliance could be placed were morale with self-sufficiency, and inferiority with submission and with neurotic tendencies. (See Table 92.) Acceptable and unacceptable morale and inferiority scores were correlated with Bernreuter scores and are presented in Table 128. It is evident that the unacceptable items are more responsible for the correlations between total scores than are acceptable items, further evidence of the greater generality of unacceptable items. The relationships for unacceptable score are, however, not appreciably different from those for total score, indicating that trends may be evaluated from total score, but that one type of item may be more responsible than the other.

TABLE 128.-TOTAL SCORES ON ACCEPTABLE AND UNACCEPTABLE ITEMS FOR MORALE AND INFERIORITY SCALES CORRELATED WITH BERNREUTER SCORES*

(University High School group; N = 37 males, 34 females.)

Items	B 4 D (Dominance-Submission		B 2 S (Self-Sufficiency)		B I N (Neurotic Tendencies)	
	Male	Female	Male	Female	Male	Female
Morale acceptable	+.210	+.287	+.221	-.042	-.030	+.290
Morale unacceptable	+.387	+.253	+.578	-.196	+.377	+.250
Inferiority acceptable	+.566	+.396	+.352	+.030	+.431	+.350
Inferiority unacceptable	+.614	+.455	+.461	+.039	+.625	+.504

*A positive correlation indicates a direct relationship between dominance or self-sufficiency or absence of neurotic tendencies and favorable attitude as defined in the text.

TABLE 129.-ACCEPTABLE AND UNACCEPTABLE SCORES CORRELATED WITH I.Q. AND HONOR POINTS FOR MORALE AND INFERIORITY SCALES

(University High School group; N = 37 males, 34 females.)

	Honor Points		I.Q.	
	Male	Female	Male	Female
Morale acceptable	+.540	-.277	+.298	-.197
Morale unacceptable	+.275	-.112	+.145	-.104
Inferiority acceptable	+.187	-.234	+.228	+.061
Inferiority unacceptable . . .	+.257	-.166	+.154	-.006

In Table 129 are given the correlations between acceptable and unacceptable morale and inferiority scores and academic achievement and I.Q. Previously (Table 93) it has been noted that the total morale score correlated +.506 with achievement in the case of men only. Here it is evident that the acceptable items carry the correlation almost entirely. This is the only instance observed in this study where acceptable items have more influence on a relationship than do unacceptable items. As was noted in connection with the adjustment scale, these correlations need to be confirmed before definite conclusions be drawn. Since the acceptable items carry this correlation, they might profitably be included in the adjustment scale (scored independently) in order to make it a still more valuable research and guidance instrument.

The available evidence points to the conclusion that the use of total score based on an equal number of each kind of item will usually reveal general trends in correlational relationships. The interpretation of such relationships will be facilitated by correlating each type of item independently with the remaining variable.

Several lines of evidence may be educed to show that the combination of acceptable and unacceptable items is not without justification.[7] First, the two

7. The statistical complications which result from use of total score, particularly in the intercorrelation field, must be kept in mind, even if the combination of the two series is justified.

series are not completely uncorrelated. Secondly, the persistence of low correlation between scores on the two types of item over several scales suggests that many personality traits may have a dual aspect, the specific and the general. Thirdly, the ideational content represents a continuity.

In the last analysis, the only satisfactory justification for combining or not combining the acceptable and unacceptable series of items within a single scale must come through validation of each series independently against outside criteria. Adequate criteria are not usually available. Nor are they in this study. The information concerning occupational security obtained from the face sheet, however, serves as a partial validation for both acceptable and unacceptable items in the morale scale. Acceptable and unacceptable morale items are related to this factor for the unemployed men of the evening classes in Table 130. The other five scales are also included in the table, since total score on all six original scales tended to be related to this variable. Both types of item show a relationship to the variable. The relationship observed when total score was considered is not a consequence of a relationship for a single type of item. What slight differences between the two types of item are apparent in Table 130 favor the unacceptable series.

SUMMARY AND INTERPRETATION

Smith in a study designed specifically to investigate the influence of form of statement, found many differences, the widespread implications of which have not been generally appreciated. The similarity of results obtained, despite pronounced differences in method, make it almost certain that the differences between acceptable and unacceptable items are fundamental and not isolated findings due to some idiosyncrasy of either investigator's technique.

So far as acceptable-unacceptable item differences are concerned, there is an important fact to consider. Smith attempted to state the essential content both acceptably and unacceptably. No such attempt

TABLE 130.-CERTAINTY OF OBTAINING EMPLOYMENT AND SCORE ON ACCEPTABLE (A.) AND UNACCEPTABLE (U.) ITEMS OF EACH SCALE*

(Evening class unemployed men.)

Degree of Certainty	N	Morale		Inferiority		Family		Law		Economic Conservatism		Education	
		A.	U.	A.	U.	A.	U.	A.	U.	A.	U.	A.	U.
Very certain	2	27.0	21.5	29.0	32.0	20.0	35.5	28.5	28.5	33.0	35.0	17.5	18.0
Certain . . .	15	27.3	25.6	32.3	29.9	22.1	27.7	26.9	26.6	35.1	35.3	29.9	23.9
Uncertain . .	34	31.4	29.1	32.7	33.8	26.2	31.5	28.5	29.0	37.2	37.6	21.3	24.4
Very uncertain	18	31.7	32.3	33.9	33.0	26.2	35.5	33.7	31.7	37.5	38.1	24.4	26.2

*Arbitrary scores used.

was made in the present study. At the outset the authors' had not included among their purposes an investigation of this subject. The findings forced its consideration.

Despite this difference, the two studies yield similar results insofar as comparable data are available. The influence of form of statement is indeed potent. Even when items are not matched for content, differences persist--differences that are in the same direction as when content is controlled. The differences found between the two types of statement are:

1. Unacceptable items yield distributions more weighted toward the "favorable" end of the scale.

2. Unacceptable items yield lower means.

3. Unacceptable items meet the criterion of internal consistency better than do acceptable.

4. Unacceptable items yield larger standard deviations.

5. Unacceptable items yield more consistent responses from test to retest.

6. Both types of item, when scored in the arbitrary fashion, correlate about equally well with total score.

7. The two types of item within a single scale correlate lower than expected on the basis of the scale's split-half reliability.

The lower means and the more skewed distribution of unacceptable items toward the favorable end of the scale are considered as evidence for the term "unacceptable' used to describe such items.

Before interpreting the remaining facts, it is necessary to draw upon additional findings of the present study. One of the most important findings is that unacceptable items are more generalized in their significance to the individual. This does not necessarily imply that they are more generalized with respect to their logical content. This general factor is adjustment.

Since unacceptable items are reacted to on the basis of the general factor, each of them measures more nearly the same thing. Or, differences in the content of unacceptable items, while having influence, do not affect the response to the extent that they do in the case of acceptable items. Some of the facts of Smith's study very clearly indicate that the acceptable items evoke a more intellectualized response. It is, then, reasonable to find that unacceptable items are more internally consistent and that they yield larger standard deviations.

Unacceptable items, being the more diagnostic of the general factor of adjustment and involving a less intellectualized response, the inference is clear that they measure something more fundamental to the individual. Hence it is reasonable to expect that there would be less change from test to retest.

Both types of item tend to measure the adjustment factor. Acceptable items, however, do so to a relatively small degree. The very fact that unacceptable items are more closely related to the adjustment factor makes inevitable a disproportionate increase in score on the unacceptable items of a single scale as the adjustment score increases. This disproportionate increase in score on unacceptable items is bound to change the position of individuals from unacceptable to acceptable series within a single scale, and a low correlation results.

The reasoning underlying the explanation of the low correlations between acceptable and unacceptable items of a single scale suggested an interesting scoring possibility. Acceptable minus unacceptable score may well be utilized as a measure of adjustment. This scoring procedure was found to arrange groups in the same order as the adjustment scale itself, and to detect some of the individuals scoring high on the adjustment scale, but not nearly all. It will undoubtedly be a useful score, but a knowledge of its exact usefulness must await future research. One question which the present data leaves unanswered is the interpretation of difference scores which do not agree with adjustment scores.

In addition, the difference score also has potential usefulness in determining the kind of reaction a scale is evoking. In both studies, Smith's particularly, there is evidence to indicate that reactions to acceptable items involve a more intellectual intellectual response. This hypothesis is supported in our study by the fact that a group of intellectual liberals scored high on the conservatism scale, at the same time gaining an excess score on the acceptable items, whereas a group who have actually been defeated by the functioning of the economic order and who may be termed emotional liberals scored equally high on the conservatism scale but gained an excess score on the unacceptable items. Because of its indirection the difference score may well prove to be an exceedingly valuable index.[8]

It has been shown that the difference between scores on acceptable and unacceptable items are an inevitable result of the closer relation of unacceptable than of acceptable items to the adjustment factor. Can the difference score be construed as a direct measure of psychological conflict? The evidence on this point is meager, but it does appear that some factor in addition to the automatic one is operating.

It is probable, in some cases at least, that the difference between the score on acceptable and unacceptable items is due to a conflict in the measurement of the general and specific traits. The individual may tend to react to the unacceptable items on the basis of his general adjustment and to the acceptable items on the basis of his specific attitude or feeling about the particular item in question. Again it may be possible, particularly in the case of a maladjusted individual, that the acceptable items are reacted to on a conventionalized basis and hence do not reflect his true position on the scale.

Which type of item is best adapted to scales of the kind we have been considering? Smith concluded that acceptable items were more useful for research instruments of this type. Were we to follow Smith's general line of reasoning, we should conclude, on the basis of the same type of evidence, that the unacceptable items were to be preferred. Knowing, however, that the unacceptable items are the more generalized in their significance, more diagnostic of adjustment, and seem to

8. Scales could be developed to maximize differences between the two types of statement. Giving the two types separately is one way of doing this.

involve fewer intellectual elements in their response, the question ceases to have a categorical answer.

An additional factor complicates the decision. Smith shows clearly that the differences between the two types of item are more pronounced when each is administered in a separate form. Whether or not this intensification of the difference is desirable can only be determined from further study. The unacceptable items given alone seem, from Smith's study, to be more disturbing to the individual. The data appear to warrant the tentative conclusion that acceptable items are to be preferred if one is interested in a relatively specific aspect of personality. If, however, one is interested in measuring a general trait, fundamental to the individual, the unacceptable item is preferable. Whether best results can be obtained from a scale consisting solely of either kind of item is problematic.

There is the further problem of whether the score on acceptable items alone will accurately predict the individual's reaction in a specific situation. The adjustment factor may well contribute to this reaction. For the present it seems preferable to use an equal number of each type of item, scoring each separately, in addition to combining them in a single score. It does not seem that acceptable and unacceptable items need to be paired for content, unless one is interested in determining the exact influence of form of statement. Utilization of both types of item provides several scores for the same individual, each of which may be independently validated. Further, the difference score provides a clue to the basis on which groups and individuals are responding. The difference score may also yield a measure of the individual's general adjustment, enabling one to evade, in part, the charge so often made against personality scales--that it is impossible properly to evaluate an individual's responses to a single scale in the absence of knowledge concerning his total personality. If Smith's suggestion that unacceptable items used alone bring about emotional disturbance in the subject is correct, the use of both types of item is further justified.

What if no differences between acceptable and unacceptable scores are found? An explanation which is not improbable can be inferred from the results presented in this chapter. The trait may not have a socially approved aspect and hence may not involve the adjustment factor. It follows that one would be measuring a highly specific aspect of personality--one that may be of social importance but that is not very fundamental to the individual's well-being. If that is the case, one need not be concerned about which type of item he uses to measure a highly specific attitude. One advantage in using an equal number of each is that it is possible to detect whether or not the responses are due to content and not in some part to form of statement, that is, whether individuals are responding on the basis of the specific aspects of the problem involved or on the basis of their adjustment.

In the case of a single scale, when a measure of the adjustment factor is not available, what is the best index of the difference between the two types of item? There are four possible measures:

1. Differences in means.
2. Differences in internal consistency and standard deviations.
3. Distribution of the difference score.
4. Correlations between the two types of item that are lower than the split-half reliability coefficients.

Of these the second and the fourth are to be preferred as furnishing the fewest exceptions in the present data. The fourth is probably the best.

While the scope of this study precluded any further analysis of the problem, the sigma equivalents for score on each type of item for the normative group of 1,000 cases have been computed and are given in the Appendix, so that norms for these scores as well as for total score will be available.

The implications of the findings of this chapter for personality measurement are legion. Many scales contain both acceptable and unacceptable items. The greater dependence of the general adjustment factor on unacceptable items, plus its widespread effects, makes plain the inherent difficulty of isolating specific trait relationships. This difficulty of isolating purely specific relationships may be one of the major reasons for the frequently disappointing character of the findings in the field of personality measurement.

The conflict between the measurement of more and less general traits, a conflict indicated by the low correlations between acceptable and unacceptable items, is of especial importance to workers in the field of personality measurement. Whenever acceptable and unacceptable items are unequally distributed in two supposedly equivalent forms (such as odd and even halves) the correlation of the two may not give a fair estimate of the reliability of the test. Split-half coefficients will be lowered by difference in form of statement. The implications for correlation of two different scales have already been considered.

In the measurement of inferiority the acceptable-unacceptable question is of particular significance. Smith points out that most inferiority scales are composed entirely of unacceptable statements. Perhaps this fact causes such scales to measure general adjustment more closely than inferiority as such.

One example, taken from Smith's data, since, so far as the authors' knowledge goes, he is the only other to have extensively studied acceptable and unacceptable statements, will suffice to suggest the importance of scoring acceptable and unacceptable items separately. Smith found that juvenile delinquents scored more unfavorably on his inventory for the measurement of inferiority feelings than did his normative group. This finding is more understandable in terms of general adjustment than in terms of inferiority feelings. A re-examination of the data may possibly show that the difference is due to excess unacceptable score and is more related to adjustment than to inferiority as such.

An additional implication of these results should be mentioned. The data reviewed in the last two chapters show clearly that personality traits differ in the generality of their organization. The specificist's argument sometimes met with that a trait consists of nothing but the sum of the reactions to the items is refuted by the data. The 16 items of the adjustment scale measured far more than is implied by their content. Further, the form of statement appears to cause considerable differences in the generality of the measure. One further point: in the present stage of uncertainty concerning the meaning of total score when acceptable and unacceptable items are combined, it would seem best not to apply a factor analysis in dealing with personality tests containing both acceptable and unacceptable items. The intercorrelations will vary according to the type of item scored. Until more is known of the meaning of total score on a scale, application of a factor analysis to items will yield more meaningful results than application of the analysis to the total score as a unit.

The finding that acceptable and unacceptable items correlate low within a scale, despite having met the requirement of the test of internal consistency, has serious implications. These will be considered in the next chapter.

GENERAL CONCLUSIONS

1. Both form and content of an item participate in determining response.

2. The terms socially acceptable and socially unacceptable are more descriptive of the differences between what Smith called positive and negative items.

3. Socially unacceptable items are more generalized in their significance to the individual, i.e., are more diagnostic of general adjustment.

4. The reactions to socially acceptable items involve a more intellectual response--intellectual in the sense that variation in content of the item is considered to a greater extent than is the case for unacceptable items. This does not mean that reactions to acceptable items are non-emotional. There is no attempt to distinguish sharply between the emotional and the intellectual response.

5. It follows from 3 and 4 that unacceptable items measure aspects of personality that are more fundamental to the individual.

6. In general, the evidence suggests that the

most useful results will be obtained by the use of an equal number of each type of item, scored separately. Further, acceptable items will probably prove to be more useful in measuring specific, relatively intellectualized aspects of personality, whereas unacceptable items will be more useful in the measurement of more emotionalized traits of fundamental importance to the individual's adjustment.

7. The difference between score on acceptable and unacceptable items has potentially great significance as an index of adjustment and as a clue to the basis on which responses are being elicited. If no differences appear for any single scale, it is probable that the trait has no socially approved aspect, i.e., it is not related to the adjustment factor.

8. The differences in results yielded by the two kinds of item make particularly difficult the interpretation of correlations between two scales. A total score, based on both, seems the best single measure in that it takes into account both general and specific factors. It may not, however, express the true relationship. For psychological interpretation correlations between like items as well as between total scores should be computed. Correlations between unlike items of different scales will be most misleading. Correlations between two scales should not be reported without information concerning the type of item in each scale.

9. Traits differ markedly in the generality of their organization in the individual.

10. It is exceedingly difficult, if not impossible, to measure a specific aspect of personality apart from the adjustment factor.

11. Personality scales should be studied more thoroughly to discover other psychological criteria, such as that uncovered in the present study, rather than investigated solely from the standpoint of reliability and validity of the particular scale.

Chapter X

A CRITICAL EXAMINATION OF THE CRITERION OF INTERNAL CONSISTENCY

The test of internal consistency is essentially the use of total score as the validating criterion for an item. As has been pointed out, it is not a new technique, having been used at least as early as 1916 by Terman. As usually applied it consists of determining the ability of an item to differentiate between extremes of the distribution of total scores. There are wide differences in the proportion of cases at the extremes which various authors have considered proper or convenient in applying the test. Likert (13), and following him, Hall (9), used the upper and lower 9 per cent. Heidbreder (10), Vernon and Allport (22), and the present authors used quartiles. Smith (16) used the upper and lower 27 per cent, and the Thurstones (21) used the 50 highest and 50 lowest papers in a group of 694 subjects, approximately 7 per cent at each extreme.

ASSUMPTION UNDERLYING USE OF THE CRITERION

An assumption underlying its use in personality measurement, while not always clearly stated, is that the items meeting the test are measures of a common variable. The Thurstones apparently regard this as self-evident from the nature of the criterion. They say (21, page 14) that the fact that their items met the test "*proves* that there is a common core of some kind *throughout* the questions that were retained . . . ."[1]

Likert, having constructed scales by the use of the criterion, uses the odd-even reliability

1. Italics not in the original text.

coefficients of the resultant scales as measures of internal consistency, and, finding them high, says (13, page 23): "These results indicate a 'cluster' or attitude variable which we are justified in treating as a unit."[1]

Now the low correlations frequently found between the acceptable and unacceptable items within a single scale, items in each series having met the test of internal consistency in terms of total score, make it improbable that this assumption is correct. The criterion of internal consistency as a method of scale construction needs to be critically studied.

The fact that the acceptable and unacceptable items are not measuring elements with a single common core can be shown in terms of the criterion of internal consistency itself. If the two types of item were measuring a common core equally well, one would expect the item discriminative values to be of approximately the same magnitude whether the quartiles were selected on the basis of acceptable item score, unacceptable item score, or total score. Table 131 shows that the discriminative values often vary widely when computed on these three different bases. The table shows the discriminative values for each morale item when quartiles are selected on each basis. Without exception the item discriminative values are appreciably higher for items of a given form when quartiles are selected on the basis of score on statements similar in form than when quartiles are selected on the basis of score on items unlike in form. Moreover, the average discriminative values of items of a given type are higher for quartiles selected on the basis of score on items of like type than for quartiles selected on the basis of total score on items of both types. It will be seen, however, that certain statements yield higher discriminative values when quartiles are selected on the basis of total score than when selected on the basis of score on items of like type only.

The drop in item discriminative values when quartiles are selected on the basis of score on items unlike in form is often great. For example, as Table 131

1. Italics not in the original text.

TABLE 131.-DISCRIMINATIVE VALUES FOR MORALE ITEMS WHEN QUARTILES ARE SEGREGATED ON BASIS OF TOTAL SCORE, ACCEPTABLE ITEM SCORE, AND UNACCEPTABLE ITEM SCORE

(Sociology I men; N = 25 in each quartile.)

Acceptable Items				Unacceptable Items			
	Quartiles Segregated on Basis of:				Quartiles Segregated on Basis of:		
Item	Total Score on 22 Items	Score on 11 Acceptable Items	Score on 11 Unacceptable Items	Item	Total Score on 22 Items	Score on 11 Acceptable Items	Score on 11 Unacceptable Items
25	1.32	1.40	.64	1	.76	.56	.92
31	1.32	1.16	.84	7	.56	.36	1.08
37	1.24	1.36	.36	13	1.28	1.08	1.64
55	1.80	1.68	1.16	19	1.36	.92	1.80
61	1.28	1.40	.76	43	.88	.48	1.32
79	1.56	1.80	.96	49	1.64	1.40	1.84
85	1.08	1.40	.40	67	.68	.60	1.00
91	1.28	1.56	.60	73	1.40	1.00	1.76
103	.60	.64	.20	97	.84	.64	1.40
109	1.36	1.32	1.12	115	1.36	.92	1.36
121	1.36	1.40	.44	127	1.04	.92	1.00
Average	1.29	1.37	.68	Average	1.07	.81	1.37

shows, item 37 yielded a discriminative value of 1.36 when quartiles were selected on the basis of score on 11 acceptable items, and only .36 when quartiles were selected on the basis of score on 11 unacceptable items. Morale item 43 yielded a scale value difference of 1.32 for quartiles segregated on the basis of score on 11 unacceptable morale items and only .48 for quartiles segregated on the basis of score on 11 acceptable items.

Considering all acceptable items in Table 131, the average item scale value difference for quartiles selected on the basis of total score is 1.29, whereas the average is 1.37 for acceptable item quartiles and only .68 for unacceptable item quartiles. The corresponding values for unacceptable items are 1.07 for total score quartiles. 1.37 for unacceptable item quartiles, and .81 for acceptable item quartiles.

Table 132 shows that these results are not confined to a single group, or a single sex, or a single scale. In this table only the average values for items of each type are given.

These tables indicate that higher average discriminative values can be anticipated in scales containing acceptable items only or unacceptable items only than in scales containing statements of both types. A considerable proportion of the items yield discriminative values so low that they would be rejected as insufficiently discriminating if ability to discriminate were determined by the magnitude of the difference between quartiles selected on the basis of score on unlike statements.

Is it possible to formulate items for the measurement of such aspects of personality as morale or inferiority feelings that will discriminate as well for quartiles segregated on the basis of score on items of unlike form as on items of like form? Table 131 gives little hope that this can be accomplished.

COMBINING UNCORRELATED SERIES OF EQUAL LENGTH

These results raise the problem of whether statistically significant item discriminative values could be obtained if items measuring two uncorrelated

TABLE 132.—AVERAGE ITEM DISCRIMINATIVE VALUES FOR ACCEPTABLE ITEMS, UNACCEPTABLE ITEMS, AND COMBINED ITEMS WHEN QUARTILES ARE SEGREGATED ON DIFFERENT BASES

(General College group; N = 25 in each quartile.)

Item Type	Morale Scale Items			Education Scale Items		
	Quartiles Segregated on Basis of:			Quartiles Segregated on Basis of:		
	Score on 11 Acceptable Items	Score on 11 Unacceptable Items	Total Score on 22 Combined Items	Score on 11 Acceptable Items	Score on 11 Unacceptable Items	Total Score on 22 Combined Items
Men:						
Acceptable	1.00	.45	.80	1.14	.75	1.03
Unacceptable	.40	1.18	1.03	.69	1.15	1.05
All Items			.91			1.04
Women:						
Acceptable	1.21	.25	1.02	1.20	.72	1.06
Unacceptable	.43	1.31	1.02	.61	1.19	1.07
All Items			1.02			1.07

variables were to be combined in a single scale. The correlations between scores on acceptable and unacceptable items are sometimes so low that it is doubtful whether they can be considered to measure the same variable. Does the criterion of internal consistency applied to items to determine discriminative values for total score quartiles provide assurance that internally consistent measures of a single variable are being obtained if the resultant discriminative values are high? To provide an answer to this question two series of items were chosen that yielded total scores correlating about zero. They were the 11 acceptable economic conservatism items and the 11 acceptable family items. The controlled sample of 100 unemployed men was utilized since the correlation between total scores on the two series was only .044 for this group. Two series of acceptable items were chosen so that the analysis would not be complicated by differences in form of item statement.

TABLE 133.-AVERAGE ITEM DISCRIMINATIVE VALUES FOR 11 ACCEPTABLE FAMILY ITEMS AND 11 ACCEPTABLE ECONOMIC CONSERVATISM ITEMS WHEN QUARTILES ARE SEGREGATED ON BASIS OF SCORE ON EACH SERIES AND ON THE TWO SERIES COMBINED

(Controlled sample of unemployed men; N = 25 in each quartile.)

Type of Item	Quartiles Segregated by Score on: 11 Family Acceptable Items	11 Economic Conservatism Acceptable Items	22 Combined Items
Family acceptable	1.34	.08	1.03
Economic conservatism acceptable	.08	1.21	.78
Combined items			.91

Items in each series discriminated well in terms of total score on the series in which they were originally placed. (See Table 133.) As is to be expected from the low correlation between total scores on the two series, the item scale value differences averaged only .08 when computed for quartiles segregated on the basis of score on the other series. The important point is that the 22 combined items yielded item scale value differences averaging .91 after the items in the two uncorrelated series were combined into a single score.[2]

It is evident that average item scale value differences exceeding 1.00 are possible when two uncorrelated series are combined into a single score. A relatively small correlation coefficient between the series will readily yield discriminative values of this magnitude, even when its extreme quartiles are used in applying the test. Moreover, if only the cases in the extreme 9 or 7 per cent of the range were utilized, as in the Likert, the Hall, and the Thurstone studies, average item scale value differences exceeding 1.00 could be obtained without the least difficulty.[3]

Figure 10 shows how it is possible to obtain fairly high average item discriminative values when items measuring two uncorrelated variables are combined into a single score. The chart is the correlation scattergram for score on 11 acceptable family items against score on 11 acceptable economic conservatism items. The quartile lines for scores in each series are indicated. The individuals in this scattergram who are in Q_1 and in Q_4 with respect to combined score on the 22 items are also marked.

It is readily apparent that combining the two uncorrelated series into a single score will place in Q_1 on combined score about an equal number who score in Q_1 on each of the single series. In addition, Q_1 on combined score contains some individuals who scored high on both series even though virtually no correlation exists between the two variables.

Figure 10 shows that of the 25 individuals in Q_1 on combined score, one was not in Q_1 on either of the single series. This individual is in area GFJK of the scattergram. Eight individuals in Q_1 on combined score were in Q_1 on the family series, but not on the economic

2. In the chapter on discriminative values (III) it was pointed out that a scale value difference of .60 was sufficient to yield critical ratios of 2 or better with 25 cases in each quartile.

3. In the experiment just discussed, the average scale value difference using extreme 9 per cent of the range, was 1.36.

FIG. 10.
CORRELATION CHART:
SCORE ON 11 ACCEPTABLE FAMILY ITEMS
VS.
SCORE ON 11 ACCEPTABLE ECONOMIC CONSERVATISM ITEMS.
$r = .04$

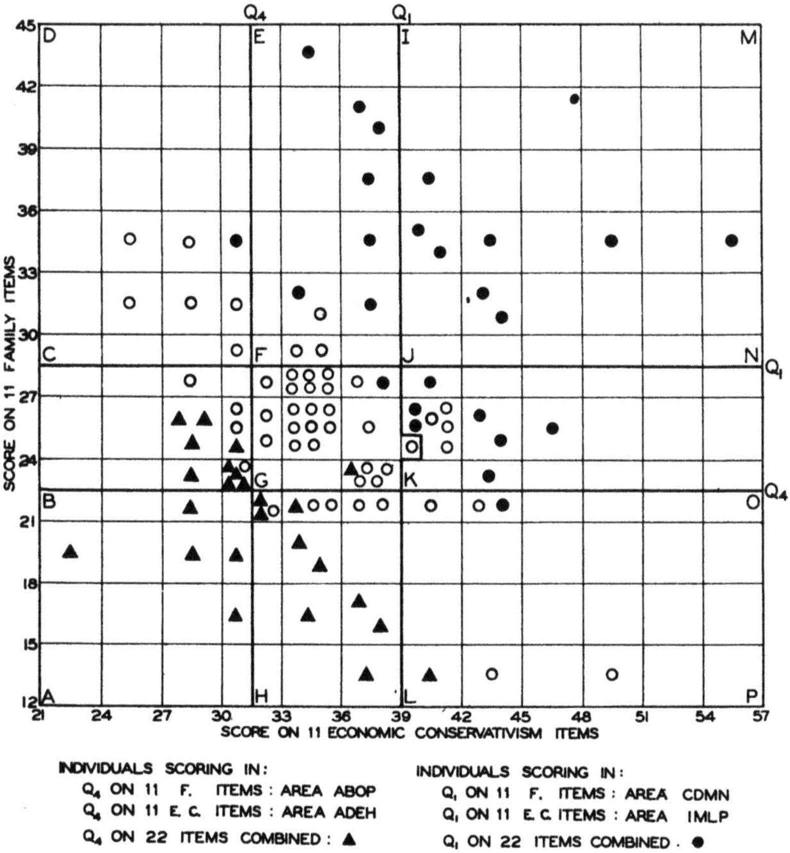

conservatism series; they are in area CDIJ. Likewise, 8 individuals were in Q_1 on combined score who were in Q_1 on the economic conservatism series but not on the family series (area JLNP). Eight individuals were in Q_1 on combined score who were in Q_1 on each of the single series (area JIMN).

In Q_4 on combined score, one individual was not in Q_4 on either of the single series (area GFJK). Nine individuals were in Q_4 on the economic conservatism series only (area BDEG). Ten individuals in Q_4 on combined score were in Q_4 on the family series but not on the economic conservatism series (area HGOP). Five individuals in Q_4 on combined score were in Q_4 on each of the single series (area ABGH).

This analysis makes it readily apparent that fairly high item discriminative values can be obtained when items in two uncorrelated series are combined in a single score as a purely mechanical result of the fact that each series yields a fairly wide range of scores, and combining the scores in the two series must yield some aggregate scores that are fairly high and some that are fairly low. The average discriminative value for items in the combined series must be lower than one or both of the average values yielded by the single series. Yet it need not be sufficiently lower to preclude obtaining item discriminative values which are above the level required for statistical significance, particularly if a small percentage of cases is selected at each extreme in applying the test.

COMBINING UNCORRELATED SERIES OF UNEQUAL LENGTH

Now that it is clear that high discriminative values are possible in the absence of correlation between scores in two series, we may ask what the result would be of loading the combined score by combining two series of unequal length. Figure 11 and Table 134 show what happened when twice as many items in one series as in another were combined in a total score. Scores on 10 acceptable economic conservatism items are plotted in the chart against score on 5 acceptable family items. Again those who score in Q_1 and Q_4 on combined score are designated on the scattergram, as are those who score in the extreme quartiles of each of the single series. The average scale value difference of the items for total combined score quartiles is .97. Combining two virtually uncorrelated series of unequal length does

FIG. 11.
CORRELATION CHART:
SCORE ON 10 ACCEPTABLE ECONOMIC CONSERVATISM ITEMS
VS.
SCORE ON 5 ACCEPTABLE FAMILY ITEMS

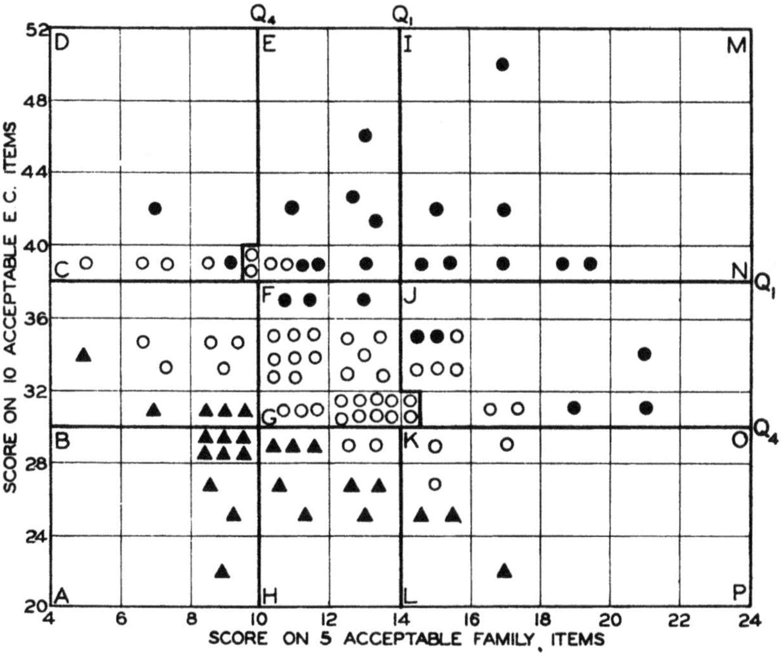

INDIVIDUALS SCORING IN:
Q_4 ON 10 E.C. ITEMS : AREA ABOP
Q_4 ON 5 F. ITEMS : AREA ADEH
Q_4 ON 15 ITEMS COMBINED : ▲

INDIVIDUALS SCORING IN:
Q_1 ON 10 E.C. ITEMS : AREA CDMN
Q_1 ON 5 F. ITEMS : AREA IMLP
Q_1 ON 15 ITEMS COMBINED : ●

not reduce average item scale value differences below those which can be obtained from two uncorrelated series of equal length combined in a single score.

Twice as many individuals in Q_1 or Q_4 on combined score were in these same quartiles of the economic conservatism series only as were in these same quartiles on the family series only. Nine individuals in Q_1 on combined score were in Q_1 on the economic conservatism

TABLE 134.-AVERAGE ITEM DISCRIMINATIVE VALUES FOR 5 ACCEPTABLE FAMILY ITEMS AND 10 ACCEPTABLE ECONOMIC CONSERVATISM ITEMS WHEN QUARTILES ARE SEGREGATED ON BASIS OF SCORE ON EACH SERIES AND ON THE TWO SERIES COMBINED

(Controlled sample of unemployed men; N = 25 in each quartile.)

	Quartiles Segregated by Score on:		
Type of Item	5 Family Acceptable Items	10 Economic Conservatism Acceptable Items	15 Combined Items
Family Acceptable	1.62	.08	.81
Economic conservatism acceptable	.03	1.21	1.03
Combined items			.97

series only (area CDIJ), whereas only 5 individuals in Q_1 on combined score were in Q_1 on the family series alone (area JLNP). In Q_4 on combined score eleven individuals were in Q_4 on the economic conservatism series only (area HGOP), whereas only five individuals were in Q_4 on combined score who were in Q_4 on the family series only (area BDEG).

Again some were in Q_1 of both series as well as on total score; they are the 8 individuals in area JIMN; and some were in Q_4 on both series as well as on total score; they are the 9 individuals in area ABGH.

Combining two series of unequal length tends to load the extreme quartiles on combined score with individuals from the extreme quartiles on the longer series in approximately the same ratio as the longer series bears to the shorter series in length. Combining the series again reduces the discriminative values of items in each series, but the reduction is greatest for items in the shorter series. That is, the items in the short series yielded much lower average differences between combined score quartiles than between quartiles on the short series. This indicates that when two relatively uncorrelated series of unequal length are combined, the chances are that a greater proportion of items in the shorter series will be rejected as insufficiently discriminating than will be rejected from the longer series, assuming that items in each series discriminate about equally well in terms of total score in their own series.

We have demonstrated that two uncorrelated series yield average item scale value differences sufficiently high to be statistically significant when combined in a single total score, and that loading the combined score will reduce the average scale value differences more in the shorter than in the longer series in comparison with averages in their original series. This means that acceptable and unacceptable items in a single scale can measure quite unlike variables and still meet the criterion of internal consistency as ordinarily applied. It also indicates that if the two types of item are unequally frequent in a preliminary form, the probability is that the disproportion will be even greater after the least discriminating items are dropped from the revised form of the scale, since the less frequent items of the one type will tend to yield lower scale value differences in terms of total score.

It is evident that the assumption underlying the test of internal consistency as usually applied is not justified. These results demonstrate that two uncorrelated series of items may be retained in the same scale if the sole criterion for inclusion is "internal consistency." While the number of uncorrelated variables that may be included in a scale constructed by the test, as usually applied, is not known, the effect of increasing the number of such variables is clear. As the number of uncorrelated items or series is increased, the average discriminative values will decrease. With a sufficient number of uncorrelated elements it will approach zero. As already pointed out, if all the items of a scale are completely uncorrelated, the range and standard deviation of total scores will also approach zero. As the proportion of correlated items is increased, individuals' responses become consistent and total scores diverge further from the mean. The effects of internal consistency are therefore evident not only in the size of item discriminative values but also in the magnitude of the standard deviations. Consequently they are also evident in the split-half reliability coefficients. Factors other than internal consistency affect the standard deviation and the reliability coefficient; these measures cannot be relied upon as sufficient measures of internal consistency.

ODD-EVEN RELIABILITY AND INTERNAL CONSISTENCY

Use of the odd-even reliability coefficient as evidence of internal consistency is not wholly warranted. The danger in using the odd-even r is nicely illustrated by the results for the family scale when it was applied to the public relief group. This scale yielded an uncorrected split-half r of .67. Scores on the acceptable and unacceptable items correlated .08 for the same group. The reason for the relatively good odd-even reliability coefficient in spite of the lack of correlation between the acceptable and unacceptable series is that the two types of item are distributed evenly between the two halves. A like situation which has not been detected may exist in scales constructed by other investigators.

EVALUATION OF THE CRITERION

Do these results imply that the technique of internal consistency is worthless? Not at all. As others have pointed out, it shows definitely whether or not the ends of the scale values for the items are consistently assigned. Existence of negative discriminative values means that weights were assigned in the reverse order from what they should have been to be consistent with the rest of the scale.

Secondly, the results of this chapter show clearly that it is a sensitive test for ascertaining which items are contributing most to the variation in the total score of the aggregate of items. If the total score is already known to be valid, the method provides a simple means for shortening a scale. Examination of the magnitude of the relationship between items having highest and lowest discriminative values will check their comparative validity. Validation of individual items against the outside criteria seems a better procedure.

Thirdly, even as usually applied in the personality field for the detection of items having a common core, it is a step in the right direction. If a series of items meet the test, it is an assurance that many uncorrelated variables are not involved. It does not, however, guarantee that the items are measuring only one major variable.

This general line of reasoning points to the fact that scales whose validity rests solely upon the ability of items to meet the test of internal consistency cannot be assumed to measure a common variable. They may be, but it depends not so much on the technique as usually applied as upon the investigator's skill or good fortune in assembling items at the outset which measure a single major variable.

It should be noted, too, that the loading or weighting which is intentionally or inadvertently introduced by the investigator into the original series of items at the outset will determine the nature of the weighting of the variables in the final scale. The weighting of the variables measured will be similar in the preliminary and final forms of the scale only if the weighting of the variables was approximately equal at the outset. If the weighting of the variables was unbalanced at the outset, the disproportion will be enhanced after items have been rejected as insufficiently discriminating.

A fourth and most important reason for not rejecting the criterion of internal consistency as worthless is the possibility of refining its application. It has already been pointed out that the use of fairly large segments of the distribution is a step in this direction. The construction of the adjustment scale illustrates an additional way of doing this. To require that only those items be retained which discriminate well in two or more rather dissimilar groups will increase the probability of obtaining true consistency. This procedure will not prevent measuring group differences, since items may discriminate equally well around different group item means. Witness the fact that 14 of the 16 adjustment items are unacceptably stated, and that 15 of the 16 discriminated in the same direction as between the controlled sample of employed and public relief groups. Other refinements can no doubt be made in the procedure.

SUMMARY

The criterion of internal consistency, while a step in the right direction, constitutes no guarantee that the resultant items are measuring a common variable, the assumption which has been made by many of its users. Even with the use of quartiles in applying the test, two uncorrelated series of items may be retained in the scale on the basis of the test. Use of lesser segments of the distribution obviously increases still further the possibility of retaining measures of uncorrelated variables. It follows that the validity of scales constructed by the method depends largely upon the investigator's judgment, skill, or good fortune in assembling at the outset items most of which do measure a common variable. In other words, the criterion selects those items that are most influential in determining the variation in total score on the original items. For this purpose it appears to be a sensitive test, although it must be borne in mind that unequal loading at the outset will result in still greater disproportion in the final scale. It is pointed out that the application of the technique may be so refined that it will come closer to providing assurance that the retained items are measures of a common variable.

Chapter XI

SEX DIFFERENCES

Sex differences have been revealed frequently in this study. Most of them have been small and of little significance when considered singly. For the most part, these differences have been only incidentally considered, not merely because the limits of the study precluded an adequate analysis but also because the data are not of such a nature that the problems indicated by them can be conclusively settled. The potential importance of certain of these sex differences make a brief discussion necessary, if only to indicate the nature of the problems.

The major sex differences that have appeared thus far in the analysis center around the adjustment scale and the difference between acceptable and unacceptable items.

THE SEX DIFFERENCE IN RELATION TO THE ADJUSTMENT SCALE

It will be recalled that in their relationship to the outside variables listed on the face sheet, the six scales as a unit tended to vary with much greater consistency for men than for women. This sex difference was so pronounced that the items of the general adjustment scale were chosen solely on the basis of male responses. The resultant scale appeared to be at least partially valid for women in that scores on all six scales varied with adjustment score for them as well as for men. It did not, however, relate itself to many face sheet variables for women, sometimes not even to those variables with which the six scales had tended to vary as a unit.

Would it be possible to select a similar scale on the basis of women's responses? To answer this question an attempt was made to construct a scale on the basis of the responses of the controlled sample of unemployed and the Sociology I women--the two groups corresponding to the male groups used in constructing the general adjustment scale. Exactly the same procedure was followed as was used in the construction of the adjustment scale. (See Chapter VIII.)

The first problem to consider is this: Are as many items discriminating well obtained from female responses? For men, 15 items discriminated 1.00 or better for the two groups, and a sixteenth item was added which discriminated better than 1.00 for one group and better than .90 for the second group. Figure 12 shows that on the basis of women's responses in the two groups, only 9 items meet the criterion of discriminating 1.00 or better for both groups--just three-fifths as many. Taking .60 as a critical level, there are 69 items for men (see Figure 8, Chapter VIII) and only 47 for women.

A similar difference is evident for one of the groups considered singly but not for the other. There are 35 items discriminating 1.00 or better for the Sociology I men, and 26 for Sociology I women; 96 items discriminating .60 or better for Sociology I men and 67 for women. For the controlled sample of unemployed there are 35 items discriminating 1.00 or better for men and 32 for women; 89 discriminating .60 or better for men and 82 for women. The sex difference is not so evident for the controlled sample of unemployed. With respect to the number of items meeting certain discriminative standards, the controlled samples of unemployed men and women are more alike than are the two sexes of the Sociology I group. They are not more alike, however, in that more of the same items are obtained from the two sexes of the controlled sample of unemployed than for the two sexes of the Sociology I group. Eleven of the items discriminating 1.00 or better for the sexes of the Sociology I group are the same and 12 are the same for the men and women of the controlled sample of unemployed--not an appreciable difference.

The most important point to note from this discussion is the greater number of items emerging on

FIG. 12.

DISTRIBUTION OF ITEM DISCRIMINATIVE VALUES IN RELATION TO TOTAL SCORE ON ALL SCALES.

FEMALE RESPONSES ONLY

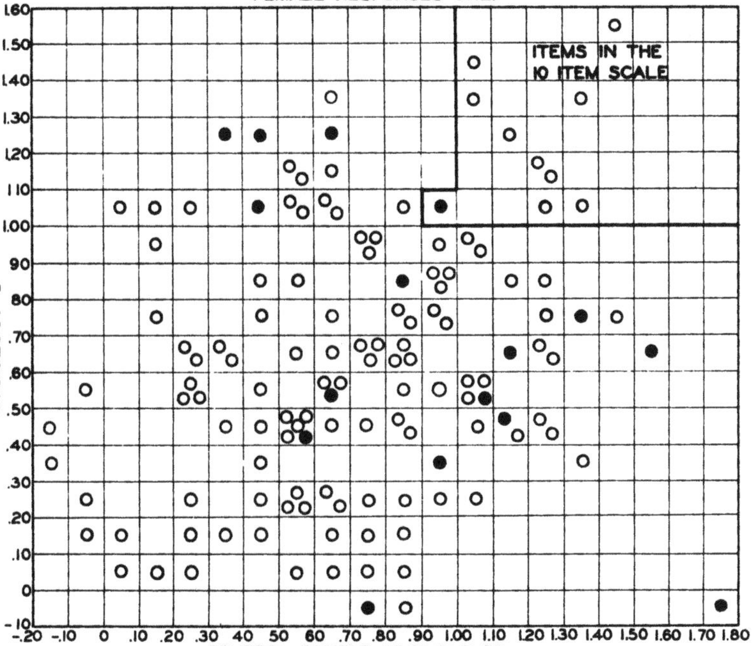

● - ITEM IN GENERAL ADJUSTMENT SCALE SELECTED ON BASIS OF MALE RESPONSES

the basis of male than on that of female responses when two samples are used as the basis of selection--15 for men and 9 for women meeting the criterion of discriminating 1.00 or better for both groups.

A 10-ITEM SCALE

In Figure 8 (Chapter VIII) the items in the 10-item scale are encircled; in Figure 12 the items of the general adjustment scale are encircled. Inspection of these figures shows that the items selected on the basis of one sex did not even come close to being selected on the basis of the other.

The 9 items that met the criterion of a Q_1-Q_4 scale value difference of 1.00 or better for both groups of women, plus one item that discriminated 1.00 for one group and .90 for the other follow:

32. IT IS EASY TO HAVE A GOOD TIME AT A PARTY.

3. HOME IS THE MOST PLEASANT PLACE IN THE WORLD.

51. IT IS HARD TO KEEP A PLEASANT DISPOSITION AT HOME.

69. THE JOYS OF FAMILY LIFE ARE MUCH OVER-RATED.

129. SO FAR AS IDEAS ARE CONCERNED, PARENTS AND CHILDREN LIVE IN DIFFERENT WORLDS.

40. ON THE WHOLE, POLICEMEN ARE HONEST.

52. COURT DECISIONS ARE ALMOST ALWAYS JUST.

58. IN THE COURTS A POOR MAN WILL RECEIVE AS FAIR TREATMENT AS A MILLIONAIRE.

65. MOST GREAT FORTUNES ARE MADE HONESTLY.

39. ONE CANNOT FIND AS MUCH UNDERSTANDING AT HOME AS ELSEWHERE.

Only one of these items, and that the least discriminative, is in the adjustment scale. There are further differences between these items and those chosen on the basis of male responses. First, only 4 of these 10 items are unacceptably stated, whereas 14 of the 16 items in the general adjustment scale are so stated. Secondly, there are marked sex differences in the scales from which the items are derived. Whereas 7 of the 16 items selected on the basis of male responses were morale items, not one selected from women's responses is derived from this scale. Of the 10 items selected on the basis of women's responses, 5 are derived from the family, 3 from the law, one from the inferiority, and one from the conservatism scale. Aside from the absence of morale items, the most conspicuous finding is that a preponderance of items are derived from the family and law scales. When the items were selected from men's responses, only one family item and one law item were obtained. The family-law relationship is obviously much more significant in the case of women. At first sight it seems strange that no morale items were obtained, since morale is known to be the most generalized scale for both sexes. (See Chapter VI.) The reason must be that the family-law relationship is sufficiently consistent to overshadow the effect of the morale scale alone.

This 10-item scale is valid in the sense that it carries with it scores on all six scales. (See Table 135.) The relationship with the family and law scales is the most pronounced, as is only to be expected from the preponderance of items these two scales contribute. It is also noticeable that the 10-item scale carries with it scores on all six scales for men. Markedly different scales are obtained on the basis of the responses of each sex singly, yet each scale seems partially applicable to the other sex.

The limits of the study precluded an adequate analysis of the 10-item scale. Tentative efforts in this direction were made, and certain general conclusions will be offered for the guidance of those interested in studying it further. The negative character of the results does not justify the inclusion of more tables in a work already overburdened with them.

The 10-item scale correlates with the general adjustment scale to the extent of .62 for men and .50 for women.[1] This result is to be expected on the basis of Table 135, which shows that the 10-item scale carries with it scores on all six scales, just as the adjustment score did. The adjustment scale, however, seems to be fundamental in this relationship. If those individuals are considered who score high and low on the 10-item scale only, this relationship tends to disappear, whereas it is even more pronounced for those who score high and low on the adjustment scale only. For those

1. General College, 100 of each sex.

TABLE 135.-RELATIONSHIP OF THE SCORES ON THE 10 ITEMS SELECTED ON THE BASIS OF WOMEN'S RESPONSES TO MEAN STANDARD SCORE ON EACH SCALE

(N = 25 in each quartile.)

Scores on 10 Items	General Adjustment*	Morale	Inferiority	Family	Law	Economic Conservatism	Education
			General College Men				
Q_1	55.68	54.88	50.72	57.16	60.00	48.60	54.08
Q_2	51.88	51.32	50.60	52.24	54.64	49.00	50.48
Q_3	44.96	45.56	49.68	45.80	49.72	45.96	48.04
Q_4	42.20	42.68	42.04	42.04	44.84	43.36	47.04
Q_1-Q_2 . .	13.48	12.20	8.68	15.12	15.16	5.24	7.04
			General College Women				
Q_1	54.56	52.96	52.56	58.44	58.56	49.72	56.96
Q_2	49.12	50.96	51.16	50.28	50.88	48.44	48.44
Q_3	47.84	47.16	47.92	43.92	46.80	47.96	49.72
Q_4	40.16	42.52	42.44	40.68	41.12	45.08	44.08
Q_1-Q_4 . .	14.40	10.44	10.12	17.76	17.44	4.64	12.88

*These items were selected on the basis of male responses.

individuals who score high and low on the 10-item scale only, the only scales that vary with it to an appreciable degree are the family and law scales.

In a further effort to see whether the 10-item scale had any meaning, it was related to some of the face-sheet variables. The evidence was entirely negative. Within the limits of the study no dependable relationship was uncovered. The scale may be useful and may add to the significance of the survey, but the authors have no indication of what its significance may be. No study has been made of its reliability. Since it contains only 10 items, high reliability coefficients cannot be expected.

In brief, the effort to develop a scale comparable to the general adjustment scale on the basis of women's responses was not successful. The main findings are that there is a striking sex difference and that a scale (the general adjustment scale) can be selected on the basis of the responses of one sex, be partially valid for the other sex, and yet its items cannot be selected on the basis of the other sex's responses. As a matter of fact, both scales would appear valid for both sexes if the test of internal consistency, as usually applied, was all that was needed for evidence. The average discriminative value of the 10-item scale for men is 1.248; the average discriminative value of the adjustment items for women is 1.030 (General College, 25 in each quartile).

THE SEX DIFFERENCE IN RELATION TO ACCEPTABLE AND UNACCEPTABLE ITEMS

The differences between acceptable and unacceptable items, altho clearly present for women, are less pronounced. There are at least three lines of evidence for this sex difference: (1) women in the most unfavorable adjustment quartile score higher on the acceptable items than do men, while men in this quartile score higher on the unacceptable items (see Table 111); (2) difference between score on acceptable and score on unacceptable items shows a smaller unacceptable excess for Q_1 adjustment women (see Table 122); and (3) the acceptable-unacceptable difference score, when the items of a single scale were utilized, did not correspond as closely with the adjustment score for women as for men. (See Table 124.) If more evidence is needed to prove the close association of the acceptable-unacceptable item problem, it is furnished by a study of those items of the survey on which the sexes differ significantly. A difference of .20 in mean score on an item yields a D/σ diff. ratio approaching 3.00 when groups of 500 are dealt with. There are 22 items on which there is a difference of .20 or greater between the 500 men and 500 women of the standardizing group. Of these, 11 yield higher scores for males and 11 for females. These items, together with the D/σ diff. ratios, are given on the following page. Acceptable items are indicated by A., unacceptable by U.

ITEM SEX DIFFERENCES

Type of Item	Item No.	Scale		D/σ diff.
			MEN SCORE MORE UNFAVORABLY THAN WOMEN	
U.	1	Morale	THE FUTURE IS TOO UNCERTAIN FOR A PERSON TO PLAN ON MARRYING.	2.78
U.	49	Morale	NO ONE CARES MUCH WHAT HAPPENS TO YOU.	3.04
U.	99	Family	PARENTS ARE INCLINED TO BE TOO OLD-FASHIONED IN THEIR IDEAS.	3.28
U.	105	Family	MEMBERS OF THE FAMILY ARE TOO CURIOUS ABOUT ONE'S PERSONAL AFFAIRS.	4.26
U.	88	Law	A HUNGRY MAN HAS A RIGHT TO STEAL.	3.24
A.	94	Law	ALL LAWS SHOULD BE STRICTLY OBEYED BECAUSE THEY ARE LAWS.	3.28
U.	100	Law	LAWS ARE SO OFTEN MADE FOR THE BENEFIT OF SMALL SELFISH GROUPS THAT A MAN CANNOT RESPECT THE LAW.	3.61
A.	112	Law	IT IS DIFFICULT TO BREAK THE LAW AND KEEP ONE'S SELF RESPECT.	3.28
U.	95	Economic conservatism	WHEN A RICH MAN DIES, MOST OF HIS PROPERTY SHOULD GO TO THE STATE.	2.94
U.	60	Education	THERE ARE TOO MANY FADS AND FRILLS IN MODERN EDUCATION.	3.48
U.	90	Education	HIGH SCHOOL COURSES ARE TOO IMPRACTICAL.	4.24
			WOMEN SCORE MORE UNFAVORABLY THAN MEN	
U.	43	Morale	THE DAY IS NOT LONG ENOUGH TO DO ONE'S WORK WELL AND HAVE ANY TIME FOR FUN.	4.67

Type of Item	Item No.	Scale		D/σ diff.
U.	67	Morale	THESE DAYS ONE IS INCLINED TO GIVE UP HOPE OF AMOUNTING TO SOMETHING.	3.15
A.	79	Morale	THE YOUNG MAN OF TODAY CAN EXPECT MUCH OF THE FUTURE.	5.65
A.	44	Inferiority	IT IS EASY TO KEEP UP ONE'S COURAGE.	3.38
A.	50	Inferiority	IT IS EASY TO IGNORE CRITICISM.	5.00
U.	68	Inferiority	IT IS HARD TO DO YOUR BEST WHEN PEOPLE ARE WATCHING YOU.	4.64
A.	80	Inferiority	IT IS EASY TO FEEL AS THOUGH YOU HAD A WORLD OF SELF-CONFIDENCE.	6.97
A.	128	Inferiority	IT IS EASY TO LOSE CONFIDENCE IN ONE'S SELF.	4.33
A.	21	Family	IN PLANS FOR THE FUTURE, PARENTS SHOULD BE GIVEN FIRST CONSIDERATION.	3.38
A.	27	Family	A MAN SHOULD BE WILLING TO SACRIFICE EVERYTHING FOR HIS FAMILY	5.74
A.	45	Family	ONE OWES HIS GREATEST OBLIGATION TO HIS FAMILY.	5.25

The striking fact about these items is that 9 of the 11 on which men score higher are unacceptably stated, while 8 of the 11 on which women score higher are acceptably stated. In terms of responses to these items, this means that women tend to disagree with or reject both types of item, whereas men tend to agree with or accept both types of item. This will be clear if one recalls how the item weights were assigned. Agreement with an unacceptable item received the high or unfavorable weight, whereas disagreement with an acceptable one received this weight. Women score higher on acceptable items, that is, tend to disagree with them, and lower on the unacceptable items, that is, tend to disagree with them. The reverse is true of men. They tend to agree with both types of item.

This is most clearly the case for those items on which there is a statistically significant sex difference, but the tendency is evident for all items. Table 114 shows that women take the 1 and 2 position (strongly agree and agree) less often for every scale than do men on acceptable items, whereas they take the 4 and 5 positions (disagree and strongly disagree) more often than men on four of the six scales. Women take the 1 and 2 positions (strongly disagree and disagree) more often on unacceptable items of three of the six scales, whereas they take the 4 and 5 positions (agree and strongly agree) less often on items of five of the six scales.

DISCUSSION

There can be little question of the importance of the sex differences noted in this chapter. What are their significance? The data do not provide a clear answer. One or two hypotheses may be ventured more as a guide for future work than as representing the authors' convictions. Consider, first, the evidence for the hypothesis that women's responses in the personality field are less generalized than men's.

The facts on which this hypothesis is based are as follows: 1. Fewer items of generalized significance are obtained from women's than from men's responses. 2. The morale scale, known to be the most generalized of the six scales, furnishes no item to the 10-item scale. 3. For the group of 500, the multiple R of the morale scale with the remaining scales (excluding economic conservatism) is .73 for men and .65 for women. 4. The correlation between the general adjustment and the 10-item scale is .62 for men and .50 for women (r's not corrected for attenuation).[2] If the

2. The statistician will no doubt inquire why these r's are not corrected for attenuation, contending that the observed difference may be a function of the lesser reliability of the scales for women. A moment's consideration will show that it is not

hypothesis is sound, this difference is to be expected. Two generalized scales should correlate lower for females if personality is less generally organized around a central core. 5. One of the most convincing findings concerning acceptable-unacceptable item differences is that unacceptable items are more generalized in their significance. Fourteen of the 16 items of the general adjustment scale are unacceptably stated whereas but 4 of the items of the 10 item scale are so stated. 6. Separation of parents appeared to be more closely related to the six scales for women than for men. (See Table 76.) This sex difference is reversed when the adjustment scale is considered. (See Table 101.) If women's responses are not highly generalized, it cannot be expected that the relationships will show up as clearly when a general scale is used. 7. To substantiate the argument that this sex difference is one of organization of personality, sex differences were found to be relatively infrequent in mean item scores and even less frequent on the items contained in either the adjustment or 10-item scale. There are 22 items on which there is a statistically significant sex difference between means. Of these, 11 yield higher scores for males and 11 for females. None of the items showing a sex difference are in the 10-item scale, and only 4 are in the adjustment scale. Of the 4, 2 show higher scores for men and 2 for women.

These data consistently point in the direction of greater organization of personality around a central generalized core among men than among women. Some generality in organization is characteristic of both sexes.

(Footnote Continued) justifiable to so correct these r's. In Chapter V the dependence of the standard deviation and hence of the reliability coefficient on the discriminative power of the items was demonstrated. Hence, if these r's are corrected for attenuation, what is being done is to correct the scale for its inapplicability to a particular group. Since this is exactly the point at issue here, correction for attenuation is not justified. Correction for attenuation would be justified if it could be demonstrated that the scales are really less reliable for one group than for the other, and not merely less applicable.

If this is granted, the hypothesis may be carried one step further in an effort to account for these findings. It will probably be conceded that, on the average, women's experience is more restricted than men's. It follows that their opportunity for organization of personality in a generalized pattern by environmental pressures is less. So long as women are economically dependent on either husband or father, the major part of their lives will revolve around domestic affairs. Hence it is only to be expected that a preponderance of family and law items would emerge in a general scale selected on the basis of women's responses. It is possible, however, that this sex difference in organization may reflect biological factors as well as differences in experience.

There are, however, some facts that do not support the hypothesis that women's personality is less generalized than men's. The multiple R's in Chapter VI, and the analysis of discriminative values (see Chapter III) do not completely fit this theory. The high school controlled sample, the women of which show higher multiple R's than men and for whom the average scale value differences of items in scales other than their own are greater than for men, provides a conspicuous exception. It is possible that environmental differences are greater for women in dissimilar groups than for men, and hence personality integration may vary more.

There is some evidence, also, that women's personality may be organized around a different core, the family and law scales particularly being more closely associated, and the inferiority scale at times appearing associated with this complex. Differences in experience might well account for this. The differences in the scales derived from the responses of the two sexes would support this hypothesis.

An additional hypothesis may be derived from the associations of the sex difference with the acceptable-unacceptable item differences. In addition to being more generalized, unacceptable items state the socially disapproved side of the case. It may be that it is a greater step to take the socially disapproved side on unacceptable items than to take it on acceptable items. The evidence that unacceptable items arouse more emotional response suggests that this is the case. Women may be less aggressive in their reactions toward the conventional restrictions--or toward authority in general, and hence tend to score lower on unacceptable items. That means on the law scale are slightly lower for women in five of six comparisons fits this hypothesis. (See Table 19.) Further, in the items on which the sexes differ significantly, not one law item is found on which women score more unfavorably, while there are 4 such for men. Also, the two family items on which men score more unfavorably suggest reaction against authority, whereas the two family items on which the women score more unfavorably do not.

If economic conservatism is looked upon as conformity to the prevailing social order, the fact that women tend to remain conservative under most adverse circumstances whereas men do not may also be interpreted in this light.

It is emphasized that these are tentative hypotheses, any or all of which may be completely or partially sound. They are presented merely as suggestive for further investigations. The search for sex differences in the field of personality organization rather than in mean differences may be particularly fruitful.

One of the findings of this chapter has implications for the application of the test of internal consistency. The 10-item scale is seemingly applicable to men in terms of the average discriminative values after it has been selected. Likewise, the general adjustment scale seems to be applicable to women on this same basis. Yet the scales cannot be selected from the responses of the other sex. This raises the question whether it is justifiable to consider high discriminative values of a final scale when applied to another group as evidence of the "validity" of the scale for that particular group. A better procedure would be to apply all items to both groups to determine whether the same ones can be selected by means of the test. The authors followed the first procedure in the analysis in Chapter III before the data on internal consistency, uncovered in this study, were available. Were they to repeat this work, they would utilize more than one group in the selection of items for each scale, as was done for the adjustment scale.

SUMMARY

In this chapter sex differences in relation to the general adjustment scale and the acceptable-unacceptable item differences were discussed. On the basis of women's responses in the two groups corresponding to the male groups used in the construction of the general adjustment scale, it was not possible to construct a similar instrument for women. It was also noted that the items on which women scored significantly higher were preponderately acceptable, whereas those on which men scored higher were preponderately unacceptable. Three general hypotheses are offered, none of which completely accounts for all the facts: women's responses are less generally organized around a central core; they are organized around a different core; in general they are less rebellious against authority. The question is raised whether it is sufficient to apply the final items of a scale to a new group to test for internal consistency or whether we should apply all the items to both groups to determine whether the same items can be selected from both. The latter procedure seems preferable.

Chapter XII

GROUP DIFFERENCES WITH PARTICULAR REFERENCE TO THE EFFECTS OF UNEMPLOYMENT

The determination of significant differences between groups is made difficult by the findings of the preceding chapter relating to scores on acceptable and unacceptable items. The tendency for scores made on unacceptable items to vary with general adjustment has been noted, and the problem has been raised as to which score is more truly indicative of attitude in a specific sphere. Since the problem has not been solved, we cannot always be certain that a higher mean standard score on a given scale signifies more than general maladjustment. To be reasonably certain that differences between groups are significant, it seems necessary that both acceptable and unacceptable item scores shall deviate in the same direction as does mean standard score in a particular group comparison.

DIFFERENCES BETWEEN TOTAL SCORES OF EMPLOYED AND UNEMPLOYED MEN

The group comparisons of major interest are those between employed and unemployed, since the detection of such differences was a major purpose in the construction of the scales. The two principal unemployed groups are the youthful unemployed in the unemployed controlled sample and the older unemployed men receiving public relief.. The youthful unemployed in the controlled sample are roughly comparable with the members of the employed controlled sample in education, occupational status of parent, and age.

The men receiving public relief, we have pointed out, are older married men with dependent children. Fifty of the men are married, one is a widower, and one is divorced. Forty-eight of the 52 men have one or more children. Ten men are between 20 and 29 years of age, nineteen between 30 and 39, sixteen between 40 and 49, four between 50 and 59, and three are over 60. Twenty-six men, or 50 per cent, are in semi-skilled or unskilled occupations (classes V, VI, or VII in the occupational classification discussed in Chapter II). Four of the men were in occupational class II, nineteen in class III, 1 in class IV, and two were unclassifiable.

These men on public relief were given the scales in groups of two or three as they waited in a relief office. They were already on relief. They were told that this study was an effort to determine how unemployed men actually felt about certain questions, and that their answers would not affect their status. The anonymity of the scales made a particularly favorable impression on this group.

These 52 men receiving public relief are too few to warrant the assumption that they are a representative sample of the entire population on public relief. They were taken from one relief office, which serves a large territory, little of which is within two miles of the central business district and none within a mile. They were not slum residents nor chronic dependents. The mean time that had elapsed since the last regular employment was 22 months, so these men were largely mid-depression cases. Twenty-five per cent had been unemployed for three years or longer, 37 per cent had been unemployed for one year or less. The scales were given in February, 1934.

An unemployed group of comparable age distribution, educational background, and occupational distribution was not obtained. The mean scores for these men on relief will be compared with those for the younger employed and unemployed male groups. Relationships between age, education, occupational status, and scores on the various scales will be examined for men in the public relief group.

The mean standard scores for the three groups just mentioned are given below. The numbers of cases in this comparison are: controlled sample of employed,

100; controlled sample of unemployed, 100; dependents on public relief, 52. The N remains the same in all later comparisons unless otherwise stated.

	General Adjustment	Morale	Inferiority	Family	Law	Economic Conservatism	Education
Controlled sample of employed	49.15	47.70	49.97	49.57	50.41	50.47	50.65
Controlled sample of unemployed	52.06	49.93	48.77	51.09	49.04	53.32	49.37
Dependents on public relief	57.98	53.52	45.44	47.17	51.67	59.04	52.96

Less favorable mean scores for the two unemployed groups than for the employed are confined to the general adjustment, morale, and economic conservatism scales. General adjustment score was found in an earlier chapter to yield larger differences in relation to face sheet data than did the morale scale. Since the items in the general adjustment scale are very general and are varied in ideational content, it seems probable that the cumulative effects of depression experience on many phases of personality are being reflected in these scores.

The unemployed seem more radical in their economic views than discouraged concerning the prospects for the future. Seventy-seven per cent of the public relief men exceeded the mean score of the men in the controlled sample of employed on the economic conservatism scale, whereas 73 per cent exceeded the mean score for the controlled sample of employed men on the morale scale. At the time the scales were given, CWA projects were being widely instituted, and a knowledge of these may have colored estimates of the immediate future. The D/σ diff. ratios for the differences between these three male groups on the three scales are shown below. In each comparison the first mentioned group scores less favorably:

		General Adjustment	Morale	Economic Conserv-atism
Dependents on public relief	-- Controlled sample of employed	4.09	2.94	4.64
Dependents on public relief	-- Controlled sample of unemployed	2.59	1.77	3.04
Controlled sample of unemployed	-- Controlled sample of employed	1.90	1.61	1.98

These ratios indicate that the young unemployed are more similar to the young employed than to the older unemployed married men on relief. Since nearly all these young men are still residing at home, most of them are recent high school graduates, and all are enrolled in educational classes, this finding is not surprising.

It is surprising to find that inferiority score is more favorable for the dependents on public relief than for either of the other two groups. The difference between the dependents on public relief and controlled sample of employed is 2.83 times its standard error, that between dependents on public relief and controlled sample of unemployed is 2.09 times its standard error.

DIFFERENCES BETWEEN SCORES OF EMPLOYED AND UNEMPLOYED MEN ON ACCEPTABLE AND UNACCEPTABLE ITEMS

Are the differences confined to standard total score or will they be manifest in scores on acceptable and unacceptable items? The data are given below for the three groups in arbitrary scores on unacceptable items.

	Morale	Inferiority	Family	Law	Economic Conservatism	Education
Controlled sample of employed	25.95	31.98	30.48	29.05	32.96	24.36
Controlled sample of unemployed . . .	27.74	32.13	31.93	29.02	35.38	24.43
Dependents on public relief	30.25	32.38	31.00	31.04	39.94	26.35

The mean scores are higher on every scale for the dependents on public relief than for the controlled sample of employed, but the largest differences are again those on the morale and economic conservatism scales. The differences between controlled sample of unemployed and controlled sample of employed in mean morale score is 2.06 times its standard error, that between dependents on public relief and controlled sample of employed groups is 3.10 times its standard error, while that between dependents on public relief and controlled sample of unemployed groups is 2.04 times its standard error.

The difference between controlled sample of unemployed and controlled sample of employed groups in economic conservatism score yields a critical ratio of 2.52, that between dependents on public relief and controlled sample of employed a ratio of 5.88, and that between dependents on public relief and controlled sample of unemployed groups a ratio of 3.80. There can be little doubt of the statistical significance of these differences. None of the remaining smaller differences on other scales in this comparison meets the test of statistical significance. The higher scores for dependents on public relief men than for controlled sample of employed men on every scale are probably due largely to generalized maladjustment rather than to less favorable attitudes in every specific sphere. A critical test of the differences so far as particular scales are concerned is whether they persist when scores on acceptable items are considered. The scores on acceptable items are:

	Morale	Inferiority	Family	Law	Economic Conservatism	Education
Controlled sample of employed	29.06	34.05	25.49	30.10	34.74	23.73
Controlled sample of unemployed	29.40	32.72	25.61	28.78	35.29	22.45
Dependents on public relief	30.33	29.77	22.31	29.35	36.67	23.52

The effect of form of statement on the magnitude of the differences is again convincingly demonstrated by the fact that dependents on public relief men scored more favorably than controlled sample of employed men on four scales, whereas they had scored less favorably on every scale when score on unacceptable items was considered.

The scales for which a consistent trend is apparent for every type of score between young employed, young unemployed, and older unemployed are the morale and economic conservatism scales. The smaller magnitude of the differences for acceptable item scores may mean that reactions are more conventionalized and consequently less diagnostic. The difference between dependents on public relief and controlled sample of employed on morale and economic conservatism acceptable items yield critical ratios of 1.33 and 1.76, neither of which is statistically certain. Yet the fact that these two scales alone yield differences in the unfavorable direction for the unemployed, coupled with the statistical significance of the difference on total standard score and unacceptable item score, leaves little doubt concerning the poorer morale and greater radicalism of the unemployed.

It is interesting to find that the men on public relief score definitely more favorably on the inferiority and family acceptable items than do either the youthful unemployed or employed. The difference on inferiority items is statistically significant, the critical ratio being 4.23. The corresponding difference between means for dependents on public relief and controlled sample of unemployed groups is 2.98 times its standard error. If the unemployed are really less prone to inferiority feelings, as the difference indicates, it is probable that they have succeeded in attributing their unemployment not to personal inferiority but to a faulty economic system. They certainly believe that it is the duty of government to provide for them while unemployed if their verbal reactions mean anything. The younger unemployed also score more favorably than the youthful employed on the inferiority scale, but the difference is not statistically certain.

The more favorable score made by men dependent on public relief on the family acceptable items is statistically certain; the critical ratio for the difference between dependents on public relief and controlled sample of employed groups is 3.95. The difference between dependents on public relief and controlled sample of unemployed groups is also statistically certain, the ratio being 3.78. If family life serves as a haven in a world of insecurity and there is increased dependence upon the family for personal satisfactions, the maintenance of favorable attitudes in this sphere is readily understandable. For many, this is undoubtedly the situation.

SCORES FOR MEN ON PUBLIC RELIEF IN RELATION TO AGE, EDUCATION, AND OCCUPATIONAL STATUS

The public relief group is heterogeneous with reference to age, previous education, and occupational status. If additional samples of this population were to be taken, it is probable that scores would vary somewhat, depending upon their composition with reference to these variables. The present sample probably includes a larger proportion of men with high school training, and a greater number in the upper occupational classes than would be found in the total relief population of the city.

Age is related in this group to scores on several of the scales. The mean standard scores are given before for 24 men who are 40 years of age or older and for 28 men between 21 and 39 years.

Age	General Adjustment	Morale	Inferiority	Family	Law	Economic Conservatism	Education
40 or over . .	61.88	57.83	48.79	48.58	52.00	60.83	54.83
21-39	54.64	49.82	42.57	45.96	51.39	57.50	51.36
D/σ diff. . .	2.04	2.42	2.56				

Poorer general adjustment and greater radicalism in this group than in either the employed, youthful unemployed, or standard populations are evident for both age periods. Poor morale is most characteristic of men in the older age range. Inferiority scores for neither age period reach the standard group means, although the older men approach it.

The mean arbitrary scores on unacceptable items are given below:

Age	Morale	Inferiority	Family	Law	Economic Conservatism	Education
40 or over	32.42	33.50	32.67	31.17	41.42	28.42
21-39	28.75	31.43	29.57	30.93	38.68	24.57

The scores are again uniformly poorer for the older men. Morale and economic conservatism scores in each age period exceed those for the younger unemployed and employed groups previously discussed.

The mean arbitrary scores on acceptable items are as follows:

Age	Morale	Inferiority	Family	Law	Economic Conservatism	Education
40 or over . . .	32.67	31.42	22.13	29.58	36.96	23.58
21-39	28.32	28.35	22.46	29.14	36.43	23.46
D/σ diff. . . .	2.74					

The differences are again uniformly in favor of the younger men, but are smaller than in the unacceptable score comparison. This is probably due to the fact that the unacceptable item scores reflected the poor general adjustment of the older men, as well as their positions on the individual scales.

The next variable to be considered is previous education. General adjustment, morale, law, and education scores show much larger differences in relation to previous education than in relation to age. The differences are in favor of the better educated. Mean standard scores for 28 men with eighth-grade training or less are compared below with those for 24 men with ninth grade training or more:

Education	General Adjustment	Morale	Inferiority	Family	Law	Economic Conservatism	Education
8 grades or less	63.39	58.64	47.25	48.68	55.78	58.93	57.54
9 grades or more	52.04	47.54	43.33	45.42	46.88	59.17	47.62
D/σ diff. . . .	3.10	3.40			2.78		3.33

Scores are poorer on five of the six scales for the less educated men. Discontent with the prevailing economic order, however, is not confined to any educational level in this group. There is little doubt of the statistical significance of the differences in relation to previous education in this group on the general adjustment, morale, law, and education scales.

The mean arbitrary scores on unacceptable items in relation to previous education are as follows:

Education	Morale	Inferiority	Family	Law	Economic Conservatism	Education
8 grades or less	33.21	34.11	32.11	32.89	40.78	29.78
9 grades or more	26.79	30.38	29.71	28.88	38.96	22.33
D/σ diff. . . .	3.31	2.26		2.43		3.98

The results are consistent with those found when mean standard scores were considered. The scores are again poorer on all scales for the less well educated, but the economic conservatism scale yields a negligible difference.

All scales except the economic conservatism yield poorer scores for the less well educated when arbitrary scores on acceptable items are considered. These scores follow:

Education	Morale	Inferiority	Family	Law	Economic Conservatism	Education
8 grades or less	31.86	30.14	22.89	31.32	35.68	24.82
9 grades or more	28.12	29.33	21.62	27.04	37.83	22.00
D/σ diff. . . .	2.43			2.34		

These differences are smaller than those found in the unacceptable item comparison.

With scarcely an exception poorer mean scores have been found to be characteristic of the older men and the less well educated in the public relief group. The differences on the economic conservatism scale, however, have been small in relation to age and education. Occupational status, too, is definitely associated with scores on certain of the scales for this group. But the differences are less striking than those found in relation to education. In the occupational comparison, men in classes II, III, and IV (as classified in Chapter II) are combined to yield an N of 26, while the N for classes V, VI, and VII is 24. Two men could not be classified. The mean standard scores in relation to occupational status are:

Occupational Classes	General Adjustment	Morale	Inferiority	Family	Law	Economic Conservatism	Education
V-VI-VII. . .	61.15	56.69	46.96	47.35	52.30	59.04	56.27
II-III-IV . .	54.29	49.71	44.33	47.08	50.96	59.42	49.08
D/σ diff. . .	1.81	1.95					2.29

All mean scores except that on the economic conservatism scale are poorer for the men in the lower occupational strata. Inferiority, family, and law score differences are of no consequence. The relationships for the general adjustment, morale, and education scales are more reliable. The size of the significance ratios is small, since the small N in the comparison requires a very large difference to establish statistical certainty.

The scores on unacceptable items are:

Occupational Classes	Morale	Inferiority	Family	Law	Economic Conservatism	Education
V-VI-VII	32.35	34.04	31.27	31.12	40.46	28.58
II-III-IV . . .	27.96	30.71	30.33	30.79	39.58	23.67
D/σ diff. . . .	2.03	1.97				2.37

Although the differences on all scales are in favor of the men in the higher occupational strata, the critical ratios are again small.

Scores on acceptable items are poorer on four scales for men in classes V, VI, and VII. The economic conservatism and family scales are the exceptions, as is evident from these statistics:

Occupational Classes	Morale	Inferiority	Family	Law	Economic Conservatism	Education
V-VI-VII	31.27	30.04	22.23	29.85	36.08	24.85
II-III-IV . . .	28.96	29.92	22.83	28.96	37.50	22.00

Summing up these differences in relation to occupation, we find that poor morale is more characteristic of the semi-skilled and unskilled laboring men, but radicalism is not limited to any occupational strata. Poorer general adjustment and poorer attitudes toward law and education seem also to be more common among men in the lower occupational strata.

The question arises whether any one of the three variables--age, education, or occupational status --accounts for all the differences. Poorer education and lower occupational status are definitely associated. To answer this question, the group was subdivided so that only a single variable varied in a comparison. First, the scores for men over 40 years of age were compared with those for men under 40, occupation and education being controlled. The mean scores below are restricted to men with 9 years or more of educational training and to men in occupational classes II, III, or IV. There are 4 men over 40 and 10 under 40.

Age	General Adjust-ment	Mo-rale	Infe-rior-ity	Fam-ily	Law	Economic Conserv-atism	Educa-tion
40 or over	56.75	50.75	45.50	51.25	50.25	64.75	47.00
21-39 . . .	47.80	41.30	38.60	42.50	50.90	59.10	45.20

The generally poorer scores for older men persist when occupation and education are held roughly constant.

Will the differences in relation to education persist when occupational status and age are controlled? The mean standard scores of men with eighth-grade training or less and of men with 9 years of training or more are compared below, all men being under 40 years of age, and in occupational classes II, III, or IV. The N is 10 for men with more education and 4 for men with less education.

Education	General Adjust-ment	Mo-rale	Infe-rior-ity	Fam-ily	Law	Economic Conserv-atism	Educa-tion
8th grade or less	52.25	51.25	50.25	54.00	48.75	51.75	52.50
9th grade or more	47.80	41.30	38.60	42.50	50.90	59.10	45.20

Although the N is small, the tendency for poorer scores to be associated with less education is apparent. The men with more education score unfavorably on only a single scale, the economic conservatism.

Will poorer scores continue to be associated with lower occupational status when age and education are controlled? All the men in the following comparison of mean standard scores are over 40 years of age, and all had 8 years of education or less. There are 8 men in classes V, VI, or VII, and 6 men in classes II, III, or IV.

Occupational Classes	General Adjustment	Morale	Inferiority	Family	Law	Economic Conservatism	Education
V-VI-VII . . .	66.88	60.38	48.75	50.88	57.75	56.00	64.50
II-III-IV . .	64.83	62.00	49.17	47.33	53.00	61.50	54.67

The tendency for poorer scores on a majority of the scales to be associated with lower occupational status is still evident. The largest difference is on the education scale.

Each of the three variables considered appears to be related to scores, independently of the other two. It is regrettable that the number of cases is not larger, so that this fact might be more firmly established. It can be shown however, that when the data are so classified that the maximum effect of the three combined variables is revealed, the differences greatly exceed those found when only a single variable is considered. In the final comparison, the scores of men over 40 in occupational classes V, VI, VII who had had no high school training will be compared with those for men under 40 in occupational classes II, III, or IV who had had high school training. There are 10 men in the first group and 8 in the second.

General Adjustment	Morale	Inferiority	Family	Law	Economic Conservatism	Education
66.88	60.38	48.75	50.88	57.75	56.00	64.50
47.80	41.30	38.60	42.50	50.90	59.10	45.20

There is almost a two sigma difference between scores on the general adjustment, morale, and education scales, and the difference in the inferiority score exceeds one sigma. Proof that radicalism is not confined to any age, education, or occupational level in the public relief group is provided by the sharp contrast between this score and other scores for the more favorably situated.

ITEM DIFFERENCES BETWEEN EMPLOYED AND UNEMPLOYED MEN

Confirmation of the fact that the major differences between employed and unemployed are in the spheres of morale and economic conservatism comes from a comparison of means for the three groups on individual items. There were 31 items which yielded differences in item means exceeding four-tenths of a point on the five-point alternative-response item scale between public relief group and the controlled sample of employed. None of these differences yield a critical ratio of less than 2.00, and they range as high as 6.42. These items are listed in Table 136, and the amount of the difference between the means for the public relief group and the controlled sample of employed is indicated. The item means for the controlled sample of unemployed are also given, although the differences between the means for the controlled samples of unemployed and employed are usually not statistically certain. The most convincing evidence that unemployment is associated with less favorable responses on these items is not the size of the critical ratios but the fact that for 27 of the 31 items, the means for the controlled sample of unemployed fall between those for the controlled sample of employed and the public relief group. Logically the young unemployed can be expected in their attitudes to be intermediate between the young employed group and the older unemployed group with dependent children.

The 27 items that yield a perfectly consistent trend as between the three groups in the order of the magnitude of the difference as given in Table 136 are:

47. THE GOVERNMENT OUGHT TO GUARANTEE A LIVING TO THOSE WHO CAN'T FIND WORK.

5. THE GOVERNMENT SHOULD TAKE OVER ALL LARGE INDUSTRIES.

63. ONE BECOMES NERVOUS AT HOME.

101. IF OUR ECONOMIC SYSTEM WERE JUST, THERE WOULD BE MUCH LESS CRIME.

19. LIFE IS JUST ONE WORRY AFTER ANOTHER.

11. LABOR SHOULD HAVE MUCH MORE VOICE IN DECIDING GOVERNMENT POLICIES.

1. THE FUTURE IS TOO UNCERTAIN FOR A PERSON TO PLAN ON MARRYING.

7. IT IS DIFFICULT TO THINK CLEARLY THESE DAYS.

22. THE SENTENCES OF JUDGES IN COURTS ARE DETERMINED BY THEIR PREJUDICES.

29. POVERTY IS CHIEFLY A RESULT OF INJUSTICE IN THE DISTRIBUTION OF WEALTH.

58. IN THE COURTS A POOR MAN WILL RECEIVE AS FAIR TREATMENT AS A MILLIONAIRE.

49. NO ONE CARES MUCH WHAT HAPPENS TO YOU.

97. LIFE IS JUST A SERIES OF DISAPPOINTMENTS.

125. MONEY SHOULD BE TAKEN FROM THE RICH AND GIVEN TO THE POOR DURING HARD TIMES.

89. LABOR DOES NOT GET ITS FAIR SHARE OF WHAT IT PRODUCES.

31. TIMES ARE GETTING BETTER.

14. IT IS DIFFICULT TO SAY THE RIGHT THING AT THE RIGHT TIME.

13. THE FUTURE LOOKS VERY BLACK.

53. LARGE INCOMES SHOULD BE TAXED MUCH MORE THAN THEY ARE NOW.

77. WITHOUT SWEEPING CHANGES IN OUR ECONOMIC SYSTEM, LITTLE PROGRESS CAN BE MADE IN THE SOLUTION OF SOCIAL PROBLEMS.

119. A MAN SHOULD BE ALLOWED TO KEEP AS LARGE AN INCOME AS HE CAN GET.

127. THERE IS REALLY NO POINT IN LIVING.

4. THE LAW PROTECTS PROPERTY RIGHTS AT THE EXPENSE OF HUMAN RIGHTS.

118. ON THE WHOLE, LAWYERS ARE HONEST.

73. THERE IS LITTLE CHANCE FOR ADVANCEMENT IN INDUSTRY OR BUSINESS UNLESS A MAN HAS UNFAIR PULL.*

100. LAWS ARE SO OFTEN MADE FOR THE BENEFIT OF SMALL SELFISH GROUPS THAT A MAN CANNOT RESPECT THE LAW.

65. MOST GREAT FORTUNES ARE MADE HONESTLY.

*An item from Hall's scale.

TABLE 136.—MEAN ITEM SCORES FOR CONTROLLED SAMPLE OF EMPLOYED MEN, CONTROLLED SAMPLE OF UNEMPLOYED MEN, AND PUBLIC RELIEF GROUP ON ITEMS YIELDING GREATEST DIFFERENCES IN FAVOR OF EMPLOYED IN EMPLOYED-RELIEF GROUP COMPARISON

Item	Scale	Form of State-ment	Mean Item Score			Difference Employed-Relief Group
			Em-ployed (C)*	Unem-ployed (C)	Relief Group	
47	Economic Conservatism	U.**	2.72	3.24	3.94	1.22
5	Economic Conservatism	U.	2.59	2.73	3.64	1.05
63	Family	U.	2.17	2.59	3.02	.85
101	Economic Conservatism	U.	3.07	3.26	3.88	.81
19	Morale	U.	2.42	2.45	3.20	.78
11	Economic Conservatism	U.	3.34	3.57	4.06	.72
1	Morale	U.	2.75	3.32	3.44	.69
7	Morale	U.	2.33	2.53	3.00	.67
22	Law	U.	3.24	3.58	3.88	.67
29	Economic Conservatism	U.	2.89	3.14	3.54	.65
58	Law	A.***	3.24	3.58	3.88	.64
49	Morale	U.	2.14	2.39	2.74	.60
97	Morale	U.	2.21	2.39	2.80	.59
125	Economic Conservatism	U.	2.72	3.02	3.30	.58
6	Education	U.	2.30	2.17	2.88	.58
89	Economic Conservatism	U.	3.67	3.78	4.22	.55
31	Morale	A.	2.11	2.36	2.66	.55
14	Inferiority	U.	2.82	2.99	3.34	.52
13	Morale	U.	1.97	2.32	2.48	.51
10	Law	U.	2.14	2.12	2.64	.50
53	Economic Conservatism	U.	3.52	3.81	4.02	.50
77	Economic Conservatism	U.	3.12	3.21	3.62	.50
119	Economic Conservatism	A.	3.06	3.27	3.52	.50
127	Morale	U.	1.73	1.92	2.22	.49
4	Law	U.	2.81	3.04	3.22	.46
55	Morale	A.	2.04	1.89	2.48	.44****
131	Economic Conservatism	A.	3.12	2.86	3.56	.44
118	Law	A.	2.90	2.94	3.32	.42
73	Morale	U.	2.85	2.93	3.26	.41****
100	Law	U.	2.81	3.04	3.22	.41
65	Economic Conservatism	A.	3.41	3.51	3.82	.41

*(C) = controlled sample.
**Unacceptable.
***Acceptable.
****Items from Hall's Occupational Morale Scale.

It is interesting to find that the item on which the men receiving public relief differ most from the employed is the government should guarantee a living to those who can't find work. Seventy-six per cent of these men strongly agree or agree with the proposition, 12 per cent are doubtful, while 12 per cent disagree or strongly disagree. Since the aid they are receiving is viewed as an obligation of government, it is understandable why the receipt of relief has not led to an increase of inferiority feelings.

The belief that poverty and crime are consequences of injustice in the distribution of wealth is shared by a majority of the unemployed. The consensus of opinion is greater among them that labor is being deprived of its fair share in the distribution of wealth than among the employed, although as a matter of fact the consensus of opinion in the standard group of 1,000 was in accord with that of the unemployed.

The low esteem in which possessors of great wealth are held is clearly revealed in the extent to which the proposition, most great fortunes are made honestly, is rejected. This is consistent with their indorsement of the proposition, large incomes should be taxed much more than they are now. The same attitude toward the possessors of large fortunes is held by a majority of the standard group of 1,000, although to a lesser degree. Another expression of the same point of view is evident in the rejection of item 119, a man should be allowed to keep as large an income as he can get.

It is interesting to find that a majority of the unemployed do not agree that the future looks very black, although a greater number of them than of the employed agree. Twelve per cent of the older unemployed men agree with the statement, there is really no point in living, which is a greater proportion than was found in any other group.

We have noted earlier the tendency of the older unemployed to be more favorable in their family attitudes than the young unemployed or employed. Yet more of these older unemployed men (48 per cent) feel nervous at home. In the past it has been almost a violation of our mores for an able-bodied man to be at home when others are working, and the monotony of having little or nothing to do must indeed be irksome. Moreover, despite their belief in the obligation of the government to provide for those who can't find work, many doubtless wish to conform to the social role of the father as breadwinner. Inability to live up to the role which an individual thinks other members of the family expect of him can easily induce nervous feelings at home.

Discontent with the prevailing economic system is accompanied by greater distrust of our courts. The men on public relief do not feel that a poor man will receive as fair treatment "as a millionaire" in our courts. In fact, only 16 per cent agreed with this proposition. They do not agree as to whether prejudices determine the sentences of judges; 36 per cent agreed, 38 per cent disagreed, and 26 per cent were undecided. That laws protect property rights at the expense of human rights is a view agreed to or strongly agreed to by 58 per cent of the men on public relief. These men do not think that on the whole, lawyers are honest, only 32 per cent agreed or strongly agreed with this proposition. It is difficult to perceive why distrust of the integrity of lawyers should be associated with unemployment, but the same tendency is evident among the younger unemployed. Perhaps the view is closely related to the attitude revealed in the statement, "Laws are so often made for the benefit of small selfish groups that a man cannot respect the law", which was agreed to or strongly agreed to by 48 per cent of these men. In short, many undoubtedly regard both lawmakers and lawyers as subservient to the wishes of selfish minorities.

Let us consider now the four statements that yielded significant differences between the public relief group and the controlled sample of employed, but which were more favorably responded to by men in the controlled sample of unemployed than by men in either of the other two groups. These statements are:

6. A MAN CAN LEARN MORE BY WORKING FOUR YEARS THAN BY GOING TO HIGH SCHOOL.

10. A PERSON SHOULD OBEY ONLY THOSE LAWS WHICH SEEM REASONABLE.

55. ANY MAN WITH ABILITY AND WILLINGNESS TO WORK HARD HAS A GOOD CHANCE OF BEING SUCCESSFUL.

131. OUR ECONOMIC SYSTEM IS CRITICIZED TOO MUCH.

It will be recalled that a majority of our youthful unemployed men were high school graduates. Seventy-three per cent of the men in the controlled sample of unemployed were high school graduates, whereas only 27 per cent of the men on public relief were high school graduates. The 14 men on public relief who had completed high school did not score less favorably on item 6 than did the men in the controlled samples of employed and unemployed. In fact, the item mean score for these 14 men was 2.14, which is more favorable than the item means for either of the other two groups. The unfavorable mean on item 6 for the public relief group as a whole is therefore associated with the fact that a majority were not high school graduates.

The young unemployed in the controlled sample of unemployed have a great deal of respect for the value of education. Proof of this is the fact that the item yielding the greatest difference between the controlled samples of employed and unemployed is item 24, a good education is a great comfort to a man out of work, which yields an item mean of 2.54 for the men in the controlled sample of unemployed and 3.21 for the controlled sample of employed. Presumably they feel that this will give them a competitive advantage when employment opportunities exist.

It is difficult to find a logical explanation for the greater acceptance among the men in the controlled sample of unemployed of the statement, "Our economic system is criticized too much", in view of their acceptance of the proposition that "poverty is chiefly a result of injustice in the distribution of wealth." This is the only logical inconsistency among the item differences which are statistically significant.

It is interesting to find that the youthful unemployed still believe, at least to a greater extent than do either the employed or the older unemployed, that ability and willingness to work will lead to "success." A reasonable interpretation is that these young men have their lives before them and undoubtedly a majority feel that they will eventually be able to make a satisfactory vocational adjustment. The older men on public relief have had more occupational opportunities and more of them have failed. This failure, it would seem from the inferiority scores for the men on public relief as well as from their response to item 55, is not attributed to lack of ability or willingness to work.

Item 55, it will be recalled, is one of the three items from O. Milton Hall's Occupational Morale Scale (9) that were incorporated in the present morale scale. The means for the three groups on these items are:

	Item 55	Item 73	Item 115[1]
Controlled sample of employed . . .	2.04	2.85	2.29
Controlled sample of unemployed . .	1.89	2.93	2.23
Dependents on public relief	2.48	3.26	2.32

Two of these items, 55 and 73, yield critical ratios higher than 2.00 as between dependents on public relief and controlled sample of employed groups. The critical ratio for item 55 is 2.48, that for item 73 is 2.11. Hall's item 55 is one of the 4 in Table 134 which failed to yield a consistent trend for the three groups compared. However, it is evident that all three yield differences in the expected direction, and that the critical ratio would probably be statistically certain if the N were larger in the public relief group.

Thus far we have discussed the items on which the dependents on public relief scored less favorably than either the youthful employed or the unemployed. Of

1. These items are numbered 28, 5, and 34 in O. Milton Hall's Confidential Survey of Engineers' Opinions, Appendix B, op. cit. His means calculated from data in Appendix B are:

	Item		
	28(55)	5(73)	34(115)
Employed engineers . . .	2.21	2.44	2.80
Unemployed engineers . .	2.73	3.25	3.24

the 31 items yielding differences in means between dependents on public relief and controlled sample of employed groups of four-tenths of a point on the five-point scale, reference to Table 136 shows that the greatest number, 12, were in the economic conservatism scale, 10 were in the morale scale, 6 in the law, and 1 in each of the other three scales. Table 136 also shows that 24 of the 31 items were unacceptably stated, a further proof of the great importance of form of statement.

The method of selecting the 16 items in the general adjustment scale as described in Chapter VIII produced a scale in which a majority of the items, 11 of 16, are diagnostic of unemployment to the extent required for inclusion in Table 136. That 11 of the 16 items yielded critical ratios of 2.00 or better as between dependents on public relief and controlled sample of employed groups, although neither of these groups was utilized in the selection of items for that scale, is further validation of the general adjustment scale. In fact, the differences between these two groups are in the expected direction on 15 of the 16 items of the general adjustment scale, albeit the differences are not statistically significant for 4 of these items. The only item that did not yield a difference in the expected direction in this comparison was, <u>one cannot find as much understanding at home as elsewhere</u>, for which the dependents on public relief group mean is 2.38 as compared with 2.42 for the controlled sample of employed group.

ITEMS ON WHICH MEN ON PUBLIC RELIEF SCORE FAVORABLY

Consider now the items on which the men on public relief scored more favorably than the controlled sample of employed men. There were 14 items on which the difference between dependents on public relief and controlled sample of employed men amounted to four-tenths of a point or more on the five-point item response scale. The means for controlled sample of employed, controlled sample of unemployed, and dependents on public relief groups on these 14 items are given in Table 137. In the order of the magnitude of the difference, they are:

104. IT IS NO TRICK TO BE THE LIFE OF THE PARTY.

8. IT IS EASY TO EXPRESS ONE'S IDEAS.

20. ONE CAN USUALLY KEEP COOL IN IMPORTANT SITUATIONS.

68. IT IS HARD TO DO YOUR BEST WHEN PEOPLE ARE WATCHING YOU.

50. IT IS EASY TO IGNORE CRITICISM.

3. HOME IS THE MOST PLEASANT PLACE IN THE WORLD.

27. A MAN SHOULD BE WILLING TO SACRIFICE EVERYTHING FOR HIS FAMILY.

81. ONE SHOULD CONFIDE MORE FULLY IN MEMBERS OF THE FAMILY.

21. IN PLANS FOR THE FUTURE, PARENTS SHOULD BE GIVEN FIRST CONSIDERATION.

99. PARENTS ARE INCLINED TO BE TOO OLD-FASHIONED IN THEIR IDEAS.

45. ONE OWES HIS GREATEST OBLIGATION TO HIS FAMILY.

64. PERSONAL CIRCUMSTANCES SHOULD NEVER BE CONSIDERED AN EXCUSE FOR LAW-BREAKING.

70. A MAN SHOULD TELL THE TRUTH IN COURT REGARDLESS OF CONSEQUENCES.

24. A GOOD EDUCATION IS A GREAT COMFORT TO A MAN OUT OF WORK.

It is immediately apparent that these items are predominantly inferiority and family scale items. Eleven of the 14 are from one or the other of these two scales. It will be recalled that inferiority and family scales were the only scales to yield significant differences in favor of the dependents on public relief on acceptable item scores. Further, it is important that the only scales that contribute no item to the list are the morale and economic conservatism scales.

Consider further the fact that 12 of the 14 items are acceptable in form, whereas 24 of the 31 items on which the public relief men scored less favorably in

TABLE 137.-MEAN ITEM SCORES FOR CONTROLLED SAMPLE OF EMPLOYED MEN, CONTROLLED SAMPLE OF UNEMPLOYED MEN, AND PUBLIC RELIEF GROUP ON ITEMS YIELDING GREATEST DIFFERENCES IN FAVOR OF THE RELIEF GROUP IN RELIEF GROUP--EMPLOYED SAMPLE COMPARISON

Item	Scale	Form of State- ment	Item Mean Score			Difference Relief- Group Employed
			Em- ployed (C)*	Unem- ployed (C)	Relief Group	
104	I.	A.**	3.57	3.17	2.70	.87
8	I.	A.	3.11	3.01	2.30	.81
20	I.	A.	3.03	2.81	2.34	.69
68	I.	U.***	3.37	3.45	2.68	.69
50	I.	A.	3.53	3.60	2.92	.61
3	F.	A.	2.06	2.09	1.46	.60
27	F.	A.	2.38	2.51	1.78	.60
81	F.	A.	2.49	2.54	1.96	.53
21	F.	A.	3.20	2.78	2.70	.50
99	F.	U.	3.14	3.22	2.66	.48
45	F.	A.	2.17	2.22	1.72	.45
64	L.	A.	2.76	2.66	2.32	.44
70	L.	A.	2.23	2.18	1.80	.43
24	E.	A.	3.21	2.54	2.78	.43

*(C) = controlled sample.
**Acceptable.
***Unacceptable.

Table 136 were unacceptably stated. This is additional evidence of the importance of form of statement.

Another important fact in Table 137 is that the trend as between controlled sample of employed, controlled sample of unemployed, and public relief men is less often consistent than in the previous comparison. In fact, complete consistency in trend is apparent on exactly half of the 14 items. The 7 items to yield consistent trends are:

104. IT IS NO TRICK TO BE THE LIFE OF THE PARTY.

8. IT IS EASY TO EXPRESS ONE'S IDEAS.

20. ONE CAN USUALLY KEEP COOL IN IMPORTANT SITUATIONS.

21. IN PLANS FOR THE FUTURE, PARENTS SHOULD BE GIVEN FIRST CONSIDERATION.

99. PARENTS ARE INCLINED TO BE TOO OLD-FASHIONED IN THEIR IDEAS.

64. PERSONAL CIRCUMSTANCES SHOULD NEVER BE CONSIDERED AN EXCUSE FOR LAW-BREAKING.

70. A MAN SHOULD TELL THE TRUTH IN COURT REGARDLESS OF CONSEQUENCES.

Of the 7 items on which the controlled sample of unemployed men do not yield a mean which is intermediate between those of the controlled sample of employed and public relief groups, the difference between controlled sample of employed and controlled sample of unemployed men is statistically certain on just one item, a good education is a great comfort to a man out of work. On this item the controlled sample of unemployed men are more favorable than either the public relief or controlled sample of employed groups.

DIFFERENCES BETWEEN EMPLOYED AND UNEMPLOYED WOMEN

Let us consider next the differences between controlled sample of employed and controlled sample of unemployed female groups. The mean standard scores for the groups of 100 are:

	General Adjustment	Morale	Inferiority	Family	Law	Economic Conservatism	Education
Controlled sample of employed	49.62	49.87	51.79	52.49	49.29	50.19	48.66
Controlled sample of unemployed	52.29	53.23	51.78	50.88	47.95	50.29	51.58
D/σ diff. . . .	2.67	2.35					2.09

The poor general adjustment and morale scores of the unemployed women are consistent with our findings for men. It is interesting to find that the pronounced radicalism among older unemployed men and the marked tendency in the same direction among the younger unemployed men is absent among these younger unemployed women. Do the differences persist when unacceptable items are considered? The scores are as follows:

	Morale	Inferiority	Family	Law	Economic Conservatism	Education
Controlled sample of employed	27.17	32.69	31.16	28.28	32.80	22.85
Controlled sample of unemployed . . .	28.76	33.81	30.78	28.09	33.42	24.89
D/σ diff.						2.54

The largest difference is that on the education items. The difference in morale score, while it is in the expected direction, is not statistically significant, nor are any of the other differences.

The scores on acceptable items for the two groups are:

	Morale	Inferiority	Family	Law	Economic Conservatism	Education
Controlled sample of employed	30.68	35.18	27.97	29.87	34.60	23.50
Controlled sample of unemployed . . .	31.59	34.09	26.60	28.83	33.84	24.19

None of these differences is statistically certain. The three types of score yield consistent differences between controlled sample of employed and controlled sample of unemployed groups on the morale and education scales, although they are so small as to be almost negligible. Slightly poorer morale and slightly less favorable attitudes toward education appear to be the chief differences between the employed and unemployed female groups. It is noteworthy that family and law scores are more favorable for the controlled sample of unemployed women regardless of which type of score is considered. They are never statistically certain differences.

If we consider the items, we find that there are only 9 items on which the controlled sample of unemployed women score less favorably to the extent of three-tenths of a point on the five-point item scale. These 9 items are listed (Table 138) together with the means for the two groups. Since there were 100 in each group, the difference between means does not need to be large to yield critical ratios of 2.00 or better. Items 90, 38, and 5 in Table 138 yield the smallest differences in means, but the ratios for these items are 2.46, 2.18, and 2.01 respectively. The 9 items in the order of the difference between means are:

56. EDUCATION IS NO HELP IN GETTING A JOB TODAY.

47. THE GOVERNMENT OUGHT TO GUARANTEE A LIVING TO THOSE WHO CAN'T FIND WORK.

67. THESE DAYS ONE IS INCLINED TO GIVE UP HOPE OF AMOUNTING TO SOMETHING.

2. AFTER BEING CAUGHT IN A MISTAKE, IT IS HARD TO DO GOOD WORK FOR A WHILE.

55. ANY MAN WITH ABILITY AND WILLINGNESS TO WORK HARD HAS A GOOD CHANCE OF BEING SUCCESSFUL.

31. TIMES ARE GETTING BETTER.

90. HIGH SCHOOL COURSES ARE TOO IMPRACTICAL.

38. MEETING NEW PEOPLE IS USUALLY EMBARRASSING.

5. THE GOVERNMENT SHOULD TAKE OVER ALL LARGE INDUSTRIES.

Seven of 9 items are unacceptably stated. The morale scale furnished the largest number, 3; none are from the family or law scale. Four of the 9 items (47, 55, 31, and 5) are among the 31 that yielded the greatest differences between the public relief and controlled sample of employed male groups.

These results indicate that the differences between the employed and unemployed female groups tested were slight. Perhaps the items in the scales were not

TABLE 138.-MEAN ITEM SCORES FOR CONTROLLED SAMPLE OF EMPLOYED WOMEN AND CONTROLLED SAMPLE OF UNEMPLOYED WOMEN ON ITEMS YIELDING LESS FAVORABLE SCORES FOR THE UNEMPLOYED GROUP

(N = 100 in each group.)

Item	Scale	Form of Statement	Item Means		Difference
			Employed	Unemployed	
36	Education	U.*	1.83	2.30	.47
47	Economic Conservatism	U.	2.75	3.18	.43
67	Morale	U.	2.81	3.19	.38
2	Inferiority	U.	2.89	3.27	.38
55	Morale	A.**	1.91	2.25	.34
31	Morale	A.	2.22	2.54	.32
90	Education	U.	2.24	2.55	.31
38	Inferiority	U.	2.04	2.34	.30
5	Economic Conservatism	U.	2.71	3.01	.30

*Unacceptable.
**Acceptable.

well chosen to reveal unemployment differences for females. It seems more likely that a majority of the unemployed women in these classes for the unemployed care less whether they find employment than do the men. Virtually all are residing with their parents and a considerable proportion are recent high school graduates who have never been employed. Presumably marriage rather than employment is the goal of a considerable number. One suspects that many who reported themselves as unemployed are not active candidates for employment, but are attending these classes for other than vocational reasons.

These unemployed women score more favorably than do the employed to the extent of the three-tenths of a point on the five-point item scale on the following items:

Item	Scale	Item Means: Controlled Sample of Employed	Item Means: Controlled Sample of Unemployed	Difference
15	Family	2.34	1.95	.39
110	Inferiority	3.51	3.14	.37
45	Family	2.80	2.44	.36
58	Law	3.65	3.30	.35
81	Family	2.77	2.47	.30
65	Economic Conservatism	3.63	3.33	.30

These items are the following:

15. ONE OUGHT TO DISCUSS IMPORTANT PLANS WITH MEMBERS OF THE FAMILY.

110. IT IS EASY TO KEEP PEOPLE FROM TAKING ADVANTAGE OF YOU.

45. ONE OWES HIS GREATEST OBLIGATION TO THE FAMILY.

58. IN THE COURTS A POOR MAN WILL RECEIVE AS FAIR TREATMENT AS A MILLIONAIRE.

81. ONE SHOULD CONFIDE MORE FULLY IN MEMBERS OF HIS FAMILY.

65. MOST GREAT FORTUNES ARE MADE HONESTLY.

One gains the impression that these young women confide in their parents and still look to them for guidance.

In passing, we note that all 6 items on which unemployed women score more favorably are acceptably stated, whereas 7 of the 9 items on which they score definitely less favorably were unacceptably stated. In this regard the findings are consistent with those for the men. The chief differences between the findings for the two sexes are that employed and unemployed women differ less in their scores than do male groups, and that women when unemployed do not readily turn to radical economic views. In fact, it appears that thinking in the field of economic affairs is largely foreign to them and, like women in the standard group of 1,000, they are inclined to check the undecided response on items in this scale. There is some indication that they are more disposed to become unfavorable in their attitude toward education than to become critical of the established economic order. Like men, they are more discouraged than the employed and feel that it is the obligation of government to care for the unemployed.

STUDENTS IN THE DEPRESSION

It is difficult to tell how much the depression has altered the attitudes of students, since comparable data from the pre-depression period are lacking. During 1931 and 1932 many students were forced to postpone or abandon their university training for financial reasons. During the school year 1933-34 federal aid was extended to a limited number of students who had been forced to discontinue their university training during the two preceding years. An estimate of the effects of financial reverses which interrupted university training can be secured by comparing the scores for a group of federal-aid students with those for other university students.

Sixty men receiving federal aid and housed in a university dormitory were given the scales. The university group most nearly comparable with these federal-aid men is the male group enrolled in Sociology I classes. The mean age for the Sociology I group was 20.2, that for the federal-aid men, 22.0. The federal-aid students were, on the average, about a year further along in their university training. The principal difference, however, between the groups was in the occupational status of the father. As the federal-aid students required financial aid to attend the university, more were from homes of lower occupational status. The distribution of the two groups in terms of the occupational classification described in Chapter II is as follows:

Occupational Class	Federal-Aid Men (N = 60)	Sociology I Men (N = 100)
I	6.7	14.0
II	11.7	23.0
III	13.3	18.0
IV	25.0	4.0
V	15.0	19.0
VI	8.3	3.0
VII	3.3	1.0
Unclassified .	16.7	18.0

The proportions from the professional and business executive classes (I and II) were less than half as large in the federal-aid group as in the sociology group. A much greater percentage of the federal-aid students were from agricultural homes (Class IV). After the differences in score between the two groups are presented, they will be further evaluated in terms of these differences in occupational status of parents.

The mean standard scores for the two groups are:

	General Adjust-ment	Morale	Infe-rior-ity	Family	Law	Economic Conserv-atism	Educa-tion
Sociology I Men	49.96	50.36	47.91	49.54	50.88	49.14	53.91
Federal-Aid Men	53.17	51.25	47.25	52.40	57.95	59.03	52.00
D/σ diff. .					3.92	4.75	

The major differences are in law and economic conservatism scores. The mean law score for the federal-aid men is three-fourths of a sigma above the standard mean, whereas their economic conservatism scores average almost a whole sigma above the standard mean. The differences between these groups on these two scales are, of course, statistically significant. Do these differences persist when mean arbitrary scores on acceptable and unacceptable items are considered?

	Unacceptable Items		Acceptable Items	
	Law	Economic Conservatism	Law	Economic Conservatism
Sociology I men . . .	28.67	31.65	31.18	34.79
Federal-aid men . . .	32.15	37.25	34.03	39.25
D/σ diff.	3.89	4.87	2.91	2.20

These differences are too large to be other than certain. The federal-aid students as a group regard both legal and economic institutions less favorably than do the men in other university groups tested.

Can these differences be accounted for in terms of occupational selection? The mean standard scores for the sons of fathers in each occupational class are given for the two groups below:

Occupational Class	Law Scores: Sociology I Men Mean	N	Law Scores: Federal-Aid Men Mean	N	Economic Conservatism Scores: Sociology I Men Mean	N	Economic Conservatism Scores: Federal-Aid Men Mean	N
I	48.57	14	46.00	4	43.71	14	54.00	4
II	49.43	23	56.14	7	48.52	23	57.29	7
III	52.89	18	54.38	8	49.00	18	57.00	8
IV	56.75	4	59.20	15	54.25	4	59.20	15
V.	51.00	19	59.44	9	48.53	19	60.22	9
VI	49.67	3	67.20	5	49.67	3	61.00	5
VII	65.00	1	58.50	2	65.00	1	68.00	2
Unclassified	52.56	18	58.90	10	47.17	18	59.80	10

The differences between the groups cannot be ascribed to occupational selection. There is a tendency, however, for scores to vary with the occupational status of the father. This is particularly evident for federal-aid students on the economic conservatism scale.

It is readily understandable why as a group these men are radical. It is more difficult to explain why their attitude toward legal institutions should be relatively unfavorable. It will serve little purpose to consider the differences on individual items, since the federal-aid men score less favorably on every single item in the economic conservatism scale, and on 21 of

22 in the law scale. Of 22 items which yielded differences of four-tenths of a point or more on the five-point item scale, 15 are in the economic conservatism scale and 7 in the law scale. Thirteen are unacceptably stated, and 9 are acceptably stated. The preponderance of unacceptable items is less marked than in the previous comparisons. The probable explanation is that the federal-aid men were less generally maladjusted than were the men in the unemployed groups. Their general adjustment score, it will be recalled, was 53.17.

Why are there no significant differences in morale score between the sociology and federal-aid students? Probably the fact that the federal-aid men have been given aid to return to school has restored their morale. They have ample reason to be encouraged, since the prospect of continuing their university training is undoubtedly a very pleasant one for a majority of these students. Their radicalism and unfavorable attitude toward legal authority appear to be more permanent effects of their experience, and will probably take much longer to alter.

SUMMARY

Greater discontent with the economic order is the most consistent and striking difference between employed and unemployed men revealed in these group comparisons. This discontent among the unemployed receiving relief is not confined to any age, educational, or occupational stratum. If anything, those more favorably situated with reference to these variables are the more discontented.

Poorer general adjustment has been found to characterize the unemployed. The magnitude of general maladjustment is greatest among men from the lower occupational strata, among older men, and among men with least education. These findings are in accord with those in Chapter VII, which indicated that the experience of unemployment affected personality adversely in proportion to the number of unfavorable factors already present in the life history or environmental situation of the individual.

Poorer morale, too, is characteristic of the unemployed as a group. Discouragement and a sense of hopelessness is greatest among men in the semi-skilled and unskilled groups, among older men, and among the men with the least education. It is much more prevalent among the older men on relief than among the younger unemployed men who are continuing their educational training in special classes for the unemployed or in evening school. The extent of poor morale among young unemployed men who did not affiliate with the special classes is not known, since such persons were not tested.

Our data indicate that unemployed men are not characterized by feelings of inferiority. In fact, such feelings are less common among them than among the employed. Perhaps these reactions among the unemployed are rationalizations, but it seems more probable that these men firmly believe that their unemployment can be ascribed wholly to the economic situation and not to personal deficiencies.

There is no evidence that family attitudes have suffered among either the youthful unemployed or the men on relief. Evidence in Chapter VII indicated that family tensions in families of the youthful unemployed were accentuated by unemployment when the normal family equilibrium had already been disturbed by such factors as death or unemployment of a parent. Approximately half of the unemployed men on relief agree that "one becomes nervous at home", but the sense of obligation to and identification with this primary group seems to be greater than among the employed. This is reasonable in that the unemployed probably find their greatest personal satisfaction in experiences in the primary group, where being unemployed does not exclude participation.

A pronounced sex difference was found. The association between radicalism and unemployment was confined almost entirely to men. Thinking in this field seems largely foreign to these women, and they seem slightly more disposed to develop unfavorable attitudes toward education than toward the economic system.

Students forced to discontinue their university training for economic reasons who were permitted to return by federal grants of aid were found to be more discontented with our legal and economic institutions than were other university students or the youthful unemployed.

The differences between the responses of the employed and the unemployed to individual items provided logical validation for the scales, particularly for the general adjustment scale. One of the most striking differences was the preponderance of unacceptable items in all comparisons where adverse depression effects were noted. This evidence amply justifies the emphasis placed on the importance of form of statement in Chapter IX and points to the urgent need for further research in this field.

Chapter XIII

GENERAL SUMMARY

The initial aim of this study was to investigate the effect of unemployment on personality and family relationships. It was desired to develop scales that would be applicable to young people at the adolescent level as well as to adults. The six original scales were designed to measure morale, feelings of inferiority, family adjustment, economic conservatism, attitudes toward law, and the value of education. A seventh scale, called a General Adjustment scale, was developed out of the others during the course of the study. The scales were administered to approximately 3,000 individuals and were found to be applicable and reasonably reliable in a wide range of groups. Evidence is presented that points to the validity of the general adjustment, morale, economic conservatism, and inferiority scales. The remaining scales may or may not be valid.

A comparison of employed and unemployed revealed that the two groups differ most consistently and most strikingly with respect to their attitudes toward the economic order. The greater discontent among the unemployed receiving public relief is not confined to any age nor to any educational or occupational stratum. If anything, those more favorably situated with respect to these variables are the more discontented. Poor general adjustment was also found to characterize this group of unemployed. The magnitude of general maladjustment was greater among the men from the lower occupational strata, among the older men, and among the men with the least education. The findings for the morale scale were similar, but the differences were less marked. Our data do not indicate that men receiving relief are characterized by feelings of inferiority or unfavorable family attitudes.

Among the younger men residing at home and attending educational classes similar, but much less striking, differences were found. As a whole this unemployed group does not seem sufficiently independent of parental support to feel appreciably the strain imposed by unemployment. When only those unemployed were considered who were not living at home, or either of whose parents was unemployed, differences again became striking. They also became striking when other unfavorable factors--such as separation of parents or overageness--were present. In other words, the effect of unemployment on young people varies in proportion to the number of other unfavorable factors present. The differences between the responses of employed and unemployed to individual items provides logical validation for the scales, particularly for the general adjustment scale.

Differences between employed and unemployed young women were small and were confined chiefly to the morale and education scales. In particular, unemployment, even in association with such factors as non-home residence, did not produce discontent with the prevailing economic order. The only factor that was clearly associated with radicalism among the women was the unemployment of either parent. Thinking in the economic field seems largely foreign to them. This is also indicated by the fact that they take the undecided position on the items of the economic conservatism scale more frequently than do men.

Although the original purpose of the study was to investigate the effects of unemployment, the nature of the data necessitated a study of problems fundamental to personality measurement. The major conclusions from this phase of the study follow.

1. The method of internal consistency, as it has usually been applied, constitutes no guarantee that the resultant items are measures of a common variable. The procedure for applying the test can be so refined that it will come closer to doing this. Use of two dissimilar groups in the selection of items is strongly recommended.

2. While individual items fluctuate widely

from group to group in their discriminative values, each scale as a whole maintains good discriminative power. This points to the conclusion that it is futile to attempt to weight items in terms of their discriminative values in the hope of improving the scoring.

3. So far as personality scales are concerned, the arbitrary method and the two sigma methods of scoring will yield virtually the same results not only relatively but also in the absolute sense. The error, no matter which score is taken as the standard, is negligible in consideration of other errors in personality measurement.

4. The method of internal consistency, when applied to two dissimilar groups, was successful in isolating items most responsible for the unit behavior of the six scales.

5. Discriminative values, standard deviations, and reliability coefficients are intimately interrelated. Because of this, caution needs to be exercised in the interpretation of reliability coefficients. Reliability coefficients and standard deviations for a particular group may be small because the scale is inapplicable to that group and not because of true homogeneity for the trait under consideration.

6. The relationship between item discriminative value and item retest coefficient was found to be small.

7. Since bimodality was greater in item response distributions for scales that are essentially personality inventories--morale, general adjustment, inferiority, and family--than on the remaining three, which are primarily social attitude scales, the frequency of bimodal items in a scale may indicate the degree to which it is measuring a trait of direct personal significance or concern to the individual.

8. Our evidence suggests that the most useful results will be obtained from the use of scales containing an equal number of acceptable and unacceptable items, each scored separately and related independently to outside variables.

9. The importance of the differences in results yielded by acceptably and unacceptably stated items can scarcely be overemphasized. Such differences

recurred in practically every analysis made. Employment-unemployment comparisons revealed that the items on which the unemployed tended to score more unfavorably were predominantly unacceptable, whereas those on which they scored more favorably were largely acceptable in form. While most of the findings with respect to form of statement are consistent for both sexes, a sex difference is particularly evident in the comparison of those items on which there is a sex difference in mean score. Women tend to score more unfavorably than do men on the acceptable items, whereas men score more unfavorably on the unacceptable items.

10. Unacceptable items are more generalized in their significance and seem to evoke a less intellectualized response. The implications of the differences in form of statement deserve extended consideration.

11. The difference between the score on acceptable and on unacceptable items has potentially great significance as an indirect measure of adjustment, as an indication of the type of reaction a scale is evoking, and possibly as a direct measure of some kind of psychological conflict.

12. The magnitude of intercorrelations between personality scales was found to vary widely, depending upon which type of items was scored.

13. While there were no marked differences in mean total score on the scales, sex differences were conspicuous in the number and nature of the outside variables with which the scales were related and in effects of form of statement. The evidence suggests that the crux of these differences lies in the integration or pattern of personality.

14. It is the hope of the authors that this study will provide an incentive to the study of personality scales for the purpose of uncovering psychological differences and characteristics of traits rather than for the sole purpose of determining reliability and validity. Further research into the effects of form of statement is particularly needed.

B I B L I O G R A P H Y

1. Allport, G. W. and Vernon, P. E. The Field of Personality. Psychol. Bull., 27: 677-730 (1930).
2. Anderson, John E. The Effect of Item Analysis on an Examination. Accepted for publication by J. Appl. Psychol.
3. Bell, H. M. The Adjustment Inventory and Manual. Stanford University Press, 1934.
4. Ezekiel, Mordecai. Methods of Correlation Analysis. New York: John Wiley and Sons, 1930. Pp. 427 + xiv.
5. Fisher, R. A. Statistical Methods for Research Workers. London: Oliver and Boyd. 2d ed., 1928. Pp. 269 + xi.
6. Goodenough, F. L., and Anderson, John E., Experimental Child Study. New York: The Century Co., 1931. Pp. 546 + xiv.
7. Green, Helen J., Berman, Isabel R., Paterson, Donald G., and Trabue, M. R. A Manual of Selected Occupational Tests. Bulletins of the Employment Stabilization Research Institute, University of Minnesota, Vol. II, No. 3. Minneapolis: University of Minnesota Press, 1933. Pp. 77.
8. Greene, H. A., Jorgensen, A. N., and Kelley, V. H. Iowa Silent Reading Test: Manual of Directions. Yonkers-on-Hudson, New York: World Book Co., 1931. Pp. 14.
9. Hall, O. Milton, Attitudes and Unemployment. Archives of Psychology, No. 165, Columbia University, 1934. Pp. 65.
10. Heidbreder, E. Measuring Introversion and Extroversion. J. Abn. and Soc. Psychol., 21: 120-134 (1926).
11. Hull, Clark L. Aptitude Testing. Yonkers-on-Hudson, New York: World Book Co., 1928. Pp. 535 + xiv.
12. Kelley, Truman. Statistical Method. New York: The Macmillan Co., 1923. Pp. 389 + xi.

13. Likert, Rensis. A Technique for the Measurement of Attitudes. Archives of Psychology, No. 140. Columbia University, 1932. Pp. 55.
14. McCall, W. A. Proposed Uniform Method of Scale construction. Teachers' College Record, 22: 31-41 (1921).
15. Rosenthal, Solomon P. Change of Socio-Economic Attitudes under Radical Motion Picture Propoganda. Archives of Psychology, No. 166. Columbia University, 1934. Pp. 46.
16. Smith, R. B. The Development of an Inventory for the Measurement of Inferiority Feelings at the High School Level. Archives of Psychology, No. 144, Columbia University, 1932. Pp. 118.
17. Symonds, P. M. Diagnosing Personality and Conduct. New York: The Century Co., 1931. Pp. 602 + xvi.
18. Terman, L. M. The Measurement of Intelligence. Boston: Houghton, Mifflin Co., 1916. Pp. 362 + xviii.
19. Thorndike, E. L. An Introduction to the Theory of Mental and Social Measurements. New York: Teachers' College, Columbia University Bureau of Publications. 2d ed., revised, 1919. Pp. 277 + xi.
20. Thurstone, L. L. and Chave, E. J. The Measurement of Attitude. Chicago: University of Chicago Press, 1929. Pp. 96 + xii.
21. Thurstone, L. L., and Thurstone, Thelma. A Neurotic Inventory. J. Social Psychol., 1: 3-29 (1930).
22. Vernon, P. E., and Allport, G. W. A Test for Personal Values. J. Abn. and Soc. Psychol., 26: 231-248 (1931).
23. Yule, G. Udny. An Introduction to the Theory of Statistics. London: Charles Griffin and Co., Ltd. 9th ed., revised, 1929. Pp. 424 + xv.

A P P E N D I X

No.-----

MINNESOTA SCALE FOR THE SURVEY OF OPINIONS

Prepared by E. A. Rundquist and R. F. Sletto

Institute of Child Welfare
University of Minnesota

The following pages contain a number of statements about which there is no general agreement. People differ widely in the way they feel about each item. There are no right answers. The purpose of the survey is to see how different groups feel about each item. We should like your honest opinion on each of these statements.

Please fill in the blanks below or underline where appropriate:

1. Age------------ 2. Sex------------ 3. MARRIED SINGLE DIVORCED? 4. Date------------
5. If married, how many children have you? (If none, write 0)------------
6. How many younger sisters have you?------------ 7. How many older sisters?------------
8. How many younger brothers have you?------------ 9. How many older brothers?------------
10. Please give the ages of your brothers in the spaces below:
----- ----- ----- ----- ----- ----- ----- -----
11. Please give the ages of your sisters in the spaces below:
----- ----- ----- ----- ----- ----- ----- -----
12. Are you employed? YES NO 13. Is it a full time job? YES NO
14. If unemployed, how many months since your last regular job?--

In answering the next three questions, please state the type of work or occupation *specifically*. Examples: Owner of drugstore, owner of grocery, travelling salesman, store salesman, stenographer, bookkeeper, file clerk, plasterer, plumber, etc.

15. In what occupation have you had the most experience?--
16. What is your present occupation, if employed?--
17. What is (or was) your father's usual occupation?--
18. Is your father DECEASED RETIRED EMPLOYED UNEMPLOYED?
19. Is your mother DECEASED A HOUSEWIFE EMPLOYED UNEMPLOYED?
20. Are your parents living together? YES NO
21. Underline the highest grade you completed in regular day school or college:
Grade 1 2 3 4 5 6 7 8 High School 1 2 3 4 College 1 2 3 4
22. If, in addition, you have attended any other school, underline the number of years attended:
(A) Business College ½ 1 1½ 2
(B) Teacher's College ½ 1 1½ 2
(C) Trade School ½ 1 1½ 2
(D) Nurses' Training 1 1½ 2 2½ 3
(E) Other -- ½ 1 1½ 2
23. If you are employed, how certain are you that your employment will last through the coming year?
VERY CERTAIN CERTAIN UNCERTAIN VERY UNCERTAIN
24. If you are unemployed, how certain are you that you will find a position this year?
VERY CERTAIN CERTAIN UNCERTAIN VERY UNCERTAIN

DIRECTIONS

READ EACH ITEM CAREFULLY AND UNDERLINE QUICKLY THE PHRASE WHICH BEST EXPRESSES YOUR FEELING ABOUT THE STATEMENT. **Wherever possible, let your own personal experience determine your answer. Do not spend much time on any item. If in doubt, underline the phrase which seems most nearly to express your present feeling about the statement.** WORK RAPIDLY. **Be sure to answer every item.**

1. **THE FUTURE IS TOO UNCERTAIN FOR A PERSON TO PLAN ON MARRYING.**
Strongly agree [5] Agree [4] Undecided [3] Disagree [2] Strongly disagree [1]

2. **AFTER BEING CAUGHT IN A MISTAKE, IT IS HARD TO DO GOOD WORK FOR A WHILE.**
Strongly agree [5] Agree [4] Undecided [3] Disagree [2] Strongly disagree [1]

3. **HOME IS THE MOST PLEASANT PLACE IN THE WORLD.**
Strongly agree [1] Agree [2] Undecided [3] Disagree [4] Strongly disagree [5]

4. **THE LAW PROTECTS PROPERTY RIGHTS AT THE EXPENSE OF HUMAN RIGHTS.**
Strongly agree [5] Agree [4] Undecided [3] Disagree [2] Strongly disagree [1]

5. **THE GOVERNMENT SHOULD TAKE OVER ALL LARGE INDUSTRIES.**
Strongly agree [5] Agree [4] Undecided [3] Disagree [2] Strongly disagree [1]

6. **A MAN CAN LEARN MORE BY WORKING FOUR YEARS THAN BY GOING TO HIGH SCHOOL.**
Strongly agree [5] Agree [4] Undecided [3] Disagree [2] Strongly disagree [1]

7. **IT IS DIFFICULT TO THINK CLEARLY THESE DAYS.**
Strongly agree [5] Agree [4] Undecided [3] Disagree [2] Strongly disagree [1]

8. **IT IS EASY TO EXPRESS ONE'S IDEAS.**
Strongly agree [1] Agree [2] Undecided [3] Disagree [4] Strongly disagree [5]

9. **PARENTS EXPECT TOO MUCH FROM THEIR CHILDREN.**
Strongly agree [5] Agree [4] Undecided [3] Disagree [2] Strongly disagree [1]

10. **A PERSON SHOULD OBEY ONLY THOSE LAWS WHICH SEEM REASONABLE.**
Strongly agree [5] Agree [4] Undecided [3] Disagree [2] Strongly disagree [1]

11. **LABOR SHOULD HAVE MUCH MORE VOICE IN DECIDING GOVERNMENT POLICIES.**
Strongly agree [5] Agree [4] Undecided [3] Disagree [2] Strongly disagree [1]

12. **THE MORE EDUCATION A MAN HAS THE BETTER HE IS ABLE TO ENJOY LIFE.**
Strongly agree [1] Agree [2] Undecided [3] Disagree [4] Strongly disagree [5]

13. **THE FUTURE LOOKS VERY BLACK.**
Strongly agree [5] Agree [4] Undecided [3] Disagree [2] Strongly disagree [1]

14. **IT IS DIFFICULT TO SAY THE RIGHT THING AT THE RIGHT TIME.**
Strongly agree [5] Agree [4] Undecided [3] Disagree [2] Strongly disagree [1]

15. **ONE OUGHT TO DISCUSS IMPORTANT PLANS WITH MEMBERS OF HIS FAMILY.**
Strongly agree [1] Agree [2] Undecided [3] Disagree [4] Strongly disagree [5]

16. **IT IS ALL RIGHT TO EVADE THE LAW IF YOU DO NOT ACTUALLY VIOLATE IT.**
Strongly agree [5] Agree [4] Undecided [3] Disagree [2] Strongly disagree [1]

17. **LEGISLATURES ARE TOO READY TO PASS LAWS TO CURB BUSINESS FREEDOM.**
Strongly agree [1] Agree [2] Undecided [3] Disagree [4] Strongly disagree [5]

18. **EDUCATION HELPS A PERSON TO USE HIS LEISURE TIME TO BETTER ADVANTAGE.**
Strongly agree [1] Agree [2] Undecided [3] Disagree [4] Strongly disagree [5]

19. LIFE IS JUST ONE WORRY AFTER ANOTHER.
Strongly agree ^{5} Agree ^{4} Undecided ^{3} Disagree ^{2} Strongly disagree ^{1}

20. ONE CAN USUALLY KEEP COOL IN IMPORTANT SITUATIONS.
Strongly agree ^{1} Agree ^{2} Undecided ^{3} Disagree ^{4} Strongly disagree ^{5}

21. IN PLANS FOR THE FUTURE, PARENTS SHOULD BE GIVEN FIRST CONSIDERATION.
Strongly agree ^{1} Agree ^{2} Undecided ^{3} Disagree ^{4} Strongly disagree ^{5}

22. THE SENTENCES OF JUDGES IN COURTS ARE DETERMINED BY THEIR PREJUDICES.
Strongly agree ^{5} Agree ^{4} Undecided ^{3} Disagree ^{2} Strongly disagree ^{1}

23. FOR MEN TO DO THEIR BEST, THERE MUST BE THE POSSIBILITY OF UNLIMITED PROFIT.
Strongly agree ^{1} Agree ^{2} Undecided ^{3} Disagree ^{4} Strongly disagree ^{5}

24. A GOOD EDUCATION IS A GREAT COMFORT TO A MAN OUT OF WORK.
Strongly agree ^{1} Agree ^{2} Undecided ^{3} Disagree ^{4} Strongly disagree ^{5}

25. MOST PEOPLE CAN BE TRUSTED.
Strongly agree ^{1} Agree ^{2} Undecided ^{3} Disagree ^{4} Strongly disagree ^{5}

26. IT IS EASY TO GET ONE'S OWN WAY IN MOST SITUATIONS.
Strongly agree ^{1} Agree ^{2} Undecided ^{3} Disagree ^{4} Strongly disagree ^{5}

27. A MAN SHOULD BE WILLING TO SACRIFICE EVERYTHING FOR HIS FAMILY.
Strongly agree ^{1} Agree ^{2} Undecided ^{3} Disagree ^{4} Strongly disagree ^{5}

28. ON THE WHOLE, JUDGES ARE HONEST.
Strongly agree ^{1} Agree ^{2} Undecided ^{3} Disagree ^{4} Strongly disagree ^{5}

29. POVERTY IS CHIEFLY A RESULT OF INJUSTICE IN THE DISTRIBUTION OF WEALTH.
Strongly agree ^{5} Agree ^{4} Undecided ^{3} Disagree ^{2} Strongly disagree ^{1}

30. ONLY SUBJECTS LIKE READING, WRITING, AND ARITHMETIC SHOULD BE TAUGHT AT PUBLIC EXPENSE.
Strongly agree ^{5} Agree ^{4} Undecided ^{3} Disagree ^{2} Strongly disagree ^{1}

31. TIMES ARE GETTING BETTER.
Strongly agree ^{1} Agree ^{2} Undecided ^{3} Disagree ^{4} Strongly disagree ^{5}

32. IT IS EASY TO HAVE A GOOD TIME AT A PARTY.
Strongly agree ^{1} Agree ^{2} Undecided ^{3} Disagree ^{4} Strongly disagree ^{5}

33. PARENTS TOO OFTEN EXPECT THEIR GROWN-UP CHILDREN TO OBEY THEM.
Strongly agree ^{5} Agree ^{4} Undecided ^{3} Disagree ^{2} Strongly disagree ^{1}

34. JURIES SELDOM UNDERSTAND A CASE WELL ENOUGH TO MAKE A REALLY JUST DECISION.
Strongly agree ^{5} Agree ^{4} Undecided ^{3} Disagree ^{2} Strongly disagree ^{1}

35. THE GOVERNMENT SHOULD NOT ATTEMPT TO LIMIT PROFITS.
Strongly agree ^{1} Agree ^{2} Undecided ^{3} Disagree ^{4} Strongly disagree ^{5}

36. EDUCATION IS OF NO HELP IN GETTING A JOB TODAY.
Strongly agree ^{5} Agree ^{4} Undecided ^{3} Disagree ^{2} Strongly disagree ^{1}

37. IT DOES NOT TAKE LONG TO GET OVER FEELING GLOOMY.
Strongly agree ^{1} Agree ^{2} Undecided ^{3} Disagree ^{4} Strongly disagree ^{5}

38. MEETING NEW PEOPLE IS USUALLY EMBARRASSING.
Strongly agree ^{5} Agree ^{4} Undecided ^{3} Disagree ^{2} Strongly disagree ^{1}

39. ONE CANNOT FIND AS MUCH UNDERSTANDING AT HOME AS ELSEWHERE.
Strongly agree ^{5} Agree ^{4} Undecided ^{3} Disagree ^{2} Strongly disagree ^{1}

40. ON THE WHOLE, POLICEMEN ARE HONEST.
Strongly agree [1] Agree [2] Undecided [3] Disagree [4] Strongly disagree [5]

41. THE MORE A MAN LEARNS ABOUT OUR ECONOMIC SYSTEM, THE LESS WILLING HE IS TO SEE CHANGES MADE.
Strongly agree [1] Agree [2] Undecided [3] Disagree [4] Strongly disagree [5]

42. MOST YOUNG PEOPLE ARE GETTING TOO MUCH EDUCATION.
Strongly agree [5] Agree [4] Undecided [3] Disagree [2] Strongly disagree [1]

43. THE DAY IS NOT LONG ENOUGH TO DO ONE'S WORK WELL AND HAVE ANY TIME FOR FUN.
Strongly agree [5] Agree [4] Undecided [3] Disagree [2] Strongly disagree [1]

44. IT IS EASY TO KEEP UP ONE'S COURAGE.
Strongly agree [1] Agree [2] Undecided [3] Disagree [4] Strongly disagree [5]

45. ONE OWES HIS GREATEST OBLIGATION TO HIS FAMILY.
Strongly agree [1] Agree [2] Undecided [3] Disagree [4] Strongly disagree [5]

46. A MAN SHOULD OBEY THE LAWS NO MATTER HOW MUCH THEY INTERFERE WITH HIS PERSONAL AMBITIONS.
Strongly agree [1] Agree [2] Undecided [3] Disagree [4] Strongly disagree [5]

47. THE GOVERNMENT OUGHT TO GUARANTEE A LIVING TO THOSE WHO CAN'T FIND WORK.
Strongly agree [5] Agree [4] Undecided [3] Disagree [2] Strongly disagree [1]

48. A HIGH SCHOOL EDUCATION IS WORTH ALL THE TIME AND EFFORT IT REQUIRES.
Strongly agree [1] Agree [2] Undecided [3] Disagree [4] Strongly disagree [5]

49. NO ONE CARES MUCH WHAT HAPPENS TO YOU.
Strongly agree [5] Agree [4] Undecided [3] Disagree [2] Strongly disagree [1]

50. IT IS EASY TO IGNORE CRITICISM.
Strongly agree [1] Agree [2] Undecided [3] Disagree [4] Strongly disagree [5]

51. IT IS HARD TO KEEP A PLEASANT DISPOSITION AT HOME.
Strongly agree [5] Agree [4] Undecided [3] Disagree [2] Strongly disagree [1]

52. COURT DECISIONS ARE ALMOST ALWAYS JUST.
Strongly agree [1] Agree [2] Undecided [3] Disagree [4] Strongly disagree [5]

53. LARGE INCOMES SHOULD BE TAXED MUCH MORE THAN THEY ARE NOW.
Strongly agree [5] Agree [4] Undecided [3] Disagree [2] Strongly disagree [1]

54. OUR SCHOOLS ENCOURAGE AN INDIVIDUAL TO THINK FOR HIMSELF.
Strongly agree [1] Agree [2] Undecided [3] Disagree [4] Strongly disagree [5]

55. ANY MAN WITH ABILITY AND WILLINGNESS TO WORK HARD HAS A GOOD CHANCE OF BEING SUCCESSFUL.
Strongly agree [1] Agree [2] Undecided [3] Disagree [4] Strongly disagree [5]

56. IT IS EASY TO ACT NATURALLY IN A GROUP.
Strongly agree [1] Agree [2] Undecided [3] Disagree [4] Strongly disagree [5]

57. PEOPLE IN THE FAMILY CAN BE TRUSTED COMPLETELY.
Strongly agree [1] Agree [2] Undecided [3] Disagree [4] Strongly disagree [5]

58. IN THE COURTS A POOR MAN WILL RECEIVE AS FAIR TREATMENT AS A MILLIONAIRE.
Strongly agree [1] Agree [2] Undecided [3] Disagree [4] Strongly disagree [5]

59. MEN WOULD NOT DO THEIR BEST, IF GOVERNMENT OWNED ALL INDUSTRY.
Strongly agree [1] Agree [2] Undecided [3] Disagree [4] Strongly disagree [5]

60. **THERE ARE TOO MANY FADS AND FRILLS IN MODERN EDUCATION.**
Strongly agree [5] Agree [4] Undecided [3] Disagree [2] Strongly disagree [1]

61. **IT IS GREAT TO BE LIVING IN THESE EXCITING TIMES.**
Strongly agree [1] Agree [2] Undecided [3] Disagree [4] Strongly disagree [5]

62. **IT IS HARD TO BRING ONE'S SELF TO CONFIDE IN OTHERS.**
Strongly agree [5] Agree [4] Undecided [3] Disagree [2] Strongly disagree [1]

63. **ONE BECOMES NERVOUS AT HOME.**
Strongly agree [5] Agree [4] Undecided [3] Disagree [2] Strongly disagree [1]

64. **PERSONAL CIRCUMSTANCES SHOULD NEVER BE CONSIDERED AN EXCUSE FOR LAW-BREAKING.**
Strongly agree [1] Agree [2] Undecided [3] Disagree [4] Strongly disagree [5]

65. **MOST GREAT FORTUNES ARE MADE HONESTLY.**
Strongly agree [1] Agree [2] Undecided [3] Disagree [4] Strongly disagree [5]

66. **EDUCATION ONLY MAKES A PERSON DISCONTENTED.**
Strongly agree [5] Agree [4] Undecided [3] Disagree [2] Strongly disagree [1]

67. **THESE DAYS ONE IS INCLINED TO GIVE UP HOPE OF AMOUNTING TO SOMETHING.**
Strongly agree [5] Agree [4] Undecided [3] Disagree [2] Strongly disagree [1]

68. **IT IS HARD TO DO YOUR BEST WHEN PEOPLE ARE WATCHING YOU.**
Strongly agree [5] Agree [4] Undecided [3] Disagree [2] Strongly disagree [1]

69. **THE JOYS OF FAMILY LIFE ARE MUCH OVER-RATED.**
Strongly agree [5] Agree [4] Undecided [3] Disagree [2] Strongly disagree [1]

70. **A MAN SHOULD TELL THE TRUTH IN COURT, REGARDLESS OF CONSEQUENCES.**
Strongly agree [1] Agree [2] Undecided [3] Disagree [4] Strongly disagree [5]

71. **PRIVATE OWNERSHIP OF PROPERTY IS NECESSARY FOR ECONOMIC PROGRESS.**
Strongly agree [1] Agree [2] Undecided [3] Disagree [4] Strongly disagree [5]

72. **SCHOOL TRAINING IS OF LITTLE HELP IN MEETING THE PROBLEMS OF REAL LIFE.**
Strongly agree [5] Agree [4] Undecided [3] Disagree [2] Strongly disagree [1]

73. **THERE IS LITTLE CHANCE FOR ADVANCEMENT IN INDUSTRY AND BUSINESS UNLESS A MAN HAS UNFAIR PULL.**
Strongly agree [5] Agree [4] Undecided [3] Disagree [2] Strongly disagree [1]

74. **IT IS EASY TO GET ALONG WITH PEOPLE.**
Strongly agree [1] Agree [2] Undecided [3] Disagree [4] Strongly disagree [5]

75. **ONE'S PARENTS USUALLY TREAT HIM FAIRLY AND SENSIBLY.**
Strongly agree [1] Agree [2] Undecided [3] Disagree [4] Strongly disagree [5]

76. **A PERSON WHO REPORTS MINOR LAW VIOLATIONS IS ONLY A TROUBLE-MAKER.**
Strongly agree [5] Agree [4] Undecided [3] Disagree [2] Strongly disagree [1]

77. **WITHOUT SWEEPING CHANGES IN OUR ECONOMIC SYSTEM, LITTLE PROGRESS CAN BE MADE IN THE SOLUTION OF SOCIAL PROBLEMS.**
Strongly agree [5] Agree [4] Undecided [3] Disagree [2] Strongly disagree [1]

78. **EDUCATION TENDS TO MAKE AN INDIVIDUAL LESS CONCEITED.**
Strongly agree [1] Agree [2] Undecided [3] Disagree [4] Strongly disagree [5]

79. **THE YOUNG MAN OF TODAY CAN EXPECT MUCH OF THE FUTURE.**
Strongly agree [1] Agree [2] Undecided [3] Disagree [4] Strongly disagree [5]

80. IT IS EASY TO FEEL AS THOUGH YOU HAD A WORLD OF SELF-CONFIDENCE.
Strongly agree ^{1} Agree ^{2} Undecided ^{3} Disagree ^{4} Strongly disagree ^{5}

81. ONE SHOULD CONFIDE MORE FULLY IN MEMBERS OF HIS FAMILY.
Strongly agree ^{1} Agree ^{2} Undecided ^{3} Disagree ^{4} Strongly disagree ^{5}

82. A PERSON IS JUSTIFIED IN GIVING FALSE TESTIMONY TO PROTECT A FRIEND ON TRIAL.
Strongly agree ^{5} Agree ^{4} Undecided ^{3} Disagree ^{2} Strongly disagree ^{1}

83. ON THE WHOLE, OUR ECONOMIC SYSTEM IS JUST AND WISE.
Strongly agree ^{1} Agree ^{2} Undecided ^{3} Disagree ^{4} Strongly disagree ^{5}

84. SOLUTION OF THE WORLD'S PROBLEMS WILL COME THROUGH EDUCATION.
Strongly agree ^{1} Agree ^{2} Undecided ^{3} Disagree ^{4} Strongly disagree ^{5}

85. THIS GENERATION WILL PROBABLY NEVER SEE SUCH HARD TIMES AGAIN.
Strongly agree ^{1} Agree ^{2} Undecided ^{3} Disagree ^{4} Strongly disagree ^{5}

86. MOST PEOPLE JUST PRETEND THAT THEY LIKE YOU.
Strongly agree ^{5} Agree ^{4} Undecided ^{3} Disagree ^{2} Strongly disagree ^{1}

87. ONE FEELS MOST CONTENTED AT HOME.
Strongly agree ^{1} Agree ^{2} Undecided ^{3} Disagree ^{4} Strongly disagree ^{5}

88. A HUNGRY MAN HAS A RIGHT TO STEAL.
Strongly agree ^{5} Agree ^{4} Undecided ^{3} Disagree ^{2} Strongly disagree ^{1}

89. LABOR DOES NOT GET ITS FAIR SHARE OF WHAT IT PRODUCES.
Strongly agree ^{5} Agree ^{4} Undecided ^{3} Disagree ^{2} Strongly disagree ^{1}

90. HIGH SCHOOL COURSES ARE TOO IMPRACTICAL.
Strongly agree ^{5} Agree ^{4} Undecided ^{3} Disagree ^{2} Strongly disagree ^{1}

91. REAL FRIENDS ARE AS EASY TO FIND AS EVER.
Strongly agree ^{1} Agree ^{2} Undecided ^{3} Disagree ^{4} Strongly disagree ^{5}

92. SO MANY PEOPLE DO THINGS WELL THAT IT IS EASY TO BECOME DISCOURAGED.
Strongly agree ^{5} Agree ^{4} Undecided ^{3} Disagree ^{2} Strongly disagree ^{1}

93. FAMILY TIES ARE STRENGTHENED WHEN TIMES ARE HARD.
Strongly agree ^{1} Agree ^{2} Undecided ^{3} Disagree ^{4} Strongly disagree ^{5}

94. ALL LAWS SHOULD BE STRICTLY OBEYED BECAUSE THEY ARE LAWS.
Strongly agree ^{1} Agree ^{2} Undecided ^{3} Disagree ^{4} Strongly disagree ^{5}

95. WHEN A RICH MAN DIES, MOST OF HIS PROPERTY SHOULD GO TO THE STATE.
Strongly agree ^{5} Agree ^{4} Undecided ^{3} Disagree ^{2} Strongly disagree ^{1}

96. A MAN IS FOOLISH TO KEEP ON GOING TO SCHOOL IF HE CAN GET A JOB.
Strongly agree ^{5} Agree ^{4} Undecided ^{3} Disagree ^{2} Strongly disagree ^{1}

97. LIFE IS JUST A SERIES OF DISAPPOINTMENTS.
Strongly agree ^{5} Agree ^{4} Undecided ^{3} Disagree ^{2} Strongly disagree ^{1}

98. IT IS HARD NOT TO BE SELF-CONSCIOUS.
Strongly agree ^{5} Agree ^{4} Undecided ^{3} Disagree ^{2} Strongly disagree ^{1}

99. PARENTS ARE INCLINED TO BE TOO OLD-FASHIONED IN THEIR IDEAS.
Strongly agree ^{5} Agree ^{4} Undecided ^{3} Disagree ^{2} Strongly disagree ^{1}

100. LAWS ARE SO OFTEN MADE FOR THE BENEFIT OF SMALL SELFISH GROUPS THAT A MAN CAN NOT RESPECT THE LAW.
Strongly agree ^{5} Agree ^{4} Undecided ^{3} Disagree ^{2} Strongly disagree ^{1}

101. IF OUR ECONOMIC SYSTEM WERE JUST, THERE WOULD BE MUCH LESS CRIME.
Strongly agree 5 Agree 4 Undecided 3 Disagree 2 Strongly disagree 1

102. SAVINGS SPENT ON EDUCATION ARE WISELY INVESTED.
Strongly agree 1 Agree 2 Undecided 3 Disagree 4 Strongly disagree 5

103. ONE SELDOM WORRIES SO MUCH AS TO BECOME VERY MISERABLE.
Strongly agree 1 Agree 2 Undecided 3 Disagree 4 Strongly disagree 5

104. IT IS NO TRICK TO BE THE LIFE OF THE PARTY.
Strongly agree 1 Agree 2 Undecided 3 Disagree 4 Strongly disagree 5

105. MEMBERS OF THE FAMILY ARE TOO CURIOUS ABOUT ONE'S PERSONAL AFFAIRS.
Strongly agree 5 Agree 4 Undecided 3 Disagree 2 Strongly disagree 1

106. ALMOST ANYTHING CAN BE FIXED UP IN THE COURTS IF YOU HAVE ENOUGH MONEY.
Strongly agree 5 Agree 4 Undecided 3 Disagree 2 Strongly disagree 1

107. THE INCOMES OF MOST PEOPLE ARE A FAIR MEASURE OF THEIR CONTRIBUTION TO HUMAN WELFARE.
Strongly agree 1 Agree 2 Undecided 3 Disagree 4 Strongly disagree 5

108. AN EDUCATED MAN CAN ADVANCE MORE RAPIDLY IN BUSINESS AND INDUSTRY.
Strongly agree 1 Agree 2 Undecided 3 Disagree 4 Strongly disagree 5

109. A MAN DOES NOT HAVE TO PRETEND HE IS SMARTER THAN HE REALLY IS TO "GET BY."
Strongly agree 1 Agree 2 Undecided 3 Disagree 4 Strongly disagree 5

110. IT IS EASY TO KEEP PEOPLE FROM TAKING ADVANTAGE OF YOU.
Strongly agree 1 Agree 2 Undecided 3 Disagree 4 Strongly disagree 5

111. PARENTS KEEP FAITH IN THEIR CHILDREN EVEN THOUGH THEY CANNOT FIND WORK.
Strongly agree 1 Agree 2 Undecided 3 Disagree 4 Strongly disagree 5

112. IT IS DIFFICULT TO BREAK THE LAW AND KEEP ONE'S SELF RESPECT.
Strongly agree 1 Agree 2 Undecided 3 Disagree 4 Strongly disagree 5

113. A MAN SHOULD STRIKE IN ORDER TO SECURE GREATER RETURNS TO LABOR.
Strongly agree 5 Agree 4 Undecided 3 Disagree 2 Strongly disagree 1

114. PARENTS SHOULD NOT BE COMPELLED TO SEND THEIR CHILDREN TO SCHOOL.
Strongly agree 5 Agree 4 Undecided 3 Disagree 2 Strongly disagree 1

115. SUCCESS IS MORE DEPENDENT ON LUCK THAN ON REAL ABILITY.
Strongly agree 5 Agree 4 Undecided 3 Disagree 2 Strongly disagree 1

116. MOST PEOPLE ARE TOO CRITICAL OF ONE'S BEHAVIOR.
Strongly agree 5 Agree 4 Undecided 3 Disagree 2 Strongly disagree 1

117. PARENTS ARE TOO PARTICULAR ABOUT THE KIND OF COMPANY ONE KEEPS.
Strongly agree 5 Agree 4 Undecided 3 Disagree 2 Strongly disagree 1

118. ON THE WHOLE, LAWYERS ARE HONEST.
Strongly agree 1 Agree 2 Undecided 3 Disagree 4 Strongly disagree 5

119. A MAN SHOULD BE ALLOWED TO KEEP AS LARGE AN INCOME AS HE CAN GET.
Strongly agree 1 Agree 2 Undecided 3 Disagree 4 Strongly disagree 5

120. EDUCATION IS MORE VALUABLE THAN MOST PEOPLE THINK.
Strongly agree 1 Agree 2 Undecided 3 Disagree 4 Strongly disagree 5

121. A PERSON CAN PLAN HIS FUTURE SO THAT EVERYTHING WILL COME OUT ALL RIGHT IN THE LONG RUN.
Strongly agree 1 Agree 2 Undecided 3 Disagree 4 Strongly disagree 5

122. FEAR OF SOCIAL BLUNDERS KEEPS ONE FROM HAVING A GOOD TIME AT A PARTY.
Strongly agree 5 Agree 4 Undecided 3 Disagree 2 Strongly disagree 1

123. OBLIGATIONS TO ONE'S FAMILY ARE A GREAT HANDICAP TO A YOUNG MAN TODAY.
Strongly agree 5 Agree 4 Undecided 3 Disagree 2 Strongly disagree 1

124. VIOLATORS OF THE LAW ARE NEARLY ALWAYS DETECTED AND PUNISHED.
Strongly agree 1 Agree 2 Undecided 3 Disagree 4 Strongly disagree 5

125. MONEY SHOULD BE TAKEN FROM THE RICH AND GIVEN TO THE POOR DURING HARD TIMES.
Strongly agree 5 Agree 4 Undecided 3 Disagree 2 Strongly disagree 1

126. A HIGH SCHOOL EDUCATION MAKES A MAN A BETTER CITIZEN.
Strongly agree 1 Agree 2 Undecided 3 Disagree 4 Strongly disagree 5

127. THERE IS REALLY NO POINT IN LIVING.
Strongly agree 5 Agree 4 Undecided 3 Disagree 2 Strongly disagree 1

128. IT IS EASY TO LOSE CONFIDENCE IN ONE'S SELF.
Strongly agree 5 Agree 4 Undecided 3 Disagree 2 Strongly disagree 1

129. SO FAR AS IDEAS ARE CONCERNED, PARENTS AND CHILDREN LIVE IN DIFFERENT WORLDS.
Strongly agree 5 Agree 4 Undecided 3 Disagree 2 Strongly disagree 1

130. IT IS ALL RIGHT FOR A PERSON TO BREAK THE LAW IF HE DOESN'T GET CAUGHT.
Strongly agree 5 Agree 4 Undecided 3 Disagree 2 Strongly disagree 1

131. OUR ECONOMIC SYSTEM IS CRITICIZED TOO MUCH.
Strongly agree 1 Agree 2 Undecided 3 Disagree 4 Strongly disagree 5

132. PUBLIC MONEY SPENT ON EDUCATION DURING THE PAST FEW YEARS COULD HAVE BEEN USED MORE WISELY FOR OTHER PURPOSES.
Strongly agree 5 Agree 4 Undecided 3 Disagree 2 Strongly disagree 1

SCORING INSTRUCTIONS FOR THE MINNESOTA SCALE FOR THE SURVEY OF OPINIONS

Administration

The Survey requires between 30 and 40 minutes for all to complete it. Although the printed directions on the Survey are self-explanatory, it is advisable to read the directions aloud while the subjects are reading them silently. To secure frankness and co-operation it is well to assure the group that their opinions are valued, will be held in complete confidence, and will not affect their grades in any course or their standing with their employers or other persons of responsibility. They may be directed to fill in all the information items (name, age, sex, etc.) or to omit those that the examiner does not require for research or counseling purposes.

Scoring

The five alternative responses to each item are weighted from 1 to 5 in scoring. This method of scoring was found to yield total scores correlating above .95 with those yielded by sigma weights to item responses, and is much simpler. The weight for each response is printed in small type just above and to the right of each response in the Survey. For example, on item 1 the weights are: strongly agree, 5; agree, 4; undecided, 3; disagree, 2; strongly disagree, 1.

Enter the printed weight for each response checked by a person given the survey in the space provided for it on the tabulation sheet. Use one tabulation sheet for each person given the Survey. The sum of the weights for the 22 items of a scale is the person's raw score.

Norms

The scoring norms in the table permit conversion of raw scores into standard scores. These norms are based on the scores of 1,000 young people, 500 of each sex. The standardization group included 400 college students, 200 high school seniors, and 400 youthful employed and unemployed persons in continuation classes at the high school level. The distribution of paternal occupation for the standardization group approximates the census distribution of occupations and indicates that it is composed of a fairly representative sample of young persons between the ages of sixteen and twenty-five years. No significant differences between the scores of high school and college students were found, and the norms are adequate for both groups.

The standard scores given in the table were obtained by the McCall T-Score technique, which expresses scores in tenths of standard deviation units from the mean score for the standardization group. The mean raw score of the standardization group becomes the standard score of 50. A standard score of 60 is one standard deviation higher than the mean; a standard score of 40 is one standard deviation below the mean. Response weights to items have been so assigned that a high standard score is unfavorable.

To illustrate the use of the table, suppose an individual makes the same raw scores--say 57--on the morale, economic conservatism, and education scales. We find 57 in the raw score column. Reading to the right, we observe that the individual's standard scores are 50 on the morale scale, 40 on the economic conservatism scale, and 60 on the education scale. These scores indicate that the individual's morale is average, that he is conservative in his economic views (one standard deviation below the mean), and that his estimate of the value of education is relatively unfavorable (one standard deviation above the mean).

Report to the Authors

The authors will greatly appreciate receiving distributions of raw scores, since these will permit development of more extensive norms. Counselors in the General College of the University of Minnesota report that these scales are proving to be of considerable value to them. The comments of counselors in other institutions are desired. Address communications to the authors in care of the Institute of Child Welfare, University of Minnesota.

Price of scales: single copy $0.10; 25 for $1.50; 100 for $5.00. Address orders to the University of Minnesota Press, Minneapolis.

MINNESOTA SCALE FOR THE SURVEY OF OPINIONS

Tabulation Sheet No.________

1. Age______ 2. M F 3. M S D 4. Date__________ 5. Own children______ 6. Younger sisters______
7. Older sisters ______ 8. Younger brothers ______ 9. Older brothers______ Size of sibship__________
10-11. Sib. position ____________ 12. Emp. Y N 13. Full time Y N 14. Mos. unemp.__________
15. Ex. occup. ______________________ 16. Pres. occup. ______________________
17. Fa. occup. ______________________ 18. D R E U 19. D H E U 20. Par. tog. Y N
21. Grade 1 2 3 4 5 6 7 8 9 10 11 12 13 14 15 16
22. A B C D E {½ 1 1½ 2 2½ 3 / ½ 1 1½ 2 2½ 3} E______________________
23. Emp. VC C Unc V Unc 24. Unemp. VC C Unc V Unc

	M	I	F	L	C	E
	A B	A B	A B	A B	A B	A B
	___ 1	2___	___ 3	___ 4	5___	___ 6*
	___ 7	8___	___ 9	10___	11___	12___
	*13___	___ 14*	15___	16___	17___	___ 18
	*19___	20___	___ 21	22___	23___	24___
	25___	___ 26	___ 27	___ 28	*29___	30___
	*31___	___ 32	33___	___ 34	___ 35	___ 36*
	37___	38___	___ 39*	___ 40	___ 41	___ 42
	43___	___ 44	45___	___ 46	___ 47	48___
	*49___	50___	51___	___ 52	___ 53	54___
	___ 55	56___	57___	58___	___ 59	___ 60
	61___	62___	63___	64___	65___	66___
	67___	68___	69___	70___	___ 71	___ 72
	*73___	___ 74	___ 75	___ 76	___ 77	___ 78
	___ 79*	___ 80	81___	___ 82	___ 83	___ 84
	___ 85	___ 86*	87___	___ 88	___ 89	*90___
	___ 91	___ 92	___ 93	94___	95___	___ 96
	___ 97*	___ 98	___ 99	*100___	*101___	___102
	___103	___104	___105	___106	107___	108___
	___109	110___	___111	___112	113___	114___
	___115	___116	117___	118___	119___	120___
	121___	122___	___123	124___	___125	___126
	___127	128___	129___	130___	___131	132___
Total	___ ___	___ ___	___ ___	___ ___	___ ___	___ ___
A plus B	______	______	______	______	______	______

* General Adjustment Score________ ________

TABLE 139

STANDARD SCORE EQUIVALENTS FOR RAW SCORES
(Based on Standardisation Group of 1000)

Raw Score	Standard Score Equivalents M	I	F	L	EC	E	GA	Raw Score	Standard Score Equivalents M	I	F	L	EC	E	GA
110								62	55	46	55	53	45	65	78
109					91			61	54	45	54	52	44	64	77
108					90			60	53	44	53	51	43	63	76
107					89			59	52	43	52	50	42	62	74
106					88			58	51	42	51	49	41	61	73
105					87			57	50	41	51	48	40	60	72
104					86			56	49	40	50	47	39	59	70
103					85			55	48	39	49	46	38	58	69
102			92		84			54	47	37	48	45	37	57	68
101		86	91		83			53	46	36	47	44	36	56	66
100		85	90		82			52	45	35	46	43	35	55	65
99		84	89		81			51	43	34	45	42	34	54	64
98		83	88		80			50	42	33	44	41	33	53	62
97		82	87		79			49	41	32	43	39	32	52	61
96		81	86		78			48	40	31	42	38	31	51	60
95	90	80	85		77			47	39	30	41	37	30	49	58
94	89	79	84		76			46	38	29	40	36	29	48	57
93	88	78	84		75			45	37	28	40	35	28	47	56
92	87	77	83		74			44	36	27	39	34	27	46	54
91	86	76	82		73	96		43	35	26	38	33	26	45	53
90	85	75	81	84	72	95		42	34	25	37	32	25	44	52
89	83	74	80	82	71	94		41	33	24	36	31	24	43	50
88	82	73	79	81	70	93		40	32	23	35	30	23	42	49
87	81	72	78	80	69	92		39	31	22	34	29	22	41	48
86	80	71	77	79	68	90		38	30	21	33	28	21	40	47
85	79	70	76	78	67	89		37	29	20	32	27	20	39	45
84	78	68	75	77	66	88		36	28	19	31	26	19	38	44
83	77	67	74	76	65	87		35	27	18	30	24	18	37	43
82	76	66	73	75	64	86		34	26	17	29	23	17	36	41
81	75	65	73	74	63	85		33	25	16	29	22	16	35	40
80	74	64	72	73	62	84		32	23	15	28	21	15	34	39
79	73	63	71	72	61	83		31	22	14	27	20	14	33	37
78	72	62	70	71	60	82		30	21	13	26	19	13	32	36
77	71	61	69	70	59	81		29	20	12	25	18	12	31	35
76	70	60	68	69	58	80		28	19	11	24	17	11	30	33
75	69	59	67	67	57	79		27	18	10	23	16	10	28	32
74	68	58	66	66	56	78		26	17	9	22	15	9	27	31
73	67	57	65	65	56	77		25						26	29
72	66	56	64	64	55	76		24						25	28
71	65	55	63	63	54	75		23						24	27
70	63	54	62	62	53	74	89	22						23	25
69	62	53	62	61	52	73	87	21							24
68	61	52	61	60	51	72	86	20							23
67	60	51	60	59	50	71	85	19							21
66	59	50	59	58	49	69	83	18							20
65	58	49	58	57	48	68	82	17							19
64	57	48	57	56	47	67	81	16							17
63	56	47	56	55	46	66	79								

TABLE 140.—STANDARD SCORE EQUIVALENTS FOR SCORES ON ACCEPTABLE ITEMS

Arbitrary Score	Morale	Inferi- ority	Family	Law	Economic Conserv- atism	Educa- tion
55	97	87	99	94	89	
54	95	85	97	92	87	
53	93	84	95	90	85	
52	91	82	94	88	85	
51	90	80	92	87	81	100
50	88	78	90	85	79	99
49	86	76	89	83	77	97
48	84	75	87	81	76	95
47	82	73	85	80	74	93
46	80	71	84	78	72	91
45	78	69	82	76	70	89
44	76	68	80	74	68	88
43	74	66	78	73	66	86
42	72	64	77	71	64	84
41	70	62	75	69	62	82
40	68	61	73	67	60	80
39	66	59	72	66	59	78
38	64	57	70	64	57	76
37	62	55	68	62	55	74
36	60	54	67	61	53	73
35	59	52	65	59	51	71
34	57	50	63	57	49	69
33	55	48	61	55	47	67
32	53	47	60	54	46	65
31	51	45	58	52	44	63
30	49	43	56	50	42	61
29	47	41	55	48	40	60
28	45	40	53	47	38	58
27	43	38	51	45	36	56
26	41	36	50	43	34	54
25	39	35	48	41	32	52
24	37	33	46	40	31	50
23	35	31	44	38	29	49
22	34	29	43	36	27	47
21	32	27	41	34	25	45
20	30	26	39	33	23	43
19	28	24	38	31	21	41
18	26	22	36	29	19	39
17	24	20	34	27	17	37
16	22	19	33	26	16	36
15	20	17	31	24	14	34
14	18	15	29	22	12	32
13	16	13	27	20	10	30
12	14	12	26	19	8	28
11	12	10	24	17	6	26

TABLE 141.-STANDARD SCORE EQUIVALENTS FOR SCORES ON UNACCEPTABLE ITEMS

Arbitrary Score	Morale	Inferi- ority	Family	Law	Economic Conserv- atism	Educa- tion
55	97	90	86	100	84	
54	95	88	85	99	82	
53	94	86	83	97	81	
52	92	84	82	95	79	
51	90	83	80	93	78	100
50	89	81	79	91	76	98
49	87	79	77	89	75	96
48	85	77	76	87	73	94
47	84	76	74	85	72	92
46	82	74	73	84	70	91
45	80	72	72	82	69	89
44	79	70	70	80	67	87
43	77	69	69	78	65	85
42	75	67	67	76	64	83
41	74	65	66	74	62	81
40	72	64	64	72	61	80
39	70	62	63	70	59	78
38	69	60	61	68	58	76
37	67	58	60	66	56	74
36	65	57	58	64	55	72
35	64	55	57	62	53	71
34	62	53	56	60	52	69
33	60	51	54	58	50	67
32	59	50	53	56	48	65
31	57	48	51	54	47	63
30	55	46	50	52	45	61
29	54	44	48	50	44	60
28	52	43	47	48	42	58
27	50	41	45	47	41	56
26	49	39	44	45	39	54
25	47	37	42	43	38	52
24	46	36	41	41	36	50
23	44	34	40	39	35	49
22	42	32	38	37	33	47
21	41	30	37	35	31	45
20	39	29	35	33	30	43
19	37	27	34	31	28	41
18	36	25	32	29	27	39
17	34	24	31	27	25	38
16	32	22	29	25	24	36
15	31	20	28	23	22	34
14	29	18	26	21	21	32
13	27	17	25	19	19	30
12	26	15	24	17	18	29
11	24	13	22	15	16	27

SHORT FORM (GENERAL ADJUSTMENT AND MORALE SCALES)

This short form is presented to assist those who may wish to obtain a measure of the general adjustment factor without administering the entire survey. Some may wish to study the general factor in relation to scales other than those in the present survey.

The short form contains 31 items, which include the 22 items in the morale scale and the 16 items in the general adjustment scale. Some items are scored in both. The Survey will yield five scores: the general adjustment score, the total morale score, the score on the acceptably stated morale items, the score on the unacceptably stated morale items, and the difference between the scores on the acceptably stated and the unacceptably stated morale items. Each score should be independently related to other variables.

To obtain these scores simply transfer the number of the phrase underlined by the subject to the lines in the left-hand margin. If there are two lines to the left of the item, enter the score on each. The sum of the scores in the extreme left-hand column is the adjustment score, the sum of the next column is the score on the acceptable morale items, the sum of the next is the score on the unacceptable morale items. To obtain the total morale score, add the total scores on acceptable and unacceptable items. This may be entered on the line below and between the lines intended for the acceptable and unacceptable item scores at the end of the blank. The difference score is obtained by subtracting the unacceptable item score from the acceptable item score. When the unacceptable item score is larger, affix a minus sign to the difference. The difference score may be entered on the line to the right of those provided for the total acceptable and total unacceptable scores.

Norms in terms of standard scores are presented elsewhere in this Appendix for all scores save the difference score. These norms are based on 1000 cases, each sex being equally represented. Since the norms were derived with the items in a different context, they may not be applicable to the results secured from the short form.

Split-half reliability in the .80's may be expected for the adjustment score and the total morale score. The split-half reliability of the remaining three scores has not been investigated.

It should be noted that the general adjustment items are so arranged that scoring every other one to compute the reliability coefficient will yield forms identical to those which the authors used in computing the reliability of that scale.

The three items which were borrowed from Hall's Scale of Occupational Morale are starred (*).

The instructions for administering the short form are identical with those for the long form.

MINNESOTA SURVEY OF OPINIONS (Short Form)

E. A. Rundquist and R. F. Sletto,
Institute of Child Welfare, University of Minnesota

Name______________________ Age___ Sex_____ Date________
(Last) (First)

The following pages contain a number of statements about which there is no general agreement. People differ widely in the way they feel about each item. There are no right answers. The purpose of the survey is to see how different groups feel about each item. We should like your honest opinion on each of these statements.

READ EACH ITEM CAREFULLY AND UNDERLINE QUICKLY THE PHRASE WHICH BEST EXPRESSES YOUR FEELING ABOUT THE STATEMENT. Wherever possible, let your own personal experience determine your answer. Do not spend much time on any item. If in doubt, underline the phrase which seems most nearly to express your present feeling about the statement. WORK RAPIDLY. Be sure to answer every item.

1. TIMES ARE GETTING BETTER.
Strongly agree[1] Agree[2] Undecided[3]
___ ___ Disagree[4] Strongly disagree[5]

2.* ANY MAN WITH ABILITY AND WILLINGNESS TO WORK HARD HAS A GOOD CHANCE OF BEING SUCCESSFUL.
Strongly agree[1] Agree[2] Undecided[3]
___ Disagree[4] Strongly disagree[5]

3. IT IS DIFFICULT TO SAY THE RIGHT THING AT THE RIGHT TIME.
Strongly agree[5] Agree[4] Undecided[3]
___ Disagree[2] Strongly disagree[1]

4. MOST PEOPLE CAN BE TRUSTED.
Strongly agree[1] Agree[2] Undecided[3]
___ Disagree[4] Strongly disagree[5]

5. HIGH SCHOOL COURSES ARE TOO IMPRACTICAL.
Strongly agree^5 Agree^4 Undecided^3
Disagree^2 Strongly disagree^1

6. A PERSON CAN PLAN HIS FUTURE SO THAT EVERYTHING WILL COME OUT ALL RIGHT IN THE LONG RUN.
Strongly agree^1 Agree^2 Undecided^3
Disagree^4 Strongly disagree^5

7. NO ONE CARES MUCH WHAT HAPPENS TO YOU.
Strongly agree^5 Agree^4 Undecided^3
Disagree^2 Strongly disagree^1

8.* SUCCESS IS MORE DEPENDENT ON LUCK THAN ON REAL ABILITY.
Strongly agree^5 Agree^4 Undecided^3
Disagree^2 Strongly disagree^1

9. IF OUR ECONOMIC SYSTEM WERE JUST, THERE WOULD BE MUCH LESS CRIME.
Strongly agree^5 Agree^4 Undecided^3
Disagree^2 Strongly disagree^1

10. A MAN DOES NOT HAVE TO PRETEND HE IS SMARTER THAN HE HEALLY IS TO "GET BY."
Strongly agree^1 Agree^2 Undecided^3
Disagree^4 Strongly disagree^5

11. LAWS ARE SO OFTEN MADE FOR THE BENEFIT OF SMALL SELFISH GROUPS THAT A MAN CAN NOT RESPECT THE LAW.
Strongly agree^5 Agree^4 Undecided^3
Disagree^2 Strongly disagree^1

12. ONE SELDOM-WORRIES SO MUCH AS TO BECOME VERY MISERABLE.
Strongly agree^1 Agree^2 Undecided^3
Disagree^4 Strongly disagree^5

13. THE FUTURE LOOKS VERY BLACK.
Strongly agree^5 Agree^4 Undecided^3
Disagree^2 Strongly disagree^1

14. REAL FRIENDS ARE AS EASY TO FIND AS EVER.
Strongly agree^1 Agree^2 Undecided^3
Disagree^4 Strongly disagree^5

15. POVERTY IS CHIEFLY A RESULT OF INJUSTICE IN THE DISTRIBUTION OF WEALTH.
Strongly agree^5 Agree^4 Undecided^3
Disagree^2 Strongly disagree^1

16. IT IS DIFFICULT TO THINK CLEARLY THESE DAYS.
Strongly agree^5 Agree^4 Undecided^3
Disagree^2 Strongly disagree^1

17.* THERE IS LITTLE CHANCE FOR ADVANCEMENT IN INDUSTRY AND BUSINESS UNLESS A MAN HAS UNFAIR PULL.
Strongly agree^5 Agree^4 Undecided^3
Disagree^2 Strongly disagree^1

18. IT DOES NOT TAKE LONG TO GET OVER FEELING GLOOMY.
Strongly agree^1 Agree^2 Undecided^3
Disagree^4 Strongly disagree^5

19. THE YOUNG MAN OF TODAY CAN EXPECT MUCH OF THE FUTURE.
Strongly agree^1 Agree^2 Undecided^3
Disagree^4 Strongly disagree^5

20. IT IS GREAT TO BE LIVING IN THESE EXCITING TIMES.
Strongly agree^1 Agree^2 Undecided^3
Disagree^4 Strongly disagree^5

21. LIFE IS JUST ONE WORRY AFTER ANOTHER.
Strongly agree^5 Agree^4 Undecided^3
Disagree^2 Strongly disagree^1

22. THE DAY IS NOT LONG ENOUGH TO DO ONE'S WORK WELL AND HAVE ANY TIME FOR FUN.
Strongly agree[5] Agree[4] Undecided[3]
____ Disagree[2] Strongly disagree[1]

23. A MAN CAN LEARN MORE BY WORKING FOUR YEARS THAN BY GOING TO HIGH SCHOOL.
Strongly agree[5] Agree[4] Undecided[3]
____ disagree[2] Strongly disagree[1]

24. THIS GENERATION WILL PROBABLY NEVER SEE SUCH HARD TIMES AGAIN.
Strongly agree[1] Agree[2] Undecided[3]
____ Disagree[4] Strongly disagree[5]

25. ONE CANNOT FIND AS MUCH UNDERSTANDING AT HOME AS ELSEWHERE.
Strongly agree[5] Agree[4] Undecided[3]
____ Disagree[2] Strongly disagree[1]

26. THESE DAYS ONE IS INCLINED TO GIVE UP HOPE OF AMOUNTING TO SOMETHING.
Strongly agree[5] Agree[4] Undecided[3]
____ Disagree[2] Strongly disagree[1]

27. EDUCATION IS OF NO HELP IN GETTING A JOB TODAY.
Strongly agree[5] Agree[4] Undecided[3]
____ Disagree[2] Strongly disagree[1]

28. THERE IS REALLY NO POINT IN LIVING.
Strongly agree[5] Agree[4] Undecided[3]
____ Disagree[2] Strongly disagree[1]

29. MOST PEOPLE JUST PRETEND THAT THEY LIKE YOU.
Strongly agree[5] Agree[4] Undecided[3]
Disagree[2] Strongly disagree[1]

30. THE FUTURE IS TOO UNCERTAIN FOR A PERSON TO PLAN ON MARRYING.
Strongly agree[5] Agree[4] Undecided[3]
___ Disagree[2] Strongly disagree[1]

31. LIFE IS JUST A SERIES OF DISAPPOINTMENTS.
Strongly agree[5] Agree[4] Undecided[3]
___ ___ Disagree[2] Strongly disagree[1]

___ ___ ___ ____________________

www.ingramcontent.com/pod-product-compliance
Ingram Content Group UK Ltd.
Pitfield, Milton Keynes, MK11 3LW, UK
UKHW020230290926
15470UKWH00002B/454